THE
SONGS OF HOMER

THE
SONGS OF
HOMER

BY

G. S. KIRK, F.B.A.

Regius Professor of Greek in the University of Cambridge

CAMBRIDGE UNIVERSITY PRESS

CAMBRIDGE

LONDON · NEW YORK · MELBOURNE

Published by the Syndics of the Cambridge University Press
The Pitt Building, Trumpington Street, Cambridge CB2 1RP
Bentley House, 200 Euston Road, London NW1 2DB
32 East 57th Street, New York, NY 10022, USA
296 Beaconsfield Parade, Middle Park, Melbourne 3206, Australia

© Cambridge University Press 1962

ISBN 0 521 05890 2

First published 1962
Reprinted 1977

Printed in Great Britain
at the University Press, Cambridge

To
D. L. PAGE
and
M. I. FINLEY

CONTENTS

vii

CONTENTS

PART IV

PLURALITY AND UNITY IN HOMER

PART V

THE DEVELOPMENT AND TRANSMISSION OF THE GREAT POEMS

PART VI

THE SONGS AND THEIR QUALITIES

MAPS AND PLATES

The maps are printed on pp. x and xi. The plates are bound in as a section between pp. 406 and 409.

CRETE: Scale same as main map.

PREFACE

The Songs of Homer are the Iliad and Odyssey. I have tried to develop a comprehensive and unified view of their nature, of their relation to the oral heroic poetry of the Dark Age and beyond, and of their creation as monumental poems by two great singers in the eighth century B.C. No one who writes on Homer can either expect or deserve common assent; yet at certain points I may hope at least to have clarified the issues, at others to have introduced a kind of salutary agnosticism. The book is intended to interest not only classical scholars and students, but also amateurs of literature and oral poetry who may know no Greek. These will find four or five patches of linguistic discussion which they will simply have to skip; otherwise all Greek passages are translated. It is not only for their sake that notes and references outside the main text have been kept as few as possible. Indeed at the present stage of Homeric studies, when the systematization of archaeology and the profounder understanding of oral song have transformed the appearance of many long-established problems, much of the work of the past, valuable though it has often been, need not always be specifically mentioned.

I make no apology for the space devoted to the historical and poetical background of the poems. The Homeric poetry is the culmination of a long tradition, and without knowing as much as possible about that tradition one can hardly begin to understand (though one might still enjoy) the poetry itself. Yet old attitudes die hard; and there are many scholars who pay lipservice to the study of oral poetry, but still think that they can carve up the whole of the poems among specific contributors. Even so, not all of the old Analytical attitudes and techniques are utterly obsolete, nor all of the Unitarian. Reinterpreted, they may have their value. In part IV, for instance, I have deliberately concentrated on the internal qualities, in terms of coherence and incoherence, of the Iliad and Odyssey themselves, and have temporarily withheld attention from the probabilities of an oral tradition. In part VI, on the other hand, I have written about the poems as unities, as works of art, with questions of composition left largely in the background. On the poems as literature some things need not be said, others cannot, and disagreement there will certainly be; but I would remind one type of reader that to regard all of Homer as precisely equal in literary virtue is obviously naïve.

Whatever errors and imperfections remain in my book, many have certainly been prevented by those who read through all or part of it before publication. There cannot, indeed, be many places better than Cambridge in which to write on Homer; it contains, for example, D. L. Page, M. I. Finley and J. Chadwick, experts and friends who have given the most careful and ungrudging attention to my typescript, and the first two of whom encouraged me to write this book from the beginning. W. A. Camps, too, read the proofs and eradicated further anomalies; and so, as he has done before, did P. H. J. Lloyd-Jones in Oxford. Others to whom I owe special thanks are G. L. Huxley, Emily Vermeule and other friends at or around Harvard; and, for their help over illustrations, R. M. Cook, N. Coldstream, P. Courbin, G. Daux, V. R. d'A. Desborough, P. Devambez, M. S. Hood, E. Kunze, A. B. Lord, T. C. Skeat, F. H. Stubbings, Gladys Weinberg and N. M. Verdelis. E. R. Dodds, A. Lesky and H. Erbse are mentioned little or not at all in what follows, yet I like many others have been greatly helped by what they have written.

Finally that perennial problem, the spelling of Greek names: no single system is quite satisfactory, and the rule followed here is roughly that familiar names are given in their most familiar Latinized forms, unfamiliar ones in a more direct transliteration retaining *k* and *os*. This explains some apparent inconsistencies of place-names in the maps.

G. S. K.

CAMBRIDGE
April 1962

PART I

THE HISTORICAL BACKGROUND OF
THE HOMERIC POEMS

1

THE RISE OF MYCENAE

THE Iliad and Odyssey are set against the background of the Achaean world in the late Bronze Age; their subjects are the Trojan war and its aftermath. Yet the poems themselves did not approach their surviving monumental form until many generations later, at some time, to give the extreme limits, between the late 9th and the early 7th century B.C. Many elements of the poems reflect the conditions, not of their ostensible Mycenaean setting, but of this later period of large-scale composition in Ionia. Between the two periods came centuries of obscurity, the so-called Dark Age of Greece, through which the Achaean traditional material must have been transmitted and during which it was no doubt greatly altered or elaborated.

To comprehend the making of the Homeric poems, therefore, one must first consider the history of at least a complete millennium, from around 1600 to around 600 B.C. In a historical novel the critic has to consider both the period described and that of the author and his readers; but with traditional poems the whole intervening period, too, is vitally important. Now the assessment of this particular millennium is more than usually difficult since, apart from the Linear B inventories from Knossos, Pylos and Mycenae, the Homeric poems themselves, and a few Hittite and Egyptian references, there exists no contemporary record until the 7th century.[1] Much of the reconstruction, therefore, has to be founded on later mythological tradition, itself often derived from or at least affected by Homer, and on archaeological evidence—together, at one or two points, with the evidence of non-Greek proper names that survived into the historical age. All these kinds of evidence, particularly the first two, are erratic in scope and ambiguous of interpretation.

3

The late Bronze Age in Greece began around 1600 B.C., and its antecedents were briefly as follows. A Neolithic or late Stone Age people of unknown race, but using pottery of Near Eastern affinities, had occupied parts of central Greece and the Peloponnese from an uncertain date, perhaps in the 5th millennium B.C., until the incursion of bronze-users around 2800.[1] The term 'Helladic' is applied to the succeeding Bronze Age cultures of the mainland, with which we are chiefly concerned; 'Minoan' refers to the Bronze Age cultures of Crete, 'Cycladic' to those of the central Aegean. This earliest Bronze Age culture of the mainland is called Early Helladic. It appears to have crossed over into Greece from Asia Minor, since it has at first no northern connexions and since in the Early Helladic period a common language seems to have been spoken not only on the mainland and in Crete and the central islands but also in south-western Anatolia.[2] Between about 2000 and 1850 the Early Helladic was succeeded by a new culture known as Middle Helladic. This was introduced by people who imposed themselves by force upon the earlier population, some of whose settlements were destroyed and others rebuilt. The new people were presumably immigrants and not a resurgent pre-Helladic stock. They may have moved down into Greece from central Europe, a region into which one Indo-European tribe, the so-called Battle-axe people, had already penetrated during the Early Helladic period. It is possible, though, that they moved along the north shore of the Aegean from Asia Minor and then turned south into the Greek peninsula. One notable characteristic of their new culture was the introduction of the horse; another was wheel-made pottery, in contrast with the rougher, hand-made Early Helladic ware. The most characteristic Middle Helladic pottery was made by the so-called 'Minyan' technique, which produced a highly burnished surface giving the impression of metal. Minyan ware is usually grey, but in certain areas and at certain periods it is red, black, or yellowish.[3] A third cultural characteristic of the Middle Helladic immigrants was the fortification of towns.[4] They do not seem to have been a particularly warlike people, but unlike most of their predecessors they must have reached a stage of economic and social development at which concentrated settlements and administrative centres were possible and necessary. These would presumably require defence, at first, against a surrounding subject population. A fourth innovation was a special kind of building, the *megaron*, a gabled hall with central hearth and sometimes a small antechamber at one of the narrow ends. Although an ancestor of this architectural type had been known in Thessaly and at Troy since the third millennium, the Middle Helladic invaders were the first to use it widely in Greece.

The fifth contribution of the Middle Helladic immigrants was a new language—Greek. The Early Helladic settlers had not been Greek-speakers. So much can be inferred with certainty from the survival into the historical period of a particular class of non-Greek names—mostly local names, of rivers and mountains and inhabited settlements, but also names of flowers, trees, and even a few common artefacts. These names are characterized by a medial -*nth*- sound (or its probable equivalent -*nd*- in Anatolia) and also by medial -*ss*-. These internal consonant-groups occur in many names that do not seem to be Greek—but also in a few like ἄνθος, ἄκανθος that do. It now seems doubtful whether they should be considered as non-Indo-European— that is, as foreign to the whole language-group of which Greek is a member. Examples of such names on the Greek mainland and in the islands are: Erymanthos, Tiryns (-*nthos*), Korinthos, Kynthos; Parnassos, Hymettos (with Attic -*tt*- for -*ss*-), Kephissos, Laris(s)a; the botanical names hyakinthos, erebinthos; kyparissos, narkissos; asaminthos (a kind of bath). In Crete: Syrinthos; labyrinthos; Knos(s)os, Tylis(s)os. In Anatolia: Myndos, Labraunda (so too Lindos in Rhodes), also Xanthos; Mylasa, Telmessos. These names were used by the early Bronze Age inhabitants of these areas, but are not Neolithic remnants: that is shown by their occurrence in Crete and the Cyclades, for example in the name of Mount Kynthos in Delos, where no Neolithic remains have been found; and by their being commonest in the known areas of early Bronze Age settlement. That

Greek was introduced in the course of the transition from Early Helladic to Middle Helladic cannot be absolutely demonstrated, but since this transition represents the only strong cultural break between the earlier period when the non-Greek language of the place and vegetation-names was spoken and the late Bronze Age when, as we know from the Linear B tablets as well as by inference from Homer, Greek was certainly spoken, it is a reasonable conjecture that the introduction of the new language is to be placed at this point and associated with the Middle Helladic invaders.[1]

The Middle Helladic culture of the mainland underwent a change around 1600, when the Late Helladic period begins. The change is not nearly so drastic as that which marked the arrival of the Middle Helladic people, and its most concrete sign is the obsolescence of the widespread Minyan pottery technique. It is doubtful whether there was any large change in population; indeed the persistence of some black and yellow Minyan pottery in the earlier royal shaft-graves at Mycenae may suggest not. These graves, whose golden masks and inlaid daggers Schliemann first exposed to an astonished world, and the second group recently found in the lower town, are larger and of course far richer than the Middle Helladic cist-burials, though not essentially different from them. The gravestones which were set above some of them, in some cases carved, are, however, a new phenomenon. This funeral wealth suggests a great increase in the power of Mycenae, which had existed as a small settlement since Early Helladic times, and in particular in the extent of its foreign trade. The appearance of amber in graves proves indirect links with the far north; more important, the 16th century sees the beginning of regular commercial contacts with Egypt. The influence of Minoan Crete, for long the richest and most powerful civilization of the Aegean area, also increases. Indeed, although the Late Helladic expansion at Mycenae seems to begin slightly before the earliest date at which there is evidence for close relations with Crete, it is tempting to consider Minoan influence as a main stimulus of the new Mycenaean vitality.[2] Yet the introduction on the Greek mainland, at precisely this time, of the war-chariot, which had already been devastatingly used by the Hittites in Asia Minor, suggests the possibility of new arrivals from Asia Minor, perhaps few in number but bringing fresh resources with them. Legend tells us that Pelops, after whom the Peloponnese was thought to be named, was an immensely rich immigrant from Asia Minor who won the daughter of Oenomaus, king of Elis, by bribing his charioteer Myrtilus and so winning a famous chariot contest; Myrtilus himself may carry a name derived from the Hittite king Mursilis.[1] It is prudent to be suspicious of genealogical evidence for early Greek history—since the degree of later compression, omission and invention cannot be even approximately gauged—but this particular tradition has certain marked correspondences with what may be surmised from the archaeological evidence. Thus it is possible that the rapid and superficial change of culture which accompanies the rise of Mycenae to the supreme position in the Aegean world was produced initially by new overseas contacts with Egypt and Crete as well as with the north, and by the arrival in the Peloponnese of a small influx of Greek-speaking elements from Asia Minor, bringing chariots with them. But this must remain highly conjectural.

Knossos, the chief city in Crete, was prevented from undergoing a corresponding expansion by a disastrous earthquake which around 1570 destroyed the great palace there together with other palace towns in the island. Crete made a spectacular material recovery from this misfortune, but was not to survive much longer as an independent power. It seems probable that the Minoan motifs and techniques which become so prominent in the art of the mainland in the last part of the 16th century were the result of a large-scale emigration of craftsmen from Crete and particularly from Knossos. Even before the decipherment of the Linear B script, which has been found in Crete only at Knossos, archaeologists were beginning to think that Achaeans from the mainland, in particular from Mycenae, must have gained physical control of Knossos by the 15th century B.C., the so-called Palace period there. Large Palace-style amphoras were manufactured on the mainland as well as at Knossos, but in no other of the Cretan towns; frescoes at Knossos, but not elsewhere in Crete, show a Mycenaean interest in scenes of hunting and valour rather than in the typically Cretan natural-istic decoration; the mainland tholos-tombs finds a parallel in Knossos but not elsewhere in Crete, and so on. This association of Knossos in the 15th century with the mainland rather than with the rest of Crete lately received powerful confirmation from the discovery that the Linear B tablets are written, partly at any rate, in Greek. This strongly suggests that the last palace at Knossos, which was destroyed by human agency apparently around 1400, was controlled by Achaeans from the mainland. But in that case who destroyed Knossos? On the old hypothesis, according to which it was Knossos that ruled Mycenae between 1500 and 1400 rather than the reverse, Mycenae as the chief Achaean power was a good candidate for the role of aggressor. But why should Mycenae destroy what now transpires to be one of its own possessions—except possibly in reprisal for rebellion? It is as likely that such a rebellion itself destroyed the palace.[1] Of other possibilities an attack from other Minoan centres in Crete is almost excluded, since most of the powerful cities had themselves been sacked well before the fall of Knossos around 1400. An onslaught by pirates or a marauding fleet cannot be entirely ruled out, particularly since Knossos was never fortified. The thalassocracy or command of the sea recorded by later writers, if it was based on a genuine tradition, must have de-clined after the earthquake; and Herodotus records a story that the fleet was lost after an attack on Sicily, unlikely as this may seem.[2] The fact remains that Knossos was destroyed, and that this time there was no renaissance.

From about 1550 onwards, then, Mycenae became the focus of the greatest independent power of the Aegean world; and so it remained until the final collapse of Bronze Age Greece some four hundred years later. (All dates at this period, it need hardly be said, are approximate. Those of the earlier part of the late Bronze Age can be given with greater confidence because of cultural synchronisms with Egypt, where a chronology, because of the survival of written historical records, can be established; though even this may prove to be fallible.) In terms of culture, though not of sheer extent of influence, the first century and a half of this four-hundred-year era, when Knossos was still unsacked, was probably the most notable. Some of the greatest triumphs of the art of Mycenae belong to the beginning of this era. The famous shaft-grave daggers, for example, exemplify both the signorial taste of the mainland and the international character of much of this palace art; the former is seen in the lion-hunt, which is nevertheless expressed with the flowing Minoan technique, while the scene of cats stalking birds along a river, among papyrus reeds, is Egyptian.[1] Not long after 1500 the earliest of a new type of royal tomb was built—the *tholos* or 'beehive' tomb of which the finest example is the misnamed Treasury of Atreus. It used to be thought that this change in royal burial custom implied a change of dynasty. That need not follow; but at least it symbolizes the new magnificence and wider cultural contacts that Mycenae had acquired. Then at some time in the 15th century the technique of writing was adapted to Greek, presumably by the palace scribes at Knossos. From shortly before the fall of Knossos, however, a new style of pottery at Mycenae shows a reaction against the traditional Minoan canons. The Minoan naturalistic motifs are made smaller, more angular, and more geometrical; they are surrounded by patterns which some critics see as a revival of Middle Helladic decoration. There is a conscious avoidance of areas of undecorated surface, allied with an impercipient failure to relate the rhythm of decoration to the shape of the pot itself. By about 1250 the results are sometimes distressing, and suggest a coarser aspect of Mycenaean culture once the fruitful Cretan influence had been removed (cf. pl. 3 b). Yet the life of Crete was not entirely forgotten. The great frescoes at Tiryns still depict the bull-leaping sport of Minoan Crete, even though this had never achieved popularity on the mainland—the Achaean palaces contained, at least, no equivalent to the 'theatral area', with broad, shallow steps for spectators, of Knossos and Phaistos.

The mainland palaces differed from the Cretan in a more important matter. They possessed fortifications and towers and protected water supplies. After 1400 the walls of Mycenae were strengthened and their circuit extended, and the massive entrance known as the Lion Gate was built. At the same time the old shaft-graves within the walls (Circle A) were enclosed in a carefully constructed double stone precinct.[1] Other palaces on the mainland, like those at Amyklai and Triphylian Pylos in the Peloponnese (Nestor's Pylos in Messenia, further south, only became important in the 13th century), or Athens, Thebes and Orchomenus north of the isthmus of Corinth, are similar in culture and sometimes greater in physical extent and potentiality of natural wealth. Mycenae, however, was the political and military centre. In its immediate neighbourhood roads can be traced which radiated southwards towards Asine and the harbour of Nauplia, northwards to Sicyon and Corinth and the way over the isthmus to the palaces of central Greece. The short route south to the coast was guarded by fortress towns at Midea and Tiryns, themselves the homes of vassal kings and richly equipped with frescoes and vessels of gold and silver; while the closely associated city of Argos held control over the most fertile fields of the Argive plain.

From the time of the fall of Knossos Achaean influence grows stronger in other directions overseas. The obvious trade-routes are supported by settlements and trading stations: Rhodes, colonized by Achaeans by the 14th century, and probably Cyprus too, are staging-points to the Levant, while Cythera and Crete lie on the more direct route to Egypt. At Ugarit in Syria there is a large Achaean quarter in the harbour town, terminus of many overland caravans. Iolcus and Peparethus lie on the Troy route, Miletus provides a safe harbour on the eastern Aegean shore. To the west of Greece, in the central Mediterranean, the Achaean settlements are smaller and hard to trace, but Mycenaean pottery found its way there in some quantity.

This then is 'golden Mycenae' at the height of its greatness: a small fortress containing a palace, surrounded by houses that have left only few traces, secreted in a rocky corner of the fertile Argive plain (pl. 1 a); yet the power-centre of a complex of palaces, cities and emporia which extended through the Peloponnese and the southern part of central Greece, and overseas to the northern shores of the Aegean, Asia Minor, Cyprus and the Levant as well as to Egypt and, in smaller measure, westward to Sicily and beyond. Now both the source of Mycenae's power and the nature of its relationship with other Achaean or 'Mycenaean' palaces of the mainland are far from easy to understand. In contrast with the Minoan palaces of Crete, which were cities in miniature, Mycenae as it survives is, like Troy, a fortified hillock containing little but the royal quarters and a few dependencies. As at Troy, the industry that contributed a part at least of Mycenae's wealth must have been carried on in mud-brick houses outside the walls, and these have disappeared. The site of Mycenae, though, could never have accommodated much of a town, however compact; though there must have been small villages in the neighbourhood, some of whose inhabitants would have been shepherds and farmers, while others may have been potters and other craftsmen.[1] Pottery was a sizeable export, even discounting the fact that it survives while other products do not. Yet the finds of 'Mycenaean' pottery overseas, while they testify to the scope of Achaean trade, do not immediately suggest that this commerce was large enough to form the main support of the economy of Mycenae itself. The other palaces of the mainland were presumably self-supporting in at least the more ordinary kinds of ware, and probably had some share of the overseas trade. Other and more valuable articles of craftsmanship, notably metalwork, jewellery, and decorated furniture, were also exported from Mycenae, yet they were rivalled from the fourteenth century onwards by the products of *émigré* Achaean craftsmen in Cyprus and Ugarit or their native apprentices. As for the agricultural wealth of the Argolid, it was considerable, but also had a considerable number of settlements to supply.

It is difficult to tell how far Mycenae benefited from the resources of other palaces on the mainland. Orchomenus, and perhaps Thebes also, had a reputation for great wealth and is remembered for this in the Iliad (IX. 381);* and, although little appears of Mycenaean Thebes or Orchomenus, it is reasonable to conjecture from the nature of their sites and from comparison with the later palace at Pylos (pl. 1 b)—the fairly extensive remains of which are being systematically revealed by American and Greek archaeologists—that they were both larger and potentially more productive than Mycenae itself.[1] In fact the source of 'Mycenaean' overseas trade was not the citadel and palace of Mycenae alone, nor even Mycenae with Argos and the other settlements of the Argolid, but the loose federation of all Greek cities on the mainland. Admittedly the tablets from Pylos and Mycenae do nothing to suggest either foreign trade or very close links between the palaces, beyond what is implied by similar social, economic, administrative, and scribal systems; but the tablets, like the indications in the Odyssey, which suggest little more than personal relationships between the different rulers, apply to the period of the empire's decline and approaching end, when some disintegration is to be expected. It does not follow that the same conditions prevailed in the greater days of 1550–1300.

Presumably an important part of the wealth of Mycenae, and perhaps in lesser degree of other mainland palaces, was derived directly from Crete. That there was strong artistic and technical influence we have already seen; and it is possible that wealthier Cretans as well as craftsmen moved over to the mainland from the earthquake-ravaged island during the course of the 16th century. When Knossos came directly under Mycenaean rule her wealth began to be further drained off to the mainland. The other Cretan palaces, most of which, like Palaikastro, succumbed earlier than Knossos itself, were perhaps the objects of looting or reprisal raids by Mycenaeans based on Knossos— and by 'Mycenaeans' here I mean specifically Achaeans from Mycenae. This is conjecture; but if Mycenae was able to exploit the wealth of the unwalled Cretan palaces in this way a

* Book-numbers of the Iliad will be printed in Roman figures; references to the Odyssey will be in italicized Arabic numerals.

great many problems are eased. Crete in the late Bronze Age possessed the natural and commercial wealth that Mycenae does not seem to have had, at least in sufficient measure to account for phenomena like the treasures of the grave-circles or Agamemnon's later pre-eminence as reflected in the Iliad. What Mycenae did possess, from the beginning of the Late Helladic period, was military power; this is what its position and its architectural remains chiefly emphasize. But Mycenae must also have had the genius to assimilate the wealth and resources that good fortune and military power together thrust upon it. For it would be wrong to deny to Mycenae some peaceful gifts too. Its pottery, even after the decline of Cretan influence, and although it had its excesses, is technically good and in its simpler forms artistically quite successful (pl. 3a). Its metal-work and jewellery are more than a mere imitation of Minoan and Near Eastern models. The art of fresco-painting is one that developed as far on the mainland as in Crete; in Mycenae itself little has survived because of its rocky site, but the walls of the state apartments at Tiryns and Pylos were gorgeously decorated with hunting scenes, fishes, monkeys, griffins, birds, a lyre-player, women in procession.

The relevance of these speculations on the position of Mycenae is this. If the Achaean power of the mainland was to a large extent based on wealth and inventiveness drained off from Crete, then it is easier to understand its decline when, as we see from the artefacts, the Cretan influence was dying away and Knossos lay in ruins. If the power of golden Mycenae itself was based on military as much as commercial pretensions, if it exercised its hegemony over the other Mycenaean palaces mainly on this footing, then it is easier to see the underlying cause of the wars of aggression that progressively weakened the whole Achaean world, notably the attacks on Thebes and the siege of Troy. The dynastic position at Mycenae, as represented in Homer, is confused. Agamemnon is king of Mycenae and on that basis alone, perhaps, leader of the whole Achaean army; but he also lives in Argos and has influence in Lacedaemon, where his younger brother Menelaus is king; according to the ninth book of the Iliad, at least, he holds sway over part of Messenia. It is not clear why the other princes of Achaea join his expedition against Troy. Legend suggests an earlier undertaking by the many royal suitors of Helen, and some kind of promise is mentioned by Homer; but Thucydides considers it to have been elicited rather by Agamemnon's pre-eminent power.[1] The Iliad and the Odyssey reveal a society, or a distillation of different societies, in which the rulers of the cities of Achaean Greece were bound to each other not so much by kinship, which operated in certain cases, as by an elaborate system of gift-giving, which imposed reciprocal obligations without formal alliances or the necessity for a hierarchy of states.[2] At the same time Agamemnon is recognized in the poems as the supreme Achaean king, with an agreed authority which cannot be explained simply on the basis of family relationships or semi-commercial obligations. It is possible, then, that Mycenae had for long been the accepted military leader of the mainland cities. It seems to have initiated the attack on Knossos, as it certainly did that on Troy. The expeditions of the Seven against Thebes and of their more successful sons were undertaken from Argos. We do not know the excuse for the assault on Knossos, but mythology offers matrimonial and dynastic reasons for the other two onslaughts. The common factor of all three cases is probably the richness of the city under attack; although Thebes, being an Achaean and not a foreign city, must have provided some additional pretext. Mycenae, having had the lion's share of the Cretan loot, and possessing fewer natural facilities than some of the other Greek states for keeping itself in the manner to which it had grown accustomed, was the natural initiator of these wars of plunder; and was able to make itself unpleasant to any other city—like, perhaps, Thebes itself—which refused to join in on the basis of an uneven division of spoils.

While Minoan Crete and then the Achaean powers of the mainland were dominating the Aegean area in the middle and late Bronze Age, the interior of Asia Minor was controlled by the Hittites—an Indo-European people who entered the peninsula around 1900, at the very time when the Greek-speaking Middle Helladic people were moving into Greece and the Troy VI people were arriving at Troy. The Hittite civilization grew to become a powerful and impressive one, especially under Suppiluliumas around 1350, during the era of Mycenae's greatness.[1] The palace at the Hittite capital at Hattusas (the modern Boghaz Keui) was a maze of rooms and magazines grouped around a large central court, as at Knossos; other Near Eastern palaces of the middle and late Bronze Age are roughly similar, and this was undoubtedly a widespread type which reflects the associations of these cultures, directly or indirectly, with the civilizations of the Euphrates valley. A large archive of clay tablets at Boghaz Keui can now be read, and shows the existence there of a highly centralized palace economy of the type also indicated for Nuzi, Alalakh, Mari, Knossos and Pylos. The Hittite empire collapsed around 1200 after costly struggles against Egypt and a period of increasing quarrels with smaller subject-states in Asia Minor itself. One of the peoples mentioned in the Hittite tablets is the Akhkhijawa, who were evidently centred outside Asia Minor but had interests along its south-western and southern coasts—interests which were pursued now with the approval, now with the extreme disapproval of the Hittite king.[2] Scholars now tend to accept the name Akhkhijawa as referring to the Akhaiwoi or Achaeans, which is what the Mycenaean Greeks, according to Homer, most commonly called themselves. The Achaeans of the Hittite tablets, though, seem mostly to have belonged to a settlement outside the Greek mainland; the likeliest place for them is perhaps Rhodes. Rhodes undoubtedly had ambitions on the Lycian coast, and these were probably reflected in the fight in the Iliad between Sarpedon of Lycia and Tlepolemos of Rhodes; and it is significant too that in parts of Pamphylia, in the historical period, a form of Greek was used which is akin to the Arcadian and Cypriot dialects, themselves certain relics of 'Mycenaean' or late Bronze Age Greek.

The Hittites never controlled the extreme north-western tip of Asia Minor; for there had been established there ever since early in the 3rd millennium B.C. a strongly fortified town called Ilios or Troy.[1] Troy was captured by invaders, not the Hittites, at the time when the Hittites themselves were spreading over the north and centre of Asia Minor. This new population, inhabitants of the sixth successive town to be built on the same site (Troy VI), established themselves so strongly in their advantageous new home that they avoided embroilment with the Hittites and are almost—perhaps wholly—ignored on the surviving Hittite tablets. Troy stood at the western entrance to the Dardanelles, and at the crossing of a not very important route from the north down the Asia Minor coast. This position might have brought a certain prosperity from early times; in the 2nd millennium B.C., however, it seems doubtful whether Troy took much part in trade with the interior. It is now probable from the American re-excavation of the site, where Schliemann's original dig, in the early days of scientific archaeology, had played havoc with the stratification, that the power and wealth of the city were greatly increased by the new population; and that this wealth was based not so much on tolls exacted from passing traders, as used to be thought, as on textile production and the rearing of horses. The fortified part of Troy occupied a very small site devoted to the royal palace and its appendages; as at Mycenae, most of the population must have lived outside the walls. The finds from the new excavation suggest that its commerce was directed west rather than east: fragments of more than 700 imported Mycenaean pots were discovered in the very limited area of fresh exploration, while eastern products were virtually lacking. This wealthy city was destroyed, apparently by earthquake, soon after 1300, to be quickly succeeded by a poorer settlement built on and among the ruins by the survivors. This settlement, known as Troy VII a, was in its turn destroyed only a generation or two later; the excavators place this event somewhere around 1240–1230. This time the destruction was caused not by earthquake but by invasion: there are human bones in the streets and a systematic devastation such as could only be caused by a full-scale sack. After the disaster a few survivors clung on until they

too succumbed to a new attack by a band of barbarous northerners. A short while longer, and the age-old site lay abandoned
until the late 8th century B.C.

The Iliad and Odyssey and the universal tradition of the
Greeks tell us that Troy was sacked after a long (though
doubtless exaggerated) siege by Achaeans under the leadership
of Agamemnon king of Mycenae. According to the most
influential ancient calculation this took place in 1184—or, to
use the widest limits, after 1300 and before 1100.[1] Only one of
the major historical destructions of Troy accords with this
tradition: that which put an end to Troy VIIa probably
around 1230 or 1240. Much else conspires to show that in this
case, as in so many others, mythological tradition was based on
historical fact. An arrow-head found in one of the streets was of
Mycenaean type; and relations with the Achaean world seem to
have been strained since the earlier part of the thirteenth
century, when Mycenaean imports almost ceased. Moreover
the destruction of Troy VIIa came at the end of a long siege, as
traditionally did Agamemnon's conquest; so much is shown by
the crowding of hastily built huts within the walls and the mass
of storage jars newly sunk in the floors. Admittedly there is no
indication of Trojan loot in the graves and ruins of the Achaean
cities; but this is because the booty would consist of women,
horses, and precious metalwork which, since it did not match
that of Mycenae in technique at this period, would be melted
down.

A certain simultaneity of events begins to appear. Greek-
speakers enter the peninsula around 1900, and at just about
this period another Indo-European people, the Hittites, move
into Asia Minor and a new population takes possession of Troy.
Add to this that the Trojans of Troy VI, like the Middle
Helladic people of mainland Greece, used the highly distinctive
Minyan pottery technique, and two related possibilities present
themselves: first, that the Troy VI people, though not identical
with the Hittites, were of the same Indo-European stock and
were propelled into Asia Minor by the same current of migration; and secondly, that the similarities of Troy VI and Middle

Helladic culture imply some degree of racial kinship between Trojans and Achaeans. Unfortunately nothing is known about the language of Troy VI and VII a; no tablets have been found like those used for records or inventories by the Hittites or by the Achaeans once they had learned the art of writing from the Minoans of Crete. It is possible that the Trojans did not know this art. At any rate no reason is so far known why their language should not have been of Indo-European type. It is possible, then, that the Middle Helladic Greek-speakers of the Greek mainland and the Trojans of Troy VI were related to each other, although their immediate past had been different enough to produce many superficial divergences of culture. In this case the contrast between Greek Achaeans and barbarian Trojans, well exemplified in Herodotus, would be misleading. The cultural differences would be explained not only by the distinct experiences of the two tribes before they reached their eventual homelands, but also by the difference between the populations they overruled and absorbed. For just as the Middle Helladic people must have been significantly altered by the traditions and way of life of their Early Helladic predecessors and subjects, so must the citizens of Troy VI and VII a have been affected, not only culturally but also physically, by the earlier stock that built and peopled the first five settlements at Troy. Equally important would be Troy's comparative isolation from her neighbours during the 2nd millennium, at a time when Mycenae underwent a tremendous cultural revolution through contact with Crete, a quite distinct and probably non-Indo-European civilization. There must also have been Minoan–Mycenaean intermarriage to complicate still further the racial ingredients of the Achaeans. The probability of ethnic affinity between Achaeans and Trojans will be considerably increased if the newly extended archaeological exploration of Asia Minor confirms a recent suggestion, so far based mainly on surface finds, that the Middle Helladic people who brought the Greek language to Greece came not from the region of the Hungarian plains but through Asia Minor, then round the north shore of the Aegean or straight across the sea.[1]

A racial kinship between Trojans and Achaeans would admittedly explain certain things in Homer: the fact, for example, that apart from Priam's oriental addiction to concubinage, and the vociferousness of the Trojan army (though that is mainly due to the allies), the customs and religion of the Trojans, and indeed most of their names, are much the same as those of the Greeks. Naturally this is largely due to poetic simplification. But if the Trojans really had always been remembered as 'barbarians' in the Greek sense—non-Greek in their speech, that is, and therefore in their customs—then we might expect to find many of their peculiarities emphasized by the epic poets in order to increase the dramatic and pictorial effect of their songs. Carried too far, this would admittedly reduce the heroic dimensions of the whole expedition; but it could be carried much further than it is in our Iliad and Odyssey. Apart from the similar customs there are one or two surprising genealogical connexions between Homeric Achaeans and Trojans, which would perhaps be more intelligible if the two nations were closely related.[1] Yet such coincidences may be due to the limitations of poetic invention where proper names are concerned; we can see, in fact, that in Homer minor Trojans are often given the same names as minor Achaeans. A surprisingly large proportion of 'Homeric' names found in the Pylos tablets, names belonging to Pylians of the 13th century, were attached to Trojans, not Achaeans, in the Iliad—which may suggest, however, not that historical Trojans did have Greek names but that epic minstrels used names with which they were familiar in their own cities for minor and fictitious characters whether Greek or non-Greek.[2]

Another striking common factor in the history of the eastern Mediterranean area during the second millennium is the relative frequency of disastrous earthquakes. Tradition tells us virtually nothing of these great cataclysms. Can we really believe, then, that so many famed cities, including Knossos and other Cretan centres around 1570 and Troy VI around 1275, were so drastically afflicted by earthquakes as to cause major breaks in cultural and political development? I think we can.

In ideal conditions the archaeological record distinguishes between destruction by earthquake and human destruction: in the former case there are cracked and neatly tumbled walls and no sign of preceding siege or military preparation. Fire and looting occur with both agencies. At first archaeologists were reluctant to admit that it was primarily an earthquake that destroyed Knossos in the 16th century, though the material evidence strongly suggests it. Yet in the past forty years there have been effective new demonstrations of the power and frequency of earthquakes in the central and eastern Mediterranean: Messina and Corinth in the early nineteen-twenties, the Ionian Island towns, Santorin/Thera and parts of Thessaly in the past decade; and at some time in the 2nd millennium B.C. Thera was literally split in pieces by a cataclysmic earthquake or volcanic explosion. It is not hard to imagine the effect on a crowded, over-centralized palace-state like Knossos, especially when neighbouring states were prone to respond to the catastrophe not with medicines and blankets but with murder and the lust for loot.

The palaces of the Mycenaean world were fortunate enough to escape this kind of destruction. Most of them, like Mycenae itself, were not situated directly on the earthquake-belt. The downfall of the Achaean culture, on the contrary, was probably caused by economic stagnation leading to internal wars, and by the gradual pressure of a new wave of Greek-speakers, the Dorians, who had been infiltrating southwards from northwest Greece at least since the 13th century. Mycenae's end was paralleled not only by that of other mainland cities but also by the destruction of Boghaz Keui, Ugarit and Alalakh. Here too the eclipse of long-established local cultures was caused by economic difficulties leading to destructive wars of aggression, which in turn so much weakened the central power that it was unable to defend itself against new, land-hungry invaders.

How far, it may be asked at this point, was the civilization which forms the background of the Homeric poems really a heroic age? Was Hesiod right to insert between the bloodthirsty age of bronze and his own squalid era an age of heroes when

most things were good? Was life between wars in late Bronze
Age Greece as settled and prosperous as the descriptions of
Pylos and Sparta in the third and fourth books of the Odyssey
would have us believe? In a sense these are misleading questions, since the 'Mycenaean' civilization covered a vast period
of time—as long as that between Columbus and the present
day—and varied greatly in quality. The traditions used by
Homer compressed this period into a matter of three or four
generations, as tradition does, and selected from different
phases of it as well as from the totally different life of post-
Mycenaean Greece. In a few matters the Iliad and Odyssey
probably reflect the great days of the 16th, 15th and 14th
centuries, the days of the shaft-grave kings and their successors
of the tholos-tombs, of the builders of the great wall and the
Lion Gate, when Mycenae stood at the head of an expanding
empire, heir to the wealth and maritime power of Crete, with
the resources of the mainland behind her and the eastern trade
temporarily within her grasp. But more often Homer reproduces qualities more suited to the following centuries, when life
was more circumscribed and more precarious, trade more
difficult, and little further was to be had from Crete; when
Asia Minor and Syria were themselves in turmoil and Egypt
hostile. Differences in natural wealth between the Mycenaean
palaces must now have made themselves felt, encouraging
jealousy and dynastic quarrels. The too-easy riches of the past
and the cumbrous administration of the palaces led to a decline
that can rightly be called a decadence, the victims of which
tried the remedy of looting, both outside the empire and within
it, in order to keep themselves going. Homer's portrait of his
chief characters, complex as it is, roughly coincides with what
we might expect of an amalgam of qualities from these two very
different epochs—and from that which followed. Agamemnon
the supreme ruler of 'Argos and many islands' is most probably
derived, tortuously and indirectly, from memories of the great
period; Agamemnon the leader of an uneasy and at times dis-
obedient expedition against Troy, which had earlier been a
good customer for Mycenaean exports, belongs to the age of

disintegration. Many elements in the poems stem from this later age, and it is natural that memories of the more distant past should be fewer and less specific. The individual voyages of opportunism or plunder, like those undertaken by Menelaus after the fall of Troy or by the Odysseus of the false tales in the Odyssey, belong to the end of the Mycenaean age and to the succeeding Dark Age; so probably do the anarchical behaviour of Thersites, the cattle raids and counter-raids of Nestor's reminiscences in the Iliad, and the costly resistance of his Pylians against the northern invaders symbolized by Heracles.[1]

It would be easy to over-emphasize the degree of disruption implied in the Homeric poetry. The selfish individualism of some of the chief heroes was no doubt exaggerated during the development of the tradition. Not all the symptoms of imperial decay would apply at one and the same time, and no doubt many individuals, perhaps even including singers of poetry, managed to lead relatively tranquil lives in the last generation of Pylos or even of Mycenae. Since Ventris's decipherment of the Linear B tablets we can assess more realistically, in the chapter which follows, some of the conditions of life in an Achaean palace shortly before its fall.

2

THE LINEAR B TABLETS
AND LIFE IN A LATE MYCENAEAN
PALACE-STATE

THE tablets were inscribed shortly before the destruction of the edifices in which they were found; they were baked by the fires that swept through the palaces or their outbuildings. Pylos has produced the greatest number of complete tablets, Knossos the next, and Mycenae disappointingly few so far.[1] It is possible to learn more about Pylos, then, than about the other two palaces, which were in other respects more important. The Pylos tablets suggest that there was no overt anarchy. The intricate organization, social and economic, was still operative; though how well it was working we cannot tell. It is a characteristic of the Mycenaean type of over-centralization that it can go wrong with extraordinary rapidity; some sort of parallel is provided by the economic chaos that overtook Egypt, and to a lesser extent the Roman empire as a whole, in the 3rd century A.D. We cannot be sure, then, that these lists of tradesmen and ships' crews and shepherds, these rations and contributions of seed and oil, these large totals of sheep and goats and pigs, are necessarily the sign of a vital economy. Comparison with the rather similar Knossian tablets of two hundred years earlier does not suggest much decline. But this is a fallible criterion, and the truth is that the tablets are too sparse in content and too obscure in detail to give even the degree of information on social and economic life that can reasonably be expected from evidence of this kind.

Before further discussion of conditions in late 13th-century Pylos two points must be emphasized. The first is simple: implausible as the minute organization of life in a Mycenaean state may seem, it is paralleled by the records of other palace civilizations in the second-millennium Near East—Boghaz Keui, Ugarit, and the Hurrian palaces of Nuzi and Alalakh. At the same time there is an intelligibility and a rationality about most of those non-Greek records which is often notably absent from the Mycenaean documents as they are presented to us.

The second point is that the investigation of the tablets, and of the language written in the Linear B syllabary, is still at an early stage. That the decipherment as Greek is correct in essentials I do not seriously doubt; though there is still a chance or two in a thousand that it is not. On the other hand the translations proposed for many of the tablets, even of the three hundred 'more interesting' ones from Pylos, Knossos and Mycenae described and interpreted by Ventris and Chadwick in their fundamental *Documents in Mycenaean Greek* (Cambridge, 1956), are admittedly provisional and in some cases highly dubious. In a case like *Documents*, no. 30 (Pylos Ae264), it is doubtful whether a translation so improbable in itself and so completely unconfirmed as Greek as 'Philaios the goat-herd (who is acting as ?) seizer has seized the cattle of Dunios' merits prolonged attention, and I have little doubt that in future editions it will be abandoned. Further, only a small proportion of tablets found up to 1955 have yielded convincing Greek even to the quite stringent pressure exerted on them by Ventris and Chadwick and other philologists working on the subject. The situation has not been changed by the comparatively small number of tablets found since then. The decipherers assert that 'There are no tablets of reasonable extent which do not give some sign of being written in Greek, though of course lists of names may well have a foreign look' (*Documents*, p. 71). We must be careful here: even of the three hundred selected tablets of *Documents* some give only the barest sign of being or containing Greek; and presumably most of the total of three thousand five hundred tablets are much less intelligible than the selected three hundred. Ventris and Chadwick also tell us that 'At least 65 per cent of the recorded Mycenaean words are proper names' (*Documents*, p. 92). The consequences we learn from the preface to the Mycenaean Vocabulary printed as Appendix 1 of *Documents*: that some 3500 tablets produce only 990 separate words, excluding apparent proper names; and, of these, 260 are mere spelling or inflectional variants. Of the remaining 630 ostensibly distinct vocabulary words found in the tablets only some 252, according to the decipherers, can be 'directly equated with Homeric or classical forms, and have corresponding meanings which fit the context of the tablets with virtual certainty'.

Yet detailed consideration shows that we cannot accept even as many as 'some 252' words, on the tablets known up till 1955, as being certainly Greek. Only about two-thirds of the total fulfil the sensible dual requirements of morphology and context that the decipherers defined. Moreover the total is not made up of 252 quite different words, but in some cases of different forms, for instance adjectival and nominal, from the same root: for example, *a-ko-ra* and *a-ko-ra-jo* (ἀγορά and ἀγοραῖος) or *da-mo* and *da-mi-jo* (δᾶμος and δάμιος). Sometimes an adjectival or verbal form is accepted largely on the basis of a previous acceptance of the noun form, or *vice versa*, so that such cases are not fully independent confirmations of Greek in the tablets. On my count the total of 252 'certain' Greek words should be reduced by at least 35 for this reason. Of the remainder only about two-thirds really fill both requirements; which gives a total of only some 150 independent lexical units that are convincing as Greek (to which a few others should probably be added from the compound personal names) out of a total of about 3500 tablets. Even assuming that only about 550 separate units can be distinguished (the decipherers say 630), apart from proper names, 150/550 or less than one-third is a disappointingly small proportion as well as a disappointingly small total. And even this is on the assumption that at least 65 per cent of distinguishable words are proper names; the ways of identifying such names are discussed by Ventris and Chadwick at *Documents*, p. 92, and though their estimate may be on the high side it does seem that every other word in the tablets as a whole is likely to fall in this category.

How is it that so few words on the tablets can be reasonably shown to be Greek? Several contributory reasons are obvious. First, in the space of four or five hundred years between the writing of the Pylos tablets and the composition of the Iliad and Odyssey, which are otherwise our earliest examples of the Greek language, many words would no doubt have fallen out of use and been forgotten. Secondly, many of the technical words connected with the social and economic organization of a Mycenaean state would be such that they might easily not chance to turn up in the whole of subsequent Greek literature (which is after all mainly 'literary' and not practical or documentary)— or rather in that part of it which survives. Thirdly, some of the words used in the tablets would be foreign loan-words, like χρυσός (gold) or χιτών (tunic), which might, unlike these, have been abandoned for native equivalents. Fourthly, in documents of this type the total number of dictionary items used might be quite small—though some of them would be used, as they are in the tablets, repeatedly. Taking the number of separate Greek words, rather than the total of their occurrences, may be to some extent misleading. Fifthly, Mycenaean dialect may in certain respects have been so different from later dialects that some of its forms would not be recognized as Greek; though this is unlikely. Sixthly, scribal errors may prevent us from recognizing a few words as Greek. It may legitimately be asked whether all these factors suffice to explain the peculiar proportional situation as it appears to exist: that fewer than one in three words on the tablets, excluding probable names, can be accepted as Greek with comparative safety.

I do not profess to know the answer to this problem, if it really is a problem. On present evidence it seems most unlikely that the decipherment itself is wrong, except possibly in the value of some of the rarer signs which do not greatly affect the issue. The laxity of the Mycenaean spelling rules does not help, since it increases, rather than diminishes, the occurrence of apparent Greek words. One possibility that deserves consideration is that some of the tablets, or at least some of the words on some of the tablets, are written not in Greek but in

some other language. This possibility was too hastily rejected by
the decipherers (*Documents*, pp. 71-2). They were concerned
chiefly with the suggestion of Merlingen that the Greeks were a
subject-class, keeping accounts for foreign rulers; or of Andrews,
that the scribes were foreigners who did not know Greek
properly and so used many unrecognizable barbarisms. I agree
that the former theory is historically implausible; but the idea
of some, if not all, the scribes of the tablets being foreigners
should not be rejected outright or categorized as irrelevant. It
should lead to the conclusion, however, not that the Greek of
the tablets is unintelligible because it is full of mistakes, but
that, although the scribes could write Greek good enough for
the purpose, they may sometimes have inserted words in their
original language or even written whole tablets in it. Historically this is not improbable: Linear B is a script adapted from
the earlier Linear A, which was used for writing the 'Minoan'
language, whatever that was—certainly not Greek. The
adaptation was presumably carried out by scribes to some
extent bilingual, after the hypothetical domination of Knossos
by Mycenae around 1500; it is probable that these were Minoan
scribes rather than Greeks who had suddenly learned Minoan.
The Achaeans seem to have taken over the palace at Knossos
as a going concern, and would presumably have left the
accounting activities more or less unaltered, though perhaps
insisting that some accounts should be done in Greek. Thus
Minoan scribes would probably be left, in the main, in control.
It is highly probable, too, that many Cretan craftsmen left
Crete for the mainland during the whole period between the
earthquake and the final destruction of Knossos; and not unlikely that scribes would be among these, carrying the new
accounting technique to the rich palaces of the mainland. Such
recondite skills tend to be preserved within families, and it
would not be surprising if some at least of the men who wrote
the Pylos tablets—who were fairly numerous, however, judging
from the different handwritings, and probably not all professionals—were descended from scribes in the palace at Knossos.

Much of this is pure speculation, but I am concerned with

showing that Minoan scribes *could* have been employed in Pylos and Mycenae centuries after the fall of Knossos. To show that they might plausibly have used some Minoan words, or even have written complete tablets in Minoan, is more difficult. But two things must be remembered. First, most of the tablets were ephemeral accounts, temporary records of day-to-day transactions. A few may have been consolidated accounts such as would be produced for inspection by authority from time to time; most were much less formal—something more than *aide-mémoire*, since they were filed away, but intended chiefly for specialized scrutiny within the accounting department. Secondly, the attachment of pictorial ideograms to the verbal descriptions, which is a characteristic of the majority of the tablets, might in certain cases enable non-Minoan literates to understand the gist of the description, even if this contained scraps of the old office idiom of Knossos, retained perhaps by a kind of bureaucratic snobbery. In a sense this whole theory is a special form of the hypothesis that many foreign loan-words must have been used in the tablets. There are difficulties, however, in this hypothesis in its simple form: for example (as M. I. Finley has reminded me), many of the Greek words claimed in the decipherment are just the kind of special name or technical term for which a foreign loan-word would, on the hypothesis, be expected.

There is no point in pursuing this conjecture further.[1] It has been presented not because it is particularly attractive for its own sake but because formally it is one of very few possible explanations for the small amount of convincing Greek so far found in the tablets. The decipherers did not think the amount as small as I do, and for them the problem was correspondingly less serious. It hardly exists at all for those who accept the transcription into Greek of the three hundred selected tablets in *Documents in Mycenaean Greek* as a hard core of fact, upon which complicated hypotheses can be safely constructed—an acceptance against which they were scrupulously warned by Ventris and Chadwick. It would be interesting to know whether or not there were ex-Minoans among the Mycenaean *corps* of scribes

28

and how many foreign loan-words were in common or professional use. Historically it is more important at present to understand the limitations of the tablets themselves. Even with these limitations they are documents of curious fascination. We may now turn, then, to summarize the state of the declining Mycenaean world as they seem to describe it—in particular the state of life at Pylos.

The palace of Messenian Pylos at the modern site called Ano Englianos seems to have controlled a large area of the southwestern Peloponnese. No less than 160 different place-names seem to occur on the Pylos tablets, of which most, although naturally not all, appear to be located in the domain. The ruler and head of state is called the Wanaka (later Greek Ϝάναξ, ἄναξ), the lord or king. The regular classical Greek word for king, βασιλεύς, occurs in the form qa-si-re-u, but refers to a comparatively subsidiary type of official or head-man, perhaps the head of certain semi-independent villages. Next in importance to the king seems to be the ra-wa-ke-ta, probably Lawagetas (cf. Greek λαγέτας), 'leader of the λαός or people'. He has been interpreted as a military leader, but that remains quite uncertain; though it is difficult to see what his position was—perhaps the king's heir-apparent? The king has a private te-me-no, τέμενος, 'cutting-off' or enclave, presumably of the best land, and so does the leader of the people. His enclave is perhaps one-third the size of the king's: see *Documents*, no. 152 (Pylos Er312), 'The *temenos* of the king, sowing of so much grain (?), WHEAT 30. The *temenos* of the leader of the people, sowing of so much grain (?), WHEAT 10'. This tablet goes on to specify the amount of seed associated with land held by three te-re-ta (? *telestai* or fief-holders) and with wo-ro-ki-jo-ne-jo land (? Ϝοργιωνεῖος or 'belonging to the celebrators of rites'). The word te-me-no only occurs on this one tablet; in any case it is wrong to infer that just because the king has a *temenos*, a word used mainly for 'divine precinct' in classical Greek, he must have received divine honours.[1] In Homer a *temenos* simply means 'a specially selected and reserved piece of land', whether it be held by god, king, or any favoured person.

It is impossible to assign most of the place-names to points on the map. *Pu-ro*, however, obliges by occurring quite often, thus confirming the identification with ancient Pylos. It is disappointing but not surprising that none of the tablets mentions the name of any known members of the Neleid dynasty, which according to Homer and tradition must have ruled Pylos at this period. The name of one important figure in the tablets, but probably not the king himself, is *E-ke-ra$_2$-wo*, unparalleled in Homer. Two tablets provide a list of nine places which may be important towns, or may just be villages close to the main palace; *Me-ta-pa* and *Pa-ki-ja-*, at least, occur fairly often, though they cannot be identified. The Catalogue of Ships (II. 591ff.) names nine towns in Nestor's kingdom, but these include Pylos itself, which the nine places of the tablets do not, and only one name is possibly common to both; thus the coincidence of number is fortuitous. A great many of the places on the tablets must have been small villages or hamlets, but each of these seems to have had its head-man who drew rations from and made contributions to the palace. The word which most commonly appears to mean 'head-man' or 'mayor', *ko-re-te*, has no plausible Greek equivalent. The difficulty of precisely envisaging the kinds of transaction involved is illustrated by one of the more explicit tablets (*Documents*, no. 257, Pylos Jn829) in the translation of the decipherers (the words in italics being admitted as less than certain, and *superintendents* now being generally preferred to *wives*): 'Thus the *mayors* and (their *wives*), and the vice-*mayors* and key-bearers and supervisors of *figs* and *hoeing*, will contribute bronze *for ships* and the points for arrows and spears'; there follow sixteen names of places, with the quantity of bronze to be contributed by mayor and vice-mayor of each place. That the vice-mayors, if this is really meant by *po-ro-ko-re-te*, should make separate contributions is a little odd, as is their separation from the mayors by vague 'superintendents'. The absence from the main list of places and contributions of these superintendents, the key-bearers (priestesses?—there are classical parallels for this title), and those splendid but improbable figures the supervisors of figs and hoeing, help to make one somewhat sceptical of the conjectured meaning of the whole introductory rubric. But at least bronze seems to be proportionally collected from villages or towns for some kind of centralized use, partly for manufacture of weapons. The reverse process is seen in *Documents*, no. 250 (Pylos Vn20): 'Thus the wine of *Pa-ra-we-* has been distributed', followed by nine place-names and a quantity against each. Here we may conjecture that wine from a winegrowing district was sent to the palace and reissued to places that did not have enough of their own, doubtless in exchange for their special produce or services. All this complex fetching and carrying to and from the palace, and the consequent checks that had to be made, is the result of a heavily centralized pre-monetary system.

Large contributions of commodities are made to various deities, not only by communities or officials but also by individual landowners, including the king and the leader of the people. These contributions were no doubt partly in return for distributions of seed and other commodities; it need not be assumed that they were all used for the decoration and upkeep of shrines—perhaps a part of them went towards the expenses of the palace and its civil servants, much as Athene's treasure in classical Athens could be used for state purposes.

The minuteness of many of these transactions, together with their apparent lack of perfect consistency in classification, is illustrated by, for example, *Documents*, no. 183 (Pylos Nn831), where contributions of linen (?) are specified for different inhabitants of a village: seven individual names are given, but among them come the cowherd, the mayor (?) (who gives as much as the rest together), the shepherds and the smith. That these are known by their trades and not their names may indicate some kind of trade-guild organization, as for example at Ugarit. Certainly the specialization of labour was intense. We should expect woodcutters, bronze-smiths and shipbuilders to be professionals in these fields, but unguent-boilers and chairmakers—and now, it seems, cyanus-makers at Mycenae—are surprising. The thirty-seven female bath-pourers of Pylos

(*Documents*, no. 9, Pylos Ab553) and the six sons of the head-band-makers (*Documents*, no. 12, Pylos Ad671) come as something of a shock. But in a land where the location of every pig or sheep and the exact condition of every chariot-wheel seems, in theory at least, to have been known, we have no right to be too dismayed. Perhaps the excessive classification was to some extent imposed by the scribes, and when there were no baths to be poured or water to be collected the thirty-seven 'bath-pourers' would be used in other capacities.

Many of the tablets deal with land-tenure. Land seems to have been divided into privately owned and communal, although on what basis the communal land was worked and taxed remains obscure. The suggestion has been made and accepted by some that the 'workers for the public' in Homer, the δημιοεργοί (who do not occur in the tablets), the doctors and minstrels and carpenters, were originally 'workers of communal land'.[1] This seems grossly improbable—but not much more so than some of the other speculation that has hovered as a kind of *ur*-Indo-European fog over the Pylos land-tenure tablets, the detailed meaning of which remains largely unknown.

Disappointingly little can be gathered about military activities. Much has been made of the 'rowers to go to Pleuron' in *Documents*, no. 53 (Pylos An1), but they are only sufficient to man a single ship and Pleuron *could* be almost anywhere; though it is not unlikely to be the Aetolian town, and it is probable that Dorian invaders crossed the Corinthian Gulf from that region. Again, *Documents*, no. 54 (Pylos An610) gives a total of 443 men, and the word *e-re-ta*, 'rowers', appears in the broken first line; it is probable though not certain that these men are all being detailed as rowers, forming the complement of some 15 ships at 30 to a ship. If this is so, then as the decipherers say it is a military and not a mercantile operation. Military groups seem to be mentioned in *Documents*, nos. 56–60, for example no. 58 (Pylos An564): '*o-ka* [an obscure word, possibly meaning "command" or "contingent"] of Klumenos: Perintheus, Woinewas, Antiaon, Eruthras. Fifty...*ke-ki-de* [quite obscure] men of Metapa, sixty *ku-re-we* [equally obscure] men of *U-pi-ja-ki-ri-*, and with them the Follower [*e-qe-ta*, tentatively connected with Greek ἑπέτης "follower", in the sense, otherwise unattested in Greek, of Latin *comes* = count, i.e. follower of the king] Alektruon son of Etewoklewes [= Eteocles]....' At least there are some good Greek names here. Some of these probable military formations are guarding the coast (presumably a normal precaution against pirates at any date), if *o-pi-a₂-ra* in *Documents*, no. 56 (Pylos An657) is really *ἐπι-αλα, classical ἔφαλα, 'by the sea'. The mention of women simply by foreign ethnic names, for instance the Cnidian women who are something to do with grain on *Documents*, no. 26 (Pylos An292), suggests that they were war booty or the descendants of war booty; a word for 'female captive' might appear on *Documents*, no. 16 (Pylos Ad686). Slaves belonging to individual men are certainly mentioned on the tablets, and it would be surprising if much of the labour force was not composed of captives and their progeny. Other military evidence is provided by the lists of equipment, including chariots and armour. Chariot-tablets are commonest from Knossos (see pl. 2 b), though various types and conditions of chariot-wheels are listed at Pylos. Homer reveals that chariots were easily taken to pieces and sometimes stored without wheels (*Il.* v. 722), and this is confirmed beyond doubt by the separate ideograms at Knossos for complete chariots, wheel-less chariots, and chariot-frames without wheels, pole, or pole-stay. A possible total of over 400 chariots is suggested by the Knossos archive—a substantial but not massive figure, probably incomplete, which suggests that Knossos in the 15th century had been fully militarized by its Mycenaean overlords. Lists of corslets and helmets at Pylos are very incomplete; they reveal something about the details of armour but nothing at all about the state of military activity in Pylos before its fall.

The majority of 'slaves' mentioned on the tablets are slaves belonging to gods, *te-o-jo do-e-ro* or θεοῖο δοῦλοι (cf. for example *Documents*, no. 119, Pylos Eo224); but since they are often lease-holders the decipherers suggest that they are not slaves in the full later sense but a subordinate class of free citizens, perhaps farmers of temple lands. The making of regular offerings to the gods and the integration of religion with civil life is widely exemplified on the tablets. It need come as no surprise that some of the names of divinities at Pylos are those of Olympian gods of historical Greece, many of whom were already known to be of Mycenaean derivation; but it is still a pleasant confirmation. The appearance of Greek gods at Knossos, too, is also to be expected in view of the probable Mycenaean domination, but it is surprising that there is no higher proportion of small local cults, representing in this case survivals or transformations of Minoan cults, than there is at Pylos. The following gods of the later Greek pantheon are probably mentioned at either Knossos or Pylos: Zeus, Hera, Poseidon, Athena (called Athana Potnia), Hermes (?), Artemis. Apollo and perhaps Ares do not appear as such, but Paian and Enyalios do; these were local gods, the latter certainly Cretan, which were later integrated with the more widely known deities. Demeter does not seem to occur; or at least *da-ma-te* comes in the first line of *Documents*, no. 114 (Pylos En609), but is highly unlikely from the context to be a divine name there. From Knossos comes a very satisfactory tablet (*Documents*, no. 206, Knossos Gg705) which begins 'Amnisos: one jar of honey to Eleuthia, one jar of honey to all the gods...'. Amnisos is on the coast near Knossos, and we know from Homer that Eileithyia, a female deity later associated especially with childbirth, was located there: '...in Amnisos, where is the cave of Eileithyia' (*19.188**). Others who seem to receive offerings at either place but are not known from later cults are: a dove-goddess, a priestess of the winds, Iphimedeia, Drimios. The name Dionysos occurs on two fragmentary tablets, but there is little to suggest that it is a god's and not a man's name. Some of the deities conjectured on the tablets are highly speculative, notably the 'thrice-hero' and the so-called 'lord of the house' which have been read on *Documents*, no. 172 (Pylos Tn316). Even where the names coincide with those of historical deities, the form under which they were

---

* The reader is reminded that these italicized references are to the Odyssey; Iliadic references are in the form XIX. 188.

worshipped in Mycenaean Knossos and Pylos was probably very different from that of most of their later counterparts. So much is shown by Mycenaean gems and seal-stones depicting scenes of worship; these follow the Cretan pattern, but must have had meaning for Mycenaean owners. On them we find a goddess with a young male consort, a god (and also a goddess) worshipped by dancing female votaries, a goddess flanked by animals. These aspects have certain later Greek parallels but were virtually ignored by the epic minstrels. So too the theriomorphic divinities and daimons of Crete, occasionally seen in Mycenaean works of art (cf. pl. 2 a), survived mainly as epithets like 'cow-faced' of Hera or 'owl-faced' of Athena.

This, then, in rapid survey, is the sort of thing that the tablets tell us. What light does it all throw on Homer? Many of those who have spent most time with the tablets think that they completely transfigure our understanding of the Iliad and Odyssey, while certain more sceptical critics insist that, interesting as the new evidence is, it tells us almost nothing about the content of poetry the greater part of which, certainly, was composed centuries later.[1] To me the tablets seem to tell us certain things that are relevant to Homer, but far less than might be expected even from this type of document.

One of the most important contributions of the tablets is undoubtedly to the understanding of Homeric *language*. This is an artificial language, an amalgam containing elements derived from different periods of the legendary tradition. Admittedly the language of the tablets is restricted in scope and authorship; in addition the Linear B syllabary is so cumbrous, and the spelling conventions so ambiguous in their effect, that the exact forms intended by the scribes are often a matter for speculation. Yet even a fragmentary knowledge of the late Mycenaean dialect, not to mention the highly important confirmation that Homer's Achaeans did speak Greek, is valuable for the isolation of forms that originated before the Ionian and Aeolic migrations of about 1000 B.C. from those developed as a result of later dialectal changes.

Another kind of gain might have been expected from the

elucidation of Homeric names. Yet the proper names of the tablets have fewer Homeric counterparts than might be expected. Their decipherment is often difficult, since the spelling rules, in the absence of the contextual evidence which sometimes helps in the identification of vocabulary words, preclude the certain transcription of short names. A few anticipated place-names occur, but more do not; the Knossos tablets are better in this respect than those from Pylos and Mycenae. The absence of traditional Neleid names from the Pylos records has already been observed; Achilleus may occur at Knossos, Hector at Pylos, but many other heroic names are absent. It is impossible to tell whether the names of minor Homeric characters that do occur were just common Mycenaean names also used for poetical purposes or whether they were given by parents as deliberate references to historical figures known, perhaps, through early poetry and story. Many names on the tablets are evidently not Greek, and that is interesting: they must have survived from Early Helladic times, or be Minoan names brought by migrants and refugees from Crete; or some of them were perhaps introduced from Asia Minor or the Levant at the transition from the middle to the late Bronze Age.

The political and economic situation envisaged in the Homeric poems has this important similarity to that of the late Mycenaean world: Greece is divided into more or less inde-pendent kingdoms, each based upon a palace, the home of the king and his family and many of his retainers. In Homer the old word 'lord', ἄναξ, is restricted in sense and commonly applied either to gods or to Agamemnon as supreme king of the joint Achaean expedition. Conversely the common Homeric word for the king of a community is βασιλεύς, which on the tablets seems to have described someone different, a subsidiary princeling or even a sort of mayor. If the e-qe-ta of the tablets really refers to ἐπέται, 'followers', and if these are really the special associates of the king, then these may correspond with the king's ἑταῖροι or companions in Homer—a word which does not occur on the tablets, and would involve a curious change of nomenclature. We have seen that the Lawagetas of the tablets has been interpreted by some scholars as the military leader; this may have other Indo-European parallels, but it finds no echo in Homer. It has been suggested that Menelaus shows signs of exercising this function, but nothing could be further from the situation described in the Iliad; Hector is the only possible comparison, and his position is largely explained by the advanced age of king Priam. There is no indication in Homer of the class of village head-men; these would not seem likely to have possessed warrior status—though there is now some indication that a *ko-re-te* could command an *o-ka*—but might be expected to occur in the Odyssey if the epic poets had been aware of this kind of position. In that poem, which contains many references to the peacetime life of the palace society, all that are mentioned are the king, his relations, his household servants and the few slaves who look after his estates and flocks. In Ithaca there are other noblemen, but they clearly have their own houses, smaller than the king's palace, and do not seem to be dependent on the palace except for occasional political or military leadership. In short, as M. I. Finley has pointed out in an important article, the terms for leaders and authorities in Homer and the tablets are quite distinct—except for ἄναξ and βασιλεύς, which have different applications in the two contexts.[1]

Except that kings in Homer have enclaves of choice land, τεμένη, and can award them to others, there is no reference to the complicated system of land-tenure indicated in the tablets. Of course the Iliad and Odyssey are heroic poems, and need not describe how land is held or exactly how the palace economy is maintained; nevertheless, one would expect casual references if late Mycenaean traditions had survived in bulk, and Finley has observed that similar references do occur in the Norse sagas and in early medieval epics. There may appear to be certain dim relics of that minute organization of personnel that is so marked a phenomenon of the tablets. The servants in Homer are slaves, or sometimes the equivalent of freedmen — who are not mentioned, however, on the tablets; sometimes they are war captives or were abducted, like Eumaeus the swineherd, by merchant adventurers. The female slaves look after baths, clean the palace, prepare the food, and attend the royal women; the stewardess has the key to the store-room and is responsible for its contents. The men tend the farms and flocks, carve and serve the food, or are craftsmen; a few specialized crafts or occupations are mentioned, and the Odyssey distinguishes between swineherd, goatherd and shepherd—though this is probably a distinction made in any agrarian society, and not specially Mycenaean. The total number of different occupations in the poems is relatively small, and does not suggest that the post-migration singers, at least, had any conception of the bureaucratic excesses of the world of the tablets. One occupation often cited in the Odyssey is that of ἀοιδός, *aoidos*, the singer or minstrel, who does not find a place in the tablets. Conversely Homer completely ignores scribes and the record system of the Mycenaean palaces. Many differences between the world of the tablets and that of the poems are to be expected —we should anticipate, for example, that many of the objects described by the *aoidoi* would take on the colouring of the post-Mycenaean age. But the differences in social structure, economy and specialized occupation are most striking, and undoubtedly strengthen the case of those who claim that the tablets do not throw much light on Homer, that the social and cultural background of the poems is largely post-Mycenaean, and that there was a profound change in society and institutions between the 12th century and the 10th and 9th.

In religious and military practices, too, the differences are marked. Admittedly the names of several of Homer's gods appear on the tablets, but the methods of cult (pl. 2a!) seem quite distinct. There is no sign in either the Iliad or Odyssey of the closely regulated cycle of offerings, month by month, that were made to the different gods of the Mycenaean world. On the whole the offerings to gods in Homer were made on a strictly *ad hoc* basis: no requirements, no hecatombs. Priests and priestesses naturally occur in both sources, but there are no slaves of the god and no extensive divine properties in the poems, and no divination is so far suggested in the tablets. As for military affairs, the Iliad certainly contains reminiscences of Mycenaean armour, including the body-shield and silver-studded sword—which seem to have lapsed from fashion, however, as early as 1400 (pp. 111, 114); it is not surprising, then, that the tablets and their ideograms supply certain details of armour, for example of corslets, which are valuable guides to obscure passages in Homer. Chariots, too, have become easier to understand, even though the Iliad in particular quite fails to reproduce the real function and limitations of the war-chariot, which was evidently still in practical use in the world of the tablets (pp. 124f.).

It may be said, then, that apart from Homer's correct archaizing over certain aspects of the palaces, certain facts of political geography, and one or two details of military equipment, the common features of the tablets and the Iliad and Odyssey are few, and those mainly due to basic conditions that did not alter much between c. 1200 and c. 750. At the same time some of the most unusual qualities of the civilization described by the tablets find no place in the poems. Thus the Homeric singers' knowledge of the social, institutional, political, economic and military background of the Trojan war was fragmentary and distorted, and was supplemented and overlaid by details derived from later stages of the oral tradition. All this is not to deny that the decipherment of the tablets has greatly improved our knowledge of later Mycenaean history, as it has improved that of the development of the Greek language. As a guide to the institutions described in the Homeric poems, and to the development of that poetry out of its traditional elements, they may seem—considering that many of them are roughly contemporary with the siege of Troy itself—distinctly disappointing. At the same time they clearly instruct us to look for the sources of much in Homer not in the originative period of the Trojan legendary tradition but in the subsequent stages of crystallization and elaboration in the early Iron Age.

39

3

FROM THE MYCENAEAN DECLINE
TO THE TIME OF HOMER

SIGNS of increasing economic pressure and social disintegration in Mycenaean society are to be seen in the series of aggressive enterprises of which the long and costly attack on Troy was the most important. The earliest of these enterprises, apart perhaps from the successful occupation of Knossos in the 15th century B.C., was probably the expedition of the Argonauts. The legend of the voyage of the ship Argo from Mycenaean Iolcus on the coast of Thessaly to Colchis on the Black Sea, in search of the Golden Fleece, is presumably a crystallization of historical exploration of the north-east in search of gold and other wealth. The Homeric description of Argo as 'of interest to all' (πᾶσι μέλουσα, *12. 70*), implies that it was the subject of a story, whether or not in verse, familiar at some time during the period of the epic tradition; and others of the tales of Odysseus's wanderings, apart from the penetration of the 'Clashing Rocks' in which the Argo was his predecessor, appear to be based on explorers' tales of the dangers of the Black Sea route. Jason is implied in Homer to have lived only a generation before the Achaeans who went to Troy. There is probably some chronological compression here, but at least the disputes after Jason's return may suggest that the expedition belonged to the period of dynastic dissensions rather than to the earlier great age. This was largely a North Mycenaean endeavour, though traditionally associated with many different cities.

The next Mycenaean undertaking of which memory survived, likewise placed by Homer a single generation before Troy, was a primarily southern attack on one of the greatest of the North Mycenaean palaces, Thebes. The dynastic quarrel between Eteocles and Polyneices was an extreme manifestation of the instability of the Achaean noble families, reflected in the murders of hosts and princes, the refugees from blood-pollution and the seductions of royal women, described or referred to in the poetry of Homer. Polyneices raised allies from Aetolia and the Peloponnese, especially Argos, and organized an attack on Thebes to regain his position as king. The 'Seven against Thebes' failed, but according to Homer and the Epic Cycle the sons of the Seven succeeded later in capturing the city. The legend of a second joint attack is presumably founded on some sort of historical memory, and it may suggest that hostility to Cadmeian Thebes was based on something more than a private quarrel or the failure of guest-friend obligations. Somehow Thebes must have offended the other Mycenaean cities, including those of the Peloponnese, so as to offer an excuse for repeated attempts on her famous wealth. Can she have been too friendly with peoples to the north-west, precursors of the Dorian intruders? Unfortunately we know all too little about the northern palaces and their relations with tribes on their borders. At all events Thebes was punished by eventual destruction; her wealth, divided out, cannot have lasted, since it was not long before another Achaean expedition, and on a much larger scale, was gathering at Aulis nearby.

Thucydides deduced, probably from Homer, that the Trojan expedition was on an unprecedented scale, and there is no reason to disagree with him. Troy burned in the end, but the Achaeans gained nothing in the way of permanent assets like the opening up of important new trade-routes or large areas for colonization. The inanimate booty would be quickly dissipated; captives, mostly female, were more valuable, and may have bolstered up a declining labour force for a time. Nevertheless new voyages in search of quick profits were soon undertaken, though not on the same massive scale. Egyptian records reveal that in 1225 and again c. 1194 there were serious piratical raids against the Nile delta. These were two of the peaks of a more or less continuous series of infiltrations ultimately prompted by barbarian pressure from the north. Egypt must have seemed to offer large prizes and a relatively ineffectual defence. Men of several different races took part, Hittite remnants and people from Syria and Phoenicia, the flotsam of a Levant in turmoil. Among the names mentioned in the records are those of the Akaiwasha and the Danuna. The identification of these people is a problem—the former have usually been equated with the Achaeans (Akhaiwoi), the latter with the Danaoi, another of the names used in Homer for the Mycenaean Greeks. D. L. Page has argued convincingly against the latter identification, and has also reiterated that the Akaiwasha of the Karnak inscription are described as circumcised—which the Achaeans in general cannot have been.[1] Nevertheless I suspect that these Akaiwasha *are* Achaeans of some kind, probably not from the mainland but from Rhodes, Cyprus or the Levant—one reason being that the Odyssey contains a probable reminiscence of one such raid on Egypt. In his false tale to Eumaeus at *14. 245* ff. Odysseus relates how, as a Cretan nobleman, he had set off directly after his return from Troy with a fleet of nine ships, which reached the Nile on the fifth day. Piracy of some kind was intended, as is explicitly stated in the slightly different version at *17. 424* ff.; the crews got out of hand and precipitately ravaged the nearby fields, slaying the men and capturing the women and children. Retribution came quickly, for infantry and cavalry came from the local town and killed or captured the Cretans. Such is the poetical account, and it is difficult not to compare, for example, the claim of Merneptah to have routed the Akaiwasha and other northerners who plundered Egypt in 1225. The chronology roughly fits, since Troy VII a was evidently burned around 1240–1230. Other kinds of Egyptian contact, too, survived in popular memory, as is shown by the account in books 3 and 4 of the Odyssey of how Menelaus was blown down to Egypt on his way home from Troy and spent seven years trading there, after which he returned to Greece a rich man. Presumably the chronology has been condensed once again, and this kind of tradition filtered down from the era of peaceful relations in the 15th century—rather than deriving from the re-establishment of regular Greek–Egyptian trade in the 7th.

One must not be too dogmatic about the historical significance of such enterprises. There must always have been individualists and adventurers who did not fit into the normal social structure. Such was the Cretan whom Odysseus imagined; and men like this, rather than any special economic malaise, could be the main cause of some at least of the undertakings like the voyage of the Argo or the piratical expedition to Egypt. The times must have helped, but all the same we must remember that the complex administrative system of the palaces was still working in Pylos just before its destruction. Life was apparently proceeding in an organized fashion in Mycenae when in these same years, around 1200, parts of the citadel and of the surrounding town were set on fire. According to Thucydides the Dorian incursions began about eighty years after the fall of Troy, which would mean around 1150 by the archaeological dating or around 1100 by the commonest traditional dating. The burning of Iolcus and Pylos, attacks on Mycenae and probably Athens, and the abandonment of many minor centres, all around 1200, suggest that a first wave of Dorians must have reached the Peloponnese somewhat earlier than Thucydides's date—unless, as is always possible, these disasters were the result of internal warfare, and men from north-west Greece simply moved in later to fill the gap. However, there was a tradition that the first attempt to enter the Peloponnese, under Hyllus, was checked, and that the 'Sons of Heracles', as the Dorians were called by later Greeks, agreed to wait a hundred years before moving further south.[1] I shall have more to add about these Dorian 'invasions', the nature of which is highly speculative, in chapter 6. Here it suffices to say that a branch of the Greek-speaking people must have settled in poor country to the north-west of Greece while the Middle Helladic Greeks were moving down into the peninsula. Centuries later, Illyrian movements to the north of them prodded these backward 'Dorian' Greeks southward at last—perhaps in small groups at first, but in something like a full-scale migration by the 12th century at latest. The wealth of the Mycenaean kingdoms must have acted as a magnet; and the Achaeans, progressively weakened by economic difficulties, costly wars, and internal disputes, gradually succumbed to, or were supplanted by, the more savage, dull and determined newcomers. This seems the most probable interpretation; at all events the final blow came between 1150 and 1100, when the citadel of Mycenae itself was pillaged and burned.[1] The Dorians, whose existence is proved by the West Greek dialect that established itself over extensive areas of the Peloponnese at about this time, installed themselves around the ravaged palaces, and presumably used as serf labour those ordinary Achaean citizens who had neither succumbed nor fled to the areas that evaded occupation—Arcadia, the north-west coast of the Peloponnese and the off-shore islands, Attica, and the Achaean possessions or outposts overseas.

From about 1100 to 900, a period embracing the Sub-mycenaean and Protogeometric styles of pottery, Greece was sunk in a 'Dark Age'. Her history is virtually unknown and her material culture, to judge from the rarity and comparative poverty of the physical remnants, was at a low level, especially at first. The palace system had utterly collapsed, and with it had faded out the technique of writing in the cumbrous Linear B syllabic script, a form of which continued in Cyprus alone. The art of representational drawing, already degraded in the sack-like figures of the latest Mycenaean pottery from Cyprus, Tiryns, and Mycenae itself, utterly disappears. The houses and buildings of the new Dorian 'aristocracy' must have been of mud-brick, a little larger but no more permanent than the huts of serfs and farmers. Yet even in a Dark Age life continues, which is something that historians tend to overlook. Fields are still ploughed and sown, men go hunting, see their friends and relations, even tell stories. The collapse of the palace economy, not to speak of the deficiencies of whatever crude local systems the Dorians substituted for it, must have caused a cataclysmic change in many places; yet there is no reason to believe that community life was completely disrupted or discontinued. To this important point, again, and to the qualities of life in this Dark Age, I shall return in chapter 6.

Much of the evidence for this period concerns Athens, because Athens alone of the Mycenaean palace-states escaped destruction or abandonment, and subsequently became a centre of refuge in which some faint ghost of the old Achaean civilization lived on. Athens seems to have survived two attacks, one of which roughly coincided with the burning of Mycenae towards the end of the 12th century B.C.[1] The houses on the slopes of the Acropolis were abandoned, but the citadel itself, strengthened by new fortifications and the protection of its water supply, was able to hold out. Twice repulsed, the Dorians never returned, and the Acropolis was gradually given over to religious and formal uses. The cemeteries present a picture of continuity, with a depressed period after 1100 and then a gradual overcrowding accompanied by signs of a certain mediocre prosperity. Cremation becomes the regular practice, and at the same time the somewhat rough and insensitive Submycenaean pottery, stolid in shape and decorated with hand-drawn half-circles and carelessly positioned linear patterns, develops into the more elegant black-glazed ware known as Protogeometric.[2] The half-circles and circles are now compass-drawn, and the bands of decoration are fitted more feelingly to the contours of the pot (pl. 3d). Yet the vices of urban Submycenaean (see pl. 3 c for an Argive example, and compare pl. 4b from Tiryns) and the virtues of its Protogeometric successor have been similarly exaggerated. The early Protogeometric pottery, though undeniably successful of its kind, is stark and somewhat unimaginative in its total rather monotonous effect. The praise that has been lavished on it has been almost hysterical at times; but does it really imply a culture dominated by an appreciation of natural rhythm and the correct arrangement of component parts, etc., as those who wish to find the qualities of the Homeric epic already present in pre-migration Athens would have us believe? Must one stress the obvious, that skill in making *pots* does not necessarily coincide with skill in making *poems*? What can truthfully be said is that Attic Protogeometric ware was far better than anything else

45

produced in Greece at the time; and by early in the 10th century it was being exported to many different parts of the Greek world. Together with the graves of the Kerameikos and Dipylon cemeteries it is a valuable sign that Athens, in spite of its few traces of imposing buildings, had achieved a relatively advanced state of material culture for this period, and was, in fact, the most important town in Greece.

In this crowded but not hopeless environment lived many of the refugees from the ruined sites of the Peloponnese and Thessaly and Boeotia. It was they who must have formed the nucleus of the migrations to the further shore of the Aegean which gained momentum shortly before 1000. Athens played a large part in the movement to Ionia; but according to tradition some of the Aeolic townships further north, notably Kyme, were the first to be settled.[1] From there the earliest Iron Age pottery so far found dates back only to around 725; and from Scepsis in the Troad, which according to tradition was ruled after the fall of Troy by descendants of Aeneas, it is even later. In fertile Lesbos Mycenaean pottery is overlaid by an anonymous Dark Age ware, but the exact date of the Aeolic immigrants remains to be discovered. The only fresh Aeolic settlement to be at all fully explored so far is Old Smyrna, where the excavations conducted in 1948–51 by J. M. Cook and E. Akurgal have revealed foundations of houses and Protogeometric pottery of local manufacture—not merely casual imports—dating back to around 1000 (or at least not much later) by the prevailing chronology, which may be too low.[2] Thus this settlement, at least, was well enough established to be making its own good-quality pottery on the Attic model by the central part of the Protogeometric age. Smyrna was eventually taken over by Ionians from Colophon; but equally early foundation dates cannot yet be proved for any of the fresh Ionian settlements. Miletus, however, seems to have been occupied continuously from the middle Mycenaean period onwards, and Protogeometric sherds, as well as Mycenaean and Geometric, have been found in the area of the later temple of Athene there. Klaros and Samos likewise show evidence of continuous Greek habitation from the late Bronze Age down into the Ionian period. Yet it seems improbable that Achaean survivors in Asia Minor were particularly influential as continuators of possible Mycenaean poetry, or that they played a very important part in the development of the Ionian epic. The main formulation of the story of the war against Troy presumably took place on the Greek mainland, to which most of the Achaean heroes returned. To judge from the archaeological evidence the early Iron Age descendants of the Achaeans in Asia Minor were poor, few and racially mixed. Miletus in Homer is an ally of Troy, inhabited by 'Carians of barbarian speech' (II. 867f.). This puzzling description is unlikely to refer to the pre-Mycenaean situation there, which would take us back beyond 1500; but Herodotus singled out Miletus as a place where the early Ionian settlers took exclusively Carian wives. Indeed it seems quite probable that going native was already a well-established custom when Neleus's men arrived at Miletus from Athens in the great wave of migration around 1000.[1]

Despite the lack of specific archaeological evidence for very early Ionian migration, it is appearing more and more probable that by the 10th century the traditionally earliest Ionian settlements by the coast—Ephesus, Priene, Colophon, Teos, Lebedos, Myus, as well as Miletus—were well established.[2] To these, with Samos and Chios, the others of the classical dodecapolis were soon added, with the originally Aeolic Smyrna as thirteenth; the last two are the places with which Homer was later associated. Little pottery has been found in Chios from before 800, perhaps because, as J. M. Cook has pertinently observed, the earliest Iron Age site explored there is a sanctuary and not a town.[3] A settlement date around 950–900 may be suggested by fourteen recorded ancestors on the gravestone of the Chian Heropythos, who died in the mid-5th century.[4] In Samos a sudden spate of early Geometric pottery, with other innovations, pushes the date of new immigrants there up to around 875 at latest; this too is at a sanctuary site. Unfortunately the precise date of the Panionion, the federal centre at the shrine of Poseidon on the Mycale peninsula facing Samos, cannot yet be determined.

47

Tradition suggests that it was established relatively early, and it was certainly in full existence by the 8th century. Yet one must not exaggerate the size and prosperity of these Aeolic and Ionic settlements in the first centuries of their foundation or re-foundation. Smyrna was admittedly not one of the most important, but the excavations show that before the late 8th century, when the place was ruined by an earthquake and then rebuilt on a better scale, it was little more than a collection of closely packed thatched cottages on a peninsula some four hundred yards long.[1] This confirms the acumen of archaeologists like R. M. Cook and G. M. A. Hanfmann, who had warned us not to exaggerate the wealth of Ionia before the 7th century.[2] There is nothing to suggest that for the first two or three centuries of the new occupation of the Asia Minor coast the settlements were able to do much more than consolidate their position, sometimes at each other's expense. The settlers had little contact with the interior and could not adequately exploit its resources. The islands, Chios and Lesbos and Samos, were probably in a better situation, and in Miletus, too, continuity of habitation perhaps eased relations with the indigenous people of the region. Unfortunately the archaeological exploration of this part of the world has by force of circumstance often been hurried and incomplete; even surface exploration is inadequate, and only in few sites has much attempt been made to reach the Geometric levels, let alone Protogeometric. Now that excavation is being encouraged in Turkey we may look forward to more tangible evidence about the date and condition of the early Ionic and Aeolic colonies; Smyrna is a happy augury.

The perception of the pre-eminence of Athens in the Dark Age, together with the scarcity of evidence for early Ionic and Aeolic foundations, has persuaded some critics to argue that Athens played an even more crucial part than Ionia in the development of the Homeric poems.[3] In spite of the obvious importance of the mainland (not merely Athens) for the propagation of Trojan poetry during the Dark Age, this is an exaggerated and distorted view. It depends either on ignoring the

Smyrna evidence and down-dating the Ionian migration to the 9th century, or on minimizing the specifically Ionian linguistic content of Homer, or on stressing the low cultural standards of the Ionian towns and implying that epic cannot have thrived in such conditions, or on exaggerating the culture of Protogeometric Athens, or on a combination of these. As for the first point, it is extremely unlikely, even apart from Smyrna, that the Aeolic and Ionic movements were later than the Dorian occupation of the south-eastern part of the coast of Asia Minor with its neighbouring islands. This had taken place by about the middle of the 10th century.[1] The unfavourable comparison of material standards in Ionia and Athens, on the other hand, is a useful antidote to the old habit of assuming on the basis of Homer that the material environment of Sappho or Anaximander must have obtained several hundreds of years earlier; yet it must not be exaggerated in its turn, or unthinkingly related to the possibility or impossibility of oral poetry. It is an obvious fallacy that poetry can only flourish in comfortable or luxurious surroundings. Some social stability is all that is needed; and this the Ionian towns, with their aristocratic form of government and their federal system, had probably achieved to a high degree by the 9th century and to a moderate degree before that. Small village coffee-houses have been the breeding-ground, in more modern times, of the South Slavic oral epic; are the facilities of the Ionian towns in the Protogeometric and early Geometric era likely to have been much worse? In its massive or monumental form, as we see it in Homer, the Greek epic may or may not have required the stimulus of royal or competitive performances (pp. 274 ff.); but for the earlier elaboration of those shorter songs that must have formed the basis of an Ionian oral tradition no such formal conditions were necessary. Indeed at many stages of an oral tradition not even urban surroundings are required, as will be argued in chapter 6; but this is more relevant to the possible history of the Greek tradition before its transplantation to Ionia—in which, for reasons of security, life was probably heavily concentrated on the main population centres.

Pathetically little is known about the Asia Minor settlements even after the end of the Dark Age proper—a few isolated facts, totally inadequate for the construction of a coherent picture of life there in the developed Geometric period. For this we await further help from archaeology. About Lesbos something can be read back from the fragments of Alcaeus and Sappho around 600, and Miletus had clearly achieved by then both prosperity and diverse foreign contacts. Indeed it had probably sent out colonies to the shores of the Propontis by the middle of the 8th century; but it is always doubtful how far colonization is a sign of prosperity. In any case conditions changed radically between the 8th century and the 7th, and the cities of the coast underwent social, dynastic and political vicissitudes the nature of which we can only dimly guess; these were caused or aggravated by the incursions of predatory Cimmerians from beyond the Black Sea. Thus little can be said about the conditions experienced earlier by 'Homer' and the other Ionian singers, or by the audiences for which they sang; except that the Greek towns of the eastern Aegean did not achieve real material prosperity before the 7th century, though they had probably enjoyed some considerable social stability for a couple of centuries down to that time. They were in many respects typical Greek *polis*-settlements of a conservative kind, in some of which, and certainly in Lesbos, the hereditary princely families maintained, against growing pressure, a restricted court-life derived ultimately from the distant Achaean past.

The same dismal lack of historical knowledge, beyond that of the vast colonial expansion in the 8th century to Sicily and Italy as well as to Chalcidice and Propontis in the north-east, prevents us from properly visualizing the life of other island or mainland communities which may have played some part either in the transmission of ordinary oral poetry about the Trojan war or in the propagation and elaboration of the long Ionian versions. Hesiod, who was closely familiar with the language of the Ionian singers and adopted it for his own songs, admittedly throws some light on the conditions of Boeotia in (probably) the early 7th century. Yet Hesiod's part of Boeotia, if it was typical of anything, was typical merely of the poorer agricultural regions of the mainland. Athens, for instance, which was probably an important centre for the spread of the new poetry—the product of what she liked to consider as her Ionian dependencies—had a different life and different problems. The long and widespread Lelantine war started in Euboea, probably but not certainly around 700, and involved much of the Greek world; after it Athens's lustre was temporarily dimmed, while Corinth emerged as a great mercantile competitor and Sparta, after finally subduing Messenia, began her quest for military domination of the Peloponnese. The sudden popularity from about 680 of episodes from the Trojan cycle as the subject of vase-paintings, the foundation around this time of new hero-cults associated with Agamemnon, Menelaus, Helen and Odysseus, and the presence of epic phraseology in the poetry of such widely dispersed figures as Callinus, Archilochus and Alcman, combine to suggest that a monumental Iliad and Odyssey had achieved fame in most parts of the Hellenic world before the middle of the 7th century (pp. 282–7). Yet the sad truth is that the historical and cultural background of this poetical *diaspora*, like that of the process of large-scale composition in Ionia itself, largely escapes us, and there is little to add to what may be deduced from the poems themselves and from echoes in the art and literature of the 7th century. These matters will be further considered in chapter 13.

PART II

❀

THE ORAL POET AND HIS METHODS

4

THE ORAL POET AND
HIS METHODS

ORAL poetry will play a prominent part in this book. The true oral poet—his epithet is disagreeable, but it is short and well established by use—is one who transmits and composes poetry without the aid of writing, who absorbs songs easily from others and elaborates them extempore without the help of trial versions jotted down in notebooks, and who reproduces them on demand with the aid of a fixed vocabulary and a powerful and highly trained memory. His poems are delivered to an audience by mouth, not published in books: that is the point of the description 'oral', though for the process of creation it signifies as much that this kind of poetry is learned and composed aurally, by ear.

It is a truism that literacy saps memory. In pre-literate societies, even quite unsophisticated ones, the gift of verbal memory is far more highly developed, through constant need and practice, than in societies like our own. Even amid the present welter of letters there remain a few who can learn rapidly by heart and remember what they have learned. They are quite exceptional; and differences in the natural capacity for exact verbal memory exist even in primarily illiterate societies, where the general level is much higher. Oral poets have no doubt always been drawn from an exceptional minority, and their performance far outstrips that of those who compel our admiration by quoting a complete scene of Shakespeare. More than mere learning by heart is involved, of course; yet to assimilate an epic poem of several thousand lines, or to elaborate a shorter poem to something like that length by his own additions or by transpositions from other songs, is no impossible feat for the exceptionally gifted oral singer in a largely or wholly unlettered community—as can be illustrated by specific examples from Yugoslavia or south Russia. The modern student of Homer may feel surprised about such capacities, but he must not be too incredulous.

§1. *Heroic Age and heroic poetry*

The narrative oral poet sings of the deeds of heroes, usually heroes of the past, and sometimes too of gods, giants or folk-tale figures. This heroic poetry is nearly always sung in lines with a uniform metrical pattern, a rapid and flowing rhythm like that of the Homeric hexameter or the looser decasyllable of Serbo-Croat verse. Metrical regularity is essential for learning and composing long oral poems; though in some traditions, especially those affected by Latin, quite complex factors like rhyme, alliteration or division into stanzas may be added. Even with the help of an easy and regular rhythmical framework, a restricted and standardized poetical vocabulary, and the great powers of memory of the non-literate, the oral heroic poet must almost invariably be a professional or semi-professional, one who begins his training as a boy and thereafter has constant practice.

Songs sung from memory need not only be narrative ones, though there is often little or no surviving evidence of other categories. Work-songs, dance-songs and dirges must always have had a place in the kind of culture that gave rise to the oral narrative poet, and in some societies gnomic and didactic oral poetry flourished too. Yet songs of these other genres were in most ways less important than the heroic songs: they were shorter, often less formally arranged, and less closely associated with the nobility. Two common features of nearly all kinds of oral poem, however, are that they were composed and remembered without the aid of writing and that they were sung or chanted, usually to a musical accompaniment. Poems are songs, and the Homeric word for a poet is ἀοιδός (*aoidos*) or singer, one who accompanies himself on the lyre-like instrument known in Homer as the *kitharis* or *phorminx*.

It is strange that great heroic narrative poems of comparable structure and ideology should have grown up in different periods and parts of Europe: the Homeric poems in early Iron Age Greece, the Teutonic poems, including *Beowulf* and the *Nibelungenlied*, in the 4th to the 8th centuries A.D., the Celtic narratives in Ireland and Wales (in which, however, prose saga was mixed with poetry), especially down to the 13th or 14th century, the great Norse poems and sagas which flourished from the 9th to the 13th century, and the Russian and South Slavic heroic epics which have developed from the 14th century to the present day—not to speak of Finnish heroic songs, or the *Chanson de Roland*, or the Byzantine epic of Digenes Akritas, or the much earlier and rather different Near Eastern tradition exemplified in the stories of Gilgamesh and Keret or in the Babylonian creation hymn.[1] In some of these, especially the Scandinavian and Near Eastern poems, the element of magic, demonology or folk-tale is much stronger than in Homer. In others, like the *Chanson de Roland*, writing has played some part. Yet the heroic quality and the oral quality remain predominant. The reason for the similarity of these products is that they arose from basically similar cultures; each of them derives from a Heroic Age or its immediate successor. The main components of such an age, which tends to occur in the development of many different nations, seem to be a *penchant* for warfare and adventure, a powerful nobility, and a simple but temporarily adequate material culture devoid of much aesthetic refinement. In such conditions the heroic virtues of honour and martial courage dominate all others, ultimately with depressive effects on the stability and prosperity of the society. It is usually during the consequent period of decline that the poetical elaboration of glorious deeds, deeds that now lie in the past, reaches its climax; though narrative songs are a favourite recreation of the tired warrior throughout the whole heroic period.

The Homeric epic, developed in its monumental form by about 700 B.C., is an outcome of the in most ways typical Heroic Age of the late Mycenaean period, an age which had ended, historically speaking, as far back as 1100. That a tradition of oral heroic song maintained itself for so long, and grew to so late

57

and stupendous a culmination, is surprising enough. But fortunately the final collapse of the Mycenaean system, drastic as it was, had not produced a total dispersal of population; many survivors were able to cultivate and transmit the memory of the heroic past. Another event which fortified the Greek heroic tradition throughout a post-heroic age was the submergence of writing for a period of several centuries; and this in its turn had been helped by the laborious and imprecise nature of the Mycenaean script. During the period of total illiteracy of the 11th and 10th century oral poetry would be as much a necessity of life as it ever had been before—perhaps more so. Other heroic ages in other lands tended to be followed much more rapidly by the spread of writing, and their oral traditions may have been relatively less pure; though in parts of Europe an oral tradition has continued for even longer than four hundred years, because until recently writing never touched more than a small minority of the population. Even in Mycenaean Greece only a small minority seems to have been literate; from the 7th century onwards, on the other hand, the impact of writing on the Greeks was rapid and pervasive.

In spite of these and other differences between one nation and another the concept of the Heroic Age as a recurrent phenomenon in the development of cultures, especially in Europe, is valid and useful; its isolation is largely the work of H. M. and N. K. Chadwick.[1] It allows us to understand the picture of the *aoidos* or professional singer as given in the Odyssey, and to envisage the way in which Homer himself—the first 'monumental' poet, that is—may have grown out of such a figure. It allows us, too, to credit the successors of singers like Demodocus with songs longer and more complex than those mentioned in the Odyssey, songs of the scale of *Beowulf* or the earlier Icelandic sagas. Yet the concept of the court poet of the Heroic Age must be diversified by the study of the popular or market-place poet. This is the kind that survives most tenaciously when a Heroic Age is ended and when the noblemen's houses are divided or abandoned. The court minstrel is the typical poet in the Heroic Age, but we must be careful not to regard the composers of the

58

Iliad and Odyssey as necessarily resembling that kind of singer in every respect. These poems were brought to perfection long after the Achaean Heroic Age had ended. Their audience must have included comparatively rich patrons and noblemen, but also, probably, the general populace in various kinds of gathering (see also pp. 274–81). Heroic poetry appeals to the people as well as to heroes and their descendants; and the oral poets that can be studied best, those of modern Yugoslavia, have for long been popular poets who sing in coffee-houses, not court poets. Yet their subjects are mainly heroic and aristocratic.

§2. *The language of formulas in Homer*

The case for describing Homer as an oral poet would be incomplete if it depended solely on the importance of the minstrel in other heroic or post-heroic societies, together perhaps with the description of Phemius and Demodocus in the Odyssey and the absence of writing from Greece during much of the interval between the downfall of Mycenae and the probable date of the Iliad. Some or all of these factors, however, interpreted with varying degrees of accuracy, had led many critics, even before Milman Parry, to conclude that Homer composed in a very different manner from Apollonius of Rhodes, Virgil or Milton. Furthermore the language of the poems had for long been closely scrutinized, and by the early 1920's Witte, Meister, Meillet and others had made a strong case for its classification as a formalized and traditional development, in which alternative dialect forms, for example, were chosen mainly to suit the requirements of metre. Of Parry himself, whose importance was generally overlooked until some time after his premature death in 1935, much has now been written. His contributions to Homeric scholarship are twofold: he saw the relevance of the modern oral poetry of Yugoslavia and succeeded in recording a great deal of it; and he demonstrated beyond doubt that Homer was an oral poet, depending on a gradually evolved traditional store of fixed phrases which covered most common ideas and situations—a store that was neither unnecessarily luxurious nor restrictively parsimonious.[1]

These essential qualities of the oral poet's treasury of verbal formulas were termed by Parry *economy* and *scope*. Düntzer and a few others had already recognized that the many recurrent phrases in Homer, most obviously the name-epithet formulas like 'divine Odysseus' and 'gleaming-helmeted Hector', were used in a way that was not just haphazard or unimaginative, but on the contrary was somehow essential to the poet. Parry first showed that such fixed phrases in Homer composed a system so tight and logical that it could only be the outcome of many generations of refinement. This process of refinement consisted in the rejection of the otiose—the merely decorative alternative—and the consolidation and expansion of whatever was functional and organic. Now the Homeric hexameter verse tends to be more or less self-contained in meaning; its ending usually coincides with a major or minor pause, the end of a sentence or clause or at least the point at which a predicate is divided from its subject. This means that there is plenty of opportunity for the repetition of whole lines, the verse being treated as a formula; and in fact about one-third of the verses in the Iliad and Odyssey recur at least once. It is more important, however, that the verse itself is divided into smaller sections by word-breaks which are part of its structure; and into these sections are fitted recurrent phrases or sense-units. The most important internal divisions, which must coincide with a gap between words, are the compulsory main caesura in the third foot, either male or female (i.e. after the first syllable of that foot, the 'strong' position, or after its first trochee, $- \cup$, the commoner 'weak' position); the extremely common 'bucolic' diaeresis before the fifth foot; and the word-break after the first measure of the fourth foot in many lines which contain a female, or trochaic, main caesura. The intervals between the beginning of the verse and the male caesura, or between the male, female, fourth-foot or bucolic caesuras and the end of the verse, are the main places in which standard phrases or fixed formulas are employed. Since the verse-end is marked by the fixed rhythm $- \cup \cup - \overset{\cup}{\smile}$ (as opposed to all other parts of the line, where the spondee can be substituted for the basic dactyl at will) the poet must first be sure of filling the latter part of the line. Thus the majority of fixed phrases are designed to fill out portions of the verse-end. At the beginning of the verse the commonest formula-lengths are the whole portion down to the main caesura, or less often the first one-and-a-half feet.

The following metrical scheme will clarify the different organic sections of the hexameter verse. The bold numbers refer to the examples set out beneath; the dotted lines represent the commonest word-breaks.

1 Ζεὺς ὑψιβρεμέτης,   Τρώεσσι δὲ βούλετο νίκην (XVI. 121; there are 4 other Homeric instances of the formula underlined here. Noun-epithet formulas in the first part of the verse tend to have been carried over from the preceding line).

2 Μυρμιδόνες, ἕταροι   Πηληϊάδεω ᾿Αχιλῆος (XVI. 269 +7 other instances).

3 ὣς φάτο, ῥίγησεν δὲ   πολύτλας δῖος ᾿Οδυσσεύς (5. 171 +37).

4 τὸν δ᾿ ἀπαμειβόμενος προσέφη   πολύμητις ᾿Οδυσσεύς (7. 207 +81).

5 ὣς ἄρα φωνήσας κόρυθ᾿ εἵλετο   φαίδιμος ῞Εκτωρ (VI. 494 +28).

These examples illustrate the formular use of name-epithet phrases in the first instance, though they contain other fixed phrases too. There are many other kinds of formulas, verbal or adverbial or containing ordinary nouns in a variety of cases. It is obvious that if the oral poet has at his command—that is, in his memory—a number of alternative phrases for any given concept, each of slightly different metrical value and corresponding with the main intervals to be filled in the hexameter line, a great part of his task of impromptu verse-making is achieved with the least expenditure of effort, and he can concentrate on filling up the rest of the line with other words, formulas or combinations of formulas in such a way as to express his own particular meaning.

It may be revealing to study the other formulas, as well as the name-epithet groups, in our five examples. In **1** the phrase βούλετο νίκην occupies the same position in the verse (that of the name-epithet group in **5**, between bucolic diaeresis and line-end) as it does in four other and different lines of the Iliad. One of these has βούλεο not βούλετο, but that is a typical minor variation; at the end of another line occurs ἔλπετο νίκην, which is clearly based on the same formular pattern. In one of its four occurrences elsewhere (VII. 21) βούλετο νίκην is preceded, as in **1**, by Τρώεσσι δέ. That again is a formular usage, since these words occur in the equivalent position, namely before the bucolic diaeresis, elsewhere: so Τρώεσσι δὲ φαίδιμος Ἕκτωρ / (xx. 364) and Τρώεσσι δὲ λοιγὸν ἀλάλκοι / (xxi. 138 = 250). Thus when the poet wished to express the idea 'he desired victory' he always used βούλετο νίκην at the line-end, and when he wanted to say 'for the Trojans' with a connecting particle in the latter part of the verse Τρώεσσι δέ (or τε) in that position was the natural and inevitable way of doing so. **1** is entirely composed, therefore, of three juxtaposed formulas. Short structural phrases may occur repeatedly in other sections of the verse too small to be classified among the main divisions: thus in **3** ὣς φάτο is a formula which occurs at the beginning of many other verses of the Iliad and Odyssey. The next word-group in **3**, ῥίγησεν δέ, is also a formula, though not so straightforwardly. It comes in the same position in the only other line of the Odyssey in which the verb appears, while in the Iliad it occurs seven times (including superficial variants), though usually at the very beginning of the line and not before the trochaic caesura. On the other hand other verbs of three spondees followed by δέ or τε fall naturally into the latter position. Again, in **4** the predicate in the earlier part of the line is a formula, just as much as the name-epithet group at the end: τὸν δ' ἀπαμειβόμενος προσέφη is absolutely standard for the sense 'answered him as follows', and with minor variants (τήν or τούς for τόν; -ομένη; προσεφώνεε; προσέφης) it occurs roughly 70 times in the

Odyssey and 40 in the Iliad—a difference, incidentally, which
may be significant for the question of authorship (see pp. 292 ff.).
In cases where the singer wishes to describe a metrically more
extensive subject as answering someone, then he will use a
shorter and slightly different formula:

$$\tau\grave{o}\nu \; \delta' \; \mathring{\eta}\mu\epsilon\acute{\iota}\beta\epsilon\tau' \; \mathring{\epsilon}\pi\epsilon\iota\tau\alpha \begin{cases} \pi o\lambda\acute{\upsilon}\tau\lambda\alpha\varsigma \; \delta\hat{\iota}o\varsigma \; 'O\delta\upsilon\sigma\sigma\epsilon\acute{\upsilon}\varsigma \\ \Gamma\epsilon\rho\acute{\eta}\nu\iota o\varsigma \; \acute{\iota}\pi\pi\acute{o}\tau\alpha \; N\acute{\epsilon}\sigma\tau\omega\rho \end{cases} \text{etc.}$$

This form (including τήν for τόν and so on) occurs 72 times in
the two poems. The choice of the longer or shorter 'answered'
formula is indeed somewhat arbitrary where the subject is a
major god or hero, because these can be described by either
shorter or longer alternative name-epithet phrases; but there
are many other characters whose specification requires more
than the room left by the longer predicate.

There is, in fact, amazingly little unnecessary reduplication
of formulas in Homer. To take the large number of name-
epithet phrases in the nominative case: the table on pp. 50 f. of
Parry's classic study, *L'Épithète traditionnelle chez Homère* (Paris,
1928), shows that for eleven prominent gods and heroes there
are no less than 824 uses of 55 different formulas in the Iliad and
Odyssey as a whole. These formulas, some of which are of
course very frequent (πολύμητις 'Οδυσσεύς comes 81 times), are
those which fill out the four commonest metrical segments of
the verse, namely those exemplified in 1, 3, 4, 5 above. Type 2,
covering the space from the male caesura to the verse-end, is
somewhat less common than the others, but if formulas of this
type were added the total would of course be carried above 824.
Out of the 824 uses only 15, involving only three different
formulas, are reduplicative in the sense of being exact metrical
equivalents of other commoner ones: for instance στεροπηγερέτα
Ζεύς (once only) is an unfunctional variant of Ζεὺς τερπικέραυνος
(four times). Thus in the extensive name-epithet nominative
system there is an astounding *economy* of phrases, not more than
5 per cent of reduplication. At the same time the coverage or
scope is almost equally striking. The four main parts of the verse
to be filled, in the case of these eleven prominent characters,

make a possibility of 44 name-epithet groups. Two of these positions cannot in any case be filled by particular names because of their metrical value, but out of the 42 remaining we find formulas for no less than 37, making roughly 88 per cent perfect coverage.

This degree of scope and economy cannot be accidental; nor can it be the creation of a single poet. No one singer could construct a system so rich in metrical alternatives and at the same time so closely shorn of unfunctional variation. Even a pen and paper composer would be hard pressed to achieve such a system, and to do so he would have to behave not like a poet but like a cryptographer—or a classical scholar; and his effort would be quite pointless, since the only reasonable purpose of such a construction is to enable the oral, non-literate poet both to assimilate and to increase a great stock of traditional heroic song. The system is so extensive because for generation after generation individual singers had added a fresh phrase here and another there, as the necessity of their particular contexts demanded; it is so economical, spare and thrifty because needless alternatives—a mere encumbrance to the singer—were systematically if gradually discarded. Human skills being fallible, and the creative urge not always responding to systems, a new and unfunctional alternative would naturally be added from time to time, so that the economy at any one period would never be quite complete.

Closer examination of the details of the formular system shows how it helps the poet to remember traditional verses; for if a line is divided into three familiar phrase-units, say, rather than ten or a dozen word-units, it is obviously easier to remember and reproduce. It also helps him to compose his own fresh lines with the minimum of effort. Epithets are standardized not only for people but also for many familiar objects, and once again they vary according to the portion of verse that it is desired to fill. If the idea 'of a ship' has to be expressed in the latter part of a verse, the ship will be described as 'equal', 'curved around' or 'dark-prowed' simply according as the final 2, $2\frac{1}{2}$ or $3\frac{1}{4}$ feet have to be filled—in other words, according as the phrase has to succeed the bucolic, hephthemimeral or trochaic caesura. The formulas are νηὸς ἐΐσης, νεὸς ἀμφιελίσσης and νεὸς κυανο-πρῴροιο: note that the form of the word 'ship' itself is varied solely for metrical convenience. If the case is changed, and a dative, for example, is needed after the bucolic caesura—because the other concepts to be expressed use the whole of the verse up to that point—then the epithet may have to be changed too, and νηὸς ἐΐσης becomes νηὶ μελαίνῃ. That is not because ships in the dative are any blacker and less equal than those in the genitive, nor is it because a ship in a particular context is envisaged as black rather than equal: it is black simply and solely because after the word νηί, and to fill the measure ∪ – ∪̲, we require an epithet of that value beginning with a consonant —since νηί ends in a vowel. ἐΐσῃ will not do and μελαίνῃ will. Prepositions, too, can be incorporated in these noun-epithet groups, and may require fresh epithets with new metrical values: thus 'on a ship', if it is to fill the last 2½ feet, for instance, entails replacing the standard epithet of the simple noun-epithet group in that place, namely 'curved around', by the shorter word 'hollow'—κοίλης ἐπὶ νηός in place of νεὸς ἀμφιελίσσης.

Other common types of formula express the verb, or the verb and its object, and so on, and are designed to fill either the first or the second part of the verse and often to be mated with an appropriate subject-formula in the other part. Thus αὐτὰρ ὁ μερμήριξε, or τὸν δ' αὖτε προσέειπε, or αὐτὰρ ἐπεὶ τό γ' ἄκουσε, for instance, may be followed by any 3¼-foot noun-epithet group beginning with a consonant. Such formulas are themselves often built up from shorter fixed components—thus there are many different phrases beginning with αὐτάρ: αὐτὰρ ὁ with different verbs, αὐτὰρ ἐπεί or ἐπειδή, αὐτὰρ ἔβη and so on. In the illustrative verses on p. 61 both 3 and 5 begin with ὥς, followed by φάτο and ἄρα respectively; both phrases recur in many other lines of Homer. ὣς ἄρα φωνήσας is a regular resumptive formula after a speech; and the phrase that follows in 5, κόρυθ' εἵλετο, is a formula-type in which the object of the verb may be replaced by any desired metrical equivalent, such as λίθον, γέρας, φρένας, δόρυ δ'.

The singers of the Ionian oral tradition sometimes adapted a phrase to a new position or a new use without much conscious thought, by ear and by instinct. The formula in its standard use and form had a familiar metrical value, and it seems to have been assumed, sometimes wrongly, that this value persisted even after the standard form had been slightly altered; or perhaps it would be truer to say that there was no conscious assumption of any kind, that this problem is one that often does not occur to the oral singer. Thus μερόπων ἀνθρώπων, for example, is a well-known formula, evidently developed for use in the genitive case, which occurs at the verse-end seven times in the Iliad and twice in the Odyssey. Once in the Iliad it is successfully adapted to the dative, μερόπεσσι βροτοῖσιν, but at XVIII. 288 we see that at some stage some not very careful singer required a *nominative* phrase meaning 'men' for the same part of the line, and so transposed the familiar formula into μέροπες ἄνθρωποι, thus producing a technical fault of metre. In performance the singer would presumably disguise this fault by artificially prolonging the -ες, and the audience would probably not notice the difference. Similarly many Homeric instances of hiatus—that is, of irregularly leaving a final vowel unaffected before a succeeding initial vowel—are the result of the minor adaptation of fixed phrases; though Parry exaggerated when he made this the primary cause of metrical anomalies, since many cases of hiatus are caused by the loss of digamma or other initial semi-vowels, or by the assumption of such a loss, or by a feeling that hiatus sometimes did not matter at the major divisions of the verse.[1] An analogous result of the careless placing of formulas is inappropriateness not of metre but of sense. Thus the basic idea 'with the hand' is often expressed by the formula χειρὶ παχείη, in which the epithet 'thick' helps to fill up the part of the verse following the bucolic caesura. When this epithet is applied not to the powerful fist of a warrior, which must have been its usual and so 'proper' function, but to the ladylike hand of the refined (sometimes over-refined) Penelope, the result, if it is noticed at all, is ludicrous. The same is the case with 'blameless Aegisthus' (*1. 29*) and perhaps with the revolting Irus's 'lady mother' (*18. 5*)—I am not sure that in the last case any contradiction would be felt. These are obvious and familiar cases, but there are others in which the redeployment of a formula reveals itself in more subtle ways; thus one of a pair of repeated passages may reveal itself as adapted from the other—or from the type of which the other is a fair representative—because of the forced adjustment of a component formula.

What is the minimum length of a formula? The maximum may be several complete lines, composing a passage which is repeated whenever a typical scene, like the preparation of a meal or sacrifice or the launching or beaching of a ship, is to be described. The minimum may be two words like ὡς φάτο or Τρώεσσι δέ, if we insist on the formula as a phrase-unit. But even single words have definite formular tendencies, since they gravitate strongly to certain positions in the verse according to their metrical value; and there are fewer exact metrical alter-natives of single words having a similar meaning than one would find in written poetry—though more than in the case of most formular phrases. The fixity of position of individual words within the line is indeed remarkable, though it quite escapes the notice of most readers or hearers. The longer the word the less remarkable this fixity becomes; there are only two positions which a word like φιλοπτολέμοισι, for example, can occupy without disturbing the natural articulations of the hexameter line. Yet even disyllables like ἦτορ or δῶμα show a strong preference for one or perhaps two positions in the verse, whereas there are theoretically several in which they could occur (see p. 117); and παιδός, παιδί regularly avoid the line-end (only once in 61 uses), while παῖδα and the plural forms do not. Some-times this preference is due to the fact that the word in question occurs predominantly in a particular formula, itself restricted in position. Where this is not the case the tendency toward fixity arises in part out of the pure mechanics of the hexameter verse, a subject which we do not yet fully understand; but at least a perusal of Eugene O'Neill Jr.'s article on metrical word-types in the Greek hexameter shows that the tendency had

67

reached a considerable degree of formalization or stylization in the Homeric poems.[1] Thus metrical word-values, rather than particular single words, are formular in Homer, and this apparent restriction, like that imposed by fixed phrases, was of a kind to help rapid composition rather than to hinder it. The singer begins to crystallize a thought of which the pivotal concept is 'house': he assigns δῶμα, for instance, to its preferred position, and can then confidently fit verbal and other nominal formulas round it. His verse is made with the minimum of conscious effort.

§3. *The oral tradition and the advent of writing*

I hope to have outlined the broad principles of formular composition and to have shown by a small number of examples that Homer manifests the scope and economy of a developed oral tradition. To illustrate all the complexities and potentialities of this type of composition would need a complete book; not even Parry produced such a comprehensive explanation, nor is one necessary. What is necessary is to grasp the principle. One consequence of Parry's demonstration is that every single line of the great poems must be assessed in terms of a traditional and formalized language and a traditional subject-matter. Fulsome lip-service has been paid to Parry's conclusions, and some scholars have even been tempted to make the one-sided claim that the only way in which Homeric scholarship can progress is by closer examination of the formular system. In spite of this, relatively little has been achieved since Parry died.[2]

Even less attention has been given to post-Homeric hexameter poetry from this viewpoint.[3] Hesiod's *Theogony* and the fairly copious fragments of his Catalogue poetry are composed in a distinctly Homeric style, somewhat debased but traditional in essence. There are many new phrases, some of them repeated several times and tending to become fully formular; these are confined primarily to fresh subject-matter. Where the subject is traditional—as for example in many of the Catalogue fragments—the traditional language is used, though often with drastic adaptations. The subject of *Works and Days*, on the other hand, is so different from those of the regular heroic narrative that hundreds of new words and phrases are needed. Native Boeotian poets may have developed a tradition which included didactic and gnomic poetry, so that even the non-Homeric language of *Works and Days* may still be oral and formular in character. Unfortunately there is no contemporary material for comparison, nor have the economy and scope of the new phrases been evaluated in detail; but Hesiod could well have used the aid of writing, in some way or other, in the genuine parts of this later poem. The earlier 'Homeric' Hymns, particularly those to Demeter, Apollo, and Aphrodite, are probably entirely oral. They depart from Homeric vocabulary often enough, and have many new phrases; but these, especially the decorative and lyrical ones, are in the style of certain relatively late elements in Homer, like the Beguilement of Zeus in Iliad xiv and xv, which there is no reason to associate with writing and which indeed preserve a scope and economy which preclude it. As for the few surviving fragments of the poems of the Homeric Cycle, they are for the most part easily distinguishable in style from Homer. The later Cyclic poems, like the *Telegony* of Eugammon, almost certainly belong to written literature. The earlier, like the *Aithiopis* and the *Iliou Persis* of Arctinus, may have been composed not long after 700 in the decadent oral manner of certain later expansions of Homer (pp. 204–8, 301 f.).

Nevertheless by the probable time of composition of the *Theogony*, the *Aithiopis*, and the *Hymn to Demeter*, none of which is likely to be very much later than 650, writing was reaching the point at which it could be used for literary purposes. Archilochus, who was certainly a literate composer, refers to an eclipse of the sun which must be that of 648. Moreover *graffito* inscriptions on certain unambitious pots show that writing was used in different parts of the Greek world, and sometimes for casual and inessential purposes, as early as the last decades of the 8th century. The Dipylon prize jug with a hexameter couplet to the effect that the best of the dancers ⟨? shall receive this prize⟩ is datable from its shape and decoration to around 730 (pl. 6a);[1] the Ithaca cup with another heroic verse is later, around 700, and the same is probably true of the little pot excavated in Ischia in 1954, with a couplet referring to the famous cup of Nestor in the eleventh book of the Iliad.[2] Its excavator wished to assign to it a slightly higher date on the basis of a scarab found in the same tomb—but a comparatively precious and indestructible object of that kind could have been kept for many decades before interment. Some fragments of cheap clay cups found on Mount Hymettus in Attica and bearing alphabetic inscriptions are to be placed around 700, while the Mantiklos bronze and Perachora inscriptions, which are often cited as early, could be as late as around 650.[3] The earliest painted (as opposed to incised) inscription is probably that on a fragment of a latest-Geometric plaque found by J. Boardman in Aegina: he states that 'it can...hardly be later than the decade 720–710...and could well be earlier'.[4] I venture to disagree, and place this fragment around 700. These cases suggest that the Greek alphabet must have been developed, in origin no doubt for more essential uses, at some time before 725.[5] It was derived, of course, from the Phoenician script, and had to undergo a fair degree of adaptation—notably in the diversion of some Phoenician signs to vowels, which were not expressed by separate letters in the Semitic script. For this reason the process most probably presupposes recurrent contact with a Phoenicianized culture over some years; though the possibility cannot be dismissed that some sharp-witted merchant quickly acquired the rudiments of so practical a recording system during the course of sporadic voyages overseas. Phoenician penetration of Greek waters is hard to date with security, but there is no doubt that Phoenicians were established in Cyprus from the 9th century; a Phoenician inscription of that date was found in the island and is now in the museum at Nicosia.[6] Trade from the Greek mainland with Cyprus was restored by about 800, and it is conceivable that the early 8th century and Cyprus were the time and place at which transmission of the alphabet occurred. That a derivative of the old Mycenaean syllabary was still retained in many places in

Cyprus does not seem to me (though it has seemed to many critics) to preclude this possibility. There are several other possibilities, however, including transmission through Al Mina.[1] Indeed the Phoenician script had been in widespread use from at least the beginning of the 12th century, the latest probable date of the inscription on Ahiram's tomb at Byblos; and might even have been accessible to some of the Mycenaean merchants who settled in Ugarit.[2] I do not wish seriously to suggest that the alphabet came over in the time of Mycenaean Cadmus, as Herodotus believed; I do wish to show the vagueness of our criteria and the highly provisional quality of any possible conclusions.

In any event the question whether alphabetic writing began to establish itself in Greece in the early 8th century, or earlier or later, is only of limited relevance to Homer—though it continues to occupy the attention of many Homeric scholars, who accept successive quasi-archaeological *pronunciamenti* on the topic with touching credulity. We know that writing was used for short inscriptions of a vaguely literary nature by the last decades of the 8th century; we are fairly confident that it must have been available for commercial purposes, which were presumably prior to literary ones, and perhaps for some other purposes, for some time before that. Yet we can also be sure that the Iliad and Odyssey are oral poems, composed according to an elaborate system which is quickly weakened when the poet begins to compose by writing; and that there is a sudden spate of definitely written literature from the middle of the 7th century onwards, which suggests that the new practice had invaded the literary field not long before. In its main outlines, then, the picture is relatively clear.

These factors, including the special characteristics of the oral system of formulas, are not necessarily incompatible with the suggestion that the monumental poets made notes to help them build up their complicated narrative. Personally I do not find this suggestion very attractive, because the study of oral poets in Russia and Yugoslavia shows that the stringing together of themes, with fair consistency, is not difficult for the memory-poet with

a large repertoire of songs. He does this with no noticeable
effort, much in the way in which he combines traditional
phrase-units. He is familiar not only with a mass of formular
passages describing repeated actions, but also with a mass
of traditional themes—like the affronted warrior, the list of
leaders, the heroic duel (whether ended by act of treachery or
by divine intervention), the long-lost husband, the cunning
fellow who triumphs over stronger enemies, the oppressed
prince, the way to handle suitors. The singer assembles and relates such major themes, and a mass of other and more detailed
ones, with something of the semi-automatic ease, born of long
familiarity, with which he deploys familiar phrase-formulas so
as to construct new lines. A great deal of ingenuity and creative
genius is required if he is to produce verses or plots like those of
the Iliad and Odyssey; the point is that large-scale composition,
unusual though it is, *does* lie within the competence of the
completely oral poet. Those who insist that Homer must have
had his memorandum cannot be refuted, but their insistence
seems to arise largely from their own experience as literates and
their unfamiliarity with the procedures and powers of illiterate
singers.

§4. *The oral poet's use of established themes*

This question of composition by theme is an important field of
study for the Homeric scholar and it has barely been touched so
far. The American scholar A. B. Lord has performed an
excellent service in drawing attention to its relevance, most
recently in his book *The Singer of Tales* (Cambridge, Mass.,
1960). He has concentrated more on broader themes and story-
motifs; I believe the oral poet's handling of minor typical
incidents is equally important, because it shows how the minute-
to-minute oral composition of poetry as complicated as the Iliad
and Odyssey was possible. Lord and his followers evidently do
not think that it *was* possible without the aid of writing; they
believe the Iliad and Odyssey to be oral dictated texts (see
pp. 98 ff.). Admittedly the poetry of Homer is far more complex
and far more polished in its detail and structure than the kind
of oral poetry that can be studied in modern societies. Yet just

as the Greek epic verse-unit is more complicated and tightly
controlled than its equivalent in Russian or Yugoslav oral
poetry, and yet was assuredly perfected by unaided oral singers,
so the infinitely finer texture of Homeric episode and incident
may also turn out to be within the powers of the Greek *aoidos*
or singer, unaided by dictation or notebooks or writing in any
form.

The emphasis in what follows is on the Iliad, since its
structure, though less sophisticated and chronologically simpler
than that of the Odyssey, is more detailed in terms of character
and minor incident, particularly in the minute treatment of the
events of the battlefield. This makes the Iliad seem even more
difficult than the Odyssey to envisage as the work of the oral
poet entirely unaided by writing—until one considers the
formular character of its thematic structure. The sequence of
main events is logical, well-defined and easily memorable:
Chryses, quarrel, wrath, Zeus's promise, catalogues of the
armies, duels and indefinite encounters, embassy to Achilles,
wounding of the Achaean chieftains, Trojan irruption into the
camp, Patroclus's intervention and death, renunciation of the
wrath of Achilles and his vengeance on Hector, funeral of
Patroclus, ransoming of Hector's body. The division into books
may not be early in its present form (pp. 305 f.), but many of the
present books coincide with natural articulations of the plot and
may be remembered as containing prominent and self-contained
episodes (for instance the embassy, the Doloneia, the battle by
the ships, the fight for Patroclus's body, the making of new
armour for Achilles), with which certain lesser episodes, themselves interconnected, are easily associated. It is not hard to
remember that associated with the catalogues early in the
poem are the deceitful dream sent by Zeus to Agamemnon, the
panic of the Achaeans, and the Thersites episode. Another well-
marked structural characteristic of the Iliad is the series of
delays which hold up the expected Achaean defeat between
books II and XII—for over one-third of the poem. The probable
purpose of these delays is partly dramatic, to increase tension
as the Achaeans hover on the brink of disaster, and partly

monumental, to convey the idea of a whole ten years' fighting. The
sequence of delays often has no special internal logic, but is easy
enough to remember: the duel of Paris and Menelaus in III, the
breaking of the truce and Agamemnon's inspection of his troops
in IV, the victories of Diomedes in V, Hector's return to Troy
and his encounters with Andromache, Helen and Paris in VI,
and so on.

So far this analysis of major themes only serves to show that
the broad structure of the poem is not difficult to master. It
possesses a certain simplicity which must have facilitated oral
composition as well as oral reproduction. The main themes
themselves, general as they are, must have occurred in other
heroic poems of the centuries before Homer. The catalogues of
warriors, the abstention of one crucial hero, the repression of a
potential mutiny, the duel to settle the whole issue, the mutilation of an enemy interrupted somehow by the gods: themes like
these were not the invention of Homer, or even probably of the
singers from whom he immediately derived them. They were
commonplaces of epic narrative. So too were many more
restricted motifs; and this is more important for the question of
oral composition. Let us consider a part of the poem where the
fighting is thickest and, to the casual modern reader, often
monotonous and unvariegated: books XI to XXII. Even here it
is divided up by conspicuous non-martial episodes, like the
beguiling of Zeus, the scene between Patroclus and Achilles at
the beginning of XVI, the making of Achilles's new armour by
Hephaestus, the reconciliation of Achilles and Agamemnon in
XIX. Furthermore within the battle-scenes themselves there are
certain memorable episodes, even apart from the crisis of the
death of Patroclus, which help to articulate the whole at first
sight rather amorphous mass: the wounding of the chieftains in
XI, Ajax fighting from the poops of the beached ships in XV,
the death of Zeus's son Sarpedon in XVI, Achilles's fight with
the river in XXI. Of these the second and fourth are highly
unusual and surely individual. They are not formular themes;
they are untypical. Brilliant and dramatic in content and
position, they may well be the invention of the main composer

74

himself. Most of the other incidents of fighting are far more
generic in quality, and more likely to have occurred, in one form
or another, in many different poems of warfare during the long
centuries of the epic tradition from the end of the Myçenaean
period down to the probable time of Homer in the 8th century.

The things that can happen in battle are themselves limited,
and the descriptions of them, within an oral formular convention that does not encourage variegated or introspective analysis,
are even more so. Thus two heroes, one from each side, meet
in the mêlée of battle; they utter threats and boasts; if in
chariots, they dismount; one of them hurls a spear, which
usually misses; the other reciprocates. Then there are second
spear-casts, one of which usually hits; the victor boasts, the
victim dies and his armour is stripped from him. Then the poet
moves on to a fresh incident, which may follow a similar
pattern. In this pattern there are many minor variations: the
first spear-throw may hit not its intended victim but his friend
or charioteer; swords may be drawn; the victim may be
wounded rather than killed outright, then carried to safety by
his comrades; or he may collapse in some unusual way, or with
a dying plea or threat. Yet the general course of the heroic
encounter is fixed, and the poet selects at will from a limited
range of well-known variants. Occasionally he may invent a
new one; sometimes, as when the charioteer Mydon is hit by
Antilochus at v. 580 ff. and topples from his chariot into soft
sand, where he remains for a time with his head buried and
his legs in the air, the result is strained and almost ludicrous
(pp. 177 f.). The place of a wound, the manner of a death, are
subjects for ingenious variation—but again the formular basis
is evident of the exercises within this theme.

The actual encounter is only one aspect of the fighting. Other
passages describe, often with the aid of simile, how the armies
are marshalled and move towards each other, or how one side
or the other closes up in defence, or is routed by human hero or
divine portent, and how they flee like deer; or how chariots are
driven over corpses and spattered with blood; or how Ajax is
isolated and driven back step by step; or how a hero searches

for a special companion, or a special enemy, along the bridges of war; or how a god appears on the battlefield, disguised or openly, to bring panic or advice; or how Zeus on Ida or Olympus weighs the fates of the two sides in his balance, or thunders, or hurls a thunderbolt.

These are the typical moments of warfare. Such themes are used again and again, expressed by means of different formular phrases or different combinations of such phrases, and decorated from time to time with fresh details—the names of minor warriors, for instance, of their fathers and native cities, and perhaps more graphic information about whether they were good at running, or rearing horses, or entertaining strangers. Yet even such details as these contain a strong element of the generic, and tend to be deployed in more than one specific situation. Of the minor figures some were presumably historical individuals, the majority are historical types. Away from the battlefield the pattern of incident is again rather stereotyped: the Achaean chieftains take council by the ships or in the plain; Agamemnon radiates gloom or despair, Nestor reminisces or gives curious advice, Achilles broods by his hut. Visitors are formally received, regaled with food and drink, asked for news or counsel. In Troy the beleaguered people watch from the walls, or take council together, or offer prayers to the gods; the royal women move anxiously in the background, accompanied by their servants. On Olympus, or on Mount Ida overlooking the field of war, events are a little more unpredictable—for gods are fickle, powerful and unusually mobile—but even so their range is limited: the pro-Achaean gods plot to help their favourites, or are curbed by Zeus; Hephaestus works at his forge or reconciles divine quarrels; Zeus comforts and upbraids, or mulls over his female conquests; divine chariots are prepared, divine messengers despatched; the savour of sacrifice is complacently relished. In one sense the contents of the Iliad are immeasurably vast, since they range from heaven to hell; in another they are narrowly compressed, since little happens that is outside the limited scope of the heroic mentality and heroic ideals—brave deeds in battle, the desire for honour and conquest, plundering one's enemies, honouring or trying to outdo the gods. In a sense almost nothing really unexpected happens in the Iliad. This is the result of oral composition, which depends on the use of standard language and to a large extent of fixed and traditional themes. It also gives the poem an important part of its effect of authenticity and concentration.

Standard themes do not necessarily have to be expressed in standardized or formular language. The particular application of a theme may demand that special language be used, or that established formulas be varied or adapted. Naturally certain narrow themes, like the spread of panic in an army and its turning to headlong flight, tend to be expressed in the same words, so that we find repeated lines and repeated passages. A substantial part of the Iliad and Odyssey consists of such lines, and their use was an important aid to the oral singer. Yet they are really extended verbal formulas, they aid the expression of narrative rather than the narrative structure itself. It is here that the repertory of generic incident is so important. The poet as he composes knows that he now wishes to depict Patroclus, for example, asking Achilles to allow him to fight. First he makes Patroclus say that the Argives are in desperate straits, their leaders wounded; then that Achilles is relentless, that his parents were not Peleus and Thetis but sea and rock; that if Achilles is held back by divine message or portent, yet at least he can send his friend to fight. None of this precisely recurs elsewhere in Homer; yet it is hard to doubt that each point is generic, the kind of thing that was sung on many different occasions. The poet who composed this passage as we have it in the Iliad surely did not have to work out the trope about sea and rock; this was a common way of saying that someone was hard-hearted. The poet knew this, and introduced it quite casually, along with other detailed themes, into the speech made by Patroclus. He may have had to re-create its particular expression in this place, though by means of the usual formular apparatus of phrases; the point is that the composition of the speech, in terms of what is said as well as of how it is said, is no hard task for the accomplished singer.

Patroclus's approach to Achilles is a well-marked incident, and indeed a turning-point in the development of the central plot of the Iliad. It was a point at which the poet was prepared to create his own material, where it was perhaps unlikely that large stretches of existing poetry could simply be reused. The thematic method of composition is useful here, but perhaps it is even more so in the composition and commission to memory of the countless details, none of them absolutely germane to the plot, of the humdrum progress of battle itself. The best way to show how this method works is to take a typical piece of battle-poetry and analyse it into its component episodes. For the sake of example I take a couple of hundred lines from XVI. 102 onwards, because this follows the conversation between Patroclus and Achilles to which reference has been made already. It is also part of a crucial book which probably contained much by the monumental composer himself, and much that was worked up to fit his special requirements. At XVI. 101 there is a formular summary of the scene between Patroclus and Achilles: 'thus they talked'. The scene switches to the progress of the battle: Ajax is forced back (102), subdued by Zeus and Trojans (103); his helmet rings with blows, his shield-arm aches, sweat pours down (104–11)—this is all standard thematic material, epitomizing the idea of the heroic warrior tiring under great pressure. (The word 'theme' will appear in parenthesis after other such basic motifs—or such as can be recognized from our limited knowledge of the Greek epic.) At 112f. the Muses are asked to tell the singer (theme) how fire first fell on the ships. Hector breaks Ajax's spear with his sword, Ajax throws the stump away, recognizes god's work, and retreats (114–22) (all theme); the Trojans fire a ship (122–4). Achilles is perturbed and urges on Patroclus (124–9) (theme?). Patroclus arms (130–9) (theme). The Pelian ash-spear is described (140–4) (the hero's special weapon constitutes a theme). Achilles's horses and their yoking are described (145–54) (theme). Achilles arms the Myrmidons, who assemble like wolves—a long simile (155–67) (theme). There follows a list of the Myrmidon leaders (theme), with details of birth (168–97);

the first two are from mothers seduced by a god (*theme*), the other three arc cursorily described. Achilles exhorts the Myrmidons (*theme*), reminding them of their complaints at being inactive (*theme?*) (198–210); they pack their ranks as tight as stones in a wall (211–17) (*theme*). Two leaders, Patroclus and Automedon, are conspicuous (218–20) (*theme*). Achilles gets a special cup and pours a libation (220–32) (*theme*); he prays to Zeus for Patroclus's success and safe return (233–48) (*theme?*). Zeus grants one prayer but not the other (249–56) (*theme?*). The Myrmidons swarm out to war like wasps (257–67) (*theme*); Patroclus exhorts them (*theme*) to avenge Achilles's honour (268–74); they attack (275–7) (*theme*). When the Trojans see Patroclus [in Achilles's armour] they panic (278–83) (*theme*). Patroclus casts, hits Pyraichmes (who is briefly described) in the shoulder; he falls, his men panic (284–92) (all *theme*). The Trojans retreat; simile (293–305) (*theme*). Hero kills hero—Patroclus hits Areilycus in the thigh, Menelaus hits Thoas in the chest, and so on (306–16) (*theme*). Two Achaean brothers kill two Trojan brothers (317–29) (*theme?*); the lesser Ajax takes Cleobulus alive (*theme*), but then slices off his head (*theme*), so that his sword is reddened (330–4) (*theme*). Peneleos and Lycon miss with spears and fall to with swords (*theme*); Lycon hits the other's helmet, his sword breaks (*theme*). Peneleos severs his neck, the head droops and is held on only by skin (*theme?*) (335–41). Meriones hits Acamas as he mounts his chariot, and makes him topple from it (342–4) (*theme*); Idomeneus hits Erymas in the mouth (345–50). Thus the Danaan leaders fall on the Trojans like wolves on sheep (351–7) (*theme*).

Sometimes in the above analysis a question-mark shows that there is no evidence in Homer that a particular motif is a standard one, though it seems probable on general grounds. No incident is omitted. The passage itself was chosen at random within this key book; it appears to be fairly typical of battles and preparations for battle in the Iliad. Analysis of domestic situations in the Odyssey, for example, would not be too different in result. The result is, of course, that the ratio of common or standard themes to particular, specially invented incidents is very high. To return to the beginning of the passage, it is as though these thoughts ran through the singer's mind: stubborn hero pushed back, usual signs of exhaustion; ask the Muses how fire fell on ships; the hero's spear can be broken, so that he retreats; a ship is fired. Then let Achilles urge on Patroclus in the usual way; Patroclus's arming will be detailed, of course, with a special bit on Achilles's spear; his horses must be described as usual; meanwhile Achilles can be assembling the troops—a long simile here, of course. To make it more impressive let us have a catalogue of battalions and leaders, with the usual sort of description of parentage. Naturally Achilles will exhort his troops . . . and so on. Nothing very difficult or very new in substance here, although the skilled singer, by his combination of themes and of formular language, with many new touches of his own, can be relied on to produce a passage that will be entirely satisfying and not seem stale or second-hand. This is the formular method—formular in theme as well as in language; and it is in this way that the whole Iliad, and the Odyssey too, can have been built up and repeated, though with some variation, by poets who had no concern with writing.

§5. *Originality and the formular method*

To many literate critics it has seemed very remarkable that the oral method of composition neither calls for nor allows a special choice of word, especially of decorative word, in individual cases. The use of conventional decorative epithets is an essential part of the Greek epic style, and lends to the Homeric poetry much of its rich and formal texture. Each individual character, object or event is treated as a perfect member of its species, and is expressed in the way determined as best for the species as a whole. This tendency to describe individuals in generic terms implies a certain way of looking at things: a simplified, synthetic way. It is a narrow view of a narrow facet of life, for the world of heroic manners and ideals was itself over-simplified and over-codified. One suspects that it only achieves subtlety, and then not frequently, through the reflecting genius of the greatest oral singers. No doubt the simplified technique that is demanded by sung narrative accentuated the schematizing tendency of the heroic outlook; but the result, in Homer, does not seem unnatural, because heroic life was something like that. Whether it was *exactly* like that mattered no more to Homer's audience than it does to us, since even they were separated from the events described by five hundred years. Thus the possible discrepancy between individual case and generalizing description does not detract from the Homeric poetry; on the contrary it confers a special 'archaic' directness, a powerful starkness, that more than compensates for a sacrifice of the literal realism to which, in any case, poetry cannot properly aspire.

Conspicuous and important as it is, the rigid economy and consequent generic quality of Homeric poetry should not be exaggerated. If restricted to the choice of the more specific kind of epithet for *important* people and places, Page's judgement is true: that 'The determining factor for each place was meaning, not metre (just as it was for each hero: ποδάρκης δῖος 'Αχιλλεύς is metrically equivalent to πολύτλας δῖος 'Οδυσσεύς, and μέγας Τελαμώνιος Αἴας to μέγας κορυθαίολος Ἕκτωρ): it is only within the scheme of each place (and each hero) that the law of economy is observed'.[1] Thus each major hero has certain special characteristics, and so, even outside the Catalogue, do places like golden Mycenae and Troy with its good horses and broad streets.[2] Achilles is never called much-enduring, or Odysseus swift-footed, though the exchange could be made with great ease. This, of course, is because Odysseus is *not* swift-footed, at least as we see him in the Iliad and Odyssey, while Achilles is. Obviously if there were to be no distinction of individuals in terms of their epithets the result would be a poem of extreme economy but utter confusion and boredom.[3] Certain characters, indeed, like Thersites, are described in very particular terms; they are the ones who, important as they may be in a section of the Homeric poems, had not fully established themselves in the tradition and been subjected to the traditional process of simplification. Each of the main heroes, on the other hand, is left with a bare minimum of special characteristics to be expressed in one or two standard epithets: Achilles is swift-footed, Hector has a shining helmet, Diomedes is good at the war-cry, Odysseus is cunning and much-enduring. These specific epithets are allied with generic ones like δῖος, 'divine', so as to build up a complex pattern of noun-epithet formulas which fill all or most of the crucial sections of the hexameter line. At the same time the individuality of human or divine characters in Homer is brought out by their actions and reactions, and does not depend exclusively or even primarily on their standard epithets. Nor, it should be said, are formulas of other kinds than the noun-epithet group, like formulas of action ('then he went', 'thus she addressed him', 'whirling (his spear) he threw it'), given these minimal particular features, since they are by essence generic and can be reduced to the level of single all-purpose expressions.

The prominence of repeated formulas, lines, passages and themes does not mean that Homer, the singer of the large-scale Iliad, is not original. His originality did not lie in the choice of specially appropriate epithets or phrases, but on the one hand in the whole conception and scale of the poem, on the other in the consistently fluid and adept handling of traditional phraseology—something not easy to achieve. Not every singer of his time would be capable of systematic creation, of constructing such lines as his, of extruding clumsy locutions as effectively as the main composer of the Iliad—or of the Odyssey. Moreover there is no reason to deny these composers linguistic originality in a large number of cases not covered by the phraseology of tradition. Although the absence of pre-Homeric poetry makes it quite impossible to determine which phrases that occur only once in Homer are due to the large-scale composers, we may be fairly sure that many of them, especially those which describe apparently unusual situations, are substantially new. Every creative oral poet extends, in some degree at least, the range of the traditional vocabulary and the inherited thematic material. In both the Iliad and the Odyssey there must be countless connecting passages, transitional between themes and episodes which already existed in shorter poems by previous singers; these passages were created in the traditional mould by the main composers, just as were many other descriptions of new incidents. We can be virtually certain of this; but we can be almost equally confident that, when adequate means of expression or a satisfactory account of a particular motif already existed, then the monumental singers would not alter them. Only rarely, indeed, would a traditional phrase or epithet be adapted to an entirely new use, since that entailed the abandonment of the central generic concept. Similarly there is only a mere handful of places where a fixed, traditional, generic epithet is used outside its normal formular associations and of set intent. Thus πελώριος, 'monstrous' or 'mighty', most commonly reserved for Ajax, is used twice of Achilles and once of Hector in the position (immediately before the bucolic diaeresis) in which the much more general διίφιλος, 'dear to Zeus', was evidently standard—being employed five times of Achilles and four of Hector. Examination of those passages in which the rarer but metrically equivalent epithet occurs shows that they depict Achilles or Hector as particularly full of menace; the use of this epithet, in fact, seems to be a quite deliberate and purposeful departure from the usual formular vocabulary for these heroes. Parry's examples of this kind of particularized use of language that had otherwise become traditional and generic — and some of those examples are far from certain—show how very uncommon it was in the Homeric poems.[1] The general truth remains unimpaired, that in the early Greek epic the language was to a very large extent fixed by tradition; and it is no service to Homer's powerful originality to pretend that this is not so.

§6. *The comparative study of the oral epic in Yugoslavia*

The same tendency to use generic epithets is seen in the oral epic of modern Yugoslavia. The comparative study of heroic oral poetry is a relatively new subject; interest in living traditions in Russia and Greece, as well as in Yugoslavia, developed from early in the last century onwards, and a number of poems were taken down by hand and published whether in translation or in their original language. The Yugoslav material was not neglected even then; but an accurate evaluation of the techniques and abilities of modern oral poets has only been possible since Milman Parry began in 1933 to make a systematic and extensive collection of gramophone recordings of the Yugoslav oral singers or *guslari* (pl. 8c). Parry died soon afterwards, long before his work was complete. The editing and translating of this material is a herculean task which has been admirably carried on by Parry's pupil and associate A. B. Lord. So far only the first volume of the publication has appeared: *Serbocroatian Heroic Songs*, 1 (Cambridge, Mass., 1954) (II is the Serbo-Croat version of the same material). This volume contains a full selection of songs, in English translation and with notes, from the region of Novi Pazar in the southern part of the country. It also contains some fascinating verbatim interviews with the singers themselves. The next volume, which is impatiently awaited, will contain songs from the nearby district of Bijelo Polje, including the 12,000-line epic by Parry's prize singer, Avdo Međedović, on 'The wedding of Smailagić Meho'. Certain information about this poet and his methods and songs has already appeared in A. B. Lord's *The Singer of Tales*, but since considerable disagreement is possible about the nature and extent of his creativity it is essential to have a full and accurate text before the precarious business of inferring from one period and culture to another can be carried much further.

There are unquestionably many things in common between the Homeric and the Serbo-Croatian poems. The latter are oral, and are sung by illiterate singers. They tell of the deeds of heroes, of internecine quarrels and fights over women and the continuous guerrilla warfare against the Turks from before the battle of Kosovo, in A.D. 1389, onwards. There is much repetition of lines or half-lines and much use of standard themes. The fixed epithet is fairly prominent, though not nearly so common as in Homer: dungeons for example are usually 'cold' or 'icy'. It is difficult to illustrate a 'typical' Yugoslav poem, since there is considerable variety of style and quality between different singers. Most of the poems are intoned to an accompaniment on the single-stringed *gusle*, which is bowed like a violin, in verses of ten syllables with a caesura after the fourth. To choose a passage as close as possible in subject to a common Homeric type, here is Lord's translation of part of the battle-description at the end of 'The captivity of Ðulić Ibrahim', in the version of a good singer called Salih Ugljanin:

When the two forces met, sabres flashed and blood flowed. Men's heads rolled, and dead limbs twitched. The wounded and dying groaned. One said: 'Woe, woe, do not tread upon me, comrade!' And another wailed: 'Raise me, comrade!' As is common in war, horses flew past without their riders. They cut one another to pieces until midday. Soon a cloud darkened the mountains, a cloud darkened them on all sides. They cut one another to pieces for two full days, for two days and three full nights. When the fourth morning dawned, dark clouds enveloped the mountains. The Turks came rushing down from the mountains and came out upon the plain of Zadar. A stronger force arrived from Zadar and went to meet them. Then they cut one another to pieces on the green plain; they hacked at one another a whole day until noon. A cloud covered the whole plain, and no one could recognize anyone else. Then Tale raised his arms and prayed to God that the wind might blow, that the wind might blow from the mountain, so that he might see which company was losing, which was losing and which was victorious. The wind blew and scattered the cloud....[1]

There are many versions of this song, which is a popular one and comes in the repertoire of many different *guslari*. Salih's version runs to about 1800 lines. One notices the repetitions, the conventional epithets ('dark clouds', 'green plain'), and the slight anomalies (the cloud darkening the mountains, which can be either a metaphor for a mass of troops or an omen of doom) which are common in oral poetry. The extract is a generic one, which aims at giving an impression of the whole battle. It is more successful in effect and less naïve in technique than much of the South Slavic poetry. In one sense there is more realism than in Homer: the twitching of dead limbs, the groans and entreaties of the wounded, give a vivid impression of the horrors of the battlefield, which the Homeric poems either disregard or describe in elaborate similes or set pieces too 'literary' in style to convey the stark sense of actuality achieved by the simpler Yugoslav poet. At the same time there is an effect of monotony and lack of imagination in the modern poem that only occurs rarely in Homer. One remarkable thematic parallel is the cloud over the battlefield and the prayer of the hero that it should be lifted: compare XVII. 644 ff., where Ajax cries: '...for the Achaeans themselves and their horses are covered with mist. Father Zeus, come rescue the sons of the Achaeans from under the mist, and make clear day, and grant us to see with our eyes: in the light even destroy us, since that is indeed your pleasure.' The 'mist' of the Iliad is presumably the cloud of dust raised by two struggling armies; this is clearer in the modern poem. The parallel is due simply to the fact that the dust and the difficulty of seeing must have been a recurrent factor of actual warfare, and so must the wish or prayer for its dispersal. The theme is unique in Homer, but the Yugoslav version reminds us that it probably occurred in other Greek poems that have not survived—that it is not necessarily a particular invention of the monumental composer of the Iliad.

Recognition scenes and returns of long-absent heroes are common in the Yugoslav poetry. Earlier in Salih's poem came a long description of the return home of Đulić, which has some thematic similarity with the return of Odysseus; this is one of the basic folk-tale elements all over the world.

Then Huso went to the chamber and brought him the mother-of-pearl tamboura. When Đulić took it into his hands, he plucked it and began to sing; he sang loudly and clearly and plucked it lightly. 'I do not wonder at my aged mother, as her eyes have failed her, and she cannot see her only son. Nor do I wonder at my sister Fatima. I left her long ago when she was still a child of seven years, and so she does not recognize her own brother. But I do wonder at Huso the steward. Why, Huso, shame upon you, since we lived together so many years. Do you not recognize your master, your master Đulić the standard-bearer? I am Đulić the standard-bearer himself!'[1]

Again in this scene, a particular and domestic one in contrast with the generic scene of warfare considered above, we see the leisureliness and the deliberate and stylized repetitiveness of the oral poet. The request for the special tamboura (a stringed instrument for plucking) is not properly motivated, in this version at least, and it was probably the quality of Ðulić's playing, like the manner of Odysseus's dealing with his bow, that enabled him to be recognized and accepted.

It is not for thematic similarities, however, that the detailed study of Yugoslav epic poetry is most valuable; it is for the whole method and procedure of the oral singer. Yet here some delicacy of judgement is required. These rustic singers demonstrate many of the capacities of the oral poet; they show in particular that the composition of poems of the length of the Odyssey or Iliad is not necessarily beyond the accomplishment of especially gifted singers entirely unaided by writing. Admittedly there is nothing of the length of the Homeric poems, though 'The wedding of Smailagić Meho' approaches it. There is also nothing of their quality; the Greek oral tradition reached an altogether higher level than the Yugoslav, or than any other comparable tradition including even the Norse—in certain stages of which literacy has played a part. Yet practically every aspect of the Homeric poems can be paralleled, though usually at a far lower level, in the Yugoslav. The treasury of recurrent themes and the way in which they are varied, strung together or given a new specific reference is also instructive; though the surviving Yugoslav tradition is thematically jejune, and assemblies, the reading of letters, recognitions and so on recur with tedious monotony.

One important lesson of the field experience of Parry and Lord is that literacy destroys the virtue of an oral singer: those who have learned to read in middle life invariably seem to lose their spontaneity, they become self-conscious about their oral repertoire and seek to garnish it in the manner of an indifferent pen and paper poet, making it in consequence pretentious and boring. In a strict system like the Homeric, in which the economy and scope of alternative fixed phrases reaches a very high level, the technical effects would be disastrous; this particular result is not so immediately noticeable in the laxer traditional linguistic framework of the South Slavic singers. Another lesson is that traditional themes can be accurately preserved for as long as six hundred years—roughly the time that separates the battle of Kosovo, many of the incidents and participants of which survive in the poetry recorded by Parry, from the present day. Moreover most of those themes are aristocratic in content—that is, they concern the affairs of leaders and heroes and pay little attention to the common folk. Nevertheless they have been preserved through centuries in which Yugoslavia passed through the Dark Age of a savage and tyrannical Turkish occupation, when the equipment and circumstances of nobility were annihilated and when the only leaders were those most adept at guerrilla warfare and the game of sheer survival. This is relevant to what may have happened in the Dark Age in Greece; it proves, if proof were needed, that in times of oppression and despair men do not forget the great days of the noble past, but rather remember them more tenaciously than ever. If they have oral poets, then the memory of the old kind of life can be maintained, not with complete accuracy, but in some detail.

Such are the main advantages to be gained by the Homeric scholar from the careful study of a surviving tradition of oral narrative verse. I must now draw attention to certain hazards in any such comparison, and in particular certain ways in which the Yugoslav poetry is significantly different from the Homeric. These differences mean that inferences cannot always be safely drawn directly from the techniques of the modern *guslari* to those of the Homeric singers or *aoidoi*. First of all, as has already been briefly indicated, neither the Yugoslav poetry nor any other oral poetry of which we know has anything like the strict formular system, with its high degree of economy and scope, that is exemplified throughout the Iliad and Odyssey. The Yugoslav singer has much standardized thematic material available, some of which is expressed in more or less fixed formular language. There are many fixed epithets and repeated lines and half-lines, and A. B. Lord has shown that the formular quality may be more pervasive than one at first thinks.[1] Even so there is nothing approaching the rigidity of the formular structure of the Greek *aoidos*, by far the greater part of whose phraseology, judging from the Iliad and Odyssey, was traditional. This difference implies in its turn a significant difference in the powers and technique of the two kinds of singer. It implies that the whole Greek tradition was fuller, richer and more highly organized, and had far higher potentialities for the development of large-scale poems of great linguistic and thematic complexity. It also implies that the transmission of poetry from one generation to another was potentially more exact than appears to be the case in Yugoslavia; since the more rigid the phraseology and the metre, the more important it is to reproduce it with precision—for mistakes and loose variations will immediately become conspicuous.

This leads on to the second main difference between the Greek and the Yugoslav tradition: the difference in metrical strictness. The Homeric hexameter verse is a fully developed quantitative rhythmical unit, highly conventionalized, with a logical system of elision and the resolution of long syllables. It is only susceptible to occasional and well-defined licences (though one must remember that certain anomalies may have been removed in the centuries first of oral transmission and then of critical exegesis). The Yugoslav line is a ten-syllable unit which allows considerable internal rhythmical variation, although the word-break after the fourth foot is strictly observed. Stress is more important than quantity. This in itself gives greater freedom to the singer, who at times will even add an extra beat to his line or omit a beat or abandon the poetical rhythm altogether for a line or half-line, especially when hard-pressed in some way. One cannot imagine the Homeric singer doing that. Rarely a Homeric verse will begin with a word whose first syllable is by nature short, like the preposition διά: that is probably the most violent metrical anomaly accepted in this kind of poetry, and its explanation (so it seems to me) is almost certainly that the missing weight was supplied by a strong musical chord accompanying the first syllable. The same kind of explanation seems to apply to comparable phenomena in *Beowulf*.[1] It may also give a clue to the formal looseness of the South Slavic decasyllable, since the total rhythmical effect is controlled and kept reasonably consistent mainly by the basic metrical pattern but also by the melodic accompaniment. Here, indeed, is a very obvious difference between the oral poetry of our two cultures. One has only to hear a recording of a *guslar*, with his nasal, quavering vocal line set against a simpler droning background from his primitive violin, which at the end of each verse provides an intricate transitional phrase, to feel that this is an entirely different world from the Homeric. The feeling is no doubt partly misleading; the Moslem type of music sounds very strange to most western ears, but the ancient *kitharis* accompaniment might have sounded quite strange too. It may be doubted, though, whether the Homeric *aoidos*, although he probably chanted his verses, did so in anything like the complicated professional quaver of the Moslem tradition, by which *gusle* music is strongly influenced. The most significant facts are these: the bowed *gusle* is capable of providing a continuous accompaniment, while the plucked or strummed *kitharis* is not (unless the recitation is extremely slow and the singer's fingers are excessively nimble); the line of Yugoslav poetry is determined mainly by the total number of syllables, and the metrical value of those syllables is not nearly so strict as in the Greek hexameter line; and variations within the decasyllabic verse are frequently disguised or counterbalanced by the *gusle* accompaniment. In short, the Yugoslav songs are rhythmically much looser, as they are looser in formular structure, than the Homeric epics; and their rhythm is probably more closely associated with their musical accompaniment. Thus there is far more opportunity for verbal variation in the process of transmission from one singer to another.

The natural articulations of the Serbo-Croat verse are often emphasized by the bowing of the *gusle*. So, no doubt, the natural emphases of the Homeric hexameter line were accentuated by a new note or chord on the *kitharis*, which would also be used to cover hesitations and provide other special diversions, transitions or tonal stresses. It is significant that the ῥαψῳδοί or rhapsodes of the 6th century B.C. (and they seem to have existed towards the end of the 7th also) had given up the lyre and used no musical accompaniment, but carried the long staff as their professional appurtenance. That is no doubt because they were for the most part not creative oral poets but mere reciters; they did not need the *kitharis* to provide emphasis and to conceal hesitations or to give them time to think, what they needed was something to give visible and dramatic force to *performances*—as they now were—before a large audience, performances which tended more and more to be decked out with rhetorical and emotional tricks. The staff was a simple but useful aid to this end (see further pp. 314f.).

The third great difference between the *aoidoi* and present-day *guslari* is, to put it crudely; that the former were primarily creative oral poets while the latter are primarily if not exclusively non-creative and reproductive. This is a criticism I have advanced elsewhere, and one which has not yet been fully tested against all the Serbo-Croat material, of which only a small part has been published.[1] It is certainly applicable, however, to the *guslari* from the region of Novi Pazar who are the subject of the first volume of Parry–Lord, *Serbocroatian Heroic Songs*. Apparently it has not been generally considered by Homeric scholars, and has been ignored or thought unworthy by those engaged on the comparative study of oral epic—who have never suggested that such a primary difference may exist between the ancient oral poets and those modern descendants who are commonly implied to be, on a simpler scale, their direct counterparts.

Now it is true that in one sense the distinction between 'reproductive' and 'creative' is misleading for an oral tradition. No oral singer learns a song like a schoolboy learning a passage of Virgil, and then merely reproduces it parrot-fashion: for he can only learn it with the required speed by rethinking it, to some extent at least, in his own terms and by relating it to his own formular and thematic equipment, which will differ slightly from that of his model. It is true that a song will never be reproduced in quite the same form twice over, even in a highly formulated and very strict tradition. Yet it is misleading to state that the oral singer 'has no idea of memorizing them [*sc.* his models] in a fixed form';[1] this can be refuted from the Novi Pazar singers. Some singers are much more interested in adhering closely to their model than others. Avdo Međedović, of course, was a keen elaborator. On one occasion he heard another *guslar* singing a song of several thousand lines that was 'new' to him, and although Avdo was not particularly trying to learn it he immediately afterwards gave on request a version that lengthened the first major theme, for example, from 176 lines to 558.[2] Yet he lengthened it precisely by working in analogous material from his own repertoire, material which in turn he seems to have acquired by learning from others and not by his own invention. A few words may be his own, for example occasional modernisms substituted for metrically equivalent traditional forms, and even a half-line or two. Yet this is certainly not a prominent part of his technique, nor one that on present evidence is very beneficial to it. Few of the other singers do more than shift verses and themes from one memorized song to another. In a way this is 'improvisation', yet it is still primarily 'reproductive'. It seems to me that this kind of process cannot account for the formation and growth of a complex epic tradition like the Homeric one, or even indeed the Yugoslav. There must have been periods when singers did infinitely more than Avdo in the way of creation—when it was not just a question of *elaborating* or *decorating* by the addition of themes or lines transposed from other songs, with a few necessary changes of names and detail; when it was a question rather of developing fresh themes and evolving new and more or less unparalleled episodes, requiring many new lines and newly adapted formulas for their expression. In a sense this is a qualitative, not merely a quantitative, distinction. That, then, is what I mean by a creative period, of the kind to which I am sure many of the Greek *aoidoi* belonged. It is something that can hardly be detected in the engaging but technically moribund circumstances of modern Yugoslav poetry. Thus while A. B. Lord is right in warning us against expecting to find something equivalent to a determinable literary original in the case of an oral poem, yet this kind of caution can be misapplied so as to blur certain important distinctions which can and should be made between the ideals and procedures of different oral poets. There is a continuous line between creation and reproduction in oral poetry; but merely to assert that all oral poets are both creative and reproductive, and to refuse to draw distinctions of method between poets like Homer and most of the singers whom we can study from Yugoslavia, is a dangerous over-simplification which will inevitably lead to some highly dubious conclusions about the Homeric singers.

By saying that the Novi Pazar singers are non-creative, then, I mean that the songs they sing are all songs they admit to having learned from other singers. Most of their repertoire they learned when they were quite young, and the older singers who were their source have often long been dead. It is true that they vary a song to some extent each time they sing it, even although they profess to attain great verbal accuracy and consistency. But the changes they make are not 'creative' in the true sense; they mainly consist in omitting a line, passage or short episode, or in adding one which they originally acquired in the context of a different song. These changes are examples of the *contamination* of different parts of their repertoire. Sometimes this kind of contamination may increase both the length and the merits of the song they are reproducing; in such cases a limited kind of creativity may rightly be held to apply, but not sufficient to invalidate the general proposition that these men are reproducers, not makers, of heroic narrative poems. Nor is this proposition much weakened by the extremely feeble performance put up on the apparently rare occasions when new composition is somewhat reluctantly attempted. No. 10 in *Serbocroatian Heroic Songs*, on 'The Greek war', is a composition by Salih Ugljanin based on what his comrades told him. It includes some common poetical themes and phrases, but is short and poor. 'The song of Milman Parry', by Milovan Vojičić, is almost pathetic.[1] On another occasion Salih had recited a short prose saga to Parry and was then persuaded to turn the content

93

of it into verse form; again the song was very brief and thematically inferior to the prose version, the phraseology of which
seems to be followed as closely as possible.[1] Salih appears to be
unusual in achieving even so much as that; and it is important
to recognize that all he achieves, and then under some kind of
pressure, is the indifferent and brief versification of some prose
story that is well known to him already, or is being put into his
head.

It is possible that rare singers from other regions could do
better; indeed, it is certain that Avdo Međedović could, for he
managed to expand the song of the Wedding of Smailagić
Meho into 12,000 verses at the earnest behest of Parry and his
Yugoslav assistant. That is a feat which presupposes a repertoire to draw from, and a power of combination and thematic
variation, exceeding anything known from Novi Pazar. It
remains doubtful, as I have suggested, how much real invention and creation is involved—whether the singer was able to
develop new incidents and thematic applications, even though
using the established traditional language of poetry. And yet
that kind of creativity must have existed for many generations
during the history of the Yugoslav epic tradition, just as it must
in the early Greek epic tradition—particularly, perhaps, during
the lifetimes of the main composers of the Iliad and Odyssey.
For the opportunity to assess Avdo's capacities properly we shall
have to wait for full publication of his poem, together with his
own recorded comments on it, which are sure to be of the
highest interest and importance. But in the meantime it is
absolutely certain that Avdo is untypical—Parry found no one
else like him and had to search long and hard to find a singer
even of his capacities. He may have been capable of poetical
invention up to the standard of the usual Yugoslav narrative;
most if not all of his contemporaries were not. They were the
reproductive representatives of a decaying tradition. They were
still illiterate and fully oral, and they used all the formular
devices available in their particular oral tradition—but for
memorization rather than creation in any real sense. Now it is
certain that even the greatest of the Greek *aoidoi*, even the first

singer of a colossal Iliad, whom we may call Homer, learned much from other singers. That must have been how he first built up a repertoire and learned the trade of the oral singer. To this extent the Novi Pazar *guslari* provide a parallel to his methods, though to an extent restricted by the metrical and other differences that have already been described. But he progressed far beyond this stage—as probably did many of his predecessors and contemporaries: he used his reproductive skill as a basis for a new inventive and creative skill. For this side of his activities, and it is among the most important, if not the most important, of all, the poets of modern Yugoslavia provide little direct parallel.

There is much to learn from the *guslari* (who are, alas, a dying race) that is useful for the study of Homer. But the differences which I have attempted, provisionally at times, to isolate and outline are perhaps of considerable importance, and make inferences from one oral culture to the other liable to be fallacious. Above all, the sheer difference in quality between the poet of an Iliad or Odyssey and Salih Ugljanin or even Avdo Međedović is so vast as to imply that their methods, too, may have been diverse in many important respects.

§7. *The life-cycle of an oral tradition*

It is essential, then, to distinguish at least four different stages in the life-cycle of an oral tradition; many of the confusions of modern assessments arise from a failure to do so. First comes an *originative* stage, when the idea of narrative poetry—as opposed to saga or prose narrative on the one hand, and occasional poetry like dirges and work-songs on the other—first occurs and finds expression in short, simple and technically naïve narrative songs. Not surprisingly there is no precise information about this stage for any major oral tradition, but it must have taken place in nearly every case.[1] Whether there were Serbo-Croatian heroic songs before the 14th century A.D. is not known; probably there were, and at least the originative stage in this tradition is unlikely to be much later than this period, which is so conspicuous in the content of the songs that have come down through the centuries. The possibility of an intermediary prose-saga tradition, perhaps of relatively short duration, cannot be entirely ignored. For Greece the situation is analogous: the originative stage must have come long before Homer and the 8th century B.C., because by that time the formular system had been so fully developed. It probably took place during the Mycenaean period, perhaps about the time of the Trojan war but possibly earlier. We just do not know; and again the possibility of a detailed prose tradition, for a time, complicates the issue, which will be further discussed in the next chapter.

The originative stage is the first manifestation of a long *creative* stage in which the range of narrative songs is greatly extended and the technique of memory and improvisation is refined from generation to generation. In such a period singers learn an initial repertoire from older men, but in the course of time they considerably extend this repertoire by their own inventions and improvisations. These may be applied to making radical developments of existing songs or to creating entirely new ones—always, of course, with the aid of standardized language and certain well-established heroic themes. The creative stage in Yugoslavia ended at some time in the past: probably quite recently, in the last century. Isolated original singers may always linger on for a generation or so. The main poets of the Iliad and Odyssey were clearly creative in a very high degree, and we should expect many of their contemporaries and predecessors to have been so too; but the monumental poets probably added a quite new dimension to the heroic narrative poem. In a sense this places them in a special category; but since they are atypical there is no point in distinguishing a monumental stage as a normal and significant part of all oral traditions. In any case the monumental singer—the singer who builds up, on the basis of existing songs and themes, a poem of quite exceptional scale which yet retains an overall unity—has all the positive qualities of the ordinary creative singer, presumably in the case of the singers of the Iliad and Odyssey to a very high degree; and he adds to them some special ones of his own.

The third stage is the *reproductive* one exemplified by the Novi

Pazar singers. Here the established oral techniques are still used by unlettered bards both for memorization and to facilitate the transposition, often though not always unintentional, of language or minor episodes from one acquired song to another. Yet there is little real extension of the repertoire, little or no composition of virtually fresh songs for which the singer can claim to be primarily responsible. If you ask these singers where a song comes from they answer that they learned it from someone else. Professor Lord would perhaps reply that all oral singers say this; I doubt whether Homer would have done so. Such reproductive singers must have existed for a time in Greece—particularly, one would conjecture, in the mid-7th century B.C.; but we have no direct knowledge of them. It must have been mainly through them that the Homeric poems were able to survive, not too mutilated, from the time of their composition to the time of their recording in writing—through them and through their offspring, the rhapsodes (pp. 302, 318f.), who belong to the next phase.

A fully oral reproductive stage is unlikely to last for many generations; oral poetry in these conditions soon seems unreal and old-fashioned, and begins to enter its last and *degenerate* stage. The whole process of decline is usually bound up with changing social conditions, but the spread of literacy is a specially potent factor. The reproductive poet now begins to lose control of his inherited oral techniques. Thus in Greece the 7th century B.C. saw, together with the establishment of literacy and literature, the progressive eclipse of the *aoidos* with his *kitharis* and the firm establishment of the trained reciter, the rhapsode. Like the monumental singer, the rhapsode may be a phenomenon almost unique to Greece; in fact he largely depended on the existence of large-scale poems like the Iliad and Odyssey and their lesser imitators for a living. In so far as they were oral poets at all, the rhapsodes may be classed with the most decadent and moribund of the *aoidoi* (pp. 318 f.). About these men our direct knowledge is even less; but their effects, like those of the rhapsodes, are visible in probable additions to the Homeric poems, like parts of the underworld episode of the

Odyssey and the ending of the same poem. These are weakly imitative, clumsy or fantastic in language, unobservant of the true oral conventions, eccentric in subject, and pretentious in their straining for dramatic, emotional or rhetorical effects. Some of the few extant fragments of the Epic Cycle, the poems designed to fill gaps left by Homer, show similar characteristics, which are precisely those one would expect from the literate or semi-literate successor to the oral narrative tradition. Parry and Lord tell us that the same qualities are to be observed in the recitals of city-bred prize poets in Yugoslavia. At this point the tradition is in its death agony (pl. 8b), and the only hope is full and accurate recording in writing or, more satisfactorily, on tape or records.

§8. *Oral dictated texts*

During the last ten years an old view has been regaining ground: that the Iliad and Odyssey are so long, complex and skilful that they must have been composed with some aid from writing. It is maintained that their technique is in essence an oral one, but that a written text of some kind, perhaps a much abbreviated one, must have been produced as each poem progressed. Personally I believe this to be an unnecessary hypothesis. The thematic method of composition and the richness of the system of formular phrases placed even an Iliad within the oral range of the exceptional genius that Homer surely was. Those who do not accept this seem to be motivated by nothing stronger than intuition; and the intuitions of habitual literates on this kind of question are almost valueless. In order to allow the poems to remain oral in essence, as they undeniably are, these critics have to determine some secondary and limited way in which writing can have helped the main composers. Sir Maurice Bowra suggested that Homer was a true oral poet who later learned the new art of writing, and so was able for the first time to aggregate a structure of huge dimensions.[1] Alphabetic writing was admittedly spreading through the Greek world at about the time when the Iliad was probably taking shape. Yet we have seen that in Yugoslavia, at least, the acquisition of writing invariably destroys the powers of an oral poet (so A. B. Lord, *The Singer of Tales*, pp. 131 ff.). Lord, however, shared Bowra's feeling that the Iliad and Odyssey must have been somehow helped by writing, and proposed an alternative theory: that the monumental composers, who were genuinely oral poets, and themselves illiterate, dictated their poems to a literate accomplice.[1] That this can be done without loss of quality, in some conditions at least, was shown by the experience of Parry and Lord themselves. They had certain songs written down to the singer's dictation by their Yugoslav assistant Nikola Vujnović, and the product was not inferior to versions sung at a more normal speed and recorded by phonograph—in fact usually it was slightly fuller, and, Lord thinks, superior. Of course Nikola was an unusually accomplished 'scribe' who certainly prevented many errors; even so the experiment was a revealing one. 'Oral dictated texts', then, are a practical possibility: this is also shown by the short and rather poor Cretan song dictated in 1786 by the illiterate singer Pantzelió to a literate shepherd friend.[2] More important, perhaps, certain Hurrian and Ugaritic songs of the 2nd millennium B.C. were dictated to scribes.[3] Yet there is no positive evidence whatever that dictation was used by the Homeric poets; it is of itself improbable that writing and bookmaking techniques could cope with anything on this scale at this period; and, as I think, no evidence or implication exists that such dictation was necessary for the composition of the monumental poems.

A different and more concrete argument has been adduced for oral dictated texts of the Iliad and Odyssey. It depends on the assumption that poems as complex as the Iliad and Odyssey cannot have been *transmitted* orally. Sterling Dow, for example, contended that verbatim transmission of an oral poem is unknown, and cited Bowra's judgement that 'We may therefore speak of the transmission of poems, though it is not actual poems which are transmitted but their substance and their technique'.[4] I suggest with respect that this is an exaggerated and misleading formulation, even in relation to modern oral traditions like the Russian or the Yugoslav. Indeed one can soon satisfy oneself from the Novi Pazar poets that a song can be repeated frequently, never in identical terms the whole way through but with only comparatively minor variations and with a considerable degree of verbal precision. This can apply to transmission from an older to a younger singer as well as to repetitions by the same singer. These particular poets pay lip-service to the ideal of complete accuracy in reproduction, and are under the impression that they come very close to it. They are, in fact, far too optimistic; and their very confidence and lack of self-criticism prevents them from trying to achieve a higher standard of accuracy, which certainly lies within their power. The truth remains that even within their simple and unsophisticated oral tradition, with its incomplete formular technique, poems—not merely 'substance' or 'technique'—*are* transmitted, though with some variation and contamination. In a stricter tradition like the Homeric one there is no reason why a fairly high standard of verbatim precision in transmission should not have been achieved; in fact there are serious reasons for thinking that it would be. The argument to the contrary depends first upon an extreme statement of the fluctuation of modern oral texts, and secondly on the fallacious assumption of exact parallelism between the Ionian tradition and the South Slavic.

Such evidence as exists suggests that a stable and widely accepted version of the Homeric poems was first produced in Athens during the 6th century B.C. (see pp. 306 ff.). That leaves some two hundred years, roughly five or six generations, in which on our theory they had to be transmitted, partly at least by oral means, from the probable time of their composition. Those who feel that nothing approaching verbatim transmission is possible shudder at the thought of these two centuries, and conclude that there must have been some kind of *complete* authentic text long before any possible Athenian Panathenaic version: a text, therefore, dictated by the great oral composers themselves. The weaknesses of this position have already been outlined. Yet the curious thing is that precision of transmission through these centuries should ever be envisaged as necessary or probable. The text of the Homeric poems, as it has come down

to us, suggests imperatively that at many points the transmission
through this period was *not* exact—that many post-Homeric
locutions and variants, implicating complete episodes, intruded
themselves at this time into the 'original' poetry of the monumental poets. At the root of this form of the oral-dictated-text
argument lies the sentimental and irrational feeling that our
version of Homer must be the 8th-century version itself.
Unfortunately this is unlikely to be the case. Yet while the
late-aoidic and rhapsodic stage may have polluted the text of
Homer in some respects, it may have transmitted most parts of
it with an accuracy that comparative oral scholars do not
suspect. Reproductive singers of the 7th century may have
greatly surpassed their Novi Pazar counterparts (pp. 88 ff.).
Moreover there is no clear parallel in other oral cultures to the
rhapsodic phase in the Greek epic tradition. It may very well
have been a consequence of the rhapsodic method of recitation,
directed as it was to a limited repertoire of quite unique authority, that it achieved in its time, in those less dramatic parts of
the Homeric poetry which it did not try to 'improve' or omit,
altogether higher standards of verbal accuracy than anything
to be seen in a true oral tradition. It is probable, too, that some
of the singers and reciters of these centuries used their own
special written aids, which may or may not have been conducive
to precision. I am prepared to consider, though without
enthusiasm, the written list of episodes or something like it,
even for the Homeric composers; but that is a very different
assumption from the assumption that they themselves produced,
with or without an accomplice, a more or less complete written
text as they went along.

When all is said, this important point remains: that the Iliad
and Odyssey are in essence oral poetry, the end-product of a
long tradition of songs improvised by illiterate but highly skilled
singers. In understanding this kind of tradition the Yugoslav
singers are extremely helpful, *providing their limitations are
recognized*.

PART III

❂

THE GROWTH OF THE ORAL
EPIC IN GREECE

5

THE EVIDENCE FOR
MYCENAEAN EPIC

THE Linear B tablets are exclusively devoted to economic and administrative records, and contain no indication that writing was used for literature in its wider sense. Yet we cannot therefore exclude literary activity from Achaean life. Music there certainly was, as is shown for instance by lyre-fragments found in the Mycenaean tholos-tomb at Menidi in Attica, or by the fresco in the palace at Pylos depicting a bird flying away from in front of a lyre-player.[1] It is certain that there was also song. This would include those short social songs of work, marriage and death that exist in all but the most primitive societies. There might also have been narrative songs, perhaps developed out of the social uses; for dirges and encomia tend to contain an element of biographical narrative. Now it is assumed by many Homeric scholars, especially since the resurgence of Mycenaean interest provoked by the Ventris decipherment, that there must have been Achaean—or 'Mycenaean' in its archaeological and looser sense—epic poetry, in dactylic metre, of which considerable remnants came down into Homer. This is an interesting possibility, but one which has not yet been adequately or systematically evaluated. It deserves closer examination.

The argument has been advanced that striking similarities exist in architecture, art and administration between the Achaean palaces and certain non-Greek centres of the 2nd millennium B.C. from which inscribed tablets containing poetry have been found. Mari on the Euphrates and Ugarit in Syria are conspicuous examples. Should we not therefore suppose that poetry, as well as the other things, was common to all these palace-states? Admittedly, since poetry about the gods and about certain heroic endeavours of the past was known in Ugarit, where many Achaean merchants and craftsmen lived, it is possible that the Achaeans of the mainland could have acquired the art of poetry from there if they did not already possess it. It has even been suggested, not very plausibly, that poetry was written down in the Greek palaces, but on some perishable material. These are possibilities, but no more. Certain cultural similarities do exist, but there are also a great many profound differences on which the protagonists of the international-culture argument do not dwell. Sometimes, too, they argue from similarities that have no significance because they are common to all civilized life or to human nature wherever it is found. Thus the presence in Ugarit and Alalakh of doctors, priests, goldsmiths, carpenters, cooks, herdsmen and so on is held to be an indication of the close similarity of life there with life in Mycenae; but it would also indicate a close similarity, on this argument, with life in Outer Birmingham. We are also told that the Knossos tablets may show that young female workers were trained by older ones—as though this had some unusual significance.[1]

More attractive is the suggestion that Greek epic contains themes borrowed from Near Eastern poetry. This is not so improbable as may at first seem. In 14th-century Ugarit, with its strong Mycenaean contacts, poems of several peoples— Akkadian, Sumerian and Hurrian–Hittite as well as Phoenician —were known either directly or in translation. At least two divine motifs in the *Theogony* of Hesiod must have reached Greece originally from the Levant. The Typhoeus-motif is particularly associated with Mount Casius near Ugarit; and the emasculation of Ouranos by Kronos, and the displacement in his turn of Kronos by the thunder-and-lightning god Zeus, are so close in detail to the earlier Hurrian–Hittite tale of Anu, Kumarbi and the storm-god that there must be at least a common model, certainly not a Greek one. Ugarit in the Mycenaean era is a very probable origin for the spread of such stories to Greece—more probable than the 8th-century Ionian colony of Poscideion (?), a little further north at the modern Al Mina, which would allow little time for the formular crystallization of the Hesiodic versions. If theogonical subjects could pass over to Greece from further east, so in theory could heroic themes also. Unfortunately there is no such exact similarity between Greek epic plots and oriental ones. The cases most often cited are the Gilgamesh story, which is claimed to provide many parallels with the Odyssey in particular and certainly contains a visit to the underworld; and the Ugaritic tale of Keret, whose wife left him and who subsequently besieged a city and won a princess—whether his wife or another is uncertain.[1] The underworld visit is the only motif in *Gilgamesh* that I am inclined to accept as a faintly possible model for Homer. It was a common Near Eastern theme and could have impressed travellers or settlers in Asia Minor or Syria. Another parallel with the Odyssey may be seen in the Hittite tale of King Gurpanzah, who won back his wife by shooting many princes at banquet with his magic bow.[2] One must always remember, however, that many basic folk-themes recur independently in quite separate cultures. The story of Keret is certainly not convincing as a thematic model for the Iliad. The abduction of a wife or daughter, the siege of a city, the winning of a princess—these are common motifs all over the world. Admittedly they are *combined*, both in the Iliad and in the tale of Keret— which only exists, however, in a very short, vague and fragmentary version. The possibility of influence cannot altogether be rejected; but since there was a historical siege of Troy, preceded by dynastic and inter-palace quarrels in which abductions of women were probably not unknown, then it must be admitted that the retrieval of an errant lady could have been independently described in 14th-century Ugarit, 12th-century Mycenae, or anywhere else where oral poetry flourished in Greece during the 12th, 11th or 10th centuries. Once more community of themes based on the common incidents of everyday life, like the greeting and entertainment of visitors, has no significance whatever.

Even if themes from Near Eastern poetry did reach Greece during the Mycenaean period, this would not of course prove that they were put into *poetical* form in Mycenaean Greece. They might have survived simply as stories in ordinary speech-form. There is no evidence for any formalized saga-tradition of the Norse type in Greece, but story-telling of a more casual and fluid kind must have been common in every generation and could account for the transmission and survival of stories or motifs for considerable periods of time. In fact Homer contains many descriptions of this kind of story-telling, though these descriptions are not usually recognized simply because they themselves are in verse form. Nestor's reminiscences in the Iliad, or those of Menelaus and Helen in the fourth book of the Odyssey, or more conspicuously Odysseus's narrative to the Phaeacians—these are examples of leisurely and extensive stories narrated by non-poets to a patient and receptive audience. These particular examples are concerned with the story-teller's own experiences; but Odysseus's false tales, for instance, are not, and there are many other descriptions of figures of the past—for example Tydeus, Bellerophon, Meleagros—which are elaborated far beyond the requirements of context and show an interest in story-telling for its own sake. The poet implicitly distinguishes this kind of story from those *sung* by the singers Phemius and Demodocus in the Odyssey. He does not confuse them in his own mind; on the one hand he describes an *aoidos*, or even Achilles at IX. 186 ff., singing a poem to the lyre, on the other he describes people reminiscing or telling tales in prose—though, because the Iliad and Odyssey are poems, prose here becomes poetry. It might be argued that Homer makes his characters behave artificially, much as novelists sometimes put unnaturally long speeches into the mouths of ordinary people. But this does not explain away the whole situation. Indeed there is one passage in the Odyssey where the telling of tales by a non-singer is specifically described as a means of entertainment: in book 4 of the Odyssey Helen cures the sorrows of Menelaus and of her visitors, Telemachus and Peisistratus, with a drug and says 'Now feast on, seated in the halls, and rejoice in stories (μύθοις τέρπεσθε); for I shall tell you things suitable to the occasion' (*4. 238–9*). There can be little doubt that story-telling was done much more accurately in a primarily or completely illiterate society, deeply conscious of its past, than it would be in our own culture. Without reaching the degree of schematization of Norse saga, it may yet have had considerable thematic and even verbal fixity. Such a prose tradition occasionally reveals itself even in modern Yugoslavia, existing alongside, and as occasionally ancillary to, the poetical tradition; there are at least two prose stories in *Serbocroatian Heroic Songs*, I, and these are the only versions the singer claims to know. He is persuaded to put them into verse, which he does rather badly, in a shorter form than his prose version, and following its phraseology as closely as possible.[1]

Thus information about the Mycenaean age, including the content of stories derived from Near Eastern poems, could have survived for some time in non-poetical accounts of the kind I have outlined. There can be little doubt, however, that such accounts would not exist for more than two or three generations in much detail; poetry, with its fixed lines and fixed phraseology, is transmitted much more accurately than prose, and it is in general true that the stricter and more complicated the verbal medium the greater the detail and purity with which its content is transmitted. Thus the Mycenaean or late Bronze Age material in the Homeric poems does not of itself prove that there must have been Achaean poetry to preserve it; for it might theoretically have survived for generations after the collapse of the Achaean world, to be eventually crystallized in poetry during the Submycenaean pottery phase (*c.* 1125–1050) or even during the earlier part of the succeeding Protogeometric age (*c.* 1050–880). That is the theoretical background: the practical probabilities depend on the precise character and extent of this Mycenaean information as it has come down to Homer.

First and foremost there is the Bronze Age political geography in the Achaean Catalogue in II; but beyond this almost all the Homeric poetry, including its references to earlier, pre-Trojan-war stories, is set in places which, except where they are obviously mythical, were prominent in the Mycenaean age and often lapsed into obscurity or oblivion in the disrupted and materially diminished era that followed. Similarly Martin Nilsson showed that the Greek myths originated for the most part in the Achaean era because of their close and consistent association with places like Mycenae, Pylos, Calydon, or Tiryns, which were totally unimportant after the Dorian penetration.[1] The almost complete exclusion of Dorians from the Iliad and Odyssey is another conspicuous instance of accurate archaization, of the successful avoidance of anachronism through centuries of transmission and expansion. The geographical accuracy, in particular, presupposes a well-defined and reasonably detailed tradition, whether in poetry or story, about the last centuries of the Mycenaean period. The Trojan war itself must have formed part, and possibly the most important part, of this tradition. It is of course the dominant theme in Homer; yet the actual Homeric information about the siege of Troy and its consequences is not necessarily very detailed or very extensive. The Achaeans had gathered at Aulis after the summoning of the various heroes; after a false start they reached Troy, leaving Philoctetes in Lemnos; Protesilaus was killed as he leapt ashore; the siege went on indefinitely, with occasional expeditions further afield, for nine years; then Hector was killed, then (in forward references in the Iliad or reminiscences in the Odyssey) Achilles. Troy falls to the ruse of the horse and is sacked, Priam and the rest perish, the Achaeans depart in two groups, Agamemnon is murdered when he reaches home, and so on. The basic facts are simple enough; there is a good deal of detail, but not more than could be remembered for generations by ordinary story-telling and subsequently worked up and embroidered by oral poets.

The other kind of Mycenaean information in the poems is about customs, beliefs, and—most easily distinguishable—material objects. The situation here is less informative than is generally assumed. Only a few Achaean objects or practices can be identified in the poems with any certainty. There may be more, but we cannot be sure; and ambiguous instances must be rigorously excluded from the argument. The composite bow, the handgrip-and-baldric shield—these appear sporadically in

Homer, but could be based on Bronze Age usages or on those of the much later Geometric period.[1] We are left with: the tower-like body-shield chiefly associated with Ajax, which from the evidence of archaeology became obsolete even before the Trojan war—though the Delos plaque (pl. 2 c), showing a warrior with figure-of-eight body-shield, might according to its excavators be as late as *c.* 1250 B.C.;[2] the 'silver-studded sword', which is known from both the 15th and the 7th century but which from its developed formular status in Homer must be based on the earlier period of fashion; probably the use of greaves, implied in the common formula ἐυκνήμιδες Ἀχαιοί: this should refer especially to metallic greaves, of which a few examples are known from Bronze Age graves and from no others before the hoplite period;[3] the helmet adorned with rows of boars' tusks, carefully described at x. 261 ff., which is well known from Mycenaean contexts (see e.g. the Delos plaque, pl. 2 c) but of which there is no Iron Age evidence whatever; Nestor's cup decorated with doves at xi. 632 ff., which has some similarities with a cup found by Schliemann in the fourth shaft-grave at Mycenae and cannot be adequately paralleled from later ware;[4] the silver work-basket on wheels at *4. 131* f., which is considered by J. Boardman to be inspired by Cypriot or Near Eastern wheeled trollies of the late Bronze Age rather than by early Iron Age wheeled tripods; the technique of metal inlay, described with some misunderstanding in the making of Achilles's shield in xviii and exemplified in the famous shaft-grave daggers; the almost universal assumption in the poems that bronze is the metal for swords and cutting-tools, for which iron was regularly used in the post-Achaean Iron Age (p. 182); the knowledge of the wealth of Egyptian Thebes revealed at ix. 382–4 and *4. 126–7*. To these Homeric references to the late Bronze Age should perhaps now be added the sporadic and inconsistent allusions in Homer to the θώρηξ or corslet. Some of these certainly presuppose a corslet made of bronze plates, and such a corslet has now been found in an interment at Dendra near Mycenae, together with other bronze accoutrements.[5] The house-plan envisaged in the extremely confusing descriptions of Odysseus's palace in the Odyssey is also considered by Miss D. H. F. Gray to be Mycenaean in essence;[1] yet late Bronze Age house-plans could have been reproduced, in much humbler fashion, in the early generations of the post-Achaean age. This is not splitting hairs: the case we have to examine is the case for *specifically* Mycenaean or late Bronze Age information in the Iliad and Odyssey.

Of the small number of comparatively certain or at least fairly probable Mycenaean phenomena in Homer by far the most striking are the pieces of armour—body-shield, boars'-tusk helmet, and probably bronze greaves and corslet. Unfortunately the archaeological information on this subject changes so rapidly with the excavation of new graves that a final decision is out of the question. Large parts of Miss Lorimer's account of the corslet situation, for example, are already obsolete. Yet while it is true that late Bronze Age parallels for Homeric descriptions of armour are increasing, it is also true that new finds from the very end of the Mycenaean period or from the Submycenaean period itself are making neat chronological divisions harder to apply. One of the finest of all early bronze helmets has been found by Verdelis in a *Submycenaean* grave at Tiryns (pl. 4a and p. 128). Conditions in the Dark Age did not favour rich burials, and doubtless bronze armour was normally melted down rather than placed in graves for archaeologists to discover; yet it is hard to believe that Greeks in the early Iron Age had no inkling of the metallic armour and the martial practices of their heroic ancestors, even apart from the possible survival of detailed poetical descriptions. As for armour that became obsolete even before the end of the Bronze Age, the body-shield is not so certain a case as it once seemed, and in any event its memory must have remained clear in palace frescoes and other works of art; while it is very far from improbable that an LH III silver-studded sword will one day be found. In many respects the erratic and often vague Homeric references to all these earlier objects suggest that the tradition about them was *not* precisely crystallized at many points, and therefore that the tradition was not a poetical one or at least more than fragmentary. Some continuity of tradition there obviously was, as is equally impressively demonstrated by the general Achaean colouring of the Homeric poems, by the Achaean geography and the whole background of the Trojan war. To determine more closely whether this tradition depended wholly or in part on the survival of Mycenaean poetry one must turn to a type of evidence that is more direct, more complete and less ambiguous. The only sure way of showing that the Homeric tradition had roots in heroic poetry of the Mycenaean age itself is by showing the effects of specifically 'Mycenaean' poetical language still surviving in Homer. Until the archaeological exploration of Greece is more nearly complete, and the potentialities of non-poetical traditions about a past great age have been more closely examined, it is by the study of the epic language, its names and epithets and morphology and metrical structure, that the question of late Bronze Age epic poetry can best be evaluated. Even here the results will be uncertain.

First of all the language itself. It is a mixture, an amalgam of different dialects and different periods: see further chapter 9, §2. The predominant component is Ionic, but there are many Aeolic forms and a relatively small number of words that belong to the so-called Arcado-Cypriot dialect. This was spoken in the geographically isolated regions of Arcadia and Cyprus during the classical period. Now the only time when these areas were historically connected, so as to account for their common speech, was the Mycenaean age; and there can be no doubt that Arcado-Cypriot is a survival of Greek as it was spoken in that age, at least in the southern part of Greece. One way of identifying Mycenaean words in Homer, then, is to look for forms which also survived in Arcado-Cypriot of the historical period; another is to search the more plausibly deciphered of the Linear B tablets. Yet many words that were used in Mycenaean speech evidently survived unchanged into the Greek of later dialects which developed out of Mycenaean, namely Ionic (including Attic) and Aeolic. Thus it would be foolish to argue that the word μέλι, 'honey', is a Mycenaean feature in Homer because it comes in the tablets (as me-ri)—for it is the common Greek word for 'honey', and remained so from the earliest stages of Greek to the latest. Similarly we now know that initial ππ- for π- is a Mycenaean dialect-form, not merely a later Aeolic one; but it would be wrong to maintain that words like πτόλις in Homer are direct survivals from Mycenaean, because they might still be taken from post-Mycenaean Aeolic. To take a slightly different case, the word ἄναξ, 'lord', appears on the tablets (wa-na-ka) and was also used in later Arcado-Cypriot. It is a Mycenaean word which was particularly appropriate for a supreme king, and its uses in classical Greek seem to be poetical and artificial in that they are primarily based on the frequent and familiar Homeric usage. Yet there is no absolute need for the Homeric usage to have been based on Mycenaean poetical occurrences of this word; it would undoubtedly have been preserved for generations in ordinary speech and in ritual phrases connected with the gods.[1] This kind of consideration obviously reduces the proportion of the language of Homer that could be expected to reveal signs of Bronze Age poetical origins.

What, however, if we find Mycenaean forms heavily concentrated in particular phrases? Will that not suggest that they, and the phrases in which they occur, have come from Achaean poetry? Unfortunately only one formula in all the Iliad and Odyssey has any reasonable claim, on present knowledge, to have this ancestry. That is φάσγανον ἀργυρόηλον, 'sword silver-studded', with its metrical variant ξίφος ἀργυρόηλον. Now φάσγανον and ἄργυρος are Mycenaean and occur in the tablets; ξίφος also, and perhaps ἇλος, 'stud', appear to be Mycenaean too. Of these words only φάσγανον dropped out of general use after the late Bronze Age, but it gives a distinctly Mycenaean flavour to the phrase. Moreover archaeology provides important support, for, as has been seen, the sword with silver-studded pommel has not so far been found in contexts datable between 1450 and 700.[2] It is conceivable, then, that the epithet 'silver-studded' became attached to swords as early as the great age of the Mycenaean world, surviving in this metrical phrase through the declining centuries of the Bronze Age and then through the Dark Age into the Homeric poems. Now the assured presence of even one single Mycenaean poetical phrase in Homer is sufficient to prove that there was Mycenaean poetry, probably of dactylic type and quite probably narrative in kind. It may well be that 'silver-studded sword' will eventually be judged to provide this proof. Yet the virtual absence of other identifiable phrases is almost equally significant in suggesting that direct verbal survivals from the Mycenaean to the Ionian poetical tradition were probably in any case very rare, even allowing for the consideration mentioned at the end of the preceding paragraph.[1] Another important probability is this: that certain Mycenaean words, which probably remained in common use for two or three generations after the technical end of Mycenaean civilization at the close of the 12th century, established themselves in the poetical language *after* the end of the Bronze Age simply because they provided convenient or essential metrical variants. That probably happened with the Mycenaean conjunction ἰδέ, 'and', which provides a useful metrical variant for τε and καί.[2] With another Mycenaean form, ἀμφιφορεύς, 'amphora', the case may be more complex. This long form is found on a Knossos tablet (in the plural, *a-pi-po-re-we*); the regular form in the historical period is the contracted ἀμφορεύς, and this already seems to appear on tablets from Pylos and Mycenae (*a-po-re-we*). Naturally Homer preserves the form which would fit into dactylic poetry, and takes no notice of the common but slipshod variation which would not. Yet it can be argued that since the contracted form ἀμφορεύς is already known from Pylos and Mycenae, and the full form from Knossos is at least two centuries earlier, then the ordinary speech-form at the end of the Bronze Age, and that which would have been used by Mycenaean survivors and their children in subsequent generations, would be the contracted form. Therefore Homer's knowledge of ἀμφιφορεύς might derive from poetical preservatives within the Mycenaean period itself.

There are, of course, a few other phrases which might for one reason or another be of Bronze Age origin. 'Well-greaved

THE SONGS OF HOMER

Achaeans' is one, not because of its linguistic form as such but because of its established formular status combined with the apparent absence of conspicuous greaves between the late Bronze Age and the late 8th century. Another fixed phrase of predominantly Mycenaean colouring is αἴσιμον ἦμαρ, 'apportioned day'. αἶσα, from which the adjective is derived, is by Cypriot evidence certainly Mycenaean, and was replaced in ordinary post-Mycenaean by μοῖρα. Similarly ἦμαρ (strictly ἆμαρ) is replaced by ἡμέρα and the like, and survives in poetry only because of its frequent use in Homer. Now the Ionic ἡμέρη occurs too in Homer, though less often; yet clearly the disyllabic ἦμαρ is a metrically convenient alternative which could have entered the poetical vocabulary at any time when the old Mycenaean form was still remembered. Likewise αἴσιμον is a useful metrical variant (since it begins with a vowel) to μόρσιμον, and might have been introduced for that reason. Nevertheless it is probable that this formula, too, is relatively old, and must have originated, if not within the Bronze Age itself, yet quite soon afterwards. The same applies, indeed, to certain archaic and sometimes unintelligible epithets attached in fixed formulas to Athena and Hermes: Πάλλας and ἀτρυτώνη to the former, ἀκάκητα, ἐριούνιος and διάκτορος to the latter. Some of these titles could have originated in the post-Mycenaean period in reference to localities or cults that were later forgotten; yet ἐριούνιος, at least, has Mycenaean associations, since its last element is attested for Arcadian and Cypriot. Again γλαυκῶπις, 'owl-faced', of Athena and βοῶπις, 'cow-faced', of Hera, probably look back to primitive theriomorphic cults. Images of daimons with animal shapes are common in the Mycenaean period (e.g. pl. 2a) and uncommon, though not unknown, later; but it has already been mentioned that ritual titles might survive for ages in common usage and not necessarily in poetry.

Recently it has been argued by the Dutch scholar C. J. Ruijgh that many Mycenaean words in Homer, even if they do not occur in formulas that may be considered Mycenaean, are so particularly fixed in one position in the line that they must have entered the post-Mycenaean poetical tradition with predetermined poetical associations and a particular formular function.[1] That is, they were learned from poetry of the Mycenaean age, and their old position in the metrical line determined their employment in new contexts. This is an attractive theory which deserves full investigation; but in fact the Mycenaean words in Homer seem to be little more restricted to certain positions in the hexameter line than are other and later forms of equivalent metrical value. I have already commented (pp. 67f.) that the formular tendencies of the Greek singer operated not only on phrases but also on single words, so that a word of a particular length and rhythmical character tended to be used in one special place in the verse, or possibly in one or other of two or three places. With long and metrically complex words this is not surprising; there may only be one place in the line into which they will fit. With shorter words, disyllables or trisyllables, it is very remarkable. To some extent it is caused by the natural articulations of the hexameter line and the breaks or caesuras which it demands or prefers; but even apart from this factor there is a marked tendency for words of certain shapes to gravitate to preferred positions within the verse. Thus the Mycenaean form δῶμα, house, which was replaced by οἶκος etc. in later spoken Greek, occurs predominantly before the trochaic caesura or as last word in the line; but so does κῦμα, for example, which was used in all later periods of Greek. This does not prove that the fixity of metrical word-types was *not* initiated in the Mycenaean period, but suggests rather that it was an organic feature of the Greek hexameter which began to establish itself in the early period of development *whenever that was*.

An interesting argument for the survival of Mycenaean poetical formulas has been based by Page on the Achaean Catalogue in II: for in addition to its impressively high proportion of archaeologically confirmed Mycenaean centres, many of these places are described by special and sometimes unique epithets.[2] Thus 'flowery Pyrasos' and 'many-vined Arne', for example, are distinctive and unusual, unlike the commonest place-name epithets in Homer, 'well-built', 'holy', 'lovely',

'prosperous', 'of fair women' and so on. Yet epithets even outside this Catalogue have specific content, like 'wooded', 'steep',
'mother of flocks', 'with good horses', 'with broad streets'—
the two last being common descriptions of Troy.[1] Some of
these, for towns virtually abandoned after the Bronze Age,
must have come down by tradition: men must have remembered that Troy was famous for its horses, Mycenae for its
treasure of gold. These things are not difficult to remember, and
prose tradition could account for their survival as well as
poetry. The qualities enshrined in personal epithets are likely
to have been less generally known, and Page thinks that Hector
is remembered as having a shining helmet, Achilles and Priam
as having great ashen spears, because their Mycenaean descriptions as κορυθαίολος, ἐυμμελίης and so on had survived in a
poetical tradition. Similarly it is possible that some of the
minor places with distinctive and otherwise un-Homeric
epithets in the Achaean Catalogue were too insignificant and
too completely abandoned to have been remembered in detail
except through having become crystallized in Mycenaean
poetry. Yet this conclusion is very far from certain. The
Catalogue contains a sizeable nucleus of geographical and
political information derived somehow from the Mycenaean
period, but it has also been much expanded and adapted later.
Many of the apparently distinctive epithets may have been, not
quite fictitious, but based on the general region in which the
place was known to be—for example 'windy' Enispe was in
mountainous Arcadia; others, like 'of many doves', would
apply to many or most Greek towns. Admittedly the epithets
often differ from those in the rest of the Iliad, but even those
show considerable variation and innovation. The Catalogue is
markedly different in many respects from the rest of the Iliad,
but not all these differences can be put down to its Mycenaean
substructure. It is a curious fact, for example, that 'The
Catalogue of Ships...is poor in Mycenaean names, other than
the great heroes'.[2]

Personal names in Homer are a fascinating but deceptive
subject. Those ending in -eus (Linear B e-u) are very old, and the

stems to which they are attached are sometimes difficult to explain as Greek.[1] Among the great Homeric heroes Achilleus and Odysseus have this old kind of name—and Idomeneus; usually the *-eus* names belong to heroes of the past, like Tydeus, Oineus, Peleus, Atreus, Neleus, or are attached to very minor figures. Again it could be argued that if the existence of these figures of earlier—perhaps much earlier—generations had been remembered simply in a prose tradition, their names would have been simplified or modernized; and uncelebrated names like Enueus, Otrunteus, Panopeus, would just have disappeared. There is reason to think, though, that some of this latter class are later inventions based on a recognized archaic pattern.

One last indication may be provided by the dactylic hexameter itself. As seen in Homer it is a highly developed instrument, fully and quite strictly formulated and with complex conventions. It must have taken many generations of experiment, rejection and improvement to reach this stage. Yet even formulas in Homer which must be archaic, either because they were no longer understood (like ἀμενηνὰ κάρηνα or νυκτὸς ἀμολγῷ) or because they contained obsolete syntactical constructions (like the accusative in βοὴν ἀγαθὸς Διομήδης), are metrically well-formed, and the origins of the dactylic hexameter must be placed long before the invention of these archaic locutions. Now admittedly we are dealing with a period of indefinite range—from the time of monumental composition back into the distant past—marked by no firmly fixed points. Yet the incorporation in poetry of many of the surviving details, historical or linguistic, of the Mycenaean age must presumably have happened within three or four generations of the end of that age, if not before. We have to ask ourselves, therefore, whether the Dark Age is likely to have seen the *invention* of dactylic epic poetry, as distinct from its continuation and expansion. The next chapter will show that conditions in this age were not necessarily unfavourable to the oral epic, which may indeed have undergone a great resurgence then. Yet one may well wonder whether they would have been favourable for the development of a new metre and a totally new means of expression. Unfortunately the nature of the metre itself tells us little, and its origins are shrouded in darkness. It used to be said that a dactylic measure is not well suited to Greek, which has many words containing successive long–short–long and short–short–short syllables. These can only be fitted into a long–short–short rhythm in very limited circumstances or not at all; although the Homeric tradition evidently tolerated certain licences of spelling, morphology and syntax in order to meet the difficulty (pp. 194f.). Now that it has become apparent that the contraction of adjacent short vowels is a mainly post-Mycenaean habit, we can see that the dactylic rhythm may not have been so unsuitable for Mycenaean speech as it was for the more spondaic speech of the post-Mycenaean world. The possibility remains that the metre was borrowed from some other poetical tradition. It may be noted, however, that Near Eastern poetry depended on stress rather than syllabic quantity, which seems to exclude it as a model; and that the poetry of Minoan Crete (whence the Mycenaeans learned to write), if it existed, is entirely unknown.

In summary the available evidence about the existence of Mycenaean narrative poetry is indecisive, though there are certain indications in its favour. Nothing is so far known to suggest that it was very extensive or that much of it passed verbatim into the Iron Age epic tradition which culminated in Homer. The potentialities of prose tradition in transmitting information about the Mycenaean age must not be overlooked—it usually is—and this kind of tradition is seen in action in story-telling scenes in Homer. These potentialities mean that the passage of Mycenaean *substance* into post-Mycenaean poetry does not necessarily entail a Mycenaean poetical original; though it remains true that the preservation of unimportant details presupposes crystallization in poetry quite soon after the disappearance of those details from common experience. Descendants of the last Bronze Age Achaeans would have preserved much information for two or three generations; after this length of time memories weaken and new circumstances assert themselves—unless heroic poetry comes to the rescue.

The best evidence of a developed Bronze Age poetical tradition would consist in recognizable and unambiguous Mycenaean poetical *language* surviving in Homer. There are several possible examples, but only 'silver-studded sword', descriptive as it is of an object that seems to have been obsolete since about 1400, looks at all convincing. Many of the Mycenaean words in Homer may have entered the poetical vocabulary as convenient metrical variants, and have been derived from speech-forms that continued into the Dark Age in the regions of Achaean dispersal. Other possible Mycenaean expressions may have been prose expressions in origin, like cult-titles for example, and have passed into poetry later. Yet even if the specific evidence for Mycenaean poetry is not particularly strong, it is supported by general probability. Narrative poetry is not a necessarily 'advanced' art, and it occurs in other cultures of a much lower level than the Mycenaean. It was certainly practised in some of the Near Eastern centres with which the Achaeans had trade contacts. It is not contrary to probability that the Achaeans, too, proceeded from songs of lamentation or rejoicing to narrative encomia and descriptions of heroic exploits. Furthermore it may seem improbable that the uncertain and depressed conditions of the post-Mycenaean Dark Age would have encouraged the initiation (as distinct from the proliferation) of heroic narrative song, or indeed of the elaborate dactylic measure that is already very old by the time of Homer.

About the *content* of the possible Mycenaean dactylic narrative very little can be inferred. Presumably it must have described martial exploits and adventures, like the Seven against Thebes and the voyage of the Argo; and particularly, in the period of decline, the great expedition to Troy. Odysseus's false tale in the fourteenth book of the Odyssey contains reminiscences of a piratical attack on Egypt which might very well be based on poetical memories of the land-and-sea raids of the late 13th and early 12th century B.C. (p. 42). Perhaps, too, some of the undoubtedly Achaean myths about glorious deeds against wild beasts and monsters were put into poetry. The feats of Bellerophon and Theseus, and some of those of Heracles, almost certainly go back to the Mycenaean age; so, for example, may the story in Homer of Odysseus's boar-hunt on Parnassus (*19.392*ff.). The gods, likewise, may probably have played some part in early Greek poetry. Offerings, rituals and supplications were a common part of Achaean life, to judge from the tablets and from pictures on rings and gems. It is highly likely that the idea of deities intervening personally in the affairs of mortals was a very old one, and some of the hypothetical Mycenaean songs may well have had divine characters; Hera is said at *12.72* to have protected her favourite Jason in his passage of the Clashing Rocks. The developed scenes of Olympian council in the Iliad and Odyssey probably had predecessors, but much simpler ones; incidentally there were not dissimilar scenes in Near Eastern poems like the Babylonian creation-hymn (see also p. 328). Above all, however, it is improbable that the Mycenaean narrative poems—whose very existence, it must be repeated, is still in some doubt—were extensive in subject or length. The pre-Homeric songs mentioned in Homer, as sung by Achilles before his hut or by the bards Phemius and Demodocus in the peace-time circumstances of the Odyssey, all seem to have been quite short. Three of the professional poems could be fitted into a long evening's feasting—and obviously the singing was far from continuous. The quarrel of Ajax and Achilles, the love of Ares and Aphrodite, the Wooden Horse—these are the subjects mentioned in the Odyssey. The 'Return of the Achaeans' sung by Phemius in Ithaca seems more comprehensive, but probably that is due to the vagueness of a title that properly applied to a genre rather than a particular song. The songs which generated these particular references were probably post-Mycenaean versions, and there is much that seems primarily Ionian about Demodocus in particular; but it seems unlikely that any possible Mycenaean prototypes were much longer, and probable that they were both simpler and even shorter.

The evidence of the language of Homer, so far as it can be assessed at present, suggests as has been seen that there may have been very little direct survival from Mycenaean poetry, and that even isolated Mycenaean phrases were only preserved at the most in small numbers. Sporadic Mycenaean words are a little commoner, but many of those may have entered the tradition from popular speech in the Submycenaean or early Protogeometric period and not in the Mycenaean age or through Mycenaean poetry. The cultural background depicted in the Homeric poems is not very different in implication. In most respects, as we should expect in a long-standing oral tradition, the Homeric picture is an amalgam of elements derived from different periods: some Mycenaean elements, many others derived from the three centuries following the collapse of the Mycenaean world, and a few taken from the late 9th or 8th century—the probable period of the monumental composers in Ionia. Thus some weapons are Mycenaean, others are post-Mycenaean; inhumation and cremation are sometimes conflated; the relations of the *anax* or supreme lord to the other *basilēes* or kings, and of the chief local king to other noblemen of the district as well as to subordinate free members of his household, are compendious ones reflecting some shadowy memory of Mycenaean custom but also perhaps certain developments, for example in the Ithacan situation, of the subsequent Dark Age. Clothes, cult, marriage customs and so on show a similar blend of older and newer (see e.g. p. 189).

Now some degree of contamination of the Bronze Age cultural background is what we should expect even if there had been perfect continuity with a Mycenaean poetical tradition of some considerable extent. Yet there are two Mycenaean subjects on which the Homeric poetry is heavily and extensively misleading. The first is the size and complexity of the Achaean palace and its bureaucratic administration, which have been outlined in chapter 2. There is little trace of this in the Odyssey or in the brief references to conditions in mainland Greece in the Iliad. There are slaves of both sexes, and a certain amount of specialization of function, in the palace at Ithaca, but nothing like the fantastic system of rationing and accounting, of scribes and overseers, of strictly controlled farms, storerooms, armouries and workshops, that are revealed by the

Linear B tablets. Ithaca may have been a small domain, and it may be true that there are vestiges of one or two of these characteristics; but in general it seems fair to conclude that many of the essential and distinctive qualities of life in a late Mycenaean palace had entirely passed out of the tradition.

The second discrepancy concerns chariots. The Iliad has countless descriptions of the use of chariots in war: they convey the chieftains to the battlefield from the camp, or from one part of the battle to another; to fight, the chieftains descend, but they keep their chariots near at hand so that they can retreat if wounded or outnumbered. Now not all these uses were impossible or superfluous—but they were not the *primary* purpose of chariots in other Bronze Age countries of the Near East about which evidence survives, or anywhere else: the Egyptians, the Syrians and the Hittites kept large chariot forces which made massed charges; fighting was done *from* the chariots, as at the battle of Kadesh in 1288 B.C., though there was infantry as well.[1] There are rare and exceptional signs in the Iliad that such tactics—which were admittedly more limited by the Greek terrain—were dimly remembered in some parts of the tradition (v. 19, XI. 289f., 502f.). The most interesting case is Nestor's instructions to the Pylian troops at IV. 297ff.: the chariots are to be massed in front, the infantry behind, with low-grade troops in between—'thus did the men of former time sack cities and walls' (308). Nestor is famous for his unconventional and often bizarre tactical advice, but this is explicitly a historical archaism; at least one of the poets of the developed oral tradition knew that chariots had been real fighting machines in earlier times, and not the merely convenient appurtenances of nobility that they had become by the Geometric age. The many chariots kept in the palaces at Knossos and Pylos can hardly have existed for the use described in all except these quite exceptional passages of the Iliad; in other words their true historical function in the Mycenaean age had been generally misunderstood. It had not quite disappeared from the poetical tradition, but only a faint memory survived the downfall of the Mycenaean world, a memory which was then misinterpreted by many singers. The same is the case with some extreme examples of the chariot as heroic transport; Telemachus is depicted as driving down the Peloponnese, even across the mountainous country between Pylos and Lacedaemon, by chariot, which is little short of absurd.

One important conclusion to be drawn from these two major misunderstandings is surely that *very little* Mycenaean poetry about warfare or palace life, at least, can have passed down into the post-Mycenaean epic tradition. If even no more than a few Mycenaean battle descriptions had descended verbatim, or had survived for any length of time in Dark Age poetry, this whole misconception about the use of chariots could never have been formed. Similarly the quite inaccurate Homeric picture of the Achaean noble household suggests strongly that no substantial amount of poetry on this topic, at least, survived. The argument is not worth carrying further. But it lends some support to a probability that exists on other grounds, that Mycenaean narrative poetry, if such there was, probably did not survive extensively in any literal or detailed form in the post-Mycenaean tradition. This places heavier emphasis on the poetical creativity of the Dark Age, the subject of the chapter which now follows.

6

THE POETICAL POSSIBILITIES
OF THE DARK AGE

ONE motive for seeking a late Bronze Age or Mycenaean origin for the archaic substratum of Homeric poetry has been that the early post-Mycenaean period is what is known as a Dark Age. On p. 118 of his Iliad book D. L. Page quotes judgements from Gomme, Lorimer, Beazley and Dunbabin which supplement the well-known image supplied by Gilbert Murray and recently cited by Webster.[1] There is no need to go outside the English tongue for a horrifying idea of the depths of squalor and disruption into which Greece fell at the time of the Dorian migrations. 'Disintegrated and materially degenerate', a darkness which 'far surpasses the Dark Ages which follow the fall of the Western Roman Empire', and so on—'a horror of great darkness' is a phrase that Page himself applies. No wonder this period is regarded by so many Homeric scholars as irrelevant to the creation of the Homeric poems!

I should like to suggest as a basis for discussion that such a picture may be highly misleading so far as oral poetry is concerned. Even the phrase 'Dark Age' itself contains a dangerous and little-observed ambiguity; for 'dark' implies both obscure or unknown, and gloomy or abject. The second meaning, however, is not an essential consequence of the first. There are other periods in the history of human culture about which little is known, but which there is no reason for considering as especially decadent, unhappy or devoid of song. The Greek Dark Age is certainly an obscure one, and our evidence for it is very slight. It was also without question an era which began with a serious decline of material conditions and communications consequent upon the burning and virtual abandonment of most of the main centres, leading to drastically diminished achievements in art and architecture. The Dorian invasions, so-called, are curiously inscrutable: they are guaranteed by tradition and the evidence of dialect, they coincide with the depopulation of most Mycenaean towns and palaces, but they introduce no special material characteristic beyond, possibly, the straight pin. The old idea that cremation and geometric pottery decoration are Dorian innovations is false; here is a people whose only characteristics, apart from a new accent, seem to be the power to move and to destroy. This is what archaeology at first suggests, and it is, of course, a completely inadequate picture. It is easy to be blinded by archaeological science into accepting the material remains with which it deals as a necessarily valid criterion of human activity. It may therefore be useful to summarize the evidence for the 11th and early 10th centuries B.C., with which I am primarily concerned, with deliberate emphasis on those factors which suggest that, in spite of the undoubtedly disastrous quality of the Achaean collapse, communal life sufficient to have supported oral poetry went on without serious interruption in many places of previous Mycenaean influence.[1]

By the end of the Trojan venture the Achaean world was in decline, and it was thus that the Dorian tribes, aided by internal disputes, were able to finish it off in the two main thrusts that led to the destruction of Pylos around 1200 and of Mycenae around 1125. The possible weakness of the palace-states after the exhausting and ultimately fruitless war against Troy needs special emphasis, since if that is the case then the Dorians need not have been quite the numerous and well-drilled external enemy that we have sometimes been prone to imagine.[2] And if so, then in some parts of Greece the survivors of the Mycenaean culture would have been allowed to live on more or less undisturbed, though in terribly reduced circumstances, by the Dorian intruders.

Archaeology and tradition confirm that this happened at Amyklai, in the valley of the Eurotas close to Sparta. The peculiar Protogeometric sherds found in the foundations of the temple of Apollo there probably suggest continuity of cult from Mycenaean times onwards, and, according to Strabo (VIII, 364), Ephorus gave the following account: that the Heraclid invaders of Laconia left Amyklai to the man who had betrayed Laconia to them, and who had persuaded its previous ruler to go with the (other) Achaeans to Ionia. There is some vagueness and confusion here, but it looks as though a local tradition survived according to which the population of Amyklai remained relatively undisturbed by the Dorians. Submycenaean pottery made between *c.* 1125 and *c.* 1050 has also been found in small quantities at Asine, Tiryns and probably Mycenae itself, showing that small village settlements continued on or near the ruined citadels; though Asine may have gone more or less unscathed. At Tiryns, indeed, a tomb was excavated by N. M. Verdelis in 1957 which was found to contain a good Submycenaean stirrup-jar (pl. 4b), a bronze spear-head and shield-boss and an iron dagger, and the remains of a fine and unusual, if impractical, bronze helmet (pl. 4a).[1] Even if this helmet was a late Mycenaean survival, it and the other objects in this grave suggest conditions around Tiryns quite different from those that we have usually been asked to imagine in the Submycenaean era. At Corinth and in its neighbourhood sherds have been found that suggest some kind of settled occupation in the transitional period from Submycenaean to Protogeometric, that is, not later than around 1050. At Traghanes, not far from Messenian Pylos, a Mycenaean tholos-tomb continued to be reused for burials throughout the 12th and 11th centuries, showing that even after Pylos was abandoned a group of Achaeans went on living in the area; they had not all been murdered or driven out. This is all in the Peloponnese and in the plains, where one might have expected total disruption. Many other Achaeans must have retreated to the not so very remote uplands of Arcadia, where their dialect survived; others again resorted to the foothills, not the heights, of Mount Panachaikon in Achaea, where they continued to make a local late Mycenaean pottery of which numerous examples have been found in tombs scattered over the whole area.[1] About 1050 or 1000 this last region seems to have become largely depopulated —at least there is no sign of Protogeometric pottery; though one cannot dismiss the possibility that a change in burial custom and in the durability of graves meant that casual archaeological search has not yet brought grave-goods of this era to light. It is highly significant that there is no other sign *apart* from graves of this influx into Achaea during the period of disturbance from before 1200 onwards. These were people who made their own pottery and went so far as to produce one distinctive local vase-shape. By this evidence they were by no means disorganized or utterly uncultured, yet they left no other trace of their existence. How many small Achaean communities were there, even in the Peloponnese and apart from those that we infer for Arcadia, whose grave-objects have *not* survived or been discovered, either through the nature of the terrain or because they used earth-cut graves or because of different local burial customs or because there was no convenient tholos-tomb to reuse?

North of the isthmus there is good evidence for continued occupation on a small scale at Thebes, where Submycenaean pottery has been found in inhumations outside the Electran gate, and probably also at Iolcus—which had developed so much by around 1000 B.C. that houses with stone foundations reappear.[2] It is possible that a sanctuary at Delphi was continuously maintained from the Bronze Age onwards, though the situation there is still obscure. The only undoubted example of post-Mycenaean *urban* survival is Athens. The Submycenaean cemetery in the Kerameikos contains many graves with relatively tolerable grave-goods, and provides sound support for the tradition that Athens held out against Dorian pressure.[3] Organized life continued there after the collapse of the other Mycenaean centres, not only in Athens itself but also in Salamis and in rural centres in Attica. Athens had not been among the most important palaces, although continued excavation round the slopes of the Acropolis has revealed more and more in the way of Mycenaean remains. Yet after 1100, at least, Athens became quite the most important town in Greece. Greek tradition knew that refugees from the Peloponnese, specifically from Pylos, had flowed into Athens during the generations of Dorian infiltration.[1] The introduction of cremation in Athens around 1050—it had already been used at Perati in.Attica in the preceding century—may have been the result of pressure of numbers and a landless element in the population; though the burning of bodies is a comparatively costly and difficult business.[2] It must be remembered, too, that the Pylian refugees seem to have established themselves pretty well, for King Codrus himself was a Pylian. Athens was undoubtedly crowded and poor in the Submycenaean period, but there is no cause for denying some small degree of culture to life there, let alone to aspects of life that cannot be assessed by material remains.[3] 'Submycenaean' never has been and never will be a term to call up images of great prosperity and beauty; yet we must be careful not to think that Submycenaean pottery necessarily indicates a crude, barbaric and utterly uncivilized way of life. The mere fact that much of the surviving pottery, and not only that major part of it that comes from Athens, was *decorated*, suggests that some of the civilized arts continued, though at a much reduced level. Not all decorated Submycenaean pottery is nasty and brutish or even utterly tasteless (some of it is not as tasteless as some Mycenaean IIIC or even IIIB examples: cf. pl. 3c with 3b), any more than all of the Protogeometric pottery that developed out of it and its predecessors is marvellously harmonious. A more positive indication may be found in the use of iron for tools and weapons. Here is a fact so obvious that it is liable to be forgotten: that it was the early Dark Age that saw the major technological revolution of skilled iron-working in Greece. At the end of the Mycenaean age iron was still a semi-precious and intractable metal, small quantities of which were occasionally wrought by Achaean workmen into soft finger-rings or the like. Within the next century and a half the Greeks of the early Dark Age were themselves producing knives, daggers and even swords of iron: a notable achievement, not to be acquired and practised in conditions of utter stagnation and chaos.[4] In short there is nothing whatever in the archaeological record of early Dark Age Greece to indicate that oral poetry could not have flourished there.

Dorian pressure, maintained over three or four generations, completed that disruption of close communications between the great Bronze Age palaces which had already begun by about 1300.[1] The smaller settlements like Zygouries, Korakou, Prosymna and even Aegina began to seem unsafe by the time that Pylos and Tiryns succumbed, and their occupants had doubtless crowded round the great surviving centres like Mycenae or were beginning like the Achaeans of Crete to move up into the hills.[2] Then came the second phase of aggression, and Mycenae itself fell. Some were killed, others must have fled to the mountain hamlets or drifted up through Achaea to the islands of Zacynthus, Cephallenia and Ithaca. Those who could crossed the isthmus to Athens and Boeotia, where the tide of migration had passed and where conditions may have regained relative stability. Others no doubt managed to reach Delos or Miletus, Trianda-Ialysos in Rhodes or Enkomi in Cyprus. Yet even in regions like Laconia which were to emerge as the chosen Dorian centres there were occasional settlements like Amyklai where for one reason or another habitation had continued; and in more remote areas which the Dorians left alone there must have been many small farms and communities in which men who had survived the 1130's or 1120's lived on, procreated children, tilled fields, milked goats, and even had friends and neighbours; and in which their children did the same.

This was the worst period to live through. When the grandchildren of the last survivors of Mycenae were grown up, if not even before, a new cultural inspiration flared up in Athens, which we relate with the careful technique and finer decoration of Protogeometric pottery. At about the same time the first post-Mycenaean colonies were established across the Aegean. Athens played a major part in the organization of the Ionian stream, but people joined it from Boeotia and many other parts of Greece—even a few Dorians![3] This was something different from the destitute trickle that had doubtless been flowing eastwards ever since the fall of Pylos, Iolcus, Gla and Tiryns. It was something that presupposed the re-establishment of communications over many parts of the Greek mainland, and the comparative security of the sea and islands. A similar story is told by the spread of Protogeometric pottery itself; for by soon after the middle of the 10th century Athenian exports are found in all quarters of the Greek world, and local styles based on the Attic had already emerged in the Argolid, Phocis and Boeotia, Corinthia and other areas. By 1050 possibly, 1000 probably, and 950 certainly, the true Dark Age in Greece had ended; what follows was dark in the sense of 'obscure' but not of 'degenerate'.

We have seen that even in the immediately post-Mycenaean period there were oases of presumed comparative stability where the Achaeans and their descendants lived on. Let us now look a little more closely at the implications of the Submycenaean archaeological record. Positively it reveals that certain sites continued to be inhabited without violent interruption, and that in them, and in some new sites, decorated pottery in the old Mycenaean shapes and one or two new ones continued to be made. Negatively it shows that writing on tablets disappeared, that there were no stone-built city-walls or palaces or public buildings, and that the more elaborate arts like ivory-carving and gem-engraving had temporarily died out. Now these things represent a very severe decline in urban culture, there is no denying it. At the same time we must not misunderstand the scope of these symptoms. Writing was bound to go if the palaces went; it was a cumbrous system, used so far as we can tell only for the elephantine administration of the palace-state economy. Stone-built palaces, palaces of any kind, became a thing of the past; even at Athens the Acropolis was turned into a sanctuary. Permanent public buildings, which would only have attracted Dorian looters and squatters, were in any case no longer needed, since men must have lived on the whole not in towns but in villages or hamlets. Their building material must have been primarily mud-brick, which normally leaves no archaeological trace but was a staple material all through Greek history. Because mud-brick leaves no trace we cannot therefore refuse to accept the existence of villages or their very possibility. In such villages men could have met together in their leisure hours, either in one of the larger houses or in summer in the open air, or conceivably in some even humbler precursor of the λέσχη or club mentioned by Hesiod. Even in the mountains men could meet and drink and sing songs, as they always have in Crete and many other places. There is no need to continue: much of this is speculative, but the important point is that the evidence suggests that community life *at this kind of level* continued after the fall of the great palaces and in many parts of Greece.

One of the bugbears of Homeric scholarship is something that Page has termed the 'remotely conceivable alternative', something that should not be allowed to consume too much of our time. We must now ask ourselves whether this term applies to the contention that heroic narrative poetry on the Trojan theme might either have begun, or rather first reached a stage at which much of its phraseology survived into Homer, in the centuries after 1100 rather than those before. Naturally I do not think it does apply. Those who believe that bits of Mycenaean poetry survive in Homer have to admit that, however dark they make out the Dark Age to be, *at least their Mycenaean poetry was transmitted through it.* For oral poetry to be transmitted, there have to be conditions settled enough for the singer of poems to earn at least a part of his living. To do this he must have an audience which can assemble in one place and has leisure to hear his songs. Thus the proponents of Mycenaean poetry must grant that community life and an interest in poetry did continue through the Dark Age. Yet the conditions which are essential for the *transmission* of oral poetry are also apt for its *creation*. One must not make the mistake to which many comparative students of the oral epic are prone, of confusing the non-creative oral transmitter with the creative poet (pp. 96f.). It is doubtful whether there would be any parallel for a non-creative phase interjecting itself in the course of a generally creative tradition; which would tell against the conjecture that the early Dark Age was entirely or mainly reproductive. A stronger argument is that reproductive stages do not seem to be induced by bad conditions and bad communications; on the contrary the present non-creative stage in the Novi Pazar region of Yugoslavia (p. 91) has developed in conditions that must be much better than any which prevailed during the Turkish occupation, in which creative oral poetry flourished. Other extraneous factors, however, can hasten the decline of an oral tradition; they are well described in Sir Maurice Bowra's *Heroic Poetry* (London, 1952), pp. 537 ff. All that can safely be said is that if there was anything like a Mycenaean epic, then Submycenaean Greece, if it could transmit it, could also create epic poetry of its own; and on this hypothesis there are reasons for considering the Dark Age as creative rather than merely reproductive.

Critics who presuppose a Mycenaean hexameter epic tend to avoid the implications of its transmission. It is indeed a difficult problem. Page, with the oral tradition as a whole in mind, accepted that 'each generation increased...the inherited stock'; but when he regarded the early post-Mycenaean period, 'the dismal night of the Dark Ages', he seemed to be appalled at what he found and inclined to discount it as a possible creative period.[1] Others, notably Professors Webster and Whitman, assume that *Athens* was the only place where the epic can have advanced between 1100 and 950; Whitman placed the Ionian migration very late, on imperfect evidence, and made the Attic stage correspondingly longer and more influential. It is important to emphasize the position of Athens, but it is also important not to exaggerate it. Thus Whitman wrote as follows: 'Oral poetry requires, as a *sine qua non* of survival, a continuous tradition of bard instructing bard in the formulaic techniques, and Athens is unique in providing the necessary conditions.'[2] There is some truth in this, but I cannot agree with its detailed expression. The transmission of oral poetry does not require anything so formal as what is implied by 'bard instructing bard in the formulaic techniques'. The easy, informal and almost accidental way in which a gifted bard may start his career is exemplified by the case of Salih Ugljanin, a good

134

singer from the Novi Pazar region, who told Parry that 'I began to sing once with the shepherds, and afterwards I kept on and sang at gatherings'.[1] Most of the Yugoslav singers seem to have started as boys; they liked the songs and gradually learned some of them, and in doing so, more or less unconsciously, they picked up the formular habits of oral poetry. It did not require a city for this to happen; the South Slavic parallel suggests very strongly that the oral tradition could have flourished in some parts of the Greek countryside and away from the urban conditions of Athens itself. Webster likewise concentrates solely on Athens; he thinks he sees two inventions which 'seem to have been made in the dark period. . . . These inventions must almost have been made in Athens'—both inventions being to do with oral poetry.[2] Both these critics are so strongly drawn to Athens in part because of the evidence for material culture, but in part because they are deeply impressed by the aesthetic and structural similarities between the Iliad and Attic Geometric pottery—similarities which seem to me to have been vastly overrated (see pp. 263–5).

It is important but sometimes difficult to recognize that a Dark Age, especially if it is the direct aftermath of a Heroic Age, is not necessarily a bad environment for the production of oral poetry. Oral poetry is not like architecture or gem-cutting or high-class vase-making, it does not need prosperity and good material surroundings. Sometimes it flourishes best when the opposite is the case. J. A. Notopoulos has put the matter as follows: 'Parallels for the survival of folklore and oral poetry in nations which have been conquered or governed by aliens, even amid circumstances of as great destruction as is shown in the Dorian Conquest, show that cultural vacuum is by no means the necessary result of conquest.'[3] He cites the case of the Digenes Akritas epic, which must have begun in the confused conditions round the frontiers of 8th-century Byzantium, though it is known to us in a sophisticated form of somewhat later date. A stronger parallel is provided by the Serbo-Croat tradition of Yugoslavia, which has gradually enlarged on the events of the battle of Kosovo in 1389 and the anti-Turk guerrilla warfare of

135

the centuries that followed, even though freedom, urban life, intercommunication and general security were excessively poor until recently. Conditions in Russia must have been similar during the transmission and development of the heroic poetry which told of the glories of Kiev in the 12th century; for the Mongol destruction of that city in 1240 is unlikely to have been less frightful than the Dorian movements. The truth seems to be that adverse conditions, after a period in which the heroic virtues of pride, courage and success have predominated, are often favourable to heroic poetry. However scarce are food and liquor, however harsh the invaders, songs can be sung if there is a bare minimum of shelter and village life; indeed they can be sung among refugee bands in the mountain retreats, as among the Greek Klephts; for songs about the heroic past keep alive some kind of pride and self-respect. Most of the noblemen may have perished, the houses may be poor and the pottery ungainly, but the singer can still repeat and improvise songs; and he may do so as well against this kind of background as in the *megaron* of a royal patron. Bowra has gone even further in a passage of his *Homer and his Forerunners* (Edinburgh, 1955), p. 28: '. . . we may surmise that the most important contribution made by this period was the formation of a belief in a heroic age. The waste and wreckage in Greece were so enormous that men must have turned back to the not-too-distant past and seen in its power and splendour something utterly alien to their own experience. . . . From this sense of departed glory and the imaginations which it bred the Dark Age gave to the Greeks the conception of a heroic past, and to their poetry some of its most special qualities.'

In spite of the pioneering work of H. M. and N. K. Chadwick and its important continuation by Bowra, not enough detailed attention has yet been given to the relationship between a heroic age and its aftermath.[1] H. M. Chadwick did wonders in identifying the idea of the heroic age, but it nevertheless seems probable that much of what he meant by such an age really belongs to the centuries that follow it. Indeed our knowledge of such ages, which are usually illiterate or largely so, tends to be derived almost entirely from subsequent oral poetry. Now court poetry is undoubtedly a common phenomenon in a heroic period; but Chadwick assumed that since there are no references to court minstrels in post-heroic Teutonic and Anglo-Saxon poetry, therefore the poetry of the age of decline in the 6/7th century A.D. must have been non-creative.[1] This I think is a doubtful inference, especially in view of the Russian and Yugoslav material. The Chadwicks were working under a grave handicap in that oral singers of other lands, and their methods, had been studied so little and in such a general way; and there can be small doubt that the full publication of the material collected by Parry and Lord will revolutionize comparative oral studies. Meanwhile court poetry is an important but not the only kind of creative oral verse.[2]

Regional and panegyric as it is, court poetry may often be the *basis* of a tradition which, developing through generations of material and political decay, both defines and inflates the memory of a great king or a great campaign. Bowra distinguishes three classes of heroic oral poetry: pastoral or primitive, aristocratic, and proletarian (for which 'popular' may be a simpler substitute). The first type cannot be traced in Greece, though it is exemplified for instance by much of the Kara-Kirghiz poetry. The Greek epic is seen in aristocratic surroundings in Ithaca and Phaeacia, while the Hesiod of *Works and Days*, at least, and the poet of the *Hymn to Apollo* who sings to the Ionians at Delos, exemplify the popular singer, whose songs are available at one time or another to all free males (at least) in the community. Many Homeric critics, however, have been obsessed with the idea that the developing Greek epic is essentially court poetry; while others have envisaged the religious festival as the occasion most likely to produce a monumental poem. One must be careful to distinguish the circumstances in which a *monumental* epic might be sung (these are discussed in chapter 13, §2) from those of its shorter and more normal predecessors. That is why I should like to stress popular poetry of aristocratic content but un-aristocratic and informal audience, village poetry in fact, as a possible and indeed probable component of the Greek heroic tradition in its earliest post-Mycenaean stage. There are many parallels from other cultures to show that this kind of poetry may not be inferior to the wholly aristocratic type either in skill or in complexity. This is why the exclusive emphasis on Athens in the Dark Age is potentially misleading. In the history of a national oral tradition the audience and the social status of the singer may easily change; there is nothing to prevent aristocratic poetry becoming first popular in the most informal sense, and then more organized as festival poetry. Until the time when the singer becomes a mere reproducer or uninventive rhapsode his methods and interests remain fairly constant, whatever his background. Thus oral poetry based on the battle of Kosovo was at first sung to upper-class audiences, but later, as conditions worsened under Turkish rule, the oral narrative became a popular amusement. In this case its subject-matter tended to become less aristocratic, and Marko Kraljević developed as a new popular hero with many proletarian characteristics. That is not a necessary consequence, however, and the conservation of aristocratic material depends on the richness and scope of that material and also on whether the post-heroic period provides a new heroic subject like guerrilla warfare. In Greece this did not happen; the popular singers of the Dark Age may well have concentrated on noble stories of the late Mycenaean past, and profoundly altered and improved their poetical form and expression.

7

DARK AGE ELEMENTS AND
AEOLIC ELEMENTS

I HAVE emphasized that any Mycenaean poetical phraseology that may survive in Homer—and I do not myself think
there is much of it—must have been *transmitted* through the
Dark Age of the 11th and 10th centuries, which would presuppose an active and potentially creative poetical tradition at
that time. I have also tried to show that conditions in those
centuries, poor as they undoubtedly were in most ways, were
not necessarily or even probably of the kind to have inhibited
oral heroic poetry. There are, indeed, several general and
a priori indications that the Dark Age played an important part
in the formulation and development of songs about the Trojan
war and certain other Mycenaean ventures. Yet this must
remain no more than a hypothesis until significant elements can
be distinguished in the Homeric poems themselves that can be
shown to have originated in the Dark Age and no other period.
Even then the situation would precisely resemble that of the
Mycenaean elements: Dark Age customs, institutions or objects
would have to be described in contemporary poetical language
before we could be sure that they emanated from Dark Age
poetry and were not put into poetical form later, after being
preserved by some non-poetical tradition. Obvious formulas
containing a high proportion of Dark Age language would
satisfy us, even if their content were archaeologically neutral—
but all this is rather unrealistic, since it must be admitted
straight away that we cannot at present identify even so much as
a single such formula; nor do we know much about 'Dark Age
language'. As if this were not enough, the isolation of 11th or
10th-century customs, objects or institutions is almost equally

difficult. Certain indications and suggestions we do have; and since the whole subject has hardly been touched, and is so important, and holds out some hope of advance in the future, I propose to consider these indications in greater detail. At the same time it must be emphasized the Iliad and Odyssey are in an important sense *Ionian* poems, made by 8th-century Ionian singers out of materials that had passed for generations through a primarily Ionian tradition (ch. 13, §§ 1 and 3). That must not be forgotten, and is of great significance. Yet our new certainty about the traditional, oral and mixed nature of the Homeric poetry makes the painstaking investigation of its pre-Ionian stages, hypothetical as some of it must at present be, of great relevance and interest for Homeric studies.

There are few if any practices or objects in Homer that can be seen to belong to the 11th or 10th century, or even the first half of the 9th, and not to the 12th or 8th: see pp. 183 ff. Cremation, which in any case is only envisaged as the normal peacetime custom in one or two passages of the Odyssey, established itself in the Athenian cemeteries in the 11th century but continued to be used in Ionia at least until the end of the 9th. Writing is unknown in the world depicted by Homer (except for vi. 168 ff., where it is treated as something mysterious) : that may be partly due to the assumptions of singers in the illiterate Dark Age, but there must have been conscious archaization, too, at a later stage of the tradition; and the late Mycenaean heroes may themselves have been illiterate and left writing largely to their professional scribes. Phoenicians are no help, for it now seems possible that Phoenician ships did not trade in Greek waters much before 900, and all the Phoenician references in the poems could certainly have originated after that date. Other post-Mycenaean innovations, like the use of throwing-spears, could have entered the tradition at almost any time between the 11th century and the 8th. Admittedly, if they are associated with apparently established formulas, then the chance of 8th-century origin is much lower; but such things cannot be tied down to the Dark Age proper, as opposed, for example, to the 9th century. Social and military organization looks at first sight more promising. There is undoubtedly a multitude of post-Mycenaean detail in the poems, some of it derived perhaps from the experience of founding new colonies—as has been plausibly suggested for certain details of Scherie in the Odyssey—and some probably based on developments of the 10th or 9th century, notably Nestor's advice to Agamemnon at II. 362f. to divide his troops into tribes and phratries.[1] Yet no one can yet prove that this advice did not reflect conditions of the 8th century rather than its predecessors. The sad fact is that no institution can be firmly assigned to the period in which we are interested, since we neither know precisely what its institutions were, nor can those of the immediately preceding and following periods be reconstructed with enough certainty to permit interpolation. Late Mycenaean organization, for example, was monarchical in some sense, and that of 9th-century Athens, Miletus or Lesbos predominantly aristocratic; but there were certain aristocratic aspects of the Mycenaean system and some monarchical survivals in the others—so that no peculiar mixture of the two, such as we might detect in Homer, can be necessarily assigned to the intervening centuries of the Dark Age. A similar difficulty prevents the assignment to a particular century in the intermediate tradition of the confused view of the use of chariots discussed on pp. 124f.

Should an exception be made for certain features of the situation in Ithaca? The case here is complicated by two factors: first, Mycenaean Ithaca was an outlying and provincial settlement, which may well have differed in government from the great palaces like Pylos; and secondly, the dynastic position as described in the Odyssey may have been affected by the abnormal circumstance that the established king had simply disappeared for ten years, nobody knowing whether he was dead or alive. The most striking quality of the situation is the role of Penelope: it is accepted by the other 'kings', the noble heads of household who in normal times act as the chief king's advisers in matters of state and communal interest, that, assuming Odysseus is dead, then whoever marries Penelope shall gain the paramount kingship. Laertes is old and discarded;

there is never any question of his regaining power or exerting any influence whatever. Telemachus is too young to establish any claim without special support; in a way, though, he influences the situation as male head of the household, since he can apparently insist that his mother return to her parents for re-marriage. There are many imponderables, but certain quasi-matriarchal aspects of Penelope's position are undeniable. Is it as the recipient of Odysseus's outstanding wealth that her future husband would be accepted as supreme king? There are hints of exceptional influence wielded by queen Arete in Scherie that could not be explained in quite this way. The fact remains that Penelope's position is very hard to reconcile either with what may be conjectured about the Mycenaean kingship or with the conditions governing aristocratic status in the 9th century and later. In this case, then, it seems possible that dynastic customs of the Dark Age have been imposed by singers of that period, *or their immediate successors*, on an earlier conception of Mycenaean kingship; but the part that could have been played by sheer confusion in the tradition should not be forgotten.[1]

The linguistic situation is just about equally ambiguous. Certain elements in the language of Homer can be shown to have developed after the end of the Bronze Age, and probably in the 11th and 10th centuries; yet these were elements that remained in later speech, and need not have entered the traditional poetical language in the centuries of their first development. What is required is transitional speech-forms that survive in Homer and yet had passed out of common use by the 9th century. Most forms of *contraction* fail to meet this requirement. Contraction is a largely post-Mycenaean phenomenon, which was primarily developed during the Ionic and Aeolic colonization from around 1000 onwards (see p. 197). Yet later Ionic and Aeolic speech retained many uncontracted adjacent short vowels, and not merely under the influence of the Homeric poems; so that we cannot conclude that the multitudinous Homeric instances of non-contraction were earlier than the 9th century in origin—in any case they might in theory be

Mycenaean. Similarly the dropping of the *w*-sound represented by the letter digamma (*F*), which evidently gathered momentum along with contraction, is an ambiguous criterion. Digamma was still used in Aeolic-speaking areas even after the composition of the Homeric poems, and the practice of Homeric singers of ignoring it on one occasion and observing it on another could have been formed at almost any time after the end of the Mycenaean period and before the 8th century—for again the crystallization of this linguistic tendency in established formulas suggests that it originated some time before the era of the monumental poems themselves. Once again, however, it must be emphasized that the epic language is a mixed and artificial one in which usages may be acquired from a particular place or period and reapplied in different linguistic surroundings, at another time, and elsewhere.

For one particular contraction an origin in the Dark Age has been claimed as highly probable: that is the form of the genitive singular in -*oo* that must be restored to a very small number of Homeric lines in order to give a correct rhythm, even though our texts present -*ov*.[1] It is tempting to interpret this uncontracted *o*-stem termination as an intermediate stage between Mycenaean -*o-jo*, retained in Homer as -*oio*, and the contracted -*ov* form also common in Homer and regular in later Ionic. The intervocalic sound represented by *j* in -*o-jo* might seem to have given rise to two variant treatments: either being simply ignored, so as to produce -*oo*, or being regarded as a semi-vowel and producing -*oio*. Yet we know so little about the development of all these terminations; -*oo* *could* be a Mycenaean ending, even perhaps a poetical variant, and -*o-jo* could represent, for example, -*osjo*, which might easily have a by-form -*oso* which gave rise to the later -*oo*, conceivably in a different regional speech like North Mycenaean. We may agree, however, that -*oo* in its ordinary uses is unlikely to have been post-Dark-Age: once the tendency to contraction had established itself in common speech it is extremely unlikely that the -*oo* variant would ever have asserted itself in the face of the more dominant -*oio*. Thus the most that can be prudently inferred is that the -*oo* ending arose either in the late Mycenaean period or in the post-Mycenaean Dark Age, but that it is pre-contraction. This places it fairly well before the end of the 10th century: for the fact that Attic and East Ionic treated εο, for example, differently, suggests not only that contraction was still developing after the Ionian migration but also that it was at least beginning at the time of that migration, and so around 1000 (cf. pp. 46f.,196ff.). Thus the Iliadic line II. 518, υἱέες Ἰφίτου μεγαθύμου Ναυβολίδαο, in which Ἰφίτου is metrically impossible and Ἰφίτοο must be restored (the restoration of μεγαθύμοο being possible but not essential), should possess a *terminus ante quem* of around 900. This line is almost unique in containing as well another linguistic form to which a *terminus post quem* can be assigned: for the Ναυβολίδαο type of patronymic is conspicuously absent from the Mycenaean tablets, which exclusively use the adjectival type (likewise seen in Homer) like Τελαμώνιος. Now the peoples of the new Ionian colonies had called themselves Neleidai, Basileidai, and so on, with this apparently new special patronymic form—and presumably may have done so from within a generation or so of their founding fathers. If both these *termini* are valid, and if this Iliadic verse was composed as a whole, and more or less as it stands, then it is of Dark Age composition. Now all this is quite probable; but the harsh argument remains that the -oo form *could* have been absorbed by singers as a useful metrical variant at some time when it had passed out of general use in ordinary speech, yet was still remembered from the past. The patronymic, too, remained in common use and could have been gathered into the poetical vocabulary, *separately*, at any time whatever after the Mycenaean period. T. B. L. Webster has also suggested that the formula Ἰλίοο προπάροιθε(ν) which begins three Iliadic verses (xv. 66, XXI. 104, XXII. 6) is 'a tiny piece of evidence that the Trojan war was a subject of poetry at this time' (in the Dark Age).[1] Certainly the pronunciation Ἰλίου, which is needed to preserve the metre with the received text, is almost unthinkable even by the elastic rules of the Homeric singers, and Ἰλίοο is a highly probable cure. Again, though, one must remember that linguistic archaisms were sometimes used when they were metrically convenient; and even if the -oo genitive was accepted into poetry in the Dark Age and not before, it does not follow that this particular example—or any other surviving one— must have been composed quite so early.

One particular type of *Aeolism* in Homer might appear to give an indication of its date and place of introduction into the poetical language. The researches of Porzig, Lejeune, Risch and others have shown that Aeolic is probably a development of North Mycenaean speech, just as Ionic is primarily a development of South Mycenaean.[1] Moreover the earlier and purer form of Aeolic is now seen, not surprisingly, to be that of East Thessaly (that is, the part of Thessaly least affected by later West Greek migrations), and not, as used to be thought, the speech of Lesbos and the other secondary Aeolic settlements across the Aegean. If, therefore, we could discover among the Aeolisms used by Homer forms which belonged to East Thessalian Aeolic but not to Lesbian Aeolic, then we might expect to be dealing with forms that entered the language of poetry *on the mainland*, before the establishment of the epic tradition overseas in Aeolis and Ionia. There are certain serious drawbacks to this expectation; but first let us discover which forms appear to meet the conditions. So far as I can see they are two, of which the first is much the more frequent: (1) the use of -μεν as infinitive termination, even for thematic forms. This is confined to East Thessalian and Boeotian, the latter containing elements of Aeolic and West Greek. Lesbian sometimes has -μεναι, never -μεν, Ionic has -ειν or -ναι. The Homeric singer could choose between εἰπεῖν and εἰπέμεν, or ἔμ(μ)εν, ἔμ(μ)εναι and εἶναι —very conveniently for an oral composer. (2) East Thessalian ποτί appears in Homer as well as the Ionic and Lesbian form πρός, again a great metrical convenience.[2]

Now the observation that ποτί and infinitives in -μεν are primarily mainland Aeolic, or at any rate derive from the mainland, seems an important one. Yet two qualifications must be introduced which severely limit the value of these forms as a possible criterion of date. First, our knowledge of the language

spoken in the Aeolic settlements of Asia Minor is largely based
on the Lesbian dialect of Sappho and Alcaeus in the 6th century
B.C., and certainly on no evidence earlier than the 7th century.
But since the differences between Lesbian and East Thessalian
are mainly due to Ionic influence on the former from the region
immediately to the south, it can be appreciated at once (what is
widely disregarded by writers on these dialect differences) that
'Lesbian' *as we know it* might have taken several generations to
develop its particular character. In other words the dialect of
the early Aeolic foundations in Aeolis might have remained
pure Aeolic, more or less indistinguishable from that preserved
in the later speech of East Thessaly, for some considerable time
after *c.* 1000; and ποτί and -μεν might have entered the speech
of the singers only then, and not on the mainland but in Aeolis.
The second qualification is this: it has been generally assumed
that these two forms, where they occur in Homer, are assured
Aeolisms. The fact is, though, that neither of them is peculiar to
mainland Aeolic as represented by East Thessalian; for they
occur too in the majority of west mainland dialects, of which the
principal divisions are Doric and North-west Greek. (-μεν is
only used for *a*thematic verbs in those dialects, which may or may
not be significant here.) Now these forms certainly did not enter
the epic language from Doric or North-west Greek. Yet these
dialects have several points of contact with Aeolic, for an
obvious reason: that both groups are related to earlier North
Mycenaean, either by descent (Aeolic) or as a result of geographical contiguity (West Greek). It is conceivable, then, that
ποτί and -μεν infinitives came into the language of the epic
neither from post-Mycenaean Thessaly, *nor* from Aeolis in the
years before its dialect was affected by Ionian proximity, but
from North Mycenaean itself in the late Bronze Age—for
South Mycenaean, at least, had adopted *po-si* well before the
end of the 2nd millennium.[1] This further weakens the value of
these forms as a criterion of date of composition, except within
limits wider than those of the Dark Age.

Another survival from the period before about 900 is seen in
the nominative plural of the demonstrative pronoun, for which

τοί, ταί are occasionally found in Homer as well as the commoner and later aspirated forms οἱ, αἱ. It is a great problem when and whence the τ-forms entered the epic language: the obvious possibilities are once more either that they are mainland Aeolic (and therefore Dark Age in date) or that they are Mycenaean. Yet Aeolic has οἱ, αἱ in the historical period, and there is no sign whatever of the τ. Indeed in the historical dialects τοί, ταί survive only in West Greek; but it is perfectly clear that this was the original form, from which οἱ, αἱ developed by analogy with the singular ὁ, ἁ. Now there is no direct evidence for this demonstrative, in either form, in Mycenaean; but since the Doric speech of Crete and Cyrene was exceptional in using οἱ, αἱ, in spite of Doric being West Greek, it looks as though this may have been borrowed by the Dorian immigrants from the existing South Mycenaean dialect. This leaves North Mycenaean, or a very early stage of Aeolic, as the most probable source of τοί, ταί in Homer; but much uncertainty remains.[1]

Another possible indicator may be seen in the Aeolic termination of the perfect participle, in -ων, -οντος. The only certain Homeric example is κεκλήγοντες, but it is possible that artificial forms like βεβαῶτα presuppose knowledge of this termination;[2] if so, then perfects in -ων, -οντος are probably not very recent introductions into the epic language. Otherwise, of course, they could be borrowed from later Asia Minor Aeolic, since these perfects are common to both the eastern and the mainland varieties of the dialect. At least, however, a *terminus post quem* can be applied: for e.g. -οντος is seen to be a parallel expedient to Ionic -ότος for dealing with the problem of replacing the Mycenaean termination -ϝōος once contraction gathered momentum after the end of the Bronze Age.

The linguistic evidence for Dark Age poetical composition, like the evidence for objects and culture, remains inconclusive. It does provide, however, certain hints which may support the probability of composition in this period, a probability based on the nature of oral poetry, the conditions in which it thrives, the comparative antiquity of much of the formular language of

Homer, and the preservation of words and detailed information derived ultimately from the Mycenaean age.

A wider and more important problem arises from the linguistic amalgam of the Homeric poems: the problem of how, when and where Aeolic forms entered the dialect mixture. The language of Homer is predominantly Ionic, and the poems are undoubtedly the product of a local Ionian tradition lasting at the very least for three or four generations. But there is also a noticeable minority of Aeolic forms in the poems, forms which simply were not used in the regions of Ionian speech and must have entered the epic language as a result of some kind of influence from Aeolis or the Aeolic area of the mainland. Most of these, but not all of them, provide metrical variants and exist alongside Ionic equivalents; they have obviously been retained, like certain Mycenaean forms, because of their usefulness. Yet the preservation of Aeolisms like πεμπώβολα and φῆρες, which have usable Ionic equivalents of identical metrical value (πεντώβολα, θῆρες), shows that there was some positive Aeolic influence, not merely an occasional borrowing of 'foreign' forms by Ionian singers where Ionic was inconvenient. The same might be suggested by a very small number of well-established formulas embodying Aeolic forms that cannot be replaced by an exact Ionic equivalent: for instance νύ τοι εὔαδε, ἀργεννῇσ' ὀίεσσι, possibly ζαχρηῶν, ζαφλέγεες (and so on) as first word in the verse. Yet the truth is that many forms which used to be accepted as Aeolisms have now turned up in the Linear B tablets (and others can be found in Arcadian or Cypriot), and can be recognized as forms common to both North and South Mycenaean which underwent alteration in the descendant of the latter (Ionic) and not of the former (Aeolic). These include ππ- for π-, prefixes in ἐρι- (Ionic ἀρι-), genitives in -αο, -άων (Ionic -εω, -ήων, -έων), -μι inflection of contracted verbs, patronymic adjectives like Τελαμώνιος, κε as conditional particle. Thus whenever these common forms are preserved in Homer they could be either real Aeolisms, derived from the speech of the post-Mycenaean Aeolic-speaking areas, or Mycenaean survivals—and not even necessarily *North* Mycenaean ones.

There is usually no means of telling whether such a word is an Aeolic import or a Mycenaean survival. (Of course there are many Arcado-Cypriot forms in the poems which are not reproduced in Aeolic or the other dialects, and these *are* assured Mycenaean survivals—which may still have entered the poetical language some little time after the end of the Bronze Age, pp. 113f.) Some of the formulas that one suspected of being Aeolic could be Mycenaean; and many which might be Mycenaean, like Τελαμώνιος Αἴας or ἐὺ κτίμενον πτολίεθρον, could equally well be derived from Aeolic poetry in the Dark Age. A few formulas, too, like ἐρίηρες ἑταῖροι, contain an ambiguous Aeolic or Mycenaean word (ἐρίηρες) in combination with a certainly post-Mycenaean form (ἑταῖροι, Myc. ἕταροι).

The following is the list of Homeric forms that can in my view be accepted as Aeolic and probably not Mycenaean—though it must always be remembered that our knowledge of the latter is extremely defective: (1) Infinitive forms in -μεν (cast Thessalian) and -μεναι (Lesbian)—though see pp. 145f. (2) Datives plural of consonant-stems in -εσσι—in Mycenaean only s-stems make -e-si. (3) Labials for dentals in πίσυρες, πεμπώβολα, φῆρες. (4) Digamma represented by υ in δεύομαι, εὔαδε, αὐερύω. (5) ἤμβροτον for Ionic ἤμαρτον, cf. ἀβροτάξομεν (probably a pseudo-Aeolic archaism) at x. 65. (6) ἴα for μία (-η), also ἰῷ. (7) -οντες as a perfect termination in κεκλήγοντες (see also p. 147). (8) ζα- for δια-, as in ζάθεος. Doubtful is (9), double liquids and nasals, for example ὀφέλλω, ἀολλής, ἄμμε: yet this is mainly a question of spelling, and these forms might be preferred as being closest to probable Mycenaean originals. There are one or two other possible cases; for example C. D. Buck remarks that 'The Homeric extension of σσ from ἐτέλεσ-σα to ἐκάλε-σσα is an Aeolic characteristic', but the Mycenaean form is not known and in any case the extension could conceivably be not a dialectal variant but an oral singer's licence.[1] Now these nine types of Aeolism are fairly well distributed between the two poems, with the exception of (6) and (7) which are Iliadic only (four times each). (4) and (8) are mainly Lesbian. A few other cases would probably be distinguishable if only we knew more about North Mycenaean; but only tablet-finds from sites like Iolcus are likely to supply that knowledge, and they not with complete certainty.

The list of assured Aeolisms in Homer is conspicuous for its brevity—it is much briefer in fact than has often been thought. Only (1), (2) and (9) make any serious impact on the mixed dialect of the epic. They, of course, are extremely important, though conceivable Mycenaean prototypes of (1) and (9) and the superficial nature of (9) limit their possible significance. The -εσσι dative, though, seems to have no such limitation: its extension beyond s-stems seems to be a genuine and exclusively Aeolic feature, and it is an essential substitute in many words for the Ionic termination -εσι, especially at the verse-end as in πολίεσσι or πόδεσσι: see also pp. 193f. Thus only a very small substratum of Aeolic forms can be identified in the language of Homer, but one or two of them seem to have become indispensable. Now some might conceivably have been acquired by singers from the ordinary spoken dialect of Thebes or Chios, for example; for the Ionic-speaking regions both of the mainland and of Asia Minor were geographically contiguous with Aeolic-speaking ones, and borrowing of one sort or another cannot have been difficult. Yet that would not account for the few cases where Aeolisms survive which have no special metrical function, especially if any of these seems to be embedded in a long-established formula. That is hard to assess, but it is highly probable that very few certain Aeolic usages will be shown to have had a non-Ionian poetical origin. Some, though, probably do carry this implication; and that leaves alive the problem of where and when this Aeolic poetry flourished.

The two most obvious possibilities are, first, that there was some kind of Aeolic epic tradition in the communities of Aeolis, corresponding with the earlier stages of the Ionian tradition that culminated in Homer; and secondly, that an Aeolic tradition maintained itself *on the mainland* in the Aeolic-speaking areas of Thessaly, Phocis, and possibly Boeotia. In the second case the crucial period would presumably be the earlier part of the Dark Age; for if truly Aeolic poetical elements were to enter the epic tradition from the mainland, that would presumably be before the migrations or at a time when mainland influence on the Asia Minor settlements was still very strong. Now the two obvious possibilities are not, of course, mutually exclusive: and the fact that nos. (4) and (8) in the list of Homeric Aeolisms on p. 149 are mainly Lesbian—the latter seemingly entirely so—suggests *some* influence from Aeolis. This, indeed, is only to be expected. It would be extraordinary if narrative oral poetry was planted, or grew up, in one region and not in the other. That there was some hostility between the two groups at first may well be suggested by the eventual Ionian domination of the originally Aeolic foundation of Smyrna; but there can have been no absolute cultural dividing line, and in any event we know from tradition that the migrants from Athens to Ionia were themselves mixed and included some elements, for example, from Boeotia. Wilamowitz believed that the dialect mixture of Homer reproduced the mixed historical dialect of Smyrna and northern Chios—quite an attractive idea, especially since Homer was to be closely associated with these places;[1] but one disproved by later inscriptions, which show that the Aeolisms used there were different from those used in Homer. No such neat solution is needed. The explanation for such interplay between Aeolic and Ionic as existed in the Asia Minor settlements is more likely to depend on general cultural contacts, and in particular on the habits of oral poets. Not all oral poets are peripatetic; in Yugoslavia, for instance, many of the *guslari* studied by Parry and Lord stayed all their lives in one small region, if not in one town or village. Others, however, notably the famous Ćor Huso of the last century, wandered much further afield. It is highly probable that some of the Ionian bards, too, whether they were popular singers or sang primarily for aristocratic audiences, moved slowly from place to place, within Ionia and also into the Aeolic settlements to the north. In this way they would be able to incorporate convenient speech-forms derived either from the ordinary dialect of the people or from songs they acquired from local Aeolic singers; and they would also tend to assimilate certain Aeolic themes and episodes.

Some of those themes and episodes would themselves have emanated from Aeolic centres on the mainland in the pre-migration period. In Scepsis and Lesbos, for instance, there was probably some continuity of habitation from the late Bronze Age onwards, but it is unlikely that such Achaean remnants were the main preservers of the Trojan-war tradition. The Homeric tradition itself, as seen in the Odyssey, was emphatic that the surviving Achaean heroes returned to their homes in Greece after the war. It was probably in the mainland region that the Trojan *geste* was crystallized in the popular memory, and probably there—if my arguments about the Dark Age are accepted—that it was first extensively developed by oral singers. From the mainland it returned to the shores of Asia Minor with the great migrations which from around 1050 onwards led to the establishment (or in a few cases the consolidation) of the Hellenic settlements of Aeolis and Ionia. We must ask ourselves, therefore, whether there are any predominantly north mainland elements in the plot of the Homeric poems; if there are, then there is some chance that they originated on the mainland itself. This possibility has, of course, long been considered, and the German scholar Cauer argued that much of the Iliad was based upon Thessalian incidents artificially transposed overseas.[1] This is an extreme view that won no favour; but it is nevertheless right to draw attention to the north mainland character of Achilles on the one hand and much of the Achaean Catalogue on the other. (A third factor, the localization of the gods on Mount Olympus, is not necessarily significant; for 'Olympus' was evidently a generic name for high mountains, and there is no certainty that it was the Thessalian Olympus that was necessarily envisaged in the earliest stages of the epic tradition.)

Achilles is formally the chief hero of the Iliad and the corner-stone of its plot, even though he is necessarily absent from much of the action. He comes from Phthia, to the south of the

Thessalian plain, and well within the later area of Aeolic speech. This alone makes his prominence in the Iliad surprising, because most of the other main Achaean heroes are firmly associated with the Peloponnese and the great South Mycenaean palaces. Two or three of them, admittedly, and notably Diomedes and Nestor, are known to have migrated south from North Mycenaean centres, but they are now established in the Peloponnese. The flavour of the Achaean forces in the Iliad, with the marked exception of Achilles, is conspicuously South Mycenaean. The question presents itself, therefore, whether the choice of the northerner Achilles as the greatest of the Achaean warriors was arbitrary, or whether it was determined by the prominence of Achilles, and probably the wrath-motif also, in the legend or poetry of the north mainland area—either at the end of the Bronze Age or the beginning of the Dark Age or both; or whether Achilles had *actually* been the greatest fighter at Troy, and was remembered as such even in the South Mycenaean legendary tradition. 'Arbitrary' is perhaps misleading: what could have happened, for example, is that an early Ionian poet decided to develop a song around the theme of the abstention of a great warrior, and to relate his song to the Trojan war; no great South Mycenaean warrior was remembered as having abstained from fighting in this way, and so the singer might have promoted a relatively unfamiliar north mainland king to the role of wrath and invincibility. Personally I do not find this kind of explanation very plausible; but even if it is rejected we are still left with a possible choice between Achilles as the hero of an Aeolic account which was later used by Ionic poets, and Achilles as an original and important element of the whole tradition of the Trojan war. Even in the former case the assumption of an Aeolic epos is not proved by the borrowing of Aeolic plot-material, which could theoretically be derived from non-poetical legend; such an assumption would have to be supported by signs of indigenous Aeolic poetical phraseology surviving in Homer—and this, as has been seen, is easy to suspect but hard to prove.

The Catalogue is an extraordinarily ambiguous piece of

evidence. It has been shown to contain an important core of genuine Mycenaean information about the detailed political geography of late Bronze Age Greece, as for example D. L. Page argues in the fourth chapter of his *History and the Homeric Iliad*. Yet it has undergone much subsequent expansion and adaptation: it was adapted from a list of ships and leaders assembling at Aulis to meet the purpose of describing a march-past of the Achaean army nine years later at Troy; and it was expanded by the addition of contingents that can never have formed a major element of the expedition and which fit badly into the geographical plan of the Catalogue as a whole. It is impossible to detect with any degree of security many of the points at which these expansions and adaptations begin and end. Achilles, like Odysseus and Agamemnon, is credited with a much smaller domain than in the rest of the Iliad, where his father Peleus is said to have exerted sovereignty as far north as Iolcus. It is probable, as Page argues, that the Catalogue preserves an earlier and more historical view of Achilles's domain, and that the growth of the poetical tradition caused an exaggeration of the position and influence of its chief heroes. That does not necessarily mean that the core of the Catalogue was a Mycenaean poem; but it does rather suggest that Achilles may have undergone precisely the same kind of change as Agamemnon and Odysseus, and therefore that he has not been imported into the tradition, from some separate Aeolic source, at some time after the end of the Bronze Age.

The Achaean Catalogue attaches surprising importance to the Boeotian contingent—numerically the largest of all—at the beginning of the list, and to many minor and often quite obscure contingents from the regions bordering Thessaly at the end (II. 494–510 and 729–59). The question is whether this presumably north mainland emphasis was supplied early in the legendary tradition, or whether it represents the influence of a much later Boeotian school of catalogue poetry which we might infer from the poetry associated with Hesiod, as well as from the added list of Boeotian and Aeolic heroines in the eleventh book

of the Odyssey (p. 237). This may be impossible to decide; but
Aeolic influence may be seen at a more important point, for the
Thessalian contingents originally led by Protesilaus and
Philoctetes are certainly not late elements in the Catalogue; in
fact the poetical description of them (II. 695–710 and 716–28)
has had to be adapted at a later stage—presumably not later
than the time of monumental composition, and perhaps earlier
—to meet the fact that Protesilaus was killed leaping ashore first
of all the Achaeans, while Philoctetes had to be left in Lemnos
because of his odious wound (p. 224). Now these two characters
are extremely important in extra-Homeric traditions of the
Trojan expedition, and the fate of Protesilaus, at least, is
recognized elsewhere in the Iliad too. It seems unlikely that the
credit for being first ashore would be given to a Thessalian, in a
primarily Ionic poem, unless there was some good reason.
Again the possibility of an actual historical memory cannot be
absolutely excluded; but again, too, the influence of Aeolic
patriotism, and perhaps of Aeolic songs about the Trojan war,
may be the primary cause.

To try to decide definitely, on the basis of such a tissue of
possibilities and counter-possibilities, whether there was Aeolic
epic poetry which somehow affected Homer is clearly unwise.
The issue must be left open; though the evidence of Aeolisms in
the Homeric language seems to me to increase the probability
of Aeolic heroic song not only in the colonial settlements of
post-migration Aeolis but also in the north mainland region in
the early part of the Dark Age. That there was a strong legendary tradition associated with the North Mycenaean palaces is
demonstrated by reminiscences and summaries in Homer.
Reference is made there not only to the voyage of the Argonauts
from Iolcus, but also to the famous wealth of Orchomenus and
perhaps Thebes, to some of Heracles's Boeotian associations,
and most notably, in Phoinix's cautionary story in IX, to a
local tale of Aetolia. General probability suggests that the
heroic tradition developed in roughly the same way among descendants of those Achaeans who lived in the great palaces
at Thebes, Calydon, Orchomenus and Iolcus, and among

the descendants of the Achaeans of the Peloponnese. The latter developed much of the poetry that culminated in the Ionian epos. It seems not unlikely, then, that Aeolic-speaking bards, too, played some part in the formulation of the Trojan-war tradition in the Dark Age, and that elements borrowed from their songs survived in the ultimately dominant Ionian versions.

PART IV

❂

PLURALITY AND UNITY
IN HOMER

8

SUBJECTS AND STYLES

THE possible outlines of Homeric prehistory have now been traced. In the present part I shall concentrate more on the great poems themselves, deliberately choosing as starting-point their own internal qualities rather than the known probabilities of an oral tradition. The results of the two approaches will be found to converge; and in part v it will be possible to consider explicitly many of the assumptions about the nature and development of the poems that have been provisionally made. In certain ways, then, this part will anticipate the results of part v; that is hard to avoid, in exploring the complicated network of possibilities and probabilities that surrounds the core of these problems.

The Iliad and Odyssey far exceed the normal and natural length of oral compositions, and each presupposes an unusual motive and a deliberate intention on the part of an individual to create a definitely monumental structure. It is now clear, chiefly through the examination of their formular language, that they are substantially constructed from traditional elements: traditional vocabulary, traditional fixed phrases, traditional themes and episodes. Yet these were worked together and expanded so as to form the two great epics, each of which displays as a whole an undeniable unity of technique, purpose and effect. We shall expect to find in such poems the evidence both of a single monumental plan and of the variability and disparity that characterize all traditional poetry. In other words, if the Iliad and Odyssey are both monumental and oral then they must contain signs both of unity and of plurality of authorship. This duality has been the innocent background of the over-protracted war between Analysts and Unitarians.

The succeeding chapters will consider first the different kinds of Homeric *diversity* and their implications for the character and method of composition. Then in chapter 12 the dramatic and formal *unity* of the poems will be evaluated and its implications discussed in their turn.

Some kinds of literary anomaly or incoherence are caused not by the use of disparate materials but by deliberate or unconscious alterations of style and method on the part of the composer. Unitarians have often had reason to point out that a single author may use different styles in different books or even in different parts of the same book. The oral poet has less capacity for variation than the writer, since he necessarily works with an inherited stock not merely of word-units but also of phrase-units. His expression and style are to some extent predetermined. Yet even so he can achieve different stylistic effects by his way of combining phrase-units, as well as by adaptations and new creations of his own. The phrases are usually quite short, two to five words, and this means that their effect on style is not overpowering; the sentences that can be built from them may differ in individuality and effect, they may be rhetorical or ironic, pathetic or factual, redundant or colourless. Within the broad limits of the heroic style there is much room for variation. Sometimes this variation will show the virtuosity of a single singer; sometimes it will suggest a difference of singers and perhaps even of periods.

Changes of style are often conditioned by changes of subject. The Iliad may be thought to be unusually homogeneous in subject: it is a war poem, its main scene restricted to the Trojan plain. Yet even the descriptions of fighting are astonishingly diversified, ranging from mere catalogues of victims to elaborate set-pieces with taunts and counter-taunts. Moreover the battle is only a part of the poem; the main motif is the wrath of Achilles, and when this too is left in the background there are many other different scenes and subjects to diversify the action: scenes among the gods on Olympus and Ida or human scenes in the Achaean camp or in Troy; major digressions like the making of the shield of Achilles in XVIII and the funeral games in XXIII; lists and catalogues of many kinds, whether of ships and warriors, of legendary parallels, of ancestors, gifts, horses, heroines, or Nereids; elaborate and frequent similes; summaries of other legends outside the Trojan tale—the attacks on Thebes and the prowess of Tydeus, Heracles, Meleagros and Bellerophon; detailed descriptions of sacrifices, tactical devices, the handling of ships or the preparation of heroic meals. Some of these components are inserted in the story with little regard for the ostensible chronological setting of the Iliad in the tenth year of the war. This may be due either to the superficial adaptation of a pre-existing poem like the Catalogue of Ships, which is in essence a list of Achaean contingents and leaders as they assembled at Aulis some nine years before; or to an uncritical addition after the main poem had already been constructed; or often to the legitimate latitude of a singer who would not hesitate, in the circumstances of oral poetry, to make Helen identify the Achaean chiefs for Priam in III, even though in realistic terms the Trojans must have learned to know their enemies after nine years.

In the Odyssey, with its more complex plot and its multiple setting in the palace and countryside of Ithaca, in the Peloponnese during Telemachus's journey, in Calypso's island or Phaeacia or occasionally on Olympus, there is less need for other kinds of diversification. Thus there are fewer similes than in the Iliad, where they had served to relieve the potential monotony of the battle-poetry; and fewer inorganic episodes, possibly added or elaborated after the main composition was completed, like the encounter of Glaucus and Diomedes in VI, the Doloneia in X, or the Games in XXIII. Not that the Odyssey is free from medium-scale digressions; for example the device could be used, in a poem describing the life of the palace, of reporting the songs of the court singer, Phemius in Ithaca or Demodocus in Phaeacia. Thus the song of the love of Ares and Aphrodite occupies a hundred lines of θ and part of the story of the Trojan Horse is given in more summary form in the same book. The visit of Telemachus to the palaces of Nestor and Menelaus, itself something of a digression, gave an opportunity for further reminiscences beyond the range of the main plot, particularly about the homecomings of heroes other than Odysseus. The encounter of Odysseus and the swineherd Eumaeus which fills book 14 is padded out—one may justly use an inelegant term for a tedious episode—by the longest of Odysseus's false tales and by the rather uninteresting story of how he once won the use of a warm cloak by guile. These occupy between a third and a half of the whole book. But the chief diversion in the Odyssey obviously consists of the stories of his adventures which Odysseus recounts to the Phaeacians in books 9 to 12. These, although put in the form of a reminiscence by Odysseus, form an important part of the action of the poem as a whole, and are set against a background remote not only from Ithaca or Troy or Pylos but from the whole world of ordinary experience. The adventures themselves are of plainly diverse origin. The visit to the underworld in *11*, for example, is in part a patchwork of different poems on this theme, and some of the other episodes show signs of abbreviation and were probably based on earlier poems describing the experiences of the Argonauts beyond the Dardanelles (pp. 234f.). Formally the recital of Odysseus's adventures is not completely irrelevant to the main plot, since they serve to connect the hero's departure from Troy, where his activities were known through the Iliad and perhaps through early versions of the *Aithiopis* and the *Fall of Ilios*, with his stay in Calypso's island at the point at which the Odyssey begins.

Some of these changes of subject-matter impose consequential changes of style. Sometimes a particular manner of presentation, within the limitations of oral poetry, is demanded by a particular kind of material. Thus a bare list, whether of proper names or of things, allows only insignificant variation. This is hardly a matter of true style—though we may for convenience talk of a 'catalogue-style'—but rather of a taste for a certain kind of subject. Such a taste may in itself carry implications of date: for example certain long and purely decorative catalogues in Homer, notably the list of Nereids at XVIII. 39–49, typify the love of codification that inspires the *Theogony* of Hesiod and is closely associated with Boeotia—which is prominent in the Catalogue of Ships in II and the Catalogue of Heroines in *11*—and probably belong to a relatively late stage of the oral epic. Normally style only comes into question when there is a choice of presentation, when content can be expressed in at least two different ways. Even here we must be careful to distinguish styles which might be adopted by almost any singer from those which are so individual that they are likely to belong to one particular singer or region. As an example of the first kind one may take what might be called the succinct narrative style as exemplified in the opening book of both the Iliad and the Odyssey. Each book has to set the scene and foreshadow the action as briefly and forcefully as possible; there are different ways in which this could be done and we might therefore look for a distinguishable style. The general approach of each book is indeed rather similar. An elegant and informative use is made of dialogue—Agamemnon and Chryses, Agamemnon and Achilles, Telemachus and Athene; between the speeches come passages of condensed narrative, devoid of imagery though not of all decoration, clear and uncomplicated in effect. This produces a stylistic impression slightly different from that of the bulk of the narrative in each poem, which tends to be more diffuse and is constructed from longer and more complex sentences. An example of this succinct narrative is I. 53 ff., the sequel of the plague sent by Apollo upon the Achaeans:

> ἐννῆμαρ μὲν ἀνὰ στρατὸν ᾤχετο κῆλα θεοῖο,
> τῇ δεκάτῃ δ' ἀγορήνδε καλέσσατο λαὸν 'Αχιλλεύς·
> τῷ γὰρ ἐπὶ φρεσὶ θῆκε θεὰ λευκώλενος "Ηρη·
> κήδετο γὰρ Δαναῶν, ὅτι ῥα θνήσκοντας ὁρᾶτο.
> οἱ δ' ἐπεὶ οὖν ἤγερθεν ὁμηγερέες τ' ἐγένοντο,
> τοῖσι δ' ἀνιστάμενος προσέφη πόδας ὠκὺς 'Αχιλλεύς....

For nine days through the army went the shafts of the god, and on the tenth to assembly Achilles called the host; for this in his mind did white-armed goddess Hera put, for she was troubled for the Danaans, because she saw them dying. When they, then, were assembled and gathered all together, to them, standing up, did swift-footed Achilles speak....

(In this and some others of the translations I have deliberately reproduced the Greek word-order fairly closely, regardless of elegance.) Yet we may well hesitate to associate this power of succinct narrative with a particular singer or period, even though it was a power which the main composer of each poem clearly possessed. The style implies complete mastery of the traditional language, and exemplifies the oral technique in one of its most impressive aspects; for however unusual the subject the sense is advanced rapidly, smoothly and without straining the predominantly formular language. This is seen in a technical passage like the building of Odysseus's raft in 5, for example 254–7:

> ἐν δ' ἱστὸν ποίει καὶ ἐπίκριον ἄρμενον αὐτῷ·
> πρὸς δ' ἄρα πηδάλιον ποιήσατο, ὄφρ' ἰθύνοι.
> φράξε δέ μιν ῥίπεσσι διαμπερὲς οἰσυΐνῃσι
> κύματος εἶλαρ ἔμεν· πολλὴν δ' ἐπεχεύατο ὕλην.

Within he made a mast and a yard-arm fitted to it; then he attached a rudder in order to steer the craft. He fenced it all along with willow-branches to be a bulwark against the wave, and heaped much brushwood over them.

From the brevity of this succinct narrative must be distinguished the more extreme compression of what may be called an abbreviated-reference style, which reveals itself in summaries of epic incidents lying outside the main plot of the Iliad or Odyssey. Here brevity is dictated by the desire of the poet to summarize, but the means of achieving it admit variation. Often these condensations and summary references seem to be based on other poems. They tend to contain stylized phrases which do not occur elsewhere, most of which are probably to be explained not so much as survivals from earlier poetry but as devices used by later singers to glide over familiar developments in a well-known story or to gloss over legendary incidents the details of which were unfamiliar or forgotten. This accounts for their characteristic vagueness. Thus in the abbreviated story of Bellerophon, which is told in the course of the inorganic episode of Glaucus and Diomedes in VI, Anticleia has just denounced Bellerophon to king Proitos (167 ff.):

> κτεῖναι μέν ῥ' ἀλέεινε, σεβάσσατο γὰρ τό γε θυμῷ,
> πέμπε δέ μιν Λυκίηνδε, πόρεν δ' ὅ γε σήματα λυγρά,

γράψας ἐν πίνακι πτυκτῷ θυμοφθόρα πολλά,
δεῖξαι δ᾽ ἠνώγειν ᾧ πενθερῷ, ὄφρ᾽ ἀπόλοιτο.
αὐτὰρ ὁ βῆ Λυκίηνδε θεῶν ὑπ᾽ ἀμύμονι πομπῇ.

Killing him [*sc.* Bellerophon] he [Proitos] avoided, for he had shame for this in his heart, but sent him to Lycia, and bestowed baneful signs, scratching on folded tablet many life-destroying things, and bade him show them to his [Proitos's] father-in-law, that he [Bellerophon] might be destroyed. But he went to Lycia under the blameless escort of the gods. . . .

The phrase σεβάσσατο γὰρ τό γε θυμῷ, 'he had shame for this in his heart', is used but once more in Homer, in another abbreviated reference in the same book (VI. 417). 'Baneful signs' and 'many life-destroying things', σήματα λυγρά and θυμοφθόρα πολλά, have a similar formular appearance but do not recur in Homer, where such a reference to writing is unique. Their unspecific quality, then, is due mainly to the arcane nature of what they describe. On the other hand the vagueness of another formular phrase in the same passage, 'under the blameless escort of the gods', θεῶν ὑπ᾽ ἀμύμονι πομπῇ, must be caused by the attempt either to summarize too much in too short a phrase or to cover a deficiency of precise information. What was this escort? We do not know, any more than we know what were the 'portents of the gods' which Bellerophon obeyed, θεῶν τεράεσσι πιθήσας, when he killed the Chimaera a few lines later (VI. 183). With this last phrase may be compared the equally vague and therefore not typically Homeric phrase ἐπισπόμενοι θεοῦ ὀμφῇ, 'complying with the voice of a god', at *3. 215* and *16. 96*; or at XVI. 120, of Oineus taking refuge at Argos, πλαγχθείς· ὣς γάρ που Ζεὺς ἤθελε καὶ θεοὶ ἄλλοι, 'wandering; for thus, I suppose, Zeus wished and the other gods'. Similarly the phrase 'through the destructive counsel of the gods', θεῶν ὀλοὰς διὰ βουλάς, is used of Oedipus in the catalogue of Boeotian heroines at *11. 276*. Many of these phrases concern the activity of gods, and many of the compressed episodes and reminiscences in which they occur are suggested by their language, and sometimes by their content, to belong to a relatively late stage of composition. The language of the phrases themselves is often closer to that of the Odyssey than that of the Iliad. Thus in 'blameless escort of the gods' the abstract noun πομπή does not recur in the Iliad, and even πομπός is extremely rare except in XXIV, which is markedly Odyssean in much of its vocabulary (pp. 320f.). But πομπή comes seven times in the Odyssey—not in this precise formula, but compare οὔτε θεῶν πομπῇ at 5. 32. On the other hand 'obeying the portents of the gods', which is equally vague and more certainly formular, since it recurs at IV. 398 in another typical abbreviated-reference passage describing Tydeus's mission to Thebes in the generation before the Trojan war, is not noticeably Odyssean. Apart from these vague compendious phrases a frequent characteristic of the style is its complication and general lack of clarity—another result of compression not ideally carried out. This is to be seen in some of the Nestor reminiscences and is well exemplified in the Bellerophon passage just quoted, where the reference of the personal pronouns is not immediately clear—this accounts for the clumsy parentheses in the translation—and where the rapid changes of subject are confusing. An extreme example of over-complication resulting from this kind of compression is to be seen in the highly condensed version of the story of Meleagros given in IX, and especially in the account of his wife's parentage (556ff.) part of which is translated on p. 169.

The use of vague or loose expressions, often in the second half of the verse, is not restricted to an abbreviated-reference style. Odd and imprecise language, often formular or tending to become so, occurs at intervals throughout both poems in contexts of many different kinds. Frequently such language belongs to what may be termed a tired or second-hand formular style: one from which the freshness of the best Homeric poetry is absent, in which there is an unusually high proportion of repeated lines and half-lines, and in which abundant traditional elements are combined in a turgid, imprecise and banal manner. At its best, and particularly when its subject-matter is not too familiar, this style can be restful and, by providing contrast, perhaps even helpful. So it is in the interlude of the highly charged opening book of the Iliad, where at lines 430–87

Odysseus sails off and returns Chryseis to her father. Here is a plethora of traditional phrases and of lines and half-lines which appear elsewhere and to greater effect; in addition there are genre passages with descriptions of ship-handling, sacrifice and feasting which must have been extremely familiar to the Homeric audience. In this case one notices no conspicuous imprecision or looseness of phraseology; at its worst, though, the tired style rejoices in phrases like ἦ θέμις ἐστί, 'which is lawful', used as little more than automatic and insignificant additions to fill out the line. Another cause of a stale or flaccid oral style is the use of pleonastic and pointlessly repetitious phrases like πολεμίζειν ἠδὲ μάχεσθαι (e.g. II. 452), δηθά τε καὶ δολιχόν (x. 52), κατὰ φρένα καὶ κατὰ θυμόν (e.g. xx. 264, 4. 813), οἶδέ τε καὶ δεδάηκε (8. 134), κέλομαι καὶ ἄνωγα (3. 317, unhappily suggested by 16. 433, ἀλλά σε παύσασθαι κέλομαι καὶ ἀνωγέμεν ἄλλους). In English these phrases mean 'to make war and to fight', 'for a long and lengthy time', 'in his mind and in his heart', 'knows and has learned', 'I order and bid' (suggested by 'but to cease I order you and to bid the others'). Such prosaic expressions are commoner in the Odyssey than the Iliad, and this is partly responsible for the flatter stylistic impression made by the later poem (see pp. 361 f.). Revealing in this respect are the statistics for the otiose use of an unqualified noun meaning 'with words' in association with verbs of speaking or asking, of the type ἔπεσσιν ἀμειβόμενος, 'answering with words': the Odyssey has about 28 instances, the considerably longer Iliad only about half that number. Nor is this simply due to the Odyssey's pre-dilection for the verb ἀμείβεσθαι (about 60 times as against 16 times in the Iliad); for the proportion of occurrences of the otiose dative is similar with other verbs of speaking. In the Odyssey, too, we more commonly come upon a whole sequence of lines each of which contains a single idea expressed in rather redundant language: 'When early-born, rosy-fingered dawn appeared, / then rose from his bed the holy might of Alcinous, / and then rose up divine-born Odysseus sacker of cities. / For them was leader the holy might of Alcinous / to the assembly-place of the Phaeacians, which was made for them near the ships' (*8. 1–5*). Here the relative clause of the last line, though far from exciting in itself, comes as a great relief. Of course the passage is better than much epic poetry and contains some fine phrases; but by the standards of Homer it may truly be said to exemplify a tired and second-hand style.

At other times the mishandling or misunderstanding of traditional formulas, or the loose formation of new ones on the analogy of old, leads to expressions which are, by any reasonable standards, almost nonsensical. Examples of this kind of expression are given on pp. 205 ff., where it is suggested that such misuses of the traditional phraseology were probably due to rhapsodic types of elaboration rather than to the fully creative *aoidoi*. This pretentious style, then, can probably be associated with a particular period. It is commonest in sections of the poems which seem to belong to the post-Homeric stages of composition, like the Doloneia (x) and parts of the Diomedeia (v) in the Iliad, or the Nekyia (*11*) and the added ending (*24*) in the Odyssey; but so thorough has been the mixture of tradition and innovation in the poems as a whole, and so liable to later rhapsodic elaboration were their most popular episodes, that these perverted expressions can occur even in passages which are otherwise well established in the tradition and relatively old. They are no rarer in the Iliad than in the Odyssey.

It would be mistaken to conclude, though, that what is stylistically obscure or highly complex is necessarily incompetent or meaningless. In contrast with the succinct narrative style, or the rounder and more periodic language of much of the Iliad, or the somewhat toneless effect of much of the Odyssey, one occasionally, and especially in the Iliad, finds a manner of expression so compact, so involuted in its component words and phrases, that it gives a superficial appearance of confusion. To further inspection—or, better, on further hearing—it reveals itself as sensitive, subtle, and sometimes pathetic. An example is xi. 242 f., where Trojan Iphidamas falls at the hands of Agamemnon and sleeps a brazen sleep,

οἰκτρός, ἀπὸ μνηστῆς ἀλόχου, ἀστοῖσιν ἀρήγων,
κουριδίης, ἧς οὔ τι χάριν ἴδε, πολλὰ δ' ἔδωκεν...,

pitiable, away from his wedded wife, helping his fellow-towns-men, his young wife, from whom he saw no recompense, but gave much for her....

This interweaving of themes and clauses is ultimately a result of the *paratactic* nature of Homeric poetry, that is, of the unsophisticated tendency to state logically subordinate ideas as separate, grammatically co-ordinate propositions.[1] When it is not carefully controlled this tendency can lead to confusion, as one may see from the chaotic sequence of events in the fighting at xvii. 605 ff., some of the weakest battle-narrative in the Iliad; or from the story of Meleagros, who at ix. 556 ff. 'lay by his wedded wife, fair Cleopatra, daughter of fair-ankled Marpessa daughter of Euenos, and of Ides, who was the strongest of men on earth at that time—and he against lord Phoebus Apollo took up his bow for the sake of the fair-ankled maid: her then in their halls did her father and lady mother call by the name Alkyone, because...'—and so on for another ten lines and two or three new themes before a major stop. Now the compression in this instance is probably produced by the condensation of a longer poem. The result is a special form of the abbreviated-reference style, which on this occasion has resorted not to vague generalization but to an excessive concentration of detail. Yet the rapid sequence of new ideas expressed in short clauses can be used more artfully, to give a deliberate effect of confused emotion. The best illustration is Achilles's reply to the envoys in ix; his confusion of mind, caused by his attempt to delve deeper into motives than was usual for heroes or could easily be expressed in the heroic language designed to describe their actions and passions,[2] is admirably reproduced in a complex and impulsive speech full of rapid transitions and passionate short sentences: 'Nor shall I at all compound counsel with him [*sc.* Agamemnon], nor indeed action; for thoroughly has he deceived me and transgressed against me; nor could he once again beguile me with words; let it be enough for him—but let him go to destruction his own way, for his senses has counsellor Zeus taken away. Hateful to me are the gifts of that man, and I esteem him in the portion of a splinter' (ix. 374–8).

Let us turn to a more tangible stylistic phenomenon. At certain dramatic and solemn moments in the Iliad the language becomes lofty and sonorous to match the event. One may fairly distinguish a *majestic* style from the less emphatic manner of the ordinary flow of narrative. A familiar example is Zeus's confirmation of his oath to Thetis at I. 528–30:

> Ἦ καὶ κυανέῃσιν ἐπ' ὀφρύσι νεῦσε Κρονίων·
> ἀμβρόσιαι δ' ἄρα χαῖται ἐπερρώσαντο ἄνακτος
> κρατὸς ἀπ' ἀθανάτοιο· μέγαν δ' ἐλέλιξεν Ὄλυμπον.

He spoke, and with his dark-blue brows the son of Kronos nodded; then did the lord's ambrosial locks stream forward from his immortal head; and he shook great Olympus.

Athene is described in a similar style as she prepares for battle at v. 745–7:

> ἐς δ' ὄχεα φλόγεα ποσὶ βήσετο, λάζετο δ' ἔγχος
> βριθὺ μέγα στιβαρόν, τῷ δάμνησι στίχας ἀνδρῶν
> ἡρώων, οἷσίν τε κοτέσσεται ὀβριμοπάτρη.

Into the flaming chariot with her feet she went, and grasped her spear, heavy, great, massive, with which she subdues the ranks of men, of heroes with whom she of the mighty father is wroth.

Here the first line contains a redundant expression, 'went with her feet', reminiscent of the mannerisms of the tired style, and a rather ineffective hyperbole in the description of the goddess's chariot as 'flaming'. The three lines are repeated in the eighth book, which like the fifth bears many signs of relatively late composition. There is an element of fantastic exaggeration in this style: Hector is inspired by Zeus in his attack on the Achaean ships, and

> ἀφλοισμὸς δὲ περὶ στόμα γίγνετο, τὼ δέ οἱ ὄσσε
> λαμπέσθην βλοσυρῇσιν ὑπ' ὀφρύσιν, ἀμφὶ δὲ πήληξ
> σμερδαλέον κροτάφοισι τινάσσετο μαρναμένοιο....

Foam around his mouth was formed, his eyes shone out from under dreadful brows, and about his temples terribly shook his helmet as he fought... (xv. 607–9).

The magnificent effect, which is on the brink of becoming absurd, is achieved by the use of long, sonorous words and by more than a touch of hyperbole. There is no reason for thinking

that the majestic style, if it is to be associated with one singer
or a single stage of the tradition—and this is not certain, even
if it may seem probable—is older than the monumental composer of the poem. Yet it is curiously rare, and sometimes
conspicuously absent from passages where it could have heightened the drama. Thus when Achilles approaches Hector in
book XXII his appearance is so terrible that Hector is panic-
stricken and simply takes to his heels. To motivate this panic
one might have expected an unusual and majestic description
of Achilles at this crucial moment, and indeed we are told that
he was like Enyalios the war-god, that he waved his great spear
over his right shoulder, that bronze gleamed around him like
fire or the sun. Yet these descriptive elements are too familiar to
be forceful; in sum they produce a certain effect, yet not a
particularly unusual one, and they lack the special sonority of
the majestic style. It is significant that at this high point of the
action, as at others which are essential to the basic monumental
plot, the majestic style is absent even when it might have had
something to contribute;[1] and where it appears is often in
episodes which could be elaborations. In the Odyssey the
majestic style is lacking, though fantasy and exaggeration are
to be found in the visit to the underworld or the vision of
Theoclymenus in book 20. We might have expected the revelation of Odysseus before his slaughter of the suitors to have been
recorded with something of the majestic imagery and dramatic
detail of Achilles's appearance at the trench at XVIII. 203-31.
On that occasion the Trojans thrice recoiled, and twelve of them
perished there and then. The revelation of Odysseus, however,
at an equally dramatic and structurally more important
moment, is described in these more ordinary terms:

αὐτὰρ ὁ γυμνώθη ῥακέων πολύμητις 'Οδυσσεύς,
ἆλτο δ' ἐπὶ μέγαν οὐδόν, ἔχων βιὸν ἠδὲ φαρέτρην
ἰῶν ἐμπλείην, ταχέας δ' ἐκχεύατ' ὀϊστοὺς
αὐτοῦ πρόσθε ποδῶν, μετὰ δὲ μνηστῆρσιν ἔειπεν·
Οὗτος μὲν δὴ ἄεθλος ἀάατος ἐκτετέλεσται....

But he stripped off his rags, Odysseus of many counsels, and
leapt on to the great threshold, holding bow and quiver full of

arrows, and poured out swift shafts there before his feet, and spoke to the suitors: ' *This* contest is decisively accomplished...' (*22. 1–5*).

Simple though it is, this description is not without power, and its lack of strain and artificiality accords well with the directness of traditional oral poetry.

Closely akin to the majestic style, and similarly absent in its extreme form from the Odyssey, even though it uses a vocabulary more Odyssean than Iliadic, is a decorated lyrical style which makes its appearance especially in descriptions of gods. Indeed this style is almost restricted to the single long episode of the Beguilement of Zeus by Hera, which, with its prelude and immediate consequences, occupies a substantial part of books XIII to XV. Thus when Poseidon descended from the peaks of Samothrace 'trembled the tall hills and forest under the immortal feet of Poseidon as he went' (XIII. 18f.); then at the fourth step he reached Aigai, where in his divine home in the depths of the sea he made ready his chariot and horses with golden mane, and then drove over the waves:

> ἄταλλε δὲ κήτε' ὑπ' αὐτοῦ
> πάντοθεν ἐκ κευθμῶν, οὐδ' ἠγνοίησεν ἄνακτα·
> γηθοσύνῃ δὲ θάλασσα διίστατο....

sea-beasts gambolled beneath him, coming from their lairs from all directions, nor did they fail to recognize their lord; and with rejoicing the sea stood asunder... (*27–9*).

This lyrical fantasy is paralleled by the account of the love-making of Zeus and Hera at XIV. 347–51:

> τοῖσι δ' ὑπὸ χθὼν δῖα φύεν νεοθηλέα ποίην,
> λωτόν θ' ἑρσήεντα ἰδὲ κρόκον ἠδ' ὑάκινθον
> πυκνὸν καὶ μαλακόν, ὃς ἀπὸ χθονὸς ὑψόσ' ἔεργε.
> τῷ ἔνι λεξάσθην, ἐπὶ δὲ νεφέλην ἕσσαντο
> καλὴν χρυσείην· στιλπναὶ δ' ἀπέπιπτον ἔερσαι.

For them, beneath, the divine earth brought forth new-burgeoning grass, and dewy clover and crocus and hyacinth thick and tender which kept them from the ground. In this did they lay themselves down, and clad themselves over with cloud fair and golden, and sparkling dew-drops descended.

This is fine poetry, more reminiscent of Sappho or *Midsummer Night's Dream* than of the heroic epic, and probably reflecting the sophisticated taste of Ionian audiences towards the end of the oral period. Its romantic style is a rarity in Homer, though there are hundreds of brief lyrical touches scattered throughout the poems—no less effective because they only extend to an epithet or a phrase but not amounting to a unified style.

It is for this last reason of brief and sporadic occurrence that one can hardly speak of a rhetorical style in Homer. Yet many devices of emphasis and variation, depending on the careful arrangement of words and phrases, occur regularly through the poems. Important among these are rhetorical questions by the poet, like 'Whom first, whom last, did Hector slay?' (v. 703), to introduce a list of victims, or 'Who of mortal men could relate all those sufferings?' (*3. 113*f.), to avoid going into unwanted details; appeals by the poet for divine aid or inspiration, or dramatic addresses to a particular character, for example XVI. 787, 'Then for you, Patroclus, appeared the end of life'; the emphatic repetition either of single words, like 'strongest were they that were reared of men on earth, strongest they were and with the strongest they fought' (I. 266f.), or of phrases, like 'Against him shall I go, even if his hands are like fire, his hands like fire and his might like gleaming iron' (xx. 371f.); comments by anonymous bystanders, for example II. 271, 'Thus did one say, looking towards another nearby...'; assonance and alliteration, which though sometimes fortuitous in Homer are often not—for example v. 440, φράζεο, Τυδεΐδη, καὶ χάζεο, and *1. 49*, δυσμόρῳ, ὃς δὴ δηθὰ φίλων ἄπο πήματα πάσχει; antithesis, as in αἴδεσθεν μὲν ἀνήνασθαι, δεῖσαν δ' ὑποδέχθαι (VII. 93); the deliberate word-series, as in *11. 612*, ὑσμῖναί τε μάχαι τε φόνοι τ' ἀνδροκτασίαι τε, a line which comes also in Hesiod's *Theogony*.

A number of other deliberate stylistic tricks could be added to these: for example word-plays, as when Achilles has the ash-spear of *Peleus*, from the crest of Mount *Pelion*, which he alone could wield, πῆλαι (*pēlai*) (XVI. 142ff. =XIX. 389ff.); or the Odyssean usages later developed in tragedy, ἐθέλων ἐθέλουσαν, 'he willing her willing' (3. 272) and μῆτερ ἐμή, δύσμητερ, 'my mother, no mother' (23. 97). Occasional tropes like Patroclus's rebuke to Achilles, 'Cruel man, your father was not horseman Peleus nor Thetis your mother, but the grey sea bore you, and precipitous rocks, since your mind is unyielding' (XVI. 33 ff.), are equally rhetorical in flavour. Yet in spite of all these devices there is no continuous rhetorical style, there are merely passages in which the isolated rhetoricism occurs. The Embassy to Achilles, book IX of the Iliad, might be expected to exemplify such a style if it existed, and indeed the flavour of this episode is undeniably rhetorical with its speeches of appeal, argument and rejection, employing such artifices as allegory (the Prayers) and paradigm (the story of Meleagros). But in the main this rhetorical flavour is produced by the deployment of arguments rather than the verbal quality which is an essential part of style. The same is true of the speeches and laments in the last book of the Iliad. It is tempting to consider any kind of rhetoricism as relatively late in the oral tradition, and it is undoubtedly true that some extreme examples occur in contexts which there are other grounds for identifying as accretions. Conversely rhetorical devices are absent from many stretches of the poems which possess an apparently (though perhaps deceptively) archaic simplicity. It is also true that subsequent Greek literature shows a progressive interest in rhetoric. Yet before we try to use these devices as evidence for comparative dating or different authorship we should remember that even primitive literature tends to delight in simple tropes and metaphorical artifices, on the level of the Homeric description of oars as the wings of ships or the fame of a song as reaching to the broad sky; and that the Iliad and Odyssey are by no means primitive. The most we can say, then, is that rhetoricisms seem to have been used more commonly in the later stages of the oral tradition, and that the most violent of them exemplify that love of novelty and variety which is characteristic of rhapsodic elaborations at the end of the oral period.

A similar situation is presented by the aphorisms in Homer, of which there are at least thirty in the Iliad and more in the

Odyssey. Often these compact reflections and proverbs fill a
verse or less. They are characterized by lack of decoration and
often by the omission of the copula, the use of gnomic τε and
the augmented gnomic aorist. Examples are v. 531, αἰδομένων
ἀνδρῶν πλέονες σόοι ἠὲ πέφανται, 'Of men who show regard for
each other more are saved than slain', and XII. 412, πλεόνων δέ
τε ἔργον ἄμεινον, 'Of more people, better work'. In the Odyssey,
which contains a greater number of moralizations about the
gods, there is a tendency towards longer *sententiae* of two lines or
more: see particularly *8. 167*ff., which reminds one of elegiac
moralists like Solon and Theognis:

> οὕτως οὐ πάντεσσι θεοὶ χαρίεντα διδοῦσιν
> ἀνδράσιν, οὔτε φυὴν οὔτ᾽ ἂρ φρένας οὔτ᾽ ἀγορητύν.
> ἄλλος μὲν γὰρ εἶδος ἀκιδνότερος πέλει ἀνήρ....

Thus not to all men do the gods give pleasant gifts, neither
beauty nor again intellect nor the power of speaking. For one
man is more insignificant in appearance...,

and so on. The Iliad contains one notable agglomeration of
aphorisms in the speech of Aeneas to Achilles at xx. 200–58. The
greater part of this curious speech, which is certainly not early
in composition, is devoted to superfluous genealogies; but from
242 to 255 there is a positive spate of aphorisms, eight or nine of
them, and here one might feel tempted to think of a gnomic or
moralistic style. But the result, as in most of this episode, is
chaotic and inartistic; and in fact there is no more point in
distinguishing a moralistic style than a rhetorical one. It is
nevertheless useful to be aware of the type and distribution of
aphoristic and rhetorical tendencies. The Odyssey is stronger in
the former—especially if one includes the semi-gnomic jokes,
like 'I don't think you came here on foot' of travellers to the
island of Ithaca—the Iliad in the latter; a difference which is
partly explained by their different subjects. The taste for gnomic
moralization, as for rhetoric, undoubtedly increased greatly
towards the end of the epic period, and there is a probability
that many examples in Homer are relatively late; but again the
simpler type of short generalization probably had great appeal
even at an early and unsophisticated stage of the oral epic.

The stylistic analysis of Homer is an occupation to be indulged in at one's peril. It was common in the latter half of the last century, but was done in so insensitive and careless a manner, and led to results so blatantly contradictory, that since then there has been a silent conspiracy to consider questions of style as beyond the scope of true scholarship. This approach seems to me feeble and unjustified. It is obvious enough that the estimation of literary style is an abstract and subjective activity. Yet certain stylistic differences are easily recognizable in the Iliad and Odyssey, and there could be little disagreement about, say, the decorated lyrical style of the Iliad. I have deliberately concentrated on some easily recognizable differences of stylistic effect, and have emphasized that many differences of style are likely to be due to changes of subject rather than of composer. At the same time certain stylistic effects seem particularly frequent in contexts which there are other grounds for considering as being relatively late in construction—as belonging either to the stage of monumental composition itself or to a subsequent stage of elaboration. Here the study of the means by which the effects are achieved is fruitful, and in particular the relation of such means to the traditional formular equipment of the Homeric singer. This has recently been illustrated by a useful examination of the different ways in which wounds and death are described in the Iliad. Before writing his *Verwundung und Tod in der Ilias* (Göttingen, 1956), Wolf-Harmut Friedrich decided that the only hope of detecting different personal styles was to take a subject that recurs throughout the poem and see how the description of this subject varies from context to context. Clearly the battle-poetry is the best such subject, and in particular the nature of wounds, fatal or not. These are usually described in a careful and formal way which nevertheless admits considerable variety of detail. Often the same kind of death, as when a charioteer is hit by a spear and topples from his chariot, is described in two or three different parts of the poem with slight variations. Sometimes it seems possible to say of such closely similar but not identical passages that one must be prior in composition and has been subjected to more or less appropriate variation in its other uses. Unfortunately, though, there is no justification for concluding, in a traditional poem, that the context of an apparently original description was composed earlier than that of an apparent derivative: for the derivative might itself be quite old, both it and the original may have been floating around in the tradition for a generation or more, and the passage containing the derivative version, in a poem like the Iliad, may actually have been put together before the passage containing the original.[1]

Thus the analytical results achieved by the application of Friedrich's method are limited and sometimes, no doubt, misleading. More important is his perception of a more purely stylistic tendency for the secondary variants and elaborations of recurrent martial incidents to become fantastic and improbable, despite a frequent veneer of specious realism. Thus XVI. 612f. (=XVII. 528f.) describes quite credibly how a spear, having missed its object, quivers in the ground:

> οὔδει ἐνισκίμφθη, ἐπὶ δ᾽ οὐρίαχος πελεμίχθη
> ἔγχεος· ἔνθα δ᾽ ἔπειτ᾽ ἀφίει μένος ὄβριμος Ἄρης.

it was buried in the earth, and the butt of the weapon quivered; then mighty Ares took away its force.

But at XIII. 442-4 this vignette is elaborated into something which, immediately one thinks about it, is physiologically impossible and artistically rather absurd:

> δόρυ δ᾽ ἐν κραδίῃ ἐπεπήγει,
> ἥ ῥά οἱ ἀσπαίρουσα καὶ οὐρίαχον πελέμιζεν
> ἔγχεος· ἔνθα δ᾽ ἔπειτ᾽ ἀφίει μένος ὄβριμος Ἄρης.

The spear was fixed in his heart, which in its palpitation made the butt of the weapon, also, quiver; then mighty Ares took away its force.

Similarly with two episodes involving Antilochus: at XIII. 396ff. he hit a charioteer, and 'he gasping fell from the well-wrought chariot', and Antilochus drove off the horses; but at v. 580ff. another charioteer was hit by Antilochus, and he too 'gasping fell from the well-wrought chariot'. This time, though, something fantastic happens: the victim falls head-first in soft sand

and sticks there upside-down until his horses knock him over. Again this shows a desire to elaborate the direct description, to go one better than what seems to be the traditional version. This desire is likely to be more characteristic of later singers and rhapsodes than of the main monumental composer or his predecessors. Again we must beware of abusing this conclusion and applying it mechanically to many less extreme cases, where the description of impossible events may be due not to second-hand elaboration and the desire for novelty at any price but rather to a keen poetical and dramatic imagination—as for example when a victim's eyes fall out when he is struck in the face by a spear (see also p. 343).

In short there is something to be learned from the search for different styles in Homer. Obviously, different styles do not necessarily entail different authors; it would be fantastic to imagine that the main poet of the Iliad—or indeed any competent singer—was incapable of composing in something like the majestic style, if he so wished, as well as in the succinct narrative style or the much commoner 'normal' style to which we can attach no special description. The question is whether or when he did so wish. In general, as one would expect on *a priori* grounds, poetry which may have been taken over more or less intact from the shorter epics of the pre-Homeric period tends to be simpler, more direct, less elaborate. The main composer of the Iliad probably brought an increase in subtlety and variation, but where the elaboration becomes excessive there are often grounds for seeing the operation of declining singers or rhapsodes. The Odyssey has a markedly narrower stylistic range than the Iliad, and its excesses are more strictly confined to large-scale expansions like the last book. Thus the diversity and unity that must be expected in any oral poem of monumental scope are certainly present, in stylistic terms, in the Iliad and Odyssey; the diversity carries certain strong implications for the complex oral ancestry of the poems, though often it arises simply from the diversity of parts possessed by any work of art whatever.

9

THE CULTURAL AND
LINGUISTIC AMALGAM

§1. *The archaeological criterion*

ONE of the most obvious kinds of plurality in the Iliad and Odyssey is that of the different and sometimes incompatible objects, customs and beliefs that they describe. In a few cases we may hope to assign these to a definite historical period: to be able to say, for example, that one passage may have taken shape in or soon after the Mycenaean period, since it describes a late Mycenaean object, while another is certainly much later in origin since its subject is demonstrably late Geometric and belongs to the 8th century. Once again, though, it must be emphasized that the poetical description need not have originated as early as the object described. Some of the more general Mycenaean knowledge in the poems, about the Trojan war and the use of bronze and even some of the late Bronze Age geography of Greece, may have come down through some generations in non-poetical tradition. Yet knowledge of more specific and sometimes unimportant objects, like body-shield, silver-studded sword and boar's-tusk helmet, or the wheeled work-basket and Nestor's decorated cup, suggests that some passages, at least, must have had poetical prototypes either in the Mycenaean age itself or quite soon afterwards (pp. 109–13). In a few cases Mycenaean phraseology may be identifiable, but this cannot be absolutely proved. Some of these objects, on the other hand, might have been remembered because of the survival of pictures or actual examples, rather than poetry; but it would be perverse to deny that identifiable Homeric descriptions of definitely Mycenaean objects tend to indicate a relatively very early origin for certain passages.

Exclusively Mycenaean objects or practices are unfortunately very few, and those that can be associated only with the Proto-geometric or Geometric age—the whole period from the mid-11th to the end of the 8th century—are no commoner. They consist, as it seems to me, of the following, which will be discussed in greater detail on pp. 183 ff.: the peacetime practice of cremation, the use of a pair of throwing-spears, Phoenician traders in Greek waters, and perhaps the absence of writing. Yet even these, though they probably belong neither to the very earliest nor to the very latest stage of the oral epic, are bounded by such broad limits of time that they tell us almost nothing about the process of composition. References to later phenomena, those that can be attached either to the latest Geometric or to the post-Geometric age, are more useful in this respect, since they may be able to provide a firm *terminus post quem* for poetical composition, but they are no less rare: Odysseus's brooch could belong to this category, so also Gorgon-heads and, not least important, hoplite fighting. All these will be further discussed on pp. 185 ff.[1] The one almost certain post-Geometric and therefore post-Homeric phenomenon in the poems seems to be the practice, apparently an Attic one, of sending home the cremated bones of the war dead for the relatives to care for (VII. 334 f.). It may not be rash to assume a *terminus post quem* of about 750 for all these references, the last-named being perhaps as late as the 5th century—if the Attic custom was really initiated, as F. Jacoby persuasively argued, only in 464.[2]

Thus it is legitimate to conclude that datable subject-matter, sparse as it is, at least provides a strong argument for certain passages in the poems having been composed at widely different dates. This is precisely what we should expect, indeed, from the very nature of oral poetry. Sceptics may be grateful for an additional indication; but it is the non-sceptics who can profit best from a cool and objective survey of the archaeological evidence, since it is much thinner in its scope and implications than they have been prone to believe. Martin Nilsson's fundamental book *Homer and Mycenae* (London, 1933) clarified the value of the cultural dating-criterion, but was not quite severe enough in its classification of strictly datable objects or practices; and the ambiguity of some of the evidence did not become clear even in Miss H. L. Lorimer's thorough and comprehensive *Homer and the Monuments* (London, 1950). There is no doubt that the Homeric poetry depicts an artificial cultural amalgam of elements derived from many different stages of the developing oral tradition. Our archaeological knowledge of the four or five centuries of this development is very incomplete and allows the identification of only few elements in the amalgam. The danger of assuming that a context containing one of these elements must have been composed at about the time of its archaeological date has been sufficiently underlined; but it is still worth examining the elements more closely to see how much of and which parts of the Iliad and Odyssey they chiefly concern.

Of the Mycenaean information identified on pp. 111 f., the boars'-tusk helmet occurs only in a single passage of the Doloneia. The body-shield is implied in a score of passages in the Iliad about Ajax—the archaic defensive fighter who alone of the major Achaeans is never associated with the corslet, and who regularly carries this antique armament, the shield like a wall, σάκος ἠΰτε πύργον, made out of seven ox-hides, ἑπταβόειον, behind which Teucros can crouch, peering out occasionally to shoot his arrows (e.g. VIII. 266 ff.). Ajax is undoubtedly a figure from the distant legendary past, schematized and expanded in the developing epic tradition. Otherwise only Hector and an obscure figure from Mycenae, Periphetes, are implied on a single occasion each, in VI and XV, to be carrying the cumbrous body-shield; and their shields are described not in the traditional formulas applied to Ajax—though these tend to be concentrated in the less well composed among books in which he is prominent, like VII and VIII—but in the style an archaizing singer might adopt, one who made the mistake of calling Periphetes's shield an ἀσπίς, which properly refers to the later round shield (p. 190). 'Well-greaved Achaeans' are firmly established in the formular tradition, and the more informative greaves with specifically metallic ankle-pieces occur in III, XI, XVI and XIX—though as a single formula, which might indeed be introduced almost anywhere. Silver-studded swords receive nine separate and well-distributed mentions in the Iliad and four in the Odyssey, but again this amounts to no more than thirteen uses of a single standardized phrase (pp. 114f.). Complex metal inlay comes in the description of the making of the shield of Achilles in xviii (e.g. 548f.), Nestor's dove-cup is unique and is described but briefly in a single passage of xi. The prevalence of bronze is ubiquitous, but this means little, since bronze continued to be used in the Iron Age not only for armour but also, often enough, for spear- and arrow-heads and even for axes. At least we can take the small number of casual references to iron as the material of weapons or tools to be certainly post-Mycenaean in composition.[1] On the other hand the two or possibly three references to iron as a particularly rare and precious metal look back, though as it happens from a very great distance, to the Bronze Age or the very early Iron Age: twice iron forms valuable prizes in the funeral games, each time however in an unsatisfactory and probably late though archaizing context (xxiii. 834, 850). In several other places iron is mentioned alongside bronze and gold as representing wealth, but this reveals nothing, since all metal was valuable through the whole period in question. As for the mention of less tangible Mycenaean conditions, namely Achaean geography and the Trojan war, accurate knowledge of the former seems to be largely confined to the Achaean Catalogue in ii, while knowledge of the war, though ubiquitous, is limited in scope and not very specific (p. 110). It was presumably deeply embedded in the epic tradition and no doubt in other forms of legendary memory, and we cannot say of a particular Homeric verse referring to the war that it must therefore have been composed early in the poetical tradition; though this tradition itself probably extended back at least to within a couple of generations of the fall of Troy.

Thus the most specific and most certain Mycenaean references, as well as being small in number, are also limited in the proportion of the Iliad and Odyssey which they affect. Several of them come in special contexts like the Doloneia, the Shield of

Achilles or the funeral games, and some of them could be the
work of archaizers composing relatively late in the tradition
rather than being closely copied from early poetical descriptions. They are commoner, it may be noted, in the Iliad than
in the Odyssey, but there are several possible explanations of
that: notably the Iliad's greater concern with arms and armour.

If we turn next to things and practices which are post-
Mycenaean but earlier than *c.* 700 we find serious limitations
there too. First, cremation: it became common at Athens at the
beginning of the Iron Age, *c.* 1050, though somewhat earlier in
outlying parts of Attica (p. 130). After some vicissitudes it went
out of fashion by the end of the 8th century. The Ionian cities
seem roughly to have followed suit, though the archaeological
evidence is very incomplete. There seems, then, to be a strong
presumption that references in Homer to cremation as the
regular means of disposing of the dead in peacetime will fall
within this wide period. Yet most Homeric mentions of cremation refer to the practice of an overseas army and are not
significant. There is indeed only one certain indication of
normal cremation, and that is when the ghost of Odysseus's
mother in the Nekyia assumes at *11. 218* that the burning of the
body is part of the δίκη βροτῶν, the regular practice of mortals.
It has been suggested that the didactic way in which Anticleia
here talks of cremation and its effects shows that it is something
new, in poetry at least; that must remain uncertain, but at least
this one passage of the Odyssey is post-Mycenaean—as if we did
not know it already! It is also unlikely to be post-Geometric,
and that is more valuable information.

The pair of throwing-spears is of wider application, since this
is the common though not the universal armament in the Iliad
and Odyssey. The Mycenaean weapon was the single thrusting-
spear (pl. 2 c) which was also sometimes remembered in the oral
tradition; the earliest evidence for its replacement, and that
uncertain, is the pair of spear-heads found in a single grave of
about 900 in the Athenian agora.[1] Twin spears are normal
equipment on 8th-century Attic Geometric pots—though these
may have been influenced by the heroic tradition—and were

probably adopted in a period of informal warfare in the Dark Age. They went out of fashion again with the spread of hoplite fighting, which may now be tentatively dated around the end of the 8th century (pp. 186ff.). Thus the many passages in the Iliad where two spears are carried, and a few similar armament passages in the Odyssey, may not have been composed before about 950. Many of them, however, could in theory have been composed even after the reintroduction of the single thrusting-spear, whenever that was, since the traditional language and background would be maintained as far as possible. Thus the archaistic tendency of the oral tradition reduces the usefulness of any such criterion. This can be seen too in the third post-Mycenaean but pre-orientalizing characteristic: the absence of scribes and writing, the almost total prevalence of illiteracy. The only exception is the cryptic reference to 'baneful signs' in the Bellerophon story at vi. 168: this is an abbreviated reference to an old story outside the Trojan plot, and could represent an isolated survival of a reference to Mycenaean writing; though the folded tablet is probably oriental and not Mycenaean, and the possibility of a later origin for the whole reference cannot be discounted. At least the assumption of illiteracy for the contemporaries of Achilles and Odysseus is virtually complete, even if it is explicitly exemplified only at vii. 175ff. where the Achaean heroes scratch their marks on lots and each can only recognize his own. We know that writing probably disappeared from Greece (though not from Cyprus) in the generations after the final collapse of the Achaean world, to be introduced in alphabetic form probably not earlier than the 9th century, when the first Phoenician inscription appears in Cyprus (pp. 70f.). Thus writing was unknown in the crucial formative stage of the Ionian epic, and so the epic world is made illiterate. If the monumental composer of the Odyssey—where references to writing might otherwise be expected—worked towards the end of the 8th century, then he probably knew about writing even if he did not use it; for the earliest known Greek inscription is dated around 730 (pp. 69f.). But in that case he archaized accurately and kept to the tradition. It was very easy to learn that the heroes did not have anything to do with writing—even a rhapsode would not abuse this simple rule—so really the facts about writing tell us very little about the composition of the poems.

References to the Phoenicians are more significant. Φοίνικες, Phoenicians (once in the Iliad in XXIII, five times in the Odyssey in reminiscences or false tales in *4, 13, 14, 15*) are always merchant-seamen, who in the Odyssey are usually deceitful. The land of Phoinike is mentioned twice in the Odyssean contexts, but the famous craftsmen of this land, who made wonderful textiles and silverware, are always known in Homer as Sidonians (VI. 290f., XXIII. 743, *4. 615* ff. = *15. 115* ff.). There is no evidence either in archaeology or in the poems that Phoenician ships made an extensive penetration of Greek waters. Their trade-route was Cyprus–Crete and Cythera–Sicily–Carthage, and, although archaeologists are disunited on the point, it is probable that this route was not established before 900, which may stand provisionally as an early limit for the composition of the scattered Homeric allusions. The greater hostility to them shown in the Odyssey may reflect clashes of interest in 8th-century Cyprus and Sicily, the latter of which is excluded from the Iliad and in the Odyssey, apart from *20. 383*, is confined to the probably appended last book.

Of the phenomena whose mention in the poems possibly presupposes a date of composition between about 800 and 600, the curious brooch of Odysseus, unique in Homer, comes in the nineteenth book of the Odyssey (226ff.). It is an uncertain criterion, though: Miss Lorimer argued that the model was 7th-century Etruscan, but Jacobsthal in his authoritative *Greek Pins* could find no adequate archaeological parallel and reserved judgement.[1] The golden lamp held by Athene at lines 33f. of the same book is again unique in Homer, and has been generally taken to indicate 7th-century composition; but again the criterion is uncertain. Lamps of this kind are certainly very uncommon between *c.* 1100 and *c.* 700, but that does not prevent this example from being Mycenaean, for example, or just a later rarity. References to separate, roofed temples are probably some time later than the late 9th century, before which such buildings seem to have been extremely uncommon. There are seven instances of νηός = 'temple' in the Iliad, four of them in VI referring to Athene's temple on the acropolis of Troy. Apollo also had a temple there (v. 446 and VII. 83), and the priest Chryses at I. 39 refers to roofing a temple or temples for Apollo Smintheus in the Troad. Then IX. 404 mentions the 'stone threshold' of Apollo at Pytho (Delphi), probably with reference to his temple. It is notable that all these passages come in the first nine books of the Iliad. Apollo's threshold comes also at *8. 80*, and temples occur in two other Odyssean passages, *6. 9*f. and *12. 346*f.; the former tells how Nausithous the founder of Phaeacia 'drove a wall round the city and built houses and made temples of the gods and divided out fields'—a description presumably based on the regular procedure of colonization, and possibly stimulated by the new interest in colonization in the 8th century.[1] The scarcity of temple references in the Odyssey may be compared with the situation in the somewhat later *Hymn to Apollo*, where there are no less than 16 occurrences of νηός in 546 lines.

A more precise criterion is the Gorgon-head, which comes three times in the Iliad, at v. 741, VIII. 349 and in the relatively late Arming of Agamemnon at XI. 36; also once in the Odyssey just after the late passage where Odysseus goes down to Hades itself (*11. 634*, cf. p. 236). As a decorative motif the Gorgoneion became really common in the orientalizing 7th century, though terracotta examples of possibly 8th-century date have been found at Tiryns;[2] on this evidence the four references in Homer are unlikely to have been composed before about 750.

Finally hoplite fighting is probably mentioned, as I think, in two or three passages of the Iliad, in XIII, XVI, and perhaps XII. The questions when hoplite tactics—the use of fully-armoured troops fighting in close-packed lines—first became known in Greece, and how far the Iliad was aware of such tactics, have led to great confusion in the past. Miss Lorimer reduced the confusion and concluded mainly from literary evidence and vase-paintings that these tactics were introduced early in the 7th century; but in 1953 a late Geometric bronze helmet and cuirass were found in a grave at Argos, to be dated not long after 720 (pl. 6 b); these suggest that full metallic armour, and therefore *conceivably* the new tactics with which this armour was to be so closely associated, may already have been establishing themselves in one part of the Peloponnese, at least, towards the end of the 8th century.[1] That would not prove that these tactics were familiar by then in Ionia; but it shows that we cannot safely down-date hoplite references in Homer to the post-Homeric 7th century, as some commentators have recently been tempted to do. How many such references there are, if any, is another delicate problem. References to masses of troops—to 'walls', 'lines' or 'ranks' (πύργοι, στίχες, φάλαγγες) —do not necessarily imply hoplite order, since the drawing-up of troops in lines or columns must have been a commonplace of warfare at many different periods. The duels between chieftains which are so prominent in the Iliad doubtless had some historical precedent, but not even the Iliad suggests that more or less disorganized mass-fighting among lesser mortals did not take place too. The word 'phalanx', whose precise Homeric meaning is obscure, need not of course refer to the hoplite phalanx; nor do descriptions of the gleam of bronze from such massed troops refer to the armour of hoplites[2]—rather the standard equipment of the chief heroes, itself derived in an exaggerated fashion from the partially bronze equipment of Mycenaean and immediately post-Mycenaean times, is assumed in generic descriptions of the troops at large. In two Iliadic contexts, however (XIII. 130–5 with 145–52, XVI. 211–17), troops are said to be so close-packed that they fence spear with spear, shield with shield, and the crests of their helmets touch; they are fitted together like a wall, and from their dense phalanxes they thrust out with spear and sword; their helmets and shields fit together like stones in a wall, spear presses against spear, man against man. These terms go beyond the usual vague language for general fighting, and describe a situation which must be deliberate and implies careful training. In short it is only in developed hoplite tactics that having your neighbour's shield pressing against your own is formidable to the enemy and not a dangerous nuisance to yourself. I would conjecture therefore that these passages, at least, are later than *c.* 750, though they may still belong to the 8th century; so also perhaps XII. 105, in which the description of shields as 'leathers' is an archaism which does not necessarily disturb the hoplite implication. Although it lacks absolute certainty, and is so limited in its effects, the hoplite criterion is among the more useful archaeological indications.

The conclusion must be that these roughly datable phenomena either tend to be very rare in the poems, or in two or three cases like knowledge of the Trojan war or of the two light throwing-spears are so common that they come almost everywhere. The more unusual phenomena are at least as frequent in the Iliad as in the Odyssey, and I will risk adding that, whatever the date of composition they superficially suggest, they appear more commonly—but by no means exclusively—in episodes whose final treatment appears on other grounds to be relatively late—episodes that occur predominantly in books like v, vII, vIII, x, or xxIII in the Iliad, or *11*, *19*, or *24* in the Odyssey. This reflects the greater interest, towards the end of the oral tradition, in the unusual, in what goes a little beyond the standardized range of most traditional poetry.

Other cultural rarities, but ones which cannot be archaeologically dated, tend to support this conclusion. Often, however, these apparently untraditional elements come in similes, where reference to the unheroic experience of the singer's audience is to be expected. Thus horseback riding is mentioned in similes at xv. 679ff. and *5. 371*; trumpets occur in a simile at xvIII. 219f. and a metaphor at xxI. 388, part of the Theomachy; fishing forms the substance of three similes in the Iliad and two in the Odyssey (in v, xvI, xxIV, *12* and *22*); a seated cult-image is envisaged in the narrative in vI (e.g. 92), ivory trappings in a simile at IV. 141ff. and in the narrative at v. 583. In the following cases the departure from the usual or traditional conception probably represents a relatively late development of custom or viewpoint. Normally chariots in the poems are drawn by a pair of horses; the exceptional assumption of four horses is made in books VIII and XI of the Iliad—the latter case in one of Nestor's reminiscences—and in a simile at *13. 81* ff. Normally Olympus, the dwelling-place of the gods, is envisaged as the mountain-top; at VIII. *18* ff. it is regarded as the sky. Dionysus was a relative newcomer among the Greek gods, and he occurs only in a digression in VI and in the Beguilement of Zeus in XIV, also in the Nekyia and the last book of the Odyssey. Again, the normal heroic marriage seems to have entailed the payment of a bride-price by the suitor to the bride's father, and this is seen three times in the Iliad and four in the Odyssey; but the second book of the Odyssey (*53*, *132*f., *196* = *1. 277*) implies a probably later development, the payment of a dowry by the parents to the groom, and ἕεδνα has changed its meaning from bride-price to dowry; while IX. *146*f. and *6. 159* seem to represent a conflation of elements of both systems. Finally in this class comes chariot-fighting. The normal conception, represented in scores of Iliadic passages, was that the chariot transported its hero to and from the battlefield and from one part of it to another; to fight he dismounted. In four or five passages, however, the idea of a chariot-charge has untraditionally slipped into the Iliad, namely at IV. *297*ff., V. *13*, XI. *289* and *503*, and perhaps XV. *353*ff.: see pp. *124*f. In sum these additional rarities and exceptions to the tradition confirm and extend the impression formed earlier: books IV, V, VI, VII, VIII, IX, XVIII and XXIV of the Iliad are prominent, and we may add the sophisticated episodes of the Beguilement of Zeus mainly in XIV and the Theomachy in XXI. Book XV, too, possibly obtrudes itself—a curiously uneven performance with some old similes and language. In the Odyssey, where once again the untraditional elements are less widely distributed, there is no such readily detectable emphasis on certain books, except in the case of *11* and *24*. Yet even apart from the special problems of similes (which are not always so firmly anchored in their general context as a passage of narrative may be) the method of assessment is admittedly a rough-and-ready one,

which should be used only to suggest a preliminary hypothesis
or lend support to one formed on a different basis.

The variant treatment in the poems of particular customs,
objects or beliefs, like marriage gifts and the use of the chariot,
whatever its implications for the composition of certain parts of
the poems, undeniably confirms the complex character of the
oral tradition. It shows that, although a roughly homogeneous
(though often artificial and inaccurate) view of conditions in
the heroic age had been achieved by the singers of the ripe oral
period, this view had been evolved by the progressive incorporation of different elements at different dates; and that inconsistent details were still incorporated from time to time, whether
they were anachronistic reflections of conditions known by the
singers themselves, or regional deviations, or archaisms that
chanced to survive elsewhere in the oral tradition or popular
memory.

This generalization may be strikingly illustrated in conclusion by a few passages concerned with armament, which show
how a traditional view has been adapted by later poets to a
changed conception of its subject-matter. Thus when Hector
runs back to Troy in book vi of the Iliad 'about his heels and
his neck tapped the black hide' (117)—that is, he was carrying
a tall Mycenaean-type body-shield slung across his back; but an
explanatory line has been added, '—the rim which ran round
the edge of the bossed targe' (vi. 118), by a poet who envisaged
not the old kind of hide shield but the new circular *aspis* with
a central boss. The process of confusion and conflation can be
seen even more clearly in the transference from the single
Mycenaean-type thrusting-spear to the pair of light throwing-
spears. The latter were the usual equipment in Homer, but
certain great heroes were known to have used the old type of
spear: thus when Patroclus borrowed Achilles's armour at
xvi. 130ff. he did not take his spear, 'heavy and great and
sturdy—no other of the Achaeans could wield it, but Achilles
alone...'. This is the 'Pelian ash' which Achilles inherited
from his father Peleus. Ajax and Hector, too, were remembered
to have this kind of spear; and Agamemnon, though in his

relatively recent arming-scene at the beginning of xi he takes a pair of throwing-spears, in his subsequent and more traditional-seeming *aristeia* is sometimes implied to be using a thrusting-spear, as when at 95 f. he 'stabbed with sharp spear', ὀξέι δουρὶ νύξ'.

Again, two separate stages of the tradition tended to become confused and to give rise to conflated situations which are only superficially puzzling. Thus although some heroic duels, like that of Sarpedon and Patroclus in xvi or Achilles and Aeneas in xx, are fought out consistently with two spears on each side, in others the situation changes in the course of the action. So Paris at iii. 18 is armed with a pair of spears (and also, con-fusedly, with bow and leopard-skin) when he makes his first challenge; lots are cast to determine whether he or Menelaus shall have first throw, which again presupposes throwing-spears; but in the event, after a single throw each, Menelaus draws his sword (361) and the second spear is forgotten, until he suddenly has one at 380. At xxii. 326 Hector is hit by a thrust, probably, from Achilles's spear, consistently with the reputation of the great Pelian ash; but earlier in the encounter at 273 this spear had been misused as a javelin, and Hector, too, had thrown his single spear and missed—a departure from realism, since a thrusting-spear would not have been thrown except *in extremis* and could not have been thrown far. Even more striking is the discrepancy in the fight between Odysseus and the suitors. At *22. 110*f. Telemachus fetched four shields and helmets and eight spears for himself, Odysseus, and their two helpers. Each is armed, then, with a standard pair of throwing-spears. Yet for no explained reason Melanthios on behalf of the suitors 'took out twelve shields, so many spears and so many helmets...' (*144*f.)—that is, a single spear each; and in the ensuing fight the suitors throw their single spears and Odysseus is described as using one of his throwing-spears for thrusting: 'he smote the son of Damastor in hand-to-hand fighting (αὐτοσχεδόν) with his long spear' (*293*). In this last case one may argue that in emergencies a throwing-spear could be used for thrusting; but in general there can be no doubt that the oral tradition tended to conflate the different uses of the two kinds of spear, just as it conflated the occasional surviving description of a body-shield with descriptions of the smaller shields with which singers had been familiar from at least the Submycenaean period onward. Indeed it can be seen how not only the action but also the formular language underwent adaptation: thus, as T. B. L. Webster observes in a good discussion,[1] the verse εἴλετο δ' ἄλκιμον ἔγχος ἀκαχμένον ὀξέι χαλκῷ, 'he grasped his mighty spear sharpened with keen bronze' (xv. 482), which refers to a single thrusting-spear, is adapted to describe a pair of spears as follows: εἴλετο δ' ἄλκιμα δοῦρε δύω κεκορυθμένα χαλκῷ, / ὀξέα, 'he grasped two mighty shafts crowned with bronze, keen ones' (xi. 43 f., in the relatively late Arming of Agamemnon). That the single-spear version is the older is suggested both by its considerably greater frequency in the poems and also by the language of the adaptation, in which δύω is forced and otiose after the dual form δοῦρε.

§2. *The criterion of language*

The language of Homer is an artificial amalgam of elements from different regions and different periods, including many forms invented by the singers themselves. The strictness and scope of the formular system demonstrate that it is the product of the selection and consolidation of metrical phrase-units through many generations (p. 64). The examination of dialect, word-form and syntax leads to an analogous conclusion: that the Iliad and Odyssey are the culmination of a continuous *tradition* of oral poetry, and that their linguistic components are of diverse origin both in locality and in date.

Predominantly the poems are in East Ionic Greek related to the presumed speech of 8th-century Miletus, Samos or Colophon. Thus ᾱ has become η even after ρ, ε and ι; τίθημι is sometimes inflected as a contracted verb; εἰ ἄν becomes ἤν. Ionic also has κεῖνος; genitives in -εω, -έων from a-stems, with quantitative metathesis (ᾱο > ηο > εω); athematic infinitives in -ναι, 3rd singular ἤν for ἦς, and 3rd plural aorists in -σαν; ἡμεῖς, ὑμεῖς; movable ν. These last forms, for example, are common to East and Attic

Ionic, but except for the aspiration are presumably East Ionic in Homer. So are forms shared between East Ionic and other non-Ionic dialects, like ἐών (as against Attic ὤν) or the lengthening of a vowel to compensate for the omission of a following post-consonantal Ϝ, as in ξεῖνος (ξένϜος), μοῦνος and so on.

There are certain specifically Aeolic forms, too, as was shown in chapter 7, and several which were *either* Aeolic *or* Mycenaean in origin. Two other small but less conspicuous minorities are formed by words in the Arcado-Cypriot dialect on the one hand and in the Attic variety of Ionic on the other. Of the latter the *organic* Atticisms—forms which do not simply have a superficial and easily replaceable Athenian colouring, like ἀγξηράνῃ or ἐνταῦθα (Ionic ἀγξηρήνῃ, ἐνθαῦτα), but ones which cannot be changed without destroying the metre, like ἑωσφόρος (xxiii. 226; Ionic ἠωσφόρος, Aeolic αὐώσφορος)—seem to be very few in number and were presumably placed in the poems when they came to form an important part of the Panathenaic festival in the 6th century (pp. 306ff.).[1] The *aspiration* of our texts must similarly be due to later stages of transmission outside Ionia, where aspirates were regularly omitted. Being additions or superficial corruptions, the Atticisms are not really part of the true diversity of the Homeric language. The Arcado-Cypriot forms are. The dialects of Arcadia and Cyprus in the historical period are a survival, in two geographical and political back-waters, of the kind of Greek spoken in the late Bronze Age palaces of the Peloponnese; and words in Homer which accord with these survivals, like αἶσα, φάσγανον, ἦμαρ, ἰδέ, ἠπύω, must be Mycenaean forms which entered the poetical vocabulary either during the late Bronze Age itself or in the generations after its collapse (pp. 113ff.).

As a result of this conflation of different dialect elements, the causes of which have been discussed in part iii, Ionic forms like ξυνός, ἔσαν or ἀγκυλομήτεω exist side by side with Aeolisms like ἄμμες (Ionic ἡμεῖς), πίσυρες (Ionic τέσσαρες), ἔμμεν or ἔμμεναι (Ionic εἶναι) and ἐραννός (Ionic ἐρατεινός). Usually the Aeolic form is found only where it provides a convenient metrical variant; indeed the useful and common Aeolic dative plural termination in -εσσι (on which see pp. 149f.) can be added even to an Ionic stem, as in νέεσσι. This typifies the freedom and artificiality of Homeric forms; for the oral singers felt themselves free to invent not only bastard forms like νέεσσι but also illogical ones like ἐπέεσσι.

Indeed an important part of the Homeric language consists of forms that belonged to no spoken dialect of any date but were the creation, on the analogy of real forms, of singers who were consciously or unconsciously struggling to reduce the bondage of dactylic verse. By its nature this kind of rhythm excluded words of the value ∪ ∪ ∪, – ∪ – and ∪ – – ∪, of which there are many in Greek. The singers overcame this difficulty mainly by the artificial lengthening of vowels, as in ἀθάνατος, Πειρίθοος, προθυμίῃσι, Ἀπόλλωνα, εἰλήλουθα and so on; the lengthening of ε to ει is a particularly common device perhaps based on the analogy of ξένϝος > ξεῖνος and similar forms. Naturally these lengthenings are commonest in the metrically most stringent sections of the verse, especially in the last two feet, and so we find for example πουλυβοτείρῃ /, ἠϋγένειος /, ἀπονέεσθαι /. In many other cases too the analogy of existing forms is important: τιθήμενος (for τιθέμενος) retains the vowel of τίθημι, grammatical solecism though it is; μαχειόμενος is supported by the metrical parallel of μαχησόμενος; the short α of φάος is lengthened in the formula φάεα καλά under the influence of analogous formulas like δώματα κᾱλά. Irregular case-endings, too, which do not necessarily involve lengthening, are formed artificially by analogy: εὐρέα πόντον after εὐρέι πόντῳ, ἡνιοχῆα after ἡνιόχοιο and so on. Some of these exemplify the special phenomenon of formular adaptation regardless of minor metrical or grammatical anomalies that may be produced. Sometimes, though, it must be admitted that the anomalies which arise from many of these artificial creations are not minor but rather serious. All one can say is that such changes were not found intolerable by Ionic audiences (after all, we ourselves have swallowed some really amazing poeticisms); though some of the most violent ones probably belong to the latest stages of the oral tradition, or even to the post-oral period of rhapsodic elaboration.

Apart from anomalies such as these we can be fairly sure that the singers invented many other forms, especially compounds, which were not irregular but were unknown to ordinary speech. Adjectival prefixes like καλλι- are attached to an indefinite variety of nouns to form metrically and descriptively useful epithets like καλλιπάρῃος, καλλικόμοιο, καλλιγύναικα, καλλιρέεθρον, καλλιρόοιο, καλλιχόροισι, καλλιπέδιλον. Alternatively the noun-element in these compound epithets may remain stable and the adjectival prefix may be varied: thus we find not only καλλι-πάρῃος but also μιλτοπάρῃος and χαλκοπάρῃος. This kind of variation is, in fact, a special case of formula-making applied to single words, which often enough are themselves part of a wider noun-epithet group. Increased knowledge of Mycenaean has slightly altered the picture, but Witte, who treated this matter extensively in his article on 'Homeros' in Pauly–Wissowa, was still right in holding that many of the long series of epithets formed by adding -έεις or -όεις to a noun-stem, for example κητώεσσαν, ἀστερόεις, τειχιόεσσαν, were poetical creations.

Thus, apart from the artificial mixture of dialects, many of the words and forms in Homer belonged to no spoken dialect whatever but were the creation of the epic singers themselves. They felt free to make these artificial inventions because the language of the poetry they knew was already to some extent formalized and separated from that of real life. The minimum of artificiality that no poetry can avoid was already being increased by the poetical contact of different regional dialects as well as by the survival of Mycenaean and other archaisms. Apart from still intelligible Mycenaean forms the singers retained certain hoary words and phrases of unknown antiquity whose precise meaning had been, or was in process of being, forgotten: words like ἀκάκητα, ἀτρυγέτοιο, ἰόμωροι or even ἴφθιμος, phrases like νυκτὸς ἀμολγῷ ('at the milking-time(?) of night'), ἀνὰ πτολέμοιο γεφύρας ('along the bridges of war'), ἀμενηνὰ κάρηνα ('strengthless heads'), or μήστωρες αὐτῆς ('counsellors of the war-cry'). What may happen is exemplified by the Homeric use of the obsolete word θέλυμνον. It is conceivable that this was merely a form of θέμεθλον = 'basis, foundation', with an odd transposition of consonants; but even so τετραθέλυμνον, 'four-based', is a cryptic description for a shield (xv. 479, 22. 122), and the whole phrase σάκος θέτο τετραθέλυμνον is likely to be a survival from an early stage in the tradition. 'Fore-based', προθελύμνῳ, applied to a shield is even odder—it appears in one of the rare (and relatively late: pp. 186–8) hoplite passages at XIII. 130 and seems to be the result of some kind of misunderstanding. The two other uses of προθέλυμνος in Homer more clearly exemplify the 'foundation' meaning: a wild boar tears up trees προθέλυμνα at IX. 541—this is acceptable, but when Agamemnon in the late Doloneia 'tore out from his head many hairs προθελύμνους, by the foundations', we suspect that a little-understood archaism is being comically misapplied; and in any case it is difficult to relate these uses to the shield.

The language of the Iliad and Odyssey is a composite organism. We must now, therefore, continue the inquiry begun in part III, of how far its different elements can be dated—by which is meant how far it can be determined when they are likely to have entered the Homeric dialect mixture. Comparative linguists have succeeded in assigning certain changes in Greek, and not merely dialectal ones, to broad but absolute periods. One important development for which an approximate *terminus post quem* can be inferred is contraction, the practice of amalgamating two adjacent vowel-sounds, at least one being short, into a single long vowel or diphthong. There are of course very many uncontracted words in Homer, like πόλεες, νόος, ἀέκητι, ἔπλεον, τρέει; there are many other words in which a contraction in the vulgate (or standard received text) can be resolved without difficulty into its earlier uncontracted form—for there is no doubt that the language of Homer was modernized in certain respects in the classical period, and that many contractions were made in recitation and copying which had not been there in Homer's time. Yet there are also many contracted forms which cannot be resolved without destroying the proper rhythm of the verse: forms like XIX. 95 ἄσατο (compared with ἀάται four lines before), 8. 160 ἄθλων (compared with frequent ἄεθλον), 6. 210 λούσατε (compared with frequent λοέσσατο etc.), and also cases like ὀλεῖται, ἐφόρει, χολοῦμαι, where the metrical value of the word necessarily precludes an uncontracted equivalent. That contraction is a post-Mycenaean phenomenon is strongly suggested by its absence from the Linear B tablets. Many of the commoner contractions are in fact demonstrably later than the foundation of the Ionian settlements in Asia Minor since, for example, εο contracts to ου in Attic but remains open, or becomes a sound later written as ευ, in Ionia. Therefore the tendency to coalesce these sounds must have undergone its chief development after the colonizers of the Ionian cities left Attica. Again, the classical Attic and Ionic imperative meaning 'win!' is spelt νίκα, contracted from an earlier νίκαε; but if the contraction had been made when the Ionic change of ᾱ to η was still operative the result would have been νίκη and not νίκα. Therefore this contraction is later than the completion of the ᾱ > η vowel-change; but this change had evidently not terminated by the time the Μᾶδα first impinged on the Greeks, almost certainly not before 1000 B.C., since the Ionians called them Μῆδοι, Medes. Such arguments as these suggest that the tendency to contract established itself some time later than 1000, and therefore unresolvable contractions in Homer were probably created later, perhaps considerably later, than this time.[1]

Another important change which has left its mark in the language of Homer is the disappearance of the semi-vowel digamma, ϝ, pronounced something like w. It had disappeared from Ionic by the time of the earliest inscriptions, though it continued in declining use in Aeolic down to the 6th century B.C. and later. Yet the Ionic singers of the Iliad and Odyssey still felt its presence, and often preserved its metrical effect in words from which the full sound had disappeared. Thus in the phrase καὶ ἴδε ἔργον (XVII. 179) the second and third word are treated as though they began with a consonant, and preceding final vowels are neither elided nor shortened. This is because ἴδε and ἔργον both began originally with ϝ, and their special metrical behaviour was handed down in the tradition even when their spelling and common pronunciation had changed. On the other hand there were many other words in which the original digamma was completely forgotten and left no metrical heritage; more important still, the reaction even to words like ἴδε and ἔργον was inconsistent, so that sometimes they were treated as though they began with a vowel after all: thus in IX. 374, to select one out of many Homeric examples, οὐδὲ μὲν ἔργον treats ἔργον as beginning with an ordinary vowel; there is no inkling of a special metrical effect, since the preceding μέν is not lengthened by position as it would be if the semi-consonantal digamma were on this occasion felt. Now the disappearance of digamma from normal Ionic, like the habit of contraction, came later than the completion of the ā > η change, as is shown by the fact that the classical Ionic word for 'beautiful' was κᾱλός not κηλός. The original form was κᾱλϜός, and when the digamma was dropped the α was still counted long as a relic of its lengthening by the two consonants that originally followed; yet it was not turned into η, so the tendency to forget digamma cannot have overlapped the tendency to pronounce ā as η. Thus, like contraction, the neglect of digamma is later (possibly much later) than about 1000, by the ā > η argument combined with the Mādā argument. In many cases, indeed, the loss of digamma must have preceded contraction, since many adjacent vowels subject to contraction in Homer had become adjacent through the disappearance of an internal digamma (certain kinds of intervocalic ι and σ had also dropped out earlier): thus ἀϜέκων became ἀέκων and so, by contraction, ἄκων. Many of the irresolvable contractions in Homer, then, must have been formed later than the time when digamma was still widely pronounced, and belong to the same relatively developed stratum of the poetical language as ignored digammas in words like ἔργον, ἄναξ, ἔτος, οἶνος, all of which had originally begun with this sound.

A particularly significant contraction which does not depend on the omission of an original digamma is seen in genitives singular in -ου. This is one form of the genitive of o-stems in surviving texts of Homer; the other is -οιο, an old and originally Mycenaean termination as can be seen from the form o-jo in the tablets. Now -ου cannot be contracted from -οιο, and perhaps arises, as shown on p. 143, from an earlier alternative form -οο. In certain verses of Homer this older and uncontracted form must be restored to our texts in order to rectify the metre; and in hundreds of other verses it is possible, though not compulsory, to restore either -οο or -οι' in the place of the vulgate -ου. There is little doubt that in many of these cases the contracted genitive is due to the modernization of the text of Homer in the course of its transmission; yet there are as many as nearly 800 cases in the Iliad and Odyssey together where an -ου genitive cannot be resolved into an earlier uncontracted form, as for example in the Ionic formula Κρόνου πάϊς ἀγκυλομήτεω and in many instances where it appears at the line-end: thus I. 190 παρὰ μηροῦ / cannot be read as παρὰ μηροῖ', or converted to παρὰ μηρόο without nullifying the metre.

The occurrences in Homer of irresolvable contractions and neglected digammas (in words in which the obsolescent sound was elsewhere in the tradition taken into account) are so numerous and so widely distributed that we have no right to use these comparatively developed linguistic features as anything but a broad criterion of post-Mycenaean and indeed post-migration composition. In general they seem to be a little commoner in the Odyssey than in the Iliad. Their greatest usefulness from the point of view of chronology is for demonstrating first that many passages which contain a Mycenaean word or describe an apparently Mycenaean situation or object cannot have come down in their present form from Mycenaean times, and secondly that many well-established formulas are post-migration in invention. Thus while they are consistent with the conclusion that the Homeric phraseology was formed over several centuries of poetical composition on heroic themes, they also show us that much of the formal expression of the Greek epic as we have it belongs to the period after about 1000. This indeed is to be expected, once it is concluded that the date of monumental composition was as late as the 8th century; for oral poetry, traditional and indeed archaistic though it is, cannot avoid the continuous process of slight and unconscious modernization.

Objective criteria like comparative dialect-geography, which make possible the establishment of a rough *terminus post* for a phenomenon like contraction, are unfortunately of little use for the chronology of the Greek language over the crucial period which separates the foundation of the Ionian settlements in Asia Minor from the composition and stabilization of the Homeric poems. It is impossible to distinguish accurately Homeric linguistic characteristics of around 950 from those of around 750. It is therefore important to be quite clear at this point about the difference between absolute and relative chronology, absolute and relative earliness or lateness. The terms 'relatively early' and 'relatively late', in the context of Homeric scholarship, should be applied in relation to an oral poetical tradition lasting from 1200 or 1100 down to about 700 or 650; and phrases like 'interpolation' or 'recent addition' should be understood to apply to the period after about 700 (or whenever it is thought that the main act of monumental composition was completed). There is no absolute chronology within the last half of the oral period, but, on the arguments advanced in this book, forms that seem to have been used by the monumental composer of each poem are presumably not later than 750 or 700, though their origin may of course be earlier.

In spite of the obvious need for caution, comparative philologists have a regrettable and almost universal propensity for writing about 'late' and 'recent' forms in Homer without any further qualification, even an implied one. It may reasonably be asked what these descriptions mean. Do these scholars mean 'recent' in terms of date of invention or of particular poetical application? Do they mean 'recent' in relation to the whole span of the living oral tradition—not later then than the middle of the 7th century or even the end of the 8th? Or do they mean that such forms have been added to, or inserted in, the Homeric poems after the main monumental stage of composition was accomplished, so that they are probably of 7th or even 6th-century origin? The truth seems to be that many of these critics have never asked themselves such questions at all, at least in any explicit shape. This assumption they seem to share: that the forms they are talking about are linguistically more developed than those which are 'normal', meaning 'most common', in the language of the Homeric poems as a whole. But since this 'normal' language is a traditional language, and must have established itself as a standard before 'Homer' or the date of monumental composition, then 'recent' forms in this sense might still be no later in origin than the 8th or even the 9th century. In fact, however, it is evident that many of our comparative linguists think that 'recent' or 'late' forms, as described by them, must be post-Homeric, and belong to the 7th or 6th century. Yet the truth is that with the probable exception of a very small number of organic Atticisms (which entered the poems after the 8th century and probably after the 7th, but which could be of earlier origin in themselves) there are no objective linguistic criteria whatever for determining whether a relatively late element in the Homeric language is to be dated round 800 or round 650. It seems to me that all linguistic experts should make this plain, and should also take pains to clarify what they mean on each occasion by 'early', 'recent' or 'late'.

In spite of the lack of absolute dates in the post-migration development of phonetics, morphology and syntax it is still possible, as I think, to apply two more general and more complex types of argument which will tend to establish certain untraditional linguistic phenomena in the Iliad and Odyssey in the one case as no later than the monumental composers, and in the other as post-Homeric in the sense of being later than the monumental composition of either poem.[1]

First, there is reason for thinking that many or indeed most of the forms usually implied to be post-Homeric are not post-Homeric at all. My argument takes as its starting-point G. P. Shipp's useful investigations in his *Studies in the Language of Homer* (Cambridge, 1953). Shipp discovered that in the Iliad— and the position of the Odyssey would not be radically different —a significantly high proportion of forms classed as 'late' by Pierre Chantraine in his standard *Grammaire Homérique* occur in the developed similes and, to a lesser extent, in other types of digressionary material outside the main narrative. Shipp simply marshalled the facts, which so far as the similes are concerned seem irrefutable, without drawing conclusions about the composition of the poems. It nevertheless appears that he often understood 'late' to imply 'post-Homeric'; Chantraine took this to be Shipp's meaning, and incidentally revealed what he himself often meant in describing a word or form in Homer as 'récent', when he observed of Shipp's conclusion, and as an implied criticism, that not all or most of the developed similes could have been post-Homeric additions.[1] Now with this I entirely agree, but draw from it a quite different conclusion: not that there cannot have been an exceptionally high proportion of 'late' forms in the similes, or that if there were it would be surprising and contradictory, but that *since most of the similes are highly unlikely to be post-Homeric then the forms they contain, including the so-called 'late' forms, are not post-Homeric either.* In other words I am prepared to assume on mainly non-linguistic grounds that the developed similes were not inserted after the monumental poem had come into being, but that the great majority of them, at any rate, were integrated into his poetical structure by the main composer himself or already existed in versions derived by him from other singers. General stylistic judgements on Homer are admittedly dangerous and often subjective, but here, I think, is a case where most critics would agree. Most of the similes perform a recognizable structural and dramatic function in their context, and they are deployed with taste and skill quite apart from their own intrinsic merits. In a few cases a simile may appear to have been repeated, with minor and sometimes unsuitable variation, from some other context in the poems; or a concentration of similes could have attracted the subsequent addition of others. This might conceivably be the cause of the unbroken sequence of six similes at II. 455–83, though I am unconvinced by arguments that the whole sequence could not be the design of the main composer.[2] In general the placing of the similes is good. Their internal virtues are obvious; the clarity and simplicity of their expression, in particular, except in the case of a few obviously added or expanded examples, arc not what we should consistently expect from added elaborations, either on general grounds or by comparison with the lower skill and taste employed in the probable additions considered below. If the insertion of similes were a favourite occupation of post-Homeric singers and rhapsodes, then we might expect it to have affected the Odyssey almost as much as the Iliad—in spite of which there are relatively few similes in most parts of the later poem. More important, there is no obvious tendency for 'late' forms to be concentrated in the more specialized similes, especially those concerned with untraditional subjects like melting lard or horse-riding, as against simpler and apparently more traditional types like those concerned with lions or fire. In short it seems highly probable that most of the similes are no later than the main composition of the Iliad or Odyssey—and the same would appear, though less cogently, to be true of many of the other digressions like Nestor's or Diomedes's reminiscences or Odysseus's false tales. Many of the more elaborate similes may well be the work of the main composers themselves, though the simpler types, at least, were probably used by singers of preceding generations: see also pp. 327f.

If this argument is provisionally accepted then there is a strong case for assuming that a very large proportion of the forms identified as 'late' by Chantraine and others, on the basis of their untraditional and apparently more advanced linguistic characteristics, are not post-Homeric but are simply 'late' in relation to the whole history of the oral tradition, near the end of which came the great monumental poems. Thus the occurrence in a particular passage of the kind of linguistic form that philologists tend to class as late, except possibly in the case of no more than half-a-dozen organic Atticisms, is no reason in itself for regarding the passage as a post-Homeric addition; it might, on the contrary, be a reason for regarding it as belonging to the monumental composer himself. Further work must certainly be done on this subject, especially on the similes.

If neither the strict philological criterion nor (as seen in § 1 of this chapter) the archaeological criterion can distinguish indubitable post-Homeric characteristics, except in the case of organic Atticisms, is there no possible way of identifying probable post-Homeric additions and elaborations? Do we have to fall back on plot-analysis and general stylistic impressions, so dangerous when unsupported by more objective criteria? I think not, and adduce my second general linguistic argument. This depends on the analysis of formular phraseology and on one or two reasonable assumptions about the transition from oral to literate poetry. We have seen that the examination of the form of single words does not allow the distinction of Homeric from post-Homeric (except always in the case of a few Attic forms), because of the absence of absolute dates in the development of poetical Greek from the Ionian migration to the earliest written and securely dated literature. Yet the examination of words *in the phrase*, or of phraseology, may be more helpful. It can be related to a distinction between live oral composition and what may be crudely termed post-oral composition, the transition between the two being absolutely datable, with some considerable probability, to somewhere between *c.* 650 and 600 (pp. 313f., 318f.). I would like to make a sharp distinction not so much between traditional and untraditional phraseology—since the latter may merely imply oral modernization or a personal or local idiosyncrasy—as between traditional and *anti*-traditional (a term used by D. L. Page in his *History and the Homeric Iliad*), this last expression implying not merely innovation or modernization but the definite misunderstanding or maltreatment of traditional language—in particular of the language of well-established and frequent verbal formulas. A similar distinction may be applied *mutatis mutandis*, but less profitably, to objects and practices in the poems.

My contention is that anti-traditional phraseology is almost always post-Homeric, since it was only possible to misuse the tradition and ignore the canons of the inherited technique of oral verse-making when those canons were no longer completely and actively valid, when the whole art of oral improvisation was decaying before the new practice of written verse and the new interest in a more personal kind of poetry. It is in what I called the 'degenerate' stage of an oral tradition (pp. 97f.) that ignorant or pretentious attempts to alter and improve the fixed language of the past are made. It is true, of course, that very archaic elements were occasionally misunderstood even when that tradition was still flourishing. Such are many of the examples collected by Manu Leumann in his *Homerische Wörter* —or rather, I should say, a high proportion of the small number of his examples that seem on close inspection to be really convincing. Such misunderstandings were usually of uncommon and obsolete words in potentially ambiguous traditional contexts, and they can be clearly distinguished from cases of the misuse of well-established, frequent and perfectly intelligible traditional phraseology.

Thus the singer who conceived of Zeus sending lightning to make not only rain, hail or snow but also 'in some place the great mouth of piercing war', ἠέ ποθι πτολέμοιο μέγα στόμα πευκεδανοῖο (x. 8), is unlikely to have been fully conversant with the range of alternatives proper to a Homeric simile, or even with the established 'mouth of war' metaphor. The language of x, the Doloneia, is often odd, but occasionally it seems to become the basis for something even odder: thus Odysseus and Diomedes are described in rather a good line, probably traditional, as going 'among the slaughter, among the corpses, through the weapons and black blood' (298); but the last half of this line reappears in an incongruous use at xxiii. 806, where the prize for the fight in armour at the funeral games is offered to him who 'touches innards through weapons and black blood', ψαύσῃ δ' ἐνδίνων διά τ' ἔντεα καὶ μέλαν αἷμα, a line as inept in expression as it is absurd in meaning in this context: see also p. 223. Again, the poet who at xvii. 476 used the phrase 'of immortal horses to contain the subduing and the might', ἵππων ἀθανάτων ἐχέμεν δμῆσίν τε μένος τε, cannot have been properly familiar with the traditional resources for linking traditional word-groups like ἵππων ἀθανάτων on the one hand and μένος τε at the line-end on the other; he introduces an untraditional word, δμῆσιν—that is not necessarily significant, but he uses it in an extremely awkward way. His attempt at innovation and improvement shows that he was free, too free, of the inherited instincts and restrictions of the natural singer. So too were the authors of the sentences 'among them they [*sc.* the gods] broke heavy strife', ἐν δ' αὐτοῖς ἔριδα ῥήγνυντο βαρεῖαν (xx. 55), and 'along his nostrils already keen might struck forward', ἀνὰ ῥῖνας δέ οἱ ἤδη / δριμὺ μένος προύτυψε (*24. 318*f.); and those who said of two eagles that they 'arrived to the heads of all', ἐς δ' ἱκέτην πάντων κεφαλάς (*2. 152*), meaning that they swooped low over the onlookers' heads, or who used phrases like 'put down the throat' (λαυκανίης καθέηκα, xxiv. 642) for drinking, or such clumsy locutions as *20. 23* ἐν πείσῃ, meaning 'obedient', or such pointless expansions of a formula as *15. 79* πολλὴν ἐπ' ἀπείρονα γαῖαν, 'over *much* infinite land'. The Odyssey has perhaps more expressions that are faintly ludicrous, like *11. 600* (of Sisyphus pushing the boulder) 'dust rose from his head', κονίη δ' ἐκ κρατὸς ὀρώρει, or *20. 13* 'his heart was barking within him', κραδίη δέ οἱ ἔνδον ὑλάκτει; although the Doloneia again can counter with a clear patch of the battlefield which 'showed through falling corpses', νεκύων διεφαίνετο χῶρος / πιπτόντων (x. 199f.), though it was night and no corpses whatever were falling. Obviously something like *fallen* was meant, though the manuscript tradition shows no sign of corruption and the phrase is curious even if a perfect form could be restored. There are other cases of extraordinary forms, like κούρητες meaning κοῦροι, twice in xix, or ἀνάκτεσιν (*15. 557*), φιλίων as a comparative (!) (*24. 268*), διδώσειν (*24. 314*), which suggest that we have no right to resort to emendation in all or many of these cases—that certain people connected with the creation or transmission of the Homeric poems were actually capable of using such strained and anti-traditional language. The last examples were single words, not phrases, but can be regarded as perversions of traditional formulas. More obviously so are the following cases in which a word is suddenly given a meaning absolutely different from its often-used traditional one, by an extension not so much bold as utterly insensitive: thus ἐπόρουσε means 'leapt upon', 23 times in a hostile sense in the Iliad; but at v. 793 Athene 'leapt upon' her favourite Diomedes, meaning she went to find him, and at 23. 343 sweet sleep 'leapt upon' Odysseus. Somewhat similarly ἐπιάλμενος, 'jumping on', is used of Odysseus embracing his father in the rather curious recognition scene at 24. 320 (p. 250), following immediately after the expression 'along his nostrils keen might struck forward' on which comment has already been made. Finally the verb ἐξαλαπάξαι, which is the standard word for sacking a city and occurs nine times, always in that sense, in the Iliad, is used in one extraordinary Odyssean verse (4. 176) to mean merely emptying a city of its inhabitants and removing them elsewhere, in peacetime, so as to offer accommodation for new immigrants.

The *distortion* of traditional language is sometimes associated with the *suppression* of a fixed word or phrase. Thus κούρητες at XIX. 248 is odd not only because it is a meaningless expansion of κοῦροι, but also because the standard expression (Ϝ)ελίκωπες Ἀχαιοί is here suppressed in favour of the untraditional (and in this case anti-traditional) novelty κούρητες Ἀχαιῶν. Yet the mere abandonment of a traditional locution—like the description of sea as γλαυκή instead of πολιή at XVI. 34—cannot be called anti-traditional, in my opinion, since the occasional modification of the traditional phraseology was something that took place throughout the oral period. It is only when familiar traditional phrases are utterly abused and misunderstood that we can conjecture a date at which the oral poetical tradition was seriously in decline.

The men who perpetrated many or most of the locutions cited above are unlikely in my view to have been true ἀοιδοί, creative oral poets, living when the oral tradition was still flourishing; for they have taken the traditional formular vocabulary and made out of it not the usual smooth and un-forced expression of any required idea but something that is not only unparalleled in the Homeric language but also positively alien to it, something which is strained, bizarre or on occasions almost meaningless. These are only some of the more extreme examples of anti-traditional language (see also p. 340). Special justification may be found for a few of them—that they are textual corruptions, or odd experiments—but this will not do for the great majority; and other examples can be found in the poems. Admittedly this is a dangerously subjective criterion and one that could be highly misleading if loosely or carelessly applied; but that does not detract from its value when properly handled. It will be noticed that many of the instances cited above come from sections of the poems which may be suspected on other grounds of being elaborations or expansions: the Doloneia and parts of the Diomedeia and funeral games in the Iliad, the Nekyia and the ending of the Odyssey. But they may also be found sporadically in apparently more traditional parts of the poems.

Such anti-traditional distortions must have been made for the most part by men who were closer to being rhapsodes than to being *aoidoi*, who were professional reciters of a fixed repertoire of famous poetry rather than minstrels able to improvise their own versions (see also pp. 318f.). There will inevitably be disagreement over particular instances, but I submit that the principle is correct: that anti-traditional language usually implies post-traditional composition. The composers of the Iliad and Odyssey came near the end of the active and creative oral tradition in Greece—indeed they probably unconsciously hastened its decline by producing poems great enough in quality and magnitude to provide a livelihood for the mere declaimer. Such a criterion is admittedly a poor substitute for absolute dates in the development of language, since it lacks precision and depends on a number of assumptions which are unprovable even if they seem highly probable. Until new linguistic evidence appears which provides fixed points for the development of Greek between 1000 and 650, our criterion seems to be the best there is.

That Greek *was* changing between these dates is beyond question, even if its changes cannot be securely dated. Verses created by the singers of these centuries, on the rare occasions when they went beyond the inherited language of song and introduced, perhaps unconsciously, modern usages from their own speech, will sometimes reveal new stages of linguistic development. These stages cannot be precisely dated or even set in relative order; but since they do not entail any necessary distortion or mishandling of the traditional oral apparatus there is no reason to think of them as post-Homeric or rhapsodic. Thus ὁ, ἡ, τό was originally a demonstrative pronoun, and remained so in the traditional language of the poems; on occasion, though, even in Homer, it is used as a pure definite article—its ultimate function in classical Greek—and in a number of other cases a transitional usage can be detected. This development evidently gained momentum after the Ionian migration, and we can probably say that unequivocal uses of the definite article (which was unknown to Mycenaean) came late rather than early in the oral period. Other developments, like the use of the short dative plural -οις or -ης for the normal Ionic -οισι(ν) and -ησι(ν), reflect not so much a general linguistic transition as the progressive adoption by epic singers of a useful licence. The same applies to the practice of keeping a vowel short before the combination of a mute and a liquid consonant; the name Ἀφροδίτη, for example, could not otherwise appear in dactylic hexameters. In all these cases it is easy to see which way the development or the licence is proceeding. The same is true of the use of abstract nouns. Language as it develops gradually concocts more and more abstracts; Mycenaean Greek probably had few, and the numbers grew steadily until there was an orgy of invention in the 6th to the 4th centuries B.C. Abstract forms derived from verbs or adjectives, like ὑποδεξίη, νεοίη, φύξις, σκέδασις, ἐπιφροσύνη, ἀλαωτύς are certainly commoner in the latest portions of the Homeric poems, like the Doloneia and the Nekyia, than in other and more traditional parts. Moreover the Odyssey as a whole shows a higher ratio of these later developments than the Iliad.[1] Yet they are to be found sporadically everywhere in the poems, even on occasion in what appear to be the most archaic contexts. Admittedly there is a tendency for these relatively late developments, as also for syntactical innovations like ὥς τε + infinitive = 'so that' (IX. 42, 17. 21) or μὴ οὐ after a verb of fearing

(x. 39), to come in contexts that contain other characteristics of relatively late composition or post-Homeric elaboration. It is tempting, therefore, to brand these usages as themselves relatively late in invention; and so some of them probably are. Yet it is important to remember that they provide an altogether less secure *terminus post quem* for their immediate contexts than more absolutely datable phenomena like contraction, or even anti-traditional phraseology, because their increase in 'late' passages may be due not to their own necessarily late invention but to the probability that some later oral composers were freer than their predecessors in introducing *any* kind of untraditional language.

If the various linguistic elements are disappointingly imprecise for the dating of different passages in the Iliad and Odyssey—and further work will probably produce some improvement in this respect—at least they provide exactly the kind of result that we should expect of an oral tradition. Indeed the nature of that kind of tradition confirms the difficulty of exactly distinguishing specific elements within it, whether they be cultural or linguistic, and of assigning them to different singers or even different generations.

10

STRUCTURAL ANOMALIES IN
THE ILIAD

O N E of the most obvious ways of demonstrating compound authorship lies in the careful analysis of narrative structure. If it contains inconsistencies or
illogicalities which cannot reasonably be accounted for by the
human failures of a single creator, but could have arisen through
the imperfect combination of contributions from two or more
different sources, then the conclusion must be accepted that the
whole work is not the original creation of one man.

Conclusions based on structural analysis are at least free from
the limitation of those derived from linguistic or cultural
diversity: namely that older elements in poetical language or
cultural background can often be explained as isolated
archaisms deliberately applied by later poets or even a single
later poet. In fact we found that linguistic and historical
diversity in Homer does nevertheless provide strong grounds
for assuming some stratification of authorship. Conversely the
analysis of plot and structure is evidently not without its un-
certainties and drawbacks. It has indeed been the main field
of dispute between Analysts and Unitarians, the former
attempting to show that the Iliad and Odyssey are inconsistent
with themselves at many critical points, the latter trying to
explain away these inconsistencies by arguing either that they
are the natural oversights of a single composer or that if
properly understood they are not inconsistencies at all. It may
be said of this dispute that most Analysts have been wilful and
unimaginative in claiming as radical inconsistencies many
divergences that might be explained in some other way; and
that most Unitarians have been obtuse both in refusing to

recognize certain obvious anomalies of plot and in their over-eager denunciation of inconsistencies between the Analysts themselves. At the same time it has become common ground between Analysts and many Unitarians that the Dolon episode in the Iliad, and the Nekyia and perhaps the ending of the Odyssey, which were the object of much critical suspicion even in antiquity, were probably not part of the 'original' large poems.

Conclusions based on the analysis of structure are not, then, so objective and so universally acceptable as one might hope. Moreover—and this is of the utmost importance, though I am deliberately not emphasizing this aspect in the present part— the conflicts of unity and diversity have now to be judged by what we know about the special characteristics of oral poetry. Even so, many of the old Analytical arguments about faults of structure in the two poems retain some force, even though they may not lead to the conclusions that Analysts have drawn from them; and the following pages contain a summary of the *major* inconsistencies as I see them in the plot of the Iliad and Odyssey. Nearly all these inconsistencies have been debated for many years, some of them from antiquity onwards; and what the critic can now contribute lies mainly in the rejection of uncertain examples, of which there are many, and the truer assessment of those that remain.

Broadly speaking the causes of inconsistency in oral poems can be reduced to four, of which the first is compatible with composition by a single poet, the second is unaffected by the number of composers, and the third and fourth, which may interact, presuppose contributions—perhaps in a very different ratio—by at least two poets.

(i) *Lapses of memory*. Minor errors from this cause occur in all kinds of literature and are particularly common in oral poetry, in which neither the singer nor his audience can check consistency in a continuously available text.

(ii) *Distortion in transmission*. With an oral poem it is often difficult to say where creation ends and transmission begins. To this extent there is some overlap between this cause and (iv). Yet if the Iliad and Odyssey each had a main composer, which is the conclusion to be reached in this book, then all oral recitals after their time, and the eventual recording of the poems in writing, count as transmission. An oral text is particularly prone to distortion in transmission; reasons have been given for thinking that degenerate singers and rhapsodes produced such distortion in Homer, which the first written texts were probably intended to curb (see especially ch. 9, §2 and ch. 14). Inconsistencies can have entered the text in the course of transmission either by the omission of material, or by unskilled elaboration at certain points, or by the use of variants which then entered the tradition as doublets, or by the creation or adaptation of special prologues for the separate recital of particular sequences.

(iii) *Conflation*. The conflation of, or inconsistent selection from, two or more earlier versions is an obvious source of imperfection, and is particularly easy in an oral tradition in which each singer tends to develop his own slightly different version of a particular theme. Often, too, a singer may conflate his own variant versions.

(iv) *Adaptation*. An existing poem may be inadequately altered or adapted in the production of a 'new' and personal version. This happens to some extent whenever an oral singer learns a new song. In a sense this is a special case of conflation, with only two authors, a prior and a posterior, immediately involved. Inconsistency can be produced by the interpolation of new material or the careless expansion of the old; or by its abbreviation, leading to the omission of vital connexions or of the beginning or end of a theme or episode.

Lapses of memory are usually unimportant affairs, like the resuscitation in a later book of a minor warrior killed off in an earlier one (for example Schedios, Pylaimenes, Chromios in the Iliad), or uncertainty whether a hero is in his chariot or out of it (Patroclus at XVI. 411 and 427, Diomedes at IV. 366 and 419); or as when the common troops are sent out of action, rather curiously, at XV. 305, but are still fighting and falling fourteen lines later. Such lapses are naturally commoner in the Iliad, with its mass of detail and hundreds of minor figures, than in the Odyssey. Sometimes, admittedly, a small anomaly of this kind could easily be caused by conflation or adaptation of some kind and not just by a temporary oversight: a case in point is the withdrawal of the common troops just mentioned, or when the Paeonians are 'with curved bows' and led by Pyraichmes at II. 848, but 'with long spears' and led by Asteropaeus at XXI. 155. This could represent a change of viewpoint or fresh invention, but there are so many divergences between the Achaean Catalogue in II and the rest of the Iliad that it probably has a more complex cause. Similarly the difficulty of deciding whether or not Odysseus and Diomedes are in a chariot, and if so whose, at X. 504 ff. may be due to lack of clarity in a single composer or it may suggest plural authorship of some kind. The point is that in such cases we cannot be sure, and so cannot necessarily infer composite authorship.

It is difficult to conjecture how far such lapses might extend; but the main composers of the Iliad and Odyssey were manifestly skilled, their obvious failures are few, and they are unlikely to have committed major structural errors unless under considerable provocation. Often, though, modern critics disagree about what constitutes a major error (one may also argue about how much 'provocation' is provided by monumental scale in itself). For instance Analysts have often picked out two remarks by Achilles in XI and XVI as proof that, when their contexts were composed, no embassy as it appears in IX can have been known. At XI. 609f. Achilles says 'Now I think the Achaeans will stand about my knees beseeching me', and at XVI. 72f. 'if lord Agamemnon had kindly feelings for me...'. Now this phraseology admittedly ignores book IX and its attempt at conciliation, but in my opinion it might be explicable either as a pardonable oversight by a single poet or even as a deliberate neglect by Achilles of offers which were unaccompanied by any frank admission of Agamemnon's highhandedness. Then at XVI. 83ff. Achilles tells Patroclus to sally forth to win glory for Achilles and regain Briseis with splendid gifts in addition. Here it is not particularly cogent to object that Achilles has already been offered the girl and the gifts, and refused them; for the situation has altered, the ships are in danger, Achilles changes his mind and decides to send out Patroclus—but he still wants Briseis back, and additional compensation too. The argument for multiple composition at this point has been put as strongly as possible by D. L. Page, *History and the Homeric Iliad*, pp. 307–12; but I remain sceptical. There *may* be a discrepancy, though that is a matter of opinion, and such a discrepancy *might* be caused by lapses of memory. That means that this particular incident should not be used as evidence for plural authorship, for which there is far better proof elsewhere.

Three times Achilles makes this complaint of Agamemnon: 'He has taken my prize and holds her, *himself having removed her*' (I. 356, 507, II. 240, cf. IX. 107, XIX. 89), ἑλὼν γὰρ ἔχει γέρας, αὐτὸς ἀπούρας. In reality Agamemnon did not remove Briseis in person, which is what the Greek clearly implies, but sent his heralds to do so, as indeed Achilles tells Thetis at I. 391. Can the expression 'himself having removed her' mean no more than that Agamemnon gave the orders and was responsible for removal? This becomes most unlikely when we observe that in instructing the heralds at I. 324f. Agamemnon tells them that if Achilles does not surrender the girl voluntarily 'I myself will take her in person', ἐγὼ δέ κεν αὐτὸς ἕλωμαι. Once the distinction has been made between removal by proxy and in person, all subsequent references to removal in person, if they cannot be accounted for as the mere repetition of a formula, are surely to be taken literally. So Achilles protests that Agamemnon took Briseis in person, when he did not in fact do so. The explanation of this anomaly can hardly be mere carelessness; a single poet inventing freely cannot have forgotten in the space of thirty-two lines that of the two methods of removing Briseis, by proxy or in person, Agamemnon adopted the former. On the other hand if the poet had in mind a version in which, for example, Achilles first refused to surrender the girl to the heralds and was later compelled to do so by the supreme king in person—a possibility envisaged in our poem—then the inconsistency becomes more understandable. Whether conflation or adaptation is the culprit we cannot say.

Consider now two cases of a grossly illogical turn of events. In book II of the Iliad Zeus sends a deceitful dream to Agamemnon, assuring him that if the Achaeans attack they will capture Troy (1–35). The king believes the dream and summons the council of chieftains. He reports his dream and concludes 'let us arm the Achaeans' (72); but then follows this extraordinary proposal—'but first I shall test them with words, which is the right thing to do, and shall order them to flee with the many-benched ships; and do you restrain them, from different positions, with words' (73–5). The army assembles and Agamemnon duly makes a long and convincing speech saying that they have failed and telling them to take to flight. The natural result of this direct order from the supreme commander is a headlong rush for the ships, which is only stopped by divine intervention working through Odysseus. Now Agamemnon's unheralded and quite senseless suggestion evoked no comment from other members of the council; and when the panic had been ended no mention whatever was made of Agamemnon's dream, either in answer to Thersites's strictures or in the morale-building speeches made by Nestor and Agamemnon himself. Yet at this stage the revelation of Zeus's message that Troy would fall that day should have been decisive. Would a single poet, creating freely, have introduced these anomalies, and would he have advanced the odd idea of the test of morale with such startling suddenness, only seeking to give it a spurious air of reasonableness with the incongruous formula ἣ θέμις ἐστί, 'which is the right thing to do'? I think he would not. On the other hand the superficial conflation or adaptation of earlier poetry might easily explain the situation— if, for example, Agamemnon's original suggestion came not as a prelude to an attack which he believed would be successful, but in a moment of real defeat and despair, as a development of the theme of his defeatism which is exemplified elsewhere in the Iliad (IX. 17 ff., XIV. 65 ff.).

The second case of an abrupt and improbable turn of events is seen in the formal duel in book VII. There had been one inconclusive duel already in III, followed by a treacherous breach of the truce by Trojan Pandarus. The Trojans are driven back in defeat, and then at the beginning of VII Hector issues a challenge to another duel. There is utter consternation among the Achaeans, and Agamemnon is especially apprehensive for his brother. The obvious solution for the Achaeans was to refuse the challenge, with the excellent excuse of Trojan treachery on the last occasion, and to press on with the general attack which was succeeding so well. But this does not happen, and Ajax is chosen by lot as Achaean champion. He lays out Hector with a stone-throw, but Apollo quickly gets the Trojan on his feet again (VII. 268 ff.). Now what will happen? "Then indeed they would have smitten each other at close range with swords' (273)—*if the heralds had not stopped the proceedings because of bad light*. 'Night is coming on', they say, 'it is good to obey night' (282)! Ajax says he will stop if Hector will, and so these duellers-to-the-death happily exchange pieces of equipment as souvenirs: a pretty piece of anti-climax, and almost inconceivable as untrammeled invention for a poem like the Iliad unless by a singularly mediocre poet. Here the explanation may not involve a lost version (though see pp. 284 f.), but may rather be that the duel in VII is based on the duel of Paris and Menelaus in III; like that duel it cannot end in a decisive win for either side, for that would bring the poem and the war to a premature end; but since III had already used the main incidents of any duel, and the obvious dramatic climax of the near-defeat of one contestant and his removal by a god, the author of the thematic variation in VII was reduced to a very poor second-best. Yet in this case the variation, inferior as it is in places (p. 330), might be by the same composer as the main thematic model.

Achilles's later ignoring of the embassy in IX might conceivably, as I have argued, be reconciled with creation by a single composer, but another famous anomaly in this book cannot. That is the inconsistency between the choice of three envoys to Achilles, namely Phoinix, Odysseus and Ajax (e.g. IX. 168 f.), and their approach to Achilles in the dual number— that is, with the special word-ending used in Greek for a *pair* of subjects:

τὼ δὲ βάτην παρὰ θῖνα πολυφλοίσβοιο θαλάσσης
πολλὰ μάλ᾽ εὐχομένω γαιηόχῳ ἐννοσιγαίῳ...
Μυρμιδόνων δ᾽ ἐπί τε κλισίας καὶ νῆας ἱκέσθην.

The two of them went along the shore of the boisterous sea,
both of them making many prayers to the earth-shaker...and
they both came to the huts and ships of the Myrmidons (IX.
182–3, 185).

They found Achilles, and 'the two of them went forward, and
divine Odysseus was leading' (192); Achilles greeted the pair of
them in three lines which contain four more dual forms (196–8).
What has happened to Phoinix here? He simply does not exist
in this part of the action: he was named as an envoy by Nestor—
unexpectedly, and without the required justification—and was
presumably briefed by him with the others (179); then he
quietly disappears, to reappear later in Achilles's hut, where he
makes a long and important speech and remains behind when
the others return to Agamemnon. Yet on the way to Achilles,
and in the first appearance of the envoys before him, Phoinix is
not there at all, in fact he is specifically excluded. This is an
unthinkable and impossible lapse for a single singer creating *de
novo*; it might be possible for an inferior Yugoslav *guslar*, but it
is out of the question for the highly competent, indeed brilliant,
singer to whom we owe this book of the Iliad, *if he were creating
freely*. If he were adapting or conflating earlier material at this
point then the lapse becomes understandable; Page put the
inevitable conclusion very clearly, 'that the large part played by
Phoinix in this embassy has been superimposed upon an earlier
version in which only Ajax and Odysseus were sent to plead
with Achilles'—though I do not feel that Page's subsequent
conclusions about authorship are really justified.[1] No attempted
explanation saves us from this conclusion, neither the un-
supportable argument that dual forms can stand for ordinary
plurals nor the easily refuted suggestion that Phoinix was
omitted here because he was not intended to be a full member
of the embassy.

After the unsatisfactory duel in VII Nestor proposed a truce to
bury the dead and build a wall and ditch round the Achaean

camp. It is odd that the Trojans allowed their enemies the time to build this vital fortification; but built it was and without comment (336ff., 435ff.). It has been a problem from antiquity onwards that as the fighting surges backwards and forwards across the plain the presence of this great wall is often ignored. Yet it was a formidable barrier which only fell to the tremendous attack that occupies the whole of xii. Now many cases where the wall is overlooked may be minor lapses in the narrative of a highly complex battle; yet the total absence of any mention of the wall throughout the whole of the eleventh book entails more than minor lapses. Dramatically we expect the wall to be emphasized here as a powerful factor, before its destruction in the next book. The Achaeans are routed by Hector and fall back toward the ships: 'Then there would have been ruin and irremediable deeds, and the Achaeans in their flight would have fallen among the ships...' (xi. 310f.)—no sign of their new defence and rescue, the wall and trench. Similarly Eurypylus tells Patroclus 'No longer will there be any defence of the Achaeans, but they will fall among the black ships' (823f.)—again the obvious 'defence', the wall, is utterly ignored. This strongly suggests that it had been introduced as a fresh motif to which certain stretches of existing Trojan poetry were not fully adjusted. Nestor's original suggestion of building the wall was cursory and odd, and was associated with the proposal that the burnt bones of the Achaean dead should be collected for carrying back to their children after the war. This custom is not only unparalleled in Homer, it is known from nowhere except Athens, and even there it probably began only in the 5th century (p. 180). Moreover at least one ancient text of the Iliad may have omitted the building of the wall *in the tenth year*, since Thucydides argued that the Achaeans must have won a battle immediately on arriving at Troy; otherwise, he says, they would not have been able to build the wall round their ships.[1] Athenian editors may or may not have had something to do with the events of our seventh book; but in any case it seems reasonable to conjecture that there had been at least two poetical versions of the Trojan fighting, in one of which the wall was an important factor and in the other of which it was not.

Another case where the singer seems to have imperfectly conflated two versions, or where an additional theme has been only incompletely assimilated, is Patroclus's wearing of Achilles's armour in XVI. Patroclus asks to borrow the armour (XVI. 40 ff.) in order that the Trojans may, for a time at least, mistake him for Achilles himself. Achilles grants the request, and Patroclus puts on the armour, without further reference to this disguise-motif. At 278 ff. the Trojans panic when they see Patroclus and Automedon gleaming with their weapons, thinking that Achilles has renounced his wrath (281 f.); but this does not necessarily mean that they mistake Patroclus for Achilles, for the latter must have relented even to allow Patroclus to fight. At 423–5 Sarpedon declares that he will face this man and find out who it is who is doing so much harm to the Trojans; the scholiast seems to be right in commenting that Sarpedon knows it is not Achilles but does not know if it is Patroclus. When Patroclus is finally stripped of his armour and killed there is no surprised recognition of him by the Trojans, and the arms are accepted as Achilles's without further comment. There is no glaring inconsistency in all this, merely a leaving of loose ends and a failure to work out a theme that has been foreshadowed. This is just the sort of thing that oral poets do, and it can be paralleled in many Yugoslav versions; but they do not do it as a result of free composition, but because they are conflating different songs or different versions of the same song. There is no need to look to textual corruption as the culprit, or to assume some kind of mechanical blunder by a redactor. This was the Analysts' cure; but in fact Homer himself could have sung XVI exactly as we have it, even with this slight imperfection. It is essential for our Iliad, of course, that Patroclus should have worn Achilles's armour, whether as a disguise or for some other reason, since on the loss of this armour depends the making of the new weapons for Achilles, and the marvellous description of the scenes on the Shield, in book XVIII; but it must be admitted that we hear little about the old armour once XVII is over and it has fallen into

Hector's hands. To some extent, therefore, the disguise-theme has been drawn in as a compositional expedient.

Minor inconsequences, which yet cannot easily arise from simple forgetfulness, are not infrequent in the Iliad. At XVII. 142 ff. the Lycian leader Glaucus accuses Hector of faint-heartedness and cynical neglect of his allies. Hector replies that he is not a coward, it was just that Zeus panicked him; let Glaucus stand at his side and he shall see what sort of fighter Hector is (170–82). We expect now to see the two warriors sally out together, but instead Hector egregiously bids the others to fight like men while he just slips away to put on Achilles's armour! Not long afterwards he is back, and Glaucus receives a mere passing mention along with others in an oddly insulting address to the allies: it is not for sheer numbers that he hands out gifts to them, Hector says, but to protect the Trojan women and children; let them therefore fight and if necessary die (220–8). Such minor inconsequences could be due simply to the difficulties of organizing a mass of material, though this seventeenth book bears certain marks of unusual expansion and adaptation. So does XXIV, in which for example Priam learns in a dream sent by Zeus that he must go to ransom Hector; 'And let not death nor fear trouble your mind, for such an escort shall follow with you, the Slayer of Argos' (181–2). Yet this important and comforting guarantee is utterly forgotten. Priam does not mention it to Hecuba when he tells her of the dream and defends his apparent rashness, and when, as he goes to face Achilles, he meets a delightful youth wandering about the Trojan plain in the middle of the night, who thereupon acts as his escort, it does not even occur to him that this may be Hermes in disguise. This inconsequence and other oddities in this book are due to some complex process of elaboration and conflation, which is confirmed in this case by linguistic evidence: see also pp. 320f.

In the last examples some kind of complex development is *probable*; let us return to the sphere of comparative certainty. At the beginning of XX Zeus encourages the other gods to join the fighting. They descend to the battlefield, and unusual

portents occur: Zeus thunders and Poseidon makes an earthquake that rocks Hades. Apollo faces up to Poseidon, Athene to
Ares, and so on; 'Thus went gods to face gods' (75)—and what
results? The hearer inevitably expects a description of their
collision; yet the inevitable does not happen—and the narrative
suddenly turns aside to Achilles and the human contestants.
Yet the sequel is not lost, at least for ever, for it turns up a book
later at xxi. 385 ff., where the prematurely prepared Battle of
the Gods at last takes place. The prologue and the battle have
obviously been torn asunder; they belong together and were
composed for continuous recitation. It is possible to see something of how this happened. Between the disrupted parts comes
the long and peculiar encounter of Aeneas and Achilles, filling
the rest of xx, and the brilliant battle between Achilles and the
river Scamander, filling the first half of xxi. This last battle ends
with Hera sending Hephaestus to burn up the river and make it
relinquish its fury. Hephaestus, then, is seen fighting against the
river-god. This seemed a good introduction to the clash of the
other, Olympian gods, and so the beginning of their actual
fighting is attached directly to the Hephaestus–Scamander
episode. But this meant cutting off the prologue, which could
not have been so attached. The prologue is then left (or placed)
in a more convenient position, and a new piece, the fight of
Achilles and Aeneas, is fitted in after it; two or three feeble
lines are then inserted which purport to explain why the gods
interrupted themselves (xx. 134, 154f.). That the displacement
occurred in some such way is shown by the end of the prologue,
for at 67 ff. the rival pairs of gods are as follows: Apollo and
Poseidon, Ares and Athene, Artemis and Hera, Hermes and
Leto, *Scamander and Hephaestus*. It is clear that Scamander does
not belong in these august circles, and his opposition to
Hephaestus is based on knowledge of the end of Achilles's battle
against the river. The couplet mentioning the last pair of gods
(xx. 73 f.) has probably been inserted at the very point of disruption by the singer who used the Theomachy proper as a
sequel to the river battle.

Another sign of complex creation is a marked change of

quality and relevance within the limits of a single episode. The funeral games in XXIII show such a change: the greater part of the narrative is excellent, but at 798 ff., in the descriptions of the fight in armour, the weight-put, and the archery contest, there is a lamentable decline. The idea of Ajax and Diomedes being encouraged to see which could first hit the other's fair skin (805) in a fully-armed duel is a curious one, even if we exclude with Aristarchus the next line which contemplates the victor 'touching innards through armour and black blood' (p. 205); and Leaf was right in saying that even this is not really much worse than the rest.[1] Equally unsatisfactory is the archery-contest, not least because of the two prizes the second is specified beforehand for the achievement of a million-to-one chance (which subsequently comes off, of course), the cutting of the string by which the target, a pigeon, is tethered to a ship's mast. Such miracles are common in some later non-Greek heroic traditions, but are foreign to the Greek taste. There is further support for regarding these particular episodes as added elaborations; for at the end of the chariot-race Achilles gave Nestor a prize of honour, since being old he could take no part in the contests—neither in the boxing, wrestling, javelin nor running contests (621–3). Now together with the chariot-race, which had just been concluded, this forms a list of those events which are adequately described, and excludes precisely the trio at 798 ff. which seem so objectionable. This could be due to chance; even so it stands out that 798–883 have been interpolated, leaving the javelin-contest and its graceful tribute to Agamemnon with its original function of rounding off the games as a whole.

Finally we return to two inconsistencies which are far wider in scope. The first of these is the adaptation of an earlier poem to form the Achaean Catalogue in II, and its incompatibility with much of the rest of the Iliad. That the list of Achaean naval contingents and their leaders at II. 494–759 is substantially an old poem superficially adapted to the march-past of the Achaean army in the Iliad is now widely though not universally accepted; see also pp. 154f. I do not myself incline to accept Jacoby's argument that the six similes which introduce the

Catalogue are incompatible with each other and point to a
disruption of the text caused by the insertion of an interpolated
passage, nor do I agree that some of the specific place-name
epithets in the Catalogue necessarily come from Mycenaean
poetry (pp. 117f.).[1] These are debatable matters: what is
certain is, first, that the Catalogue describes many details of
Greece as it had been before the full effects of the Dorian
invasion took shape; and secondly that it has been adapted to
its present place and function in the Iliad from a list of ships,
leaders and contingents as they gathered at Aulis, and perhaps
Halos, at the start of the Trojan expedition nine years earlier.
The first point is proved by the seemingly accurate references
to minor sites like Hyrie which were totally abandoned at the
end of the Bronze Age, and conversely by the absence of any
reference to Dorian Greece—to the existence of Megara or the
Thessaloi or to the special importance of Sparta, Corinth and
Argos. The Catalogue is based on a very old poem. The second
point, the subsequent adaptation of this old poem, is shown by
the cases of Protesilaus and Philoctetes. Neither of these heroes
was at Troy during the period covered by the Iliad, the first
because he had been killed as he leapt ashore nine years earlier,
the second because he had been abandoned in Lemnos on the
way to Troy on account of his poisoned foot. Yet both had
naturally been present in the original assembly of ships at
Aulis; so we find that in the Catalogue they are mentioned in
quite standard terms as leaders of their contingents, and that in
each case there is a somewhat awkward addition to explain that
the situation has now changed. Thus of Protesilaus: 'Those who
possessed Phylake and flowery Pyrasos...of them again was
warlike Protesilaus leader—while he was alive; but then
already the black earth held him...and a Dardanian man slew
him as he leapt from his ship...yet they were not leaderless,
though they mourned their leader; but Podarces marshalled
them...' (695–704). Incidentally the passages that explain
the substitutes for Protesilaus and Philoctetes are the only ones
in which the verb 'marshalled', κόσμησε, which applies to the
actual situation of the Iliad, is used.[2]

The discrepancies between the Catalogue and the rest of the Iliad are serious and exclude the possibility of a common author having invented the whole of both. The Boeotians are utterly unimportant in the rest of the poem but they are named first, and given the largest contingent, in the Catalogue. The contingents from the later Thessaly and from some of the islands are described in detail in the Catalogue, but the rest of the poem makes little use of them. Ajax, who like Odysseus brings a mere dozen ships, is dismissed in a couple of lines, and in general the great heroes of the Iliad are diminished in stature in the Catalogue. The kingdoms of Odysseus, Achilles and Agamemnon himself are much reduced in extent: Agamemnon's realm, for example, runs north to Sicyon and does not even include the Argive plain, which belongs to Diomedes. This may have had some historical truth but it is not the situation described and implied in the Iliad at large. In the ninth book Agamemnon offers Achilles the gift of seven towns in south-west Messenia (149 ff.); these towns do not appear in the Catalogue as his or anyone else's. All this is well brought out in Page's Iliad book, as also is the important truth that despite these divergences the overwhelming majority of characters in the Catalogue, even the least important, reappear in the rest of the poem, usually with the characteristics foreshadowed in the older document.[1] Page concludes that the functions of even the lesser heroes were already fixed in poetry about the Trojan war composed very soon after the war itself—this poetry was the common source of the Catalogue on the one hand and the rest of the Iliad on the other. Now for the major heroes this may be to some extent true. Yet there is another possible explanation of the points in common between the two, and one which does not aggravate the problem of their frequent divergence; and that is the obvious one that the main composer of the Iliad, possibly he who adapted the old Aulis-poem and incorporated it in his monumental epic, *sometimes used it as a source for his minor characters*, of which there had to be many. He did not extract details of the major heroes therefrom, since the oral tradition knew about these, and had already greatly expanded their functions and kingdoms—hence the inconsistency in this respect with the Achaean Catalogue. This seems a much more probable explanation of the facts than Page's hypothesis of detailed and widely known Trojan poetry, even about minor characters, in or very shortly after the Mycenaean period.

The second of the broader inconsistencies in the Iliad does not in itself entail compound invention. It is, in short, that the 'plan of Zeus' of I. 5, his decision and his solemn oath to Thetis to avenge the insult to Achilles's honour, is so very long in fulfilment. Achilles had asked that the Achaeans should 'be penned in round the sterns of the ships, near the sea, being slain' (I. 409f.). At the beginning of II, when Zeus sends the deceitful dream to Agamemnon, we believe that this request will soon be granted; but in reality Zeus's purpose is not achieved until the end of book XV. Until then the plan of Zeus is constantly thwarted or forgotten in a long series of large-scale diversions or interruptions. Of course, if Achilles's prayer had been granted at once, there would be no Iliad in the strict sense, no summation of the whole fighting round Ilios, but merely the story of Achilles's wrath and its consequences. It was surely legitimate for the main poet to insert new themes and digressions like the Achaean catalogue, the formal duels, the viewing from the walls, the *aristeia* of Diomedes, or the embassy to Achilles, to delay the progress of the main plot and give an impression of the war as a whole. It is of course unlikely that this poet was himself the inventor of all these digressions— probably he adapted some of them from pre-existing poetry. In fact we have already seen that the Achaean catalogue and the embassy, at least, contain the marks of contamination.

The inconsistencies in the Iliad vary in scope, violence and implication. I have excluded many old but ambiguous favourites of the Analysts; not all that remain are certainly the result of compound authorship, but some of them are, and they suffice to prove, what is already evident from the nature of oral poetry and the study of language and cultural background, that the Iliad is to some considerable extent a product of many generations of oral composition. More important, these anomalies indicate certain points in the narrative structure where earlier poetical versions have been used by the main composer, and others where he or some successor has elaborated his original large-scale plan. Sizeable expansions of one kind or the other obviously took place in the first half of the poem and in its last four books. There are other sections, too, even apart from the story of Dolon in x, which like the Beguilement of Zeus in books xiv and xv may be strongly suspected of independent composition or of considerable later elaboration—but where the criterion is difference in style or ethos or language rather than any serious structural incompatibility with their broader contexts.

11

STRUCTURAL ANOMALIES IN
THE ODYSSEY

THE Odyssey has a more complex structure than the Iliad and the opportunities for minor contradictions of plot are correspondingly greater. There are, however, a number of major inconsistencies too, and these have led to complicated Analytical hypotheses about the progressive adaptation and development of earlier narrative poems. Thus the ingenious author of a recent study, Merkelbach, posits an earlier vengeance-poem (R), an older Odyssey (A), a separate Telemachy (T), and a *Bearbeiter*, a reviser or compiler, (B). Von der Mühll (1940) used a slightly simpler scheme, but he and Bethe and Schwartz and Wilamowitz, going right back to Kirchhoff in the last century, all claimed to show exactly how the different chronological stages of the poem were combined.[1] Now I am not satisfied that any of these detailed accounts is correct; indeed my belief in a pre-eminent singer for the greater part of each poem is incompatible with most Analytical explanations. More important, I am not even satisfied that their unspoken main premise is correct—that our Odyssey is made from two or three or four major elements built up in a systematic and recoverable sequence. I am not convinced that there were two or three or four elements rather than twenty or thirty or forty. The oral tradition had presumably been expanding from at least the 11th century B.C. onwards, and there could have been literally hundreds of versions of the main themes of the Odyssey by the time the monumental composer started work— for *he*, as will be seen, is the one fixed element that we have to accept. How these versions must have reacted with each other and with him, and whether his immediate sources were poems of 500 or 3000 verses, we may never know. The old-fashioned Analysts, inspired with confidence that by the grace of God no problem is insoluble, have divided up the poem between hypothetical but sternly delimited composers and into different and determinable layers of composition; but none of their accounts is really convincing in detail. It is more profitable to reserve judgement on precisely how the components of the poem are to be distributed, and to admit that within an oral tradition this may be at many points indeterminable. That there are signs of major structural inconsistency, and that some of these presuppose a complex development *of some kind* from earlier and shorter versions to the monumental epic as it was eventually recorded in writing, is the foundation on which the Analysts built—and this at least, however baroque or flimsy the edifices they have imposed on it, may be accepted as solid. The survey which follows is rather long, but being cumulative in character it can be read selectively by those who wish. In it I implicitly criticize the attitudes both of extreme Unitarians and of extreme Analysts, and try to isolate those cases in which some kind of structural anomaly or exceptional compositional complexity has to be accepted by all parties. Only when the generic cause of such an anomaly is tolerably clear—chiefly the conflation of earlier materials by the main poet, or alternatively re-working by post-Homeric singers or rhapsodes—do I necessarily draw special attention to it at this stage.

The first sign of strain appears in *1*. This book is a skilful and effective introduction to the poem as a whole, but contains one great anomaly—the advice given by Athene to Telemachus when she visits him in the guise of Mentes at *1. 269–96*. Part of this advice is logical enough: that Telemachus should consider how to drive out the suitors, then call an assembly of the Achaeans and bid the suitors return to their own homes, then take a ship and go to Pylos and Sparta for news of his father; and, if eventually he learned that Odysseus were dead, he should return home and give his mother in marriage. The rest is rather illogical: first that before departing for Pylos he should send Penelope back to her father, *if she is eager to marry*, εἴ οἱ θυμὸς ἐφορμᾶται γαμέεσθαι (*275*), and her parents should arrange a wedding; and then that, after himself giving Penelope in marriage in the event that he discovered Odysseus was dead (and also, we must understand, if Penelope had not earlier wished to return to her father's home and marry from there), he should next consider how to slay the suitors in his halls. Now although the Odyssey gives a slightly inconsistent account of Penelope's treatment of the suitors (p. 232), the audience knows perfectly well that she is *not* burning to remarry; she is the very type of the faithful wife, and the second book describes the subterfuge of the Web by which she had laboriously delayed any such decision. Athene must know this as well as the audience; there is no chance that Penelope will be eager to rush off home to her father for another wedding, and no point in Telemachus making the proposal. In the event he does not do so; a similar proposal is indeed made, but by the suitor Antinous (*2. 113*f.). This happens in the debate called by Telemachus; and it is from passages in this debate that the greater part of Athene's advice in book 1 is compiled. As for the second inconsistency, that there will be no suitors left in the palace for Telemachus to kill, after he has married off his mother, this is a piece of clumsiness or carelessness which accords well with the second-hand style and the otiose language of its immediate introduction (*1. 293*f.), but is foreign to the rest of the opening book of the Odyssey. It confirms the inference that parts, at any rate, of Athene's speech to Telemachus have been re-edited in a careless and mechanical fashion in the light of the present form of the second book.

This conclusion was reached by Kirchhoff and is accepted, together with more dubious additions, by most Analysts. It is well and clearly put by D. L. Page in chapter III of *The Homeric Odyssey*. Now the reason why Athene's advice had to be re-composed is presumably that the debate as it now stands in *2* was inconsistent in some way with the original speech in *1*. From here on I do not follow Page, who thinks that *2* suggests two incompatible versions of how Telemachus gained a ship to go to Pylos: according to one account the suitors tried to prevent him, according to the other they did not. He considers, then, that Athene's original advice was that Telemachus should keep his Pylos plans secret from the suitors, and that this is what happened in the original form of *2*. But in fact there is no compelling sign of inconsistency in our *2*, the events of which can be understood quite logically: Telemachus asks the Achaeans for a ship (*2. 212*ff.), the suitor Leocritus comments that Telemachus's friends can help his journey, but that he, Leocritus, does not think it will come off (*259–6*); Telemachus prays to Athene complaining that the Achaeans delay his journey, the suitors most of all (*265*f.)—this is a little odd, but Leocritus's words can be taken as threatening in tone. Next Athene disguised as Mentor explicitly promises Telemachus that he (she) will prepare a ship, and bids Telemachus get provisions (*285*ff.); Antinous later salutes Telemachus with suspicious cordiality and says that after all the Achaeans *will* provide a ship (*303–8*), but Telemachus replies with a mixture of imprudence and cunning, first that he will destroy the suitors somehow, secondly that he will go to Pylos as a merchant and does not require a special ship (*310–20*). That Telemachus does not now want a ship has been taken as a grave inconsistency,[1] but is not so on the interpretation outlined above: for Telemachus is by now suspicious of the suitors, and he knows that his friend Mentor is preparing a ship for him—a fact which he does not want the suitors to discover, so he misleads them by saying that he will travel on an ordinary cargo-boat. A further inconsistency is said to be that the suitors do not at first regard Telemachus's journey as disturbing, but they later talk as though they had done their best to prevent it (e.g. *4. 663–6*). This, of course, is so, but the change comes after Telemachus has overtly admitted to them, at *2. 316*f., that he is planning their destruction. In this instance, then, a Unitarian defence may be correct; at least it is possible, and the Analytical critics are not justified in assuming a major inconsistency. The case provides an exemplar of the methods adopted by the two sides in the dispute; though often the Unitarian case is weaker and more forced than here, and the Analytical case rather stronger.

Thus all we can safely say is that Athene's advice in *1* has been to some extent remodelled, probably later than the main composer, on the basis of the present *2*, probably because *2* itself had undergone some alteration in detail at some indeterminable stage of transmission. The nature of this detail is hard to guess; it *might* have been the question of whether or not Telemachus kept his journey secret; or something to do with Penelope's behaviour to the suitors, since the story of the Web is strangely at odds with Antinous's assertion that she 'gives hope to all, and makes promises to each' (*2. 91*). At least the situation presupposes some complexity of authorship at this point. Why was *2* altered? It has been suggested that our version was expanded from a simpler account in the original monumental form of the poem, so as to form a special prologue to the Journey of Telemachus when this was chosen for separate recitation.[1] That is in many ways an attractive hypothesis, but it is only one out of several possible explanations of *2*. That the journey of Telemachus would have made a good piece for separate recital is obvious; in fact many critics have argued that the whole episode had an independent origin and does not belong to the true structure of the Odyssey. Against this hypothesis in its starkest form it has been observed that the interlocking of Odysseus's wanderings and Telemachus's journey in *14/15*, one of the points at which the mechanical difficulties of interpolation would be especially apt to show, is not only not awkward, but is exceptionally skilful.[2] It strongly suggests that a single singer formed both the journey of Telemachus and the wanderings of Odysseus as we have them—though as always with considerable help from traditional songs and traditional themes. The use of earlier poetry might explain the difficulty that Telemachus does not think of asking for help from Nestor, or especially from Menelaus, in getting rid of the suitors. That is something he had threatened at *2. 317*, and the tacit omission of this intention in the course of books 3 and 4 may suggest that the core of these books was not originally designed to fit the special circumstances of Telemachus as we find him in our Odyssey—or it may suggest merely that the monumental composer has done some simplification.

The beginning of book 5 is a clearer case. Something is seriously wrong: for the proceedings in divine assembly at the opening of the poem (*1. 26*ff.) are partially repeated here in contravention of epic practice. There it was decided to send Athene to advise Telemachus, and at the same time to send Hermes to Calypso with orders to release Odysseus from her island. First Athene's visit to Telemachus is described, with its consequences; these last until the end of *4*. Now the epic way of dealing with simultaneous events is to describe first one, then the other, as though they happened successively.[1] Therefore all that is needed or expected at the beginning of *5* is for the poet to say 'Then Zeus told Hermes to go to Calypso', looking back to *1. 84*f. The most that would be permitted in the way of reminder would be a verse or two to the effect that 'for so the gods had already decided'. Instead we have a scene that is not only unnecessary and contrary to epic practice, but also utterly ignores the previous assembly of the gods and the decision already taken there. The gods are made to go through the motions of deciding the whole thing again, and Athene holds forth about Odysseus's plight as though nothing of the kind had happened before. Moreover she does so in a speech (*5. 7–20*) compounded of three sentences, each of which is taken from a pronouncement made by a quite different character—Mentor, Proteus and Medon—in the preceding books. Page is surely right in finding this patchwork an abuse of the oral convention, based though this certainly was on the use and re-use of fixed lines and phrases.[2] The case need not be argued further: it is obvious, as few things are in this field, that the repeated divine assembly has been added by someone other than the main composer, who has assembled Athene's speech out of materials known to him from the opening books of the main poem. Here Page's hypothesis of a specially composed prologue is most attractive: the second divine assembly has been inserted by a poet who wishes to recite the wanderings of Odysseus, or part of them, separately, beginning from Calypso's island; therefore he wishes to show as briefly as possible how and why Calypso was persuaded to release her lover. The original 'Then Zeus told Hermes to go to Calypso', or whatever it was, was not self-explanatory; and the first divine assembly in *1* included the instruction that Athene should visit Telemachus, which was irrelevant to a separately recited selection from the Odyssey on the Wanderings of Odysseus. Thus a special short version of the original divine assembly was patched together.

In this instance we see that something resembling the typical Analytical concept of a *Bearbeiter*, a later and conscious re-worker or adapter, is difficult at one point to avoid. Yet this instance is not itself typical—though Analysts have been encouraged by it to think that they can apply the same panacea to most other anomalies in the poems. The conflation of different *pre-Homeric* sources, on the other hand, is conspicuous in the recital of Odysseus's adventures which occupies books 9 to 12. The two longer stories of the Cyclops and the Underworld show clear signs, in different ways, of multiple creation; but even the shorter tales suggest some divergence of composition. The encounter with the Kikones is treated in a compendious, imprecise, and uncharacteristically dull manner, and is immediately followed by a pointless storm at sea (*9. 39–73*); episodes like the Laestrygonians and Scylla and Charybdis imply abbreviation at certain points, and in the latter tale the initial distinction between the *Planktai* (the Clashing Rocks) and Scylla and Charybdis themselves is not observed (compare *12. 59* ff. and *201* ff.). Moreover the adventures fall into two separate groups, the one located on the eastern confines of the Greek world, the other either unlocated or implied to be in the west. One of the very few widely accepted discoveries of Homeric analysis is that made by K. Meuli that certain of these adventures are based on stories of the voyage of the Argo to find the Golden Fleece.[1] Consider the geographical implications of Odysseus's stories: first, after the Kikones incident on the coast of Asia Minor, his ships are driven south from cape Malea for nine days before they reach the land of the Lotus-eaters—which is presumably envisaged, therefore, as somewhere on the north

African coast (*9. 80–4*). The Cyclops island is not precisely located, and the island of Aeolus is a mobile one anyway. The Laestrygonians, however, are imagined as dwelling somewhere in the north (for such is the probable implication of *10. 82–6*), and their fountain is called Artacie like that of historical Cyzicus on the Propontis, in the north-east. Circe's island, Aiaie, is said at *12. 4* to be the place where the sun rises, and lies therefore in the east or north-east, and Circe herself is the sister of Aietes, prominent in the Argonautic legend as king of Colchis at the eastern end of the Black Sea. The Hades episode is located at the boundaries of Okeanos near the community of the Cimmerians (*11. 13*ff.), and thus somewhere in the far north; though at *10. 507* Circe said that the *North* wind would drive him there—a minor slip, perhaps. Next come the Sirens, prominent in later versions of the Argonautic poetry because of their musical contest with Orpheus, who was a member of the expedition. Even more plainly Argonautic in origin is the conception of the Clashing Rocks, with which Scylla and Charybdis are rather confusedly associated in the next episode; for at *12. 69*f. Argo is specifically mentioned as the only ship to have made that dangerous passage. Next Odysseus's ship reaches Thrinacie and the herds of Helios the sun—again the east, rather than the west, is probably envisaged; at least when Odysseus is cast back thence, past Scylla and Charybdis again, he is driven on for another nine days and reaches Calypso's island Ogygie, which is nothing to do with the Argonauts and appears to be imagined in the distant west. Thus the first four adventures and the final arrival at Ogygie seem to have been added at the beginning and end of a nucleus of episodes based on legendary accounts of the Argonauts in the Black Sea region; and the longer Hades episode has been inserted, not quite smoothly as will be seen, into the whole amalgam. No doubt the Argonautic stories were derived from earlier poems on this subject, as probably were most of the other adventures, even those with a strong folk-tale element; but some were probably quite extensively re-worked by the Homeric poet, and stylistically they are very homogeneous—with the exception of palpable additions in the Nekyia, the underworld episode.

It is superfluous to go through the slight inconsistencies of the Cyclops story and their causes, since they have been dealt with in the first chapter of D. L. Page's *The Homeric Odyssey*. To take a fresh minor instance, the golden-age/noble-savage motif has been conflated with the theme of the outwitting of a lawless giant, with the consequence that in one place the Cyclopes are said to gather their crops without labour, 'trusting in the immortal gods' (*9. 107*), while at *9. 275*f. Polyphemus roundly declares that they pay no heed to Zeus or the blessed gods. Other slight inconsistencies in the description of the Cyclopic social structure have been produced by grafting the Οὖτις or No-man folk-theme on to the main blinded-giant theme. The accretion of themes produces just this type of minor inconsistency, which is not caused just by chance or simple human frailty but reveals the complexity of the whole legendary and poetical tradition.

The underworld tale that fills the eleventh book is not derived from the Argonautic tradition. On to the main conception of a Νεκυομαντεία or consultation of an oracle of the dead have been grafted typical elements of a Κατάβασις or descent into Hades, a type of poem later rather common and of which the hero was often Heracles, who according to legend went down to Hades and attacked both Cerberus and Pluto. Discrepancies in the Odyssey version may be divided into two classes: those due to rhapsodic expansion after the main part of the epic was complete, and those caused earlier when the basic underworld episode was inserted into the main narrative of the adventures. The most obvious later expansion is *11. 568–627*, which was counted as spurious by Aristarchus; for in this section Odysseus's position at the threshold of Hades, to which all the other ghosts have been attracted by the smell of blood, is suddenly ignored, and he is imagined as strolling around in the underworld itself and viewing Minos, Orion, Tityus, Tantalus and Sisyphus performing their traditional tasks there; while the description of Heracles confirms the impression that part of a later κατάβασις poem has been inserted, with little regard for Odysseus's needs and circumstances, at this point. At the end of the section Odysseus is suddenly found back by his trench. Another addition is the list of heroines who present themselves before Odysseus, irrelevantly and at considerable length, from 225 to 330. The first five of these women all have strong Boeotian, or at least Aeolic, associations; and this immediately suggests, what the surviving fragments of Hesiod's *Catalogue of Women* tend to confirm, that we are dealing with an insertion based upon, or taken direct from, the typically Boeotian genre of catalogue poetry, probably from Hesiod himself. Certainly there is no reason to think that this list of heroines is the work of the main poet of the Odyssey.

The Iliad too shows some Boeotian influence, notably in the Catalogue of Ships; but the implication need not be that all Boeotian passages in Homer are as old as the oldest parts of that Catalogue, but rather that there was a strong Boeotian school of oral poets, culminating in Hesiod and his followers, and that their versions were able at different periods and in different ways to make some impact on the Ionian epic. Even Teiresias, of course, is Theban (e.g. *10. 492*); if we argue that he too is a later addition then we argue away the whole of the Odyssean underworld scene, the whole of the eleventh book, which has been accepted as one of the chief glories of the Odyssey from antiquity onward—for Teiresias is essential to that book, and provides the only motive, albeit one not well worked out in the event, for Odysseus's journey to the borders of Hades. Indeed in the summary account of his journey to the world of the dead which Odysseus gives Penelope at *23. 322* ff. he only mentions seeing Teiresias, his own former companions, and his mother. Now the Teiresias oracle was an ancient one; such oracles were known in the old territory of mainland Greece—especially, moreover, in Boeotia—and not, with one or two doubtful exceptions, in the newer lands of Aeolis and Ionia. It is not surprising, then, that this Boeotian figure, perhaps already well-established in the North Mycenaean poetical tradition, should be taken over by the Ionian poets.

Teiresias gives two important pieces of information: that Odysseus will find trouble when he returns to Ithaca (this Odysseus seems to ignore), and that before he can finally settle down he must undertake the mysterious last journey inland, carrying an oar, until he meets someone who dwells so far from the sea that he thinks it is a winnowing-fan. There Odysseus is to plant it and sacrifice to Poseidon. Now this journey, odd as it may at first appear, implicitly contains an excellent motive— the appeasement of that wrath of Poseidon which is a recurrent theme of the Odyssey. Odysseus is to carry a symbol of Poseidon's domain, the sea, to a place where it—and presumably Poseidon himself—has never been heard of; there he is to sacrifice to the god and so, perhaps, make Poseidon's name known there. Then at last he can return home to face old age, and death finally from the sea—a reference we cannot properly understand, but which again may be connected with Poseidon. If that really is the motive of Teiresias's prophecy, then it is not adequately brought out, and we must assume that the episode has been abbreviated and somehow adapted from an earlier story. Yet that story presumably concerned Odysseus. Analysts like Merkelbach assume that there were earlier and shorter Odysseus poems which were used and expanded by a later poet; and I agree with them that some of the source-material used by the monumental poet must already have concerned Odysseus himself. In the case of the meeting with Teiresias the original point of the prophecy has been omitted or obscured, to be replaced by an ostensible point (the gaining of information about Odysseus's immediate movements) which is not consistently observed. The recondite quality of Teiresias's prophecy in its Odyssean form intrigued later singers and rhapsodes and ultimately led to the tale of Odysseus's Thesprotian adventures and the *Telegony* composed by Eugammon of Cyrene somewhere near the middle of the 6th century B.C. It is conceivable that the ending of our Odyssey, from *23. 297* onwards, is derived from these later poems, which were themselves based on hints or apparent lacunas in the Homeric version; but the arguments of Merkelbach and others, that integral parts of the story of

Odysseus as given in our Odyssey, even apart from the ending, must be subsequent to Eugammon, seem to me to have very little force.[1]

Nevertheless there are difficulties in the relation of the underworld episode as a whole, minus its obvious elaborations, to its surroundings. First, although Odysseus was sent by Circe specifically to get instructions from Teiresias on the next stages of his return home, in fact he learns very little from Teiresias on this subject, and in any case Circe herself repeats this little, together with more of her own, early in the twelfth book after Odysseus's return from Hades. Secondly, the interlude from *11. 333* to *384*, during which the tale of adventures is interrupted and the poet describes a conversation between Odysseus and his Phaeacian hosts, ignores the elaborate preparations made earlier for Odysseus's departure that night, and contains no good motive for a delay so tortuously imposed. Thirdly, the account of Elpenor's death by falling off the roof of Circe's palace, at the end of book 10, seems designed to disguise the weak motivation of the whole underworld episode, by specifically linking Odysseus's actions just before his journey to the borders of Hades with what he finds when he arrives there. The description at *10. 551* ff. certainly reveals a strained and unnatural composition: Elpenor's death is ignored by Odysseus and the rest of his comrades in a most odd way—they cannot stop because business presses, which is not really true; and when Odysseus meets the dead Elpenor in the next book he seems not to know how he had died—the feeble line *11. 58* is best explained as a later attempt to meet this difficulty. In fact the narrative of Elpenor's death at the end of *10* is derived and adapted from the explanation later offered by the dead Elpenor in *11*, just as Circe's account of what Odysseus must perform to raise the dead is derived from the narrative of what Odysseus later did.[2] Neither case is consistent with a poet freely and progressively developing his own narrative; both cases show that a pre-existing poem on Odysseus consulting the dead has been inserted into a broader account of his adventures, and has been used for the provision of anticipatory passages designed to link the two together. The Phaeacian intermezzo in *11*, incidentally, probably had the same aim of integrating an originally independent story with the action of a larger Odyssey.

The possibility remains, of course, that the singer of the originally independent underworld poem was the same as the composer of the monumental poem—that this composer used an earlier piece from his own oral repertoire as an element of his more ambitious later conception. Something similar must certainly have happened with many other episodes, in both Iliad and Odyssey, in which the inconsistencies with the surrounding poetry are both minor and more or less mechanical. Yet even the originally independent short poem may itself have been taken over and expanded or conflated from earlier poetical versions. There are *hundreds* of possibilities in this kind of situation, and it is misguided, if ingenious, to attempt to assign definite originators, definite elaborators (apart from broad distinctions between rhapsodic and pre-rhapsodic and so on), and definite relationships between them.

The action in Ithaca from *15* onwards is attended by new difficulties. First is the problem of Theoclymenus, the only character in the Iliad or Odyssey—with the possible exception of Phoinix—whom one feels to have arrived there almost by mistake. Theoclymenus is a prophet who has fled from Argos because of an unspecified manslaughter; he meets Telemachus when the latter is on the point of setting sail back from Pylos to Ithaca, and asks to be taken along. Theoclymenus's ancestor Melampus is described, though with some confusion, but he himself remains an obscure and unmotivated figure. The manner of his initial question to Telemachus (*15. 260–4*) has justifiably been characterized as ludicrous. Then when the ship arrives at Ithaca Theoclymenus asks whose hospitality he is to seek, since Telemachus is not returning immediately to the palace. Telemachus at first suggests Eurymachus, the best respected of the suitors (*15. 518*ff.)—a suggestion which has been found absurd, especially since Telemachus shortly afterwards (*540*) turns to his friend Peiraeus and, with no further reference to Eurymachus, bids him look after the stranger. The whole passage is admittedly awkward, though not intolerably so for oral poetry. Yet the entertainment of this refugee *is* something of a problem, since the suitors virtually control the palace. Why not let one of them take on the responsibility of entertaining him, then? This is Telemachus's first thought; but then Theoclymenus ingratiates himself by the favourable interpretation of an omen, and Telemachus immediately makes more definite and more hospitable arrangements for his protégé. In fact the omen is much queerer than the question of Theoclymenus's host. A hawk flies past from a favourable quarter, plucking the feathers out of a dove the while. The feathers fall between Telemachus and his ship; Theoclymenus draws Telemachus on one side and says that he has recognized the event as a portent (as though it were not obvious!), whose meaning is that Telemachus's race is most kingly of those in Ithaca and always strong (*15. 533–4*). Now Homeric omens normally have some detectable relation to the interpretation offered for them; this one has none, and the interpretation is in addition both weak and vague. Next, in book 17, Telemachus, after some pointlessly cool behaviour to Penelope, sends for Theoclymenus to the palace. The prophet's sole positive action in this book occurs when he interrupts Telemachus and his mother to declare that Odysseus is already in Ithaca preparing vengeance,

> οἷον ἐγὼν οἰωνὸν ἐϋσσέλμου ἐπὶ νηὸς
> ἥμενος ἐφρασάμην καὶ Τηλεμάχῳ ἐγεγώνευν,

as I interpreted the omen, sitting on the well-benched ship, and shouted to Telemachus (*17. 160f.*).

The second line here is a particularly awkward one, and the claim does not accord with the prophecy in *15*, which implied no more than that Telemachus's race would remain kings in Ithaca.

Theoclymenus's final appearance is in book 20, when the suitors are suddenly driven hysterical by Athene, leading him to declare that they are enveloped in darkness, that there is groaning, and blood sprinkled on the walls; that the hall is full of ghosts on their way to Erebus, the sun has gone from the sky and an evil mist has risen (*345–57*). Finally he leaves and returns to Peiraeus's house, prophesying imminent doom for the insolent suitors. Now the vision of blood and darkness is absolutely unique in Homer, for whom prophets are interpreters of signs and not Cassandra-like possessors of second sight. However dramatic it may be—and it *is* dramatic—the scene is alien to the spirit of the Homeric epos, and like the other Theoclymenus passages it abounds in strained and clumsy locutions. It is doubtful whether it, and the preceding actions of Theoclymenus in the poem, justify his presence there on purely structural grounds. There is no obvious sign that he was a traditional element in the Odysseus story or any of its possible predecessors; though it has sometimes been suggested that in some other version of the returning-warrior theme he might have represented Odysseus himself in disguise.[1] At all events in our version this explanation, if it ever applied, must have been entirely suppressed or forgotten, since Theoclymenus and Odysseus are simultaneously present in the hall of the palace in book 20. The most that can be concluded with safety is that Theoclymenus cannot have been conceived by the main poet especially for his part in the monumental Odyssey; he is an intrusive element, though when and why the intrusion was made we cannot tell. The intrusion may have taken place after the earliest large-scale version of the Odyssey had already been achieved. If so it has few possible parallels in the Odyssey, on such a scale and in relation to a new subject—except for the added ending which will be considered shortly; and there the matter is one of appending not inserting, and consequently simpler.

Two other traditional stumbling-blocks are Odysseus's disguise and the removal of the arms. That there are inconsistencies in each case is undeniable, yet I disagree with Analytical critics from Kirchhoff to Page and would classify these inconsistencies as minor ones, possibly caused not by the mechanical juxtaposition of incompatible versions but by changing intentions on the part of a single main poet—who may of course have known

different versions of his theme. At *13. 429*ff. Odysseus is transformed by Athene into an old man; he is given a quite new
physical appearance, and has to be changed back again before
Telemachus can accept him as his father, and then transformed
once again so that Eumaeus shall not recognize him (*16. 172*ff.
and *454*ff.). After this, however, the poet seems entirely to
forget that Odysseus is impenetrably disguised by divine means,
and that he needs changing back once more: the hero goes un-
recognized simply because of his beggar's clothes and because
he is older by twenty hard years than when he was last in
Ithaca. Admittedly Athene casts a special radiance over him
after his bath, at *23. 156*ff., just as she did after his bath in
Phaeacia; but this is less specific than removing the wrinkles
and restoring his hair as at *16. 175*f. Now this seems to me to be
a minor inconsistency, such as any oral poet might perpetrate
and any oral audience accept, particularly in a large-scale
poem. It is not of the same order, and does not carry the same
implications, as for example the inconsistencies in the visit to
the underworld. The same could be true of the notorious
difficulties over the removal of the arms from the hall of the
palace. At *16. 281*ff. Odysseus in Eumaeus's hut concocts a plan
with Telemachus. Odysseus will nod, and at this secret sign
Telemachus is to remove all the armour that was hung up on
the walls of the *megaron*, making appropriate excuses to the
suitors. As an afterthought Odysseus instructs him to leave two
sets behind. This is planned: what happens? The suitors go off
to bed at the end of *18*, unexpectedly leaving Telemachus and
the disguised Odysseus alone in the hall. There is now no need
for Odysseus's secret nod, since the opportunity has arisen for
them both to remove the arms without difficulty. No reference is
made to the plan formed earlier, though Odysseus's words in the
event (*19. 4*ff.) are derived from those of the plan; as is natural
enough in an oral poem. Here, however, there is no afterthought about leaving two sets of arms for themselves, which
almost leads to disaster later; on the other hand Odysseus
repeats in full the excuses to be offered to the suitors. The need
for these excuses is no longer so obvious, since the suitors are

not present while the armour is removed; but excuses will presumably be needed when the absence of the arms is noted on the next day—though as it happens the suitors notice nothing until the time for excuses is past. In fact one excuse is required forthwith, not for the suitors but for Eurycleia (*19. 18–20*). Now there is no inconsistency in all this which might not be explained by change of circumstance in the plot and by the normal lapses of the memory-poet. One poet could have invented the plan in *16* and subsequently departed from its details because he later decided to leave Odysseus alone in the hall with Telemachus. Indeed the suitors' decision to leave them is specially emphasized at *18. 420*f.—the poet's real motive, of course, being so that Odysseus and Penelope can talk together later that night. If the main poet decided on this last refinement, which is not essential to the plot, when he came to this part of his story, then he would naturally make a slight but important alteration of Odysseus's plan to remove the arms. The ancient critics marked one passage or another as spurious; but this remedy does little to heal the present case (unless the afterthought about leaving two sets of armour is a later addition, though it is hard to see why it should be), and the confusion, such as it is, in unlikely to have arisen later than the time of the main poet. Modern Analytical editors have likewise been tempted to excise, especially since many of them have thought that Athene's lamp at *19. 34*, during the actual removal of the arms, must belong to a later cultural background than that of the Homeric epic as a whole and thus betoken a later insertion in this episode (but see p. 185).

Let us pass to a more difficult problem. In the curious 'second Nekyia' of book 24 the ghost of Amphimedon tells the dead Agamemnon how the suitors come to be in Hades. In two matters his account differs significantly and surprisingly from the main narrative. First over the web woven by Penelope and secretly undone each night: the implication of what Antinous tells Telemachus at *2. 87*ff. is that Penelope had been found out some considerable time before, and since then had been employing other delaying tactics. At *24. 147–50*, however, Amphimedon is explicit that, immediately after Penelope had finished the web, Odysseus arrived in Ithaca. This chronology is more logical, more dramatic, and more consistent with other versions of this common folk-tale motif. Yet in the main narrative of the poem it has been contradicted or at the very least obscured. Apart from the second book the story is recounted by Penelope to the disguised Odysseus at *19. 137* ff., in words which seem to be derived from *2* and may have been absent from many ancient copies, and which in any case do not absolutely exclude Amphimedon's chronology. The inconsistency, then, is between *24* and *2*, between Amphimedon and Antinous. Yet Antinous's speech is confused, and the confusion could be due to later re-working: first he says that Penelope has been deceiving the suitors for nearly three years, and the fourth is at hand (*2. 89*f.); then he adds that she devised this other deceit, namely the web, which was kept up for three years and found out in the fourth. The deceptively similar time-interval may suggest a mechanical and localized expansion, but even so such expansion would have been impossible if the monumental poet had stressed that Odysseus arrived in the nick of time, once the web-stratagem had failed, as clearly as Amphimedon stressed it. There *is* an inconsistency here, then, but it need not be a very extensive one.

The second matter is more serious. At *24. 167*f. Amphimedon stated that Odysseus 'cunningly bid his wife set up for the suitors bow and grey iron',

> αὐτὰρ ὁ ἧν ἄλοχον πολυκερδείῃσιν ἄνωγε
> τόξον μνηστήρεσσι θέμεν πολιόν τε σίδηρον.

In fact, of course, this is not at all what happened in the poem: Penelope suddenly decides to arrange the contest of the axes *before* she has recognized Odysseus—she tells him of her intention, and he approves, but there is no other collusion whatever (*19. 571* ff., *21. 1* ff.). Now it is true that Amphimedon was not a party to what went on between Odysseus and Penelope, and might have wrongly inferred collusion between them, after his death. But this is not a likely explanation of the inconsistency. Moreover there are other signs in the Odyssey that another version existed, and left its mark on the main poet, in which the contest of the bow and axes was arranged jointly between Odysseus and Penelope and in which Penelope recognized her husband at a much earlier stage than in the surviving poem. First the odd episode at *18. 158*ff., where she is inspired by Athene to act provocatively towards the suitors and so become 'more honoured than before by her husband and son' (*162*). If Odysseus had not yet revealed himself his natural reaction to this performance would be one of resentful suspicion; instead we are told that he 'rejoiced because she was eliciting gifts from them and charming their heart with soothing words, *but her mind was eager for other things*':

γήθησεν δὲ πολύτλας δῖος 'Οδυσσεύς,
οὕνεκα τῶν μὲν δῶρα παρέλκετο, θέλγε δὲ θυμὸν
μειλιχίοις ἐπέεσσι, νόος δέ οἱ ἄλλα μενοίνα (*18. 281–3*).

Secondly Odysseus's insistence in the next book that if his feet are to be washed by a servant it must be by an aged retainer. This almost inevitably means Eurycleia, who will certainly recognize his scar. That is what in fact happens—yet it is not what Odysseus is depicted as wishing to happen, for at *19. 388–91* he turns his face into the shadow and fears Eurycleia may recognize him. Why then did he so carefully specify an old retainer? Probably, as has often been conjectured, for the precise purpose of being recognized and so declaring himself to Penelope during their nocturnal conversation. Thirdly Penelope's announcement of the trial of the bow, at the end of that conversation, is utterly illogical. Evidence has been accumulating all that day that Odysseus is near at hand. She may not believe Telemachus, Theoclymenus, or the disguised Odysseus, but she has just related to the last of these a recent and perspicuous dream which clearly portends the very same thing—that her husband is near and will destroy the suitors. Admittedly she thinks this dream may be false, but it would be very welcome to her and Telemachus if it were not (*19. 568*f.). She envisages the possibility, then, that it is not false; so why does she proceed in the very next line, apparently without special reason, to

announce a contest which will result in her immediate acceptance of one of the suitors? This is a serious illogicality which
supports the probability that an earlier version, in which the
contest was arranged in full collusion between husband and
wife, has been extensively but inadequately remodelled by the
large-scale composer. Lastly, when the suitors have failed to
string the bow, Penelope herself insists at surprising length that
it should be given to the stranger to try—a poorly motivated
insistence if she really thought him a humble stranger (*21.
312*ff.).

The poem contains other and less conspicuous signs of a pre-
Homeric predecessor which differed in certain important
respects: for example there are occasional and surprising
references in our poem to a real tension between Penelope and
Telemachus, and she tells the disguised Odysseus at *19. 533*f.
that Telemachus implores her to leave the palace (to remarry,
that means), since the suitors are devouring Telemachus's
possessions. In the earlier version, then, *everything* conspired to
force Penelope to remarry: the suitors themselves, the discovery of the web-stratagem, the hostility of Telemachus,
pressure by her parents (cf. *19. 158*f.). At the eleventh hour
Odysseus reveals himself, compounds with her the axe-contest
which will put bow and arrows into his hands, and removes
the weapons from the hall in preparation—all of them, no
doubt, for in this lost version it seems that all the suitors were
killed by arrows. In the description of the slaughter, brilliantly
done in our twenty-second book, it is probable that the expansions by the monumental poet have improved on his earlier
sources; but one cannot help suspecting that his other alterations have weakened the impact of a simpler and more powerful
plot.

Though the situation is by no means clear, and though other
explanations might be found for one or two of the difficulties I
have described, it remains that there are some surprising
illogicalities in books 18 to 21, especially in connexion with
Penelope's relation to Odysseus and the preparations for the
contest. These are unlikely to be random inconsequences due to

the unmotivated lapses of a single composer, since they have one quality in common: that they cease to exist once it is assumed that Odysseus makes himself known to Penelope before the planning of the contest and the removal of the arms. Such is the version presupposed by Amphimedon in *24*, itself not an earlier but a later component—which raises questions of its own about the transmission of different versions (see also p. 311).

'Aristophanes and Aristarchus make this the end of the Odyssey': that is the scholiast's comment on *23. 296*. So far as book 24 is concerned it is hard not to agree. From our point of view the poem ends perfectly naturally at the point indicated by the ancient critics, whose judgement is important if not decisive. The suitors are dead, and Odysseus and Penelope, recognized and reunited, renew the old bond of love. This reunion is the real climax of all the agony and frustration of Penelope and all the obstinacy and hardships of Odysseus, who rejected immortality itself for the hope of returning home. Athene's holding back of the dawn, Odysseus's confession of the eventual necessity for his last journey, Penelope's acceptance and the resort to bed, all these make an excellent ending. Yet one problem remains: how is the blood-guilt for the death of the suitors to be purged? What of the dead men's relatives outside the palace—how are they to be reconciled? To an audience of the classical age this would have seemed an immediate and extremely conspicuous problem. To an audience of the 8th or early 7th century it must have been no less obtrusive. It is just conceivable that it was never explicitly resolved; that it was simply assumed that the resourceful Odysseus, openly aided by a goddess and supported by all his retainers, would easily have overcome the difficulty. It is more probable, however, that the original monumental poem contained some reference to the problem—perhaps no more than a line or two to the effect that Athene would reconcile the relatives. If so, the reference has been removed in favour of an elaborate and miscellaneous addition—and an insertion even before the point at which the version favoured by Aristarchus ended; for *23. 117–52*, at least, looks forward to specific treatment of the problem of the suitors' relatives. In fact line 110 could lead straight on to line 177, with considerable improvement.

What happens in the part of the poem implicitly condemned by Aristophanes and Aristarchus? First of all, lying in bed, Odysseus summarizes his adventures for Penelope (*23. 310–41*)— a piece of indirect narrative unparalleled in Homer, the content of which, though natural enough in the assumed circumstances, serves no purpose for the audience of the poem as a whole. It reads almost like a rhapsode's mnemonic, or more plausibly like a prelude to a special recitation of the events after the departure from Calypso; or perhaps it belonged to the version in which Odysseus was recognized by Penelope before the trial of the bow. Yet there is no absolutely compelling reason for classing it as a post-Homeric addition. The last 29 lines of the book are more doubtful: Athene pointlessly hastens the dawn, Odysseus makes an odd speech to Penelope and announces his intention of visiting Laertes in a forward reference to *24*. Language is surprising as well as plot, at least in the case of ἠριγένεια used as a noun to mean 'dawn' in *347*, although its traditional and otherwise universal use is as one of the standard *epithets* of dawn; and of ἐπιτέλλω so pronounced in *361*. Book 24, however, provides more striking departures from the apparent tradition. It opens with an extraordinary scene, Hermes escorting the dead suitors to Hades. *Kyllenian* Hermes, the White Rock, the Gates of the Sun, the Community of Dreams—these accessories are absolutely unique in Homer, though we should certainly expect to have heard of some of them in the eleventh book.[1] On arrival the suitors witness a long discussion between Achilles and Agamemnon, who are strangely assumed not to have met before in Hades; the latter describes the former's funeral, the details of which, on the traditional assumption about the dead, would be known to Achilles himself. The whole meeting, though interesting enough, is utterly irrelevant to the Odyssey and to the suitors. Then comes Amphimedon's explanation to Agamemnon of the suitors' presence, an explanation which is rational except that it does not accord with the preceding poem. Suddenly the story switches back to Odysseus (*24. 205*), who finds Laertes in the fields; but instead of identifying himself it seemed better to the cunning hero 'first to test him with taunting words', πρῶτον κερτομίοις ἐπέεσσιν πειρηθῆναι (240). This bizarre plan soon drives the old man to tears; though Lord has shown that recognition-scenes in oral poetry often demand this kind of initial deception.[1] The whole scene is full of sudden transitions and untraditional details, while much of the language is positively anti-traditional: so οὐκ ἀδαημονίη σ᾽ ἔχει with the infinitive at 244, the position of ἔνεκ᾽ in 251, φιλίων as a comparative in 268, διδώσειν in 314, the phrase 'along his nostrils already keen might struck forward', 318f. (see p. 206). Next Odysseus and his father return to the latter's hall, where there is some desultory conversation with the aged servitor Dolios, third of that name in the poem—incidentally Laertes is no longer the poor recluse of 1. 189-93, but has a whole family of servants to look after him and his prosperous farm.[2] A rustic repast is served; back near the palace the relatives of the suitors look after their dead, and the ancient Eupeithes persuades one group of them to seek vengeance. Athene addresses Zeus—the transition to Olympus is not even mentioned, and its startling suddenness is unparalleled in the rest of Homer. Back again to Odysseus almost as precipitately: let someone see if the avenging relatives are coming. They are; Odysseus's party arms, and Athene fills Laertes with might so that his spear-cast kills Eupeithes outright. The rest join battle, and Odysseus would have made his enemies ἀνόστους, 'devoid of return' (528, a phrase never reused in poetry) had not Athene panicked them. Odysseus leaps in pursuit; Zeus flings a thunderbolt at Athene's feet, and she bids Odysseus stop the strife. 'Thus spake Athene, and he obeyed and rejoiced in his heart. And oaths again afterwards with both sides made Pallas Athene, daughter of aegis-bearing Zeus, in the likeness of Mentor both in stature and in speech'— and that is the end of the Odyssey! It may be judged a suitably weak and inept conclusion to a final episode that is ludicrous in its staccato leaps hither and thither, its indigestible concoction of rustics, thunderbolts, feeble old men and a goddess disguised or undisguised.

Surely those are right who believe that the whole ending of the Odyssey, and at least the final book, is a patchwork which reveals the taste, the capacity and some of the language of declining exponents of the epic in the late 7th or the 6th century, whether over-ambitious reciters or decaying singers and minor cyclical poets. The ending stands apart from the rest of the Odyssey as the Doloneia, which in every other respect greatly surpasses it, does from the Iliad.

In brief, and to anticipate somewhat, the situation seems to be as follows. Certain of the major structural anomalies in each poem are suggested by their language and by their untraditional or anti-traditional subject-matter to be caused by post-Homeric elaboration or rearrangement. Parts of the Games and the Theomachy in the Iliad (to which must be added the Doloneia, which, however, reveals no direct structural incompatibility with its surroundings simply because it is an independent unit never referred to in any other part of the poem) come in this category; so do parts of the Nekyia and the end of the Odyssey. Small embellishments and expansions of similar origin are probably quite frequent. Many inconsistencies, however, have been shown to be of a quite different kind: to be due not to post-Homeric activity—not all or even much of which, in any case, is 'editorial' in the common Analytical sense—but to the complexity of the material used by each main composer and to their inevitable difficulties in assembling different elements of their repertory into unified epics of huge length and scope. The Iliad reveals many marks of the progressive elaboration of one or two simple themes by the deliberate use of material derived from other poems about the Trojan war. Many inconsistencies arise from this kind of aggregation by a single poet deploying disparate traditional materials. The Odyssey, in spite of its more complex chronological structure, achieves more and longer stretches of completely consistent and homogeneous narrative. It also shows signs of the rather mechanical incorporation of post-Homeric summaries perhaps designed to introduce separate recitations of certain popular episodes; and of the imperfect expansion, adaptation and conflation by its monumental poet of a mode-rately full (and also more logical) vengeance poem, likewise of the compilation of adventure stories, some with a strong folk-tale content, from different sources. Plurality of structure and complexity of creation in each poem is undeniable, but it is fully compatible with the activity of the oral poet making a large-scale epic with the help of different sorts of traditional material. Each great poem was then further developed in the course of transmission.

12

THE OVERRIDING UNITY

THE various kinds of anomaly and discord in the Homeric epics have now been described, and they show clearly enough that the poems were not the free invention of one man or two distinct men but are complex entities containing elements of different date, different style, and different culture. This result is irrefutable and must never be forgotten. Yet against this pattern of diversity may be set the impression felt by every hearer and every reader, whether in ancient or modern times, that each poem is a somehow a unity—an amalgam of different elements, perhaps, but one so close as to form a new, self-contained, purposive and non-random organism. It will be prudent to discover on what this impression is based and what its implications really are for the way in which the monumental poems were composed.

The impression of unity is founded first of all on obvious common characteristics of all parts of both poems. The hexameter metre and the general theme of the Trojan war or its immediate sequel are universal throughout Homer. There is also a general community of language and dialect—not any spoken dialect but an artificial mixture chiefly of Ionic and Aeolic which itself betokens a long tradition of oral poetry. These obvious common qualities serve to suggest that the poems as a whole belong to a single oral tradition; there are no *grossly* unsuitable interpolations, and what additions may be detected are nearly all fairly skilful in one way or another. Nor has either poem been subjected, so far as we can see, to a radical rearrangement of its parts. Even the diction is comparatively homogeneous, and most passages which might ultimately be recognized as belonging to exceptionally early or late stages of the living tradition would escape the casual notice of an oral audience or even an ordinary reader. This is true even for many of those passages which have been recognized since antiquity as obvious glosses or additions. In vocabulary and syntax nearly every line of the Iliad and Odyssey conforms rather closely with the epic pattern, and even apart from metre the phraseology is readily distinguished from that of choral lyric or tragedy, for example, except in so far as these imitated epic. Even within the narrower category of hexameter epic poetry the Homeric poems possess many special characteristics which set them aside, both as a whole and in most of their parts, not only from later imitations like the *Argonautica* of Apollonius of Rhodes or earlier ones like the *Shield of Heracles* falsely attributed to Hesiod, but also from the narrative portions of the earliest 'Homeric' Hymns, from nearly all of Hesiod except some of the Catalogue poetry, and even from the fragments of the other poems, known as the Epic Cycle, which were designed to fill in those aspects of the Trojan adventure not described in the Iliad or Odyssey. There are of course, in some of the more obvious rhapsodic additions or later learned embellishments, certain Homeric exceptions to this generalization; but most of these are of short compass, and in general it is undeniable that, ignoring fine distinctions, nearly all the parts of the Homeric poems show a close resemblance to each other in ethos, diction, scale and style, as opposed to all other and later examples of Greek hexameter poetry.

If the Iliad and Odyssey belong to a single and homogeneous oral tradition, or possibly each to a separate local branch of a single tradition (ch. 13, §4), this is compatible both with the diversity of elements within each poem and with the comprehensive unity of subject and treatment. The question naturally arises whether the greater part of each poem displays such unity not only of subject and treatment but also of detailed structure that it must have been built up—to a large extent of course from traditional elements—by a single main poet. Before proceeding with this question, which will be further examined in chapter 15, it is prudent to consider the alternatives: either that the great poems do not contain sufficient unity of plot and structure to presuppose any coherent plan whatever, or that each of them could be the work, for example, of a number of poets developing a common nucleus or central theme. The first of these hypotheses can be absolutely excluded. It is quite obvious that both poems have a distinct and logically followed plot; neither of them is just a fortuitous amalgam of poetry on a common heroic theme, or even an anthology of songs about the Trojan war which might in the course of time have undergone some casual process of ordering by subject. This leaves, as the chief alternative to the assumption of a single main singer for each poem (whether or not the same one was responsible for both), the possibility of several singers, whether belonging to the same or different generations, together working up a central heroic theme—the wrath and abstention of a great hero, or the vengeance of a hero on his return from war—so as eventually to form a monumental poem.

Composition by several poets is improbable for at least two main reasons. The first concerns the possible motives and opportunities for such a group-endeavour, whether carried on in the same generation or more gradually. In chapter 13 the conclusion will be reached that, although oral poetry is by nature functional and extremely sensitive to the demands and habits of its audience, no particular function, occasion or audience that we can plausibly imagine was of itself likely to call forth an exceptionally large-scale poem. In order to account for the formation of a poem like the Iliad it is difficult not to introduce the motive of personal design and ambition by a specially gifted and famous singer, one who could to a large extent create his own audience-conditions. No collection or succession of singers is *a priori* likely to have formulated such a design and been able to carry it through. It is difficult to see, too, how a plurality of singers could have been encouraged or even allowed by the common circumstances of oral song, in popular or aristocratic gatherings, systematically to develop a single theme. The religious festival might seem a possible occasion; yet even here the right circumstances are hard, if not impossible, to envisage. A ritual song, a hymn, might be gradually extended, and this happened in the Near East though not so far as is known in Greece; but a narrative poem does not encourage indefinite simple accretions of this kind. A lay song might conceivably be elaborated through a formally established contest; but it is not easy to see why poets in competition with each other should constantly develop the same original shorter poem or theme, and a competition would soon be swamped if mere expansion was the criterion of poetic virtue. Once an exceptional large-scale poem existed, then further expansion is easy to understand—indeed it undoubtedly took place with both the Iliad and the Odyssey; but it is the original production of the truly outsize song that requires explanation. It is conceivable, too, that a great *aoidos* might dominate a festival or a region, and so acquire followers. This very probably happened. His songs might be elaborated in one way by one follower, in another way by another—but this would not lead to a systematic monumental product, unless he himself had created most of it in the first place. Only if there was a corporation, as it were, dedicated to the end of producing a large-scale poem, could such a *new* result accrue from a plurality of singers in the same generation; and this idea is so unlikely in itself, so contrary to human nature and to the probable ambitions, egocentricities and limitations of the oral singer, that I personally am prepared to reject it. In short it is difficult to see what sort of aim, function or opportunity could have induced the progressive development of a monumental epic by a plurality of singers.

The second objection to the plurality of poets lies in the kind and degree of consistency achieved. The two preceding chapters reached the conclusion that there are a number of major inconsistencies in each poem; they are significant and cannot decently be disregarded. On the other hand it is perfectly evident that the general standard of consistency, considering the length, complexity and oral composition of the poems, is rather high. Yet is it necessarily the case that a single main composer would achieve a much higher standard of structural consistency than a plurality of expanders and elaborators, if these were still creative singers? When an oral poem is learned by one singer from another it becomes a part of him; it differs little from songs of his own invention; it is rephrased in places in his own way, though in general its diction is one possessed in common by all the poets of his particular tradition. Thus if the new singer decides to expand an acquired song, he will do so just as consistently or inconsistently as he will expand a song of his own invention. Put in this form, then, this argument for a single main poet does not work; let us reconsider it. Judging from the study of modern Yugoslav poetry it appears that the achievement of consistency over *small details*, though it may gain lip-service from the singers themselves, is not regarded as particularly important. Now the most conspicuous type of inconsistency in Homer, as we have seen, is produced by contradictions or illogicalities in the development of plot. This is something which is likely to bedevil the exceptional large-scale poet, but only in slight degree the more usual kind of singer whose songs might not exceed a thousand lines or so. *His* lapses are lapses over details rather than over structure; they are relatively unimportant, though they may seem prominent to the reader. So far we have paid little attention to such minor lapses in Homer, precisely because they are common in all oral poetry and do not necessarily entail plurality of composition. The fact is, however, that the Homeric poems are remarkably free of this kind of minor inconsistency, except perhaps over details of armament; but that is a special case, since such lapses are usually caused by the use of traditional terms whose precise meaning was no longer understood. Other similar misuses of archaic material are irrelevant also, since they would be perpetrated alike by one composer or many. Rather it is cases like those of Pylaimenes and two other minor heroes in the Iliad, who are killed in one place but found alive again later, that are significant for the technique of the oral singer. Yet the name of Pylaimenes has become familiar to modern students of Homer simply because there are so few other minor lapses of this type. Occasionally, too, a warrior is implied to be in his chariot in one passage, but is described as standing near it a line or two later (pp. 213f.). Sometimes this is because the poet does not

257

describe every detail of the action, and the warrior can be understood to have dismounted in the meantime; but sometimes there is a real imprecision in the poet's mind, and this makes a good example of typical oral inexactitude. When one considers the hundreds of minor characters and minor encounters in the Iliad and the complications of the action of the Odyssey, and when one compares the much commoner anomalies of most other known oral poetry, the rarity of such lapses is striking indeed.

We may now ask, then, whether *this* kind of consistency of detail is likely to have been so regularly achieved, exceptional as it is by the apparent norms of small-scale oral poetry, by a plurality of poets. Probably not; probably this rare precision of the Iliad and Odyssey, just like their unique monumentality, should be attributed to the exceptional ability and exceptional aims of a single main composer for each; and neither the detailed precision nor the monumental scale arise out of the amalgamated talents of a series of small-scale poets. Admittedly this is a very *a priori* argument, and we cannot be certain that the Ionian singers were not much more skilled in this respect, as certainly in many others, than the later poets who can be studied. Probably, too, certain minor Homeric lapses were removed in the course of transmission. Unfortunately there is no good standard of comparison in Greek oral poetry; the *Theogony* of Hesiod is probably oral, but its untraditional subject-matter and probable later accretions makes its higher degree of minor inconsistency invalid for our purposes. In general, however, the breadth and unity of their structural conception, supported by the arguments from possible function and relatively high consistency, endorse the universal opinion of antiquity and the common reader that the Iliad and the Odyssey were each in some sense constructed by a single great poet; that there was some specially gifted singer called *Homeros* who played a predominant part in the formation of the great poems—as composer of the Iliad and as setter of the standard, probably, for the Odyssey (ch. 13, §4; ch. 17).

This apperception of unity, which must be limited by what

we have seen of the complexity and plurality of traditional poetry, should not be pressed too far. Some scholars have discovered a highly developed unity not only in the general structure but also in particular details of the poems. They have traced elaborate patterns and correspondences between one part of the Iliad or Odyssey and another, and have claimed that the main poets deliberately achieved these correspondences for the sake of dramatic effect. In the present century J. T. Sheppard's *The Pattern of the Iliad* (1922) was an influential example, for a time, of this kind of Unitarian analysis—an analysis which claimed to show that the Iliad is a very carefully elaborated composition virtually every detail of which was deliberately and subtly designed by one great poet. In a more recent study, Cedric Whitman's *Homer and the Heroic Tradition* (1958), great significance is assigned to the recurrence of themes in imagery. Agamemnon's eyes gleaming like fire at I. 104 and Achilles gleaming like a star at XXII. 26, for example, are held to imply unity of authorship because they are part of 'a remarkable pattern of associations, all centering around the theme of heroic passion and death'.[1] Even single words have been thought by some critics to carry intentional echoes of each other over quite long stretches of intervening text; yet Parry's demonstration that the Homeric poems were oral compositions, using a special formular technique, has severely diminished the probability of deliberate cross-references between many single words or fixed phrases. As for the deliberate or subconscious interreference of similes and other evocative passages, this is of course impossible either to prove or disprove. I agree with Whitman that many of the similes were deployed by the monumental poet; but fire-similes were surely popular among other singers also. In fact the 'pattern of imagery' proves the unity of the epic tradition, *not* that there was one single originator of all the contexts in which such imagery occurs. In general it seems fair to say that there are few widely separated repetitions or similarities which compel the assumption of significant cross-reference, however subtle, and that the oral principle of economy of phraseology, together with the poets' acceptance of, and indeed evident delight in, repeated lines, themes and images, is sufficient to explain most of these apparent overtones.

There are of course many explicit forecasts of future events in the poems, as well as references to, and comparisons with, past action. These factual cross-references help to hold the poems together, particularly when they occur in the course of large-scale digressions like these to be found in books II to x of the Iliad. Their significance has been emphasized by Schadewaldt, notably in his *Iliasstudien*, and some of them are listed by Webster in his *From Mycenae to Homer*.[1] They do undoubtedly suggest that each poem, in the form in which it came down to the 5th century B.C., and so with comparatively few changes to us, had been given as precise an appearance of dramatic unity as possible. Unfortunately they do not prove much more than that—contrary to what Schadewaldt and his followers have sometimes seemed to assume; they do not of themselves prove, for example, that virtually the whole of either poem is due to a single poet, or even that every broad context in which such a cross-reference occurs is necessarily an integral part of the monumental plot. Many of these reminiscences and forecasts are very brief, being contained within a line or a couplet, and many too are inorganic to their immediate context—they can be added or removed without really disturbing it. The possibility cannot be excluded, therefore, that some of them have been inserted by post-Homeric singers or rhapsodes, whether or not as part of their own elaborated passages, and that there was a progressive attempt to tighten up the rather loose structure of the Iliad (in particular) down to the time at least of the probable Panathenaic stabilization of the text. The matter need not be pursued much further: the cross-references are there, and in general they undoubtedly reinforce the impression of a single plan for each poem which has been pursued, despite digressions, with an ultimate resolution and intelligence. They do not, however, reveal much about the extent of later elaborations to this central plan; for example the end of the Odyssey, from *23. 297* onwards, contains episodes that show every sign of having been added considerably later than the composition of the bulk of the poem—yet even the suitors' descent to the underworld and the encounter between Odysseus and the relatives of the suitors contain back-references to the preceding poem. It is natural that an elaborator should attempt to bind his own contribution to the main poem by means of such cross-references. Forecasts of future action required greater subtlety, and the majority of them, though not all, are likely to be the work of the main composer.

The alleged discovery of two special kinds of correspondence in Homer deserves special examination. First, many Unitarians have claimed that the Iliad reveals a detailed symmetry of structure, working from its extremities towards its centre. Certainly the time-intervals mentioned in the first and last book are approximately equivalent: the plague sent by Apollo lasts for nine days, so does a truce for Hector's funeral, and so on. This particular symmetry does possess a certain interest, superficial though it may be; even so one must remember that, quite apart from the ancient emphasis on certain significant numbers, the formular system selected metrically convenient numerals; so that three, seven, nine, twelve and twenty are common quantities. One must also remember that the opening and closing books not unnaturally cover a wider range of action than the intervening ones, so that time-intervals of longer than a single day or night are relevant here rather than elsewhere. More serious in its implications is the claim, made in its most detailed form by Whitman in his book, that the sequence of events in I and xxiv shows an exact *reverse* correspondence.[1] His analysis may be summarized as follows:

Book i	Book xxiv
(1) Rejection of Chryses (plague and funeral pyres)	(5) Dispute among gods, Hera opposes Zeus
(2) Council of chiefs and quarrel	(4) Thetis with Zeus
(3) Thetis with Achilles, consoling him and taking message to Zeus	(3) Thetis with Achilles, consoling him and bringing message from Zeus
(4) Thetis with Zeus	(2) Achilles in council with Priam
(5) Dispute among gods, Hera opposes Zeus	(1) Funeral of Hector (funeral pyre)

The themes are described here in as favourable a way as possible to Whitman's thesis, which is that the reverse correspondence is so close that it cannot be accidental and must be the result of deliberate intention on the part of a single poet. Now Whitman admits that the similarity between theme (1) in each column is only a vague one; and I would add that (2) is equally indefinite and doubtful. Furthermore these five themes are not comprehensive in each case but omit some important incidents: in book I the taking of Briseis by the heralds, the 'interlude' of the journey to and from Chryse (Whitman himself does not seem to feel much confidence in his suggestion that it corresponds with the journey of Priam to Achilles's hut in XXIV), and the reconciliation of the gods by Hephaestus at the end; in XXIV the mutilation of Hector by Achilles, the preparations of Priam and his meeting with Hermes (the last episode, however, being expanded by later elaboration: p. 321). Another objection is that the reverse order of themes is in this case so abstruse that it could only occur to a pen-and-paper composer. The oral poet, if he needs such compositional aids, chooses more straightforward examples; while the audience, of course, like nearly all readers, would pass over such conundrums in blissful ignorance. The most important objection of all—and it is one that applies, *mutatis mutandis*, to many other discoveries of subtle correspondence—is that such similarity in theme and sequence as actually exists between the first and the last book of the Iliad may be, and probably is, the result *neither* of sheer chance *nor* of deliberate and conscious planning necessarily by a single poet, but arises from the firmly established relationships of the characters involved in each book and from the exigencies and natural sequences of the plot as a whole. The crucial observations are the following: that the epic begins with the wrath of Achilles and ends with his humanity to Priam; that Thetis is Achilles's divine mother, his natural consoler and intermediary with the gods; and that Hera supports the Achaeans and frequently quarrels with her husband. Therefore in book I the affront to Achilles causes him to invoke Thetis, who naturally consoles him and offers to represent his case to Zeus; Zeus's decision to harm the Achaeans just as naturally arouses the wrath of Hera and other pro-Achaean gods. In xxiv there is another divine quarrel, caused quite differently by horror at Achilles's mutilation of Hector, and again Hera is inevitably found in opposition to Zeus. Achilles has to be restrained, and his mother is the obvious intermediary once more; she consoles him and passes on Zeus's instructions. The correspondences here are neither fortuitous nor on the other hand entirely deliberate. Rather they arise from the general structure of the poem, its over-all plan of the wrath of Achilles and his ultimate conciliation, and also from certain typical sequences generated by the roles of Thetis, Achilles and Hera.

Given, then, that the Iliad and Odyssey maintain a certain logic in the development of their plot—which even the looser Iliad undoubtedly does—and that the first book initiates and the last book winds up the action, the kind of parallelism that has seemed so significant to Whitman and others can be plausibly explained without resorting to the improbable hypothesis of deliberate and detailed symmetry of the more recherché type. Human ingenuity has found other correspondences of the same kind, though never so apparently impressive in detail, in other books of the Iliad, working from the approximate centre of the poem towards its extremities. Anyone, if he tries hard enough, can find examples of similarity, of one type or another, in quite diverse parts of either great poem. The question is whether these signify more than a general logic of plot and character which the poems undeniably possess. There seems to me to be no reason for thinking so.

This is the first kind of over-interpretation of structural symmetry. The second aberration, as I consider it, seems to have particular appeal to the Anglo-Saxon mind; at least it has flourished for the most part in England and America. It consists in the assumption that the structure of the Iliad and Odyssey resembles the arrangement of the pediment in a Greek temple, or the pattern on a Geometric pot, or both. J. L. Myres favoured both similitudes at one time or another; Webster and Whitman have concentrated more recently on the latter.[1]

Essentially, beneath all the technicalities, the pattern said to
inhere in these different art-forms is that of the major element
flanked by two minor ones. Webster adds a further distinction,
between static and dynamic pattern, which may be ignored
here. That the Homeric poems may in many places exemplify
this kind of arrangement I do not wish to deny, for the simple
reason that this is a very common, indeed a universal way of
dealing with verbal narrative—a way implicitly illustrated by
Aristotle in his prescription of beginning, middle, and end,
since the middle portion may well be more extensive than the
other two. The reason why, in pedimental sculpture, the central
element is more conspicuous and is flanked by two balancing
groups of smaller importance is altogether different; it is the
regular triangular shape of the pediment itself, a shape imposed
by purely architectural reasons concerned with *draining water off
a roof*. In the case of Geometric pots it is not even certain that
the same kind of pattern is predominant, though in the Ripe
Geometric period a central panel of figures is often flanked by
two balancing sections of decorative frieze. This again is an
obvious and functional device determined largely by the shape
of the pot itself, chiefly the fact that it is circular in plan. Such
similarities as may exist between pots, pediments and poems
may be inherently interesting, they may be indicative of some
cosmic principle of order, but they do not allow us to interpret
one kind of craftsman in terms of another, since each is simply
obeying certain obvious demands of his own particular medium.
And yet Whitman was so certain that there is some special
connexion between the Iliad and the Geometric style of pottery
decoration developed notably in Attica that he was prepared to
argue, against all other evidence, that Geometric Athens must
have played a crucial part in forming the detailed structure of
the poem. It is undoubtedly true that certain broad cultural
ideals or presuppositions make themselves felt in different forms
of art in response to common social needs and stimuli; but the
comparison of different art-forms will rarely reveal more than
that, and in general this kind of comparative study tends to be
both tortuous and fanciful. One such common tendency may

reveal itself both in the poetry and in some of the art of the developed Geometric age: the tendency towards largeness, bulk, monumentality. Thus we find a funerary amphora as high as a man and, in the case of the Iliad and Odyssey, poems far exceeding the traditional or usual needs in length. No doubt the growing prosperity of the Greek world in the 8th century B.C. partly accounts for these happy aberrations; but within each technique long mastery of the traditional forms was another necessary precondition—one which in the case of temple buildings and sculpture was not fulfilled until a generation or so later.

One of the most important kinds of unity revealed in the poems, itself the product of complete mastery of the tradition, is unity of character. The depiction of the heroic character is limited both by the technique and aims of oral poetry and by the simplicity of heroic virtues and vices. Yet in a few cases— notably Achilles and Hector, and to some extent Odysseus and Telemachus in the Odyssey—the great epics manage to transcend these limitations. These characters achieve a complexity which has the appearance of being consistently developed as each poem progresses. Even so we must take care not to deduce too much about the methods and the scope of operation of the main poets. Achilles is absent from the action of the greater part of the Iliad, and even if it is true that his character shows a subtle unity this does not guarantee that the Catalogue of Ships or the duel of Menelaus and Paris, for example, are an integral part of the same careful plan. Nevertheless Achilles stands out as a hero in conflict with himself and with the heroic morality. It is a unique and an extraordinarily perceptive study, even if some of the subtle contradictions of his character might be the result of accretion by a plurality of poets rather than of the consistent insight of a single main composer. I do not believe many of them are; but veering attitudes in the Iliad towards Agamemnon, for example, who is presented now as a great and admirable leader, now as a manic depressive, may have a different cause; they may imply either a plurality of composers working on the main poem or the inadequate reconciliation by a monumental composer of divergent traditions about the Mycenaean king. In general, however, the argument from the consistency of the characters—and the difference between the Odysseus of the Iliad and the Odyssey shows that the epic tradition was not regularly so consistent—supports the assumption of some final inclusive unity for each poem; though like other arguments from unity of effect it does nothing to show that every line, every passage, and every major theme was placed there by the main composer.

The explicit theme of the Iliad is the wrath of Achilles, which leads to the death of Patroclus, Achilles's vengeance on Hector, and his subsequent magnanimity to Priam. Into this story has been inserted, primarily it seems by the main poet himself, a series of expansions presumably designed to give an impression of the scale and nature of the war as a whole; or it may be truer to say conversely that the wrath-plot has been imposed on a mass of Trojan poetry—the point being that the two main components of the Iliad do not seriously conflict, in spite of elements like the Beguilement of Zeus in xiv and xv whose purpose directly contradicts the promise of Zeus to Thetis. Inessential retardations such as this do not worry the listener to an oral poem, provided that they are not aggressively alien to the main theme and that they are interesting in themselves. Moreover the hearer of a monumental poem, even though not the whole of it is heard on one occasion, must inevitably reduce his normal standards of relevance; sheer bulk seems to confer a unity of its own, and what cannot be apprehended synoptically is credited with an organic structure that it may not really possess. No such excuses need be made for the Odyssey, however. It possesses a tighter structure than the Iliad, and even its digressions, like parts of the journey of Telemachus and the tales of Odysseus's adventures, are more clearly related to the central themes of Odysseus's return, vengeance, and reunion with Penelope. The end of the Odyssey is a special problem. It is almost certainly the result, in large measure at least, of post-Homeric expansion and adjustment (pp. 248 ff.); yet it does not seriously prejudice the unity of the epic as a whole or imply that this unity was seriously defective, since the Homeric poem could have ended virtually at 23. 296, or its original ending could have been suppressed by or submerged in the later expansion.

From the aesthetic point of view the *effect* of unity in the Iliad and Odyssey is what really matters, not the question of whether that effect was achieved by one, two or twenty poets. Yet the problem of composition is not irrelevant; for it is only by understanding how and why the poems were composed that one can hope to penetrate their real meaning and effect for a contemporary Greek audience. The kind of unity they possess is certainly not that of a modern work of literature, nor does it demonstrate that a single poet, and one only, was responsible for each poem. On the other hand it is no way incompatible with the hypothesis to which so many different factors point: that each poem reflects the creative endeavour of a great singer, using many traditional components and providing much of his own; and that these works were subjected to minor alteration and elaboration in the earliest centuries of their transmission. This hypothesis, and other possibilities, will be further explored in the following three chapters.

PART V

✸

THE DEVELOPMENT AND TRANSMISSION OF THE GREAT POEMS

13

THE CIRCUMSTANCES OF HOMERIC COMPOSITION

§1. 'Homer' and his region

ANTIQUITY knew nothing definite about the life and personality of Homer. Even his name was a strange one, subjected to several fantastic derivations. Yet this name, at least, was for long firmly and indisputably attached to the Iliad and Odyssey—and less firmly to certain other hexameter narrative poems not independently ascribed, like the *Thebais*, the *Cypria*, the *Hymn to Apollo*, even the trivial *Margites* and *Batrachomyomachia*. It is not surprising that these later and lesser works were attracted to Homer as the archetypal singer; and it seems probable that the singer of the Iliad, at least, was known by this name in his lifetime. Little else about Homer that is at all plausible is found in the ancient traditions whose proliferation we can trace back to near the end of the 6th century B.C.—except only that he was an Ionian particularly associated with Smyrna and Chios. The *horror vacui* that was an endemic disease of ancient biographers caused a mass of spurious details to be invented, many of them palpably based on innocent passages in the poems themselves, others supplied by local interests or designed to reconcile divergent conjectures. The commonest version to be found in the various Lives of Homer, compiled from the Hellenistic period onward but sometimes incorporating stories from the classical age, is that Homer was born in Smyrna (which became Ionic early in its history), lived in Chios and died in the insignificant Cycladic island of Ios; his name was originally Melesigenes, his father being the river Meles and his mother the nymph Cretheis; he was also descended from Orpheus and coeval with, or even a cousin of, Hesiod, with whom he had a poetical contest in Euboea.[1] Much of this information is recognizably fantastic and nearly all of it is probably worthless. Even the association with Smyrna and Chios, the latter backed by the existence there from at least the late 6th century B.C. of a rhapsodic guild called the Homeridae or 'descendants of Homer', cannot have been watertight—or there would not have been so many rival claimants, of which Kyme and Colophon were perhaps the chief but to which several others had been added by the Roman period.

The association of Homer with both Chios and Smyrna evidently goes back at least as far as Pindar; while the famous line about the generations of men (VI. 146) was quoted by Semonides of Amorgos, towards the end of the 7th century, as by 'the man of Chios'.[2] Pindar also wrote of the Homeridae as 'singers of stitched words', ῥαπτῶν ἐπέων . . . ἀοιδοί (Nem. 2, 1 f.); and the scholion on this passage stated that they were at first members of the family of Homer, but later were rhapsodes who claimed no blood descent; one of them was Kynaithos of Chios, who first declaimed the poems of Homer to the Syracusans in 504 B.C. This last piece of information is improbable as it stands; but it is less likely that the date is seriously wrong than that the nature of Kynaithos's service to the Syracusans is misconstrued. The scholiast's statement about the Homeridae seems to be for the most part speculative, but that there was some sort of guild-organization in Chios as early as the 6th century at least, claiming a special relationship with Homer, need not be doubted; and it survived there, apparently in a degenerate form, at least until Plato's time. Unfortunately we do not know the origin of these eponymous or guild connexions, or how loose and fortuitous they might be: certainly the Homerid connexion need have been no closer than that which related the doctors, the Asclepiadae, to the semi-divine Asclepius, or even the Talthybiadae to the Homeric herald Talthybius. We can at least conclude that the Chiote associations of Homer were claimed as early as the 6th century, and appeared then to have some supporting evidence.

That the two great poems were composed in Ionia, and on the

basis of formular materials developed by Ionian singers for several generations, is shown by the internal evidence of the Iliad and Odyssey themselves—and that is more reliable and more important than the uncertain speculations of later authors in antiquity. First and foremost is the predominantly Ionic dialect. It is theoretically conceivable, I suppose, that monumental composition might have taken place far outside Ionia, once Ionic had been established as the proper speech for epic, even as the Boeotian Hesiod composed in the conventional and primarily Ionic epic dialect with very few lapses. That this is a negligible possibility is confirmed not only by the external tradition but also by many signs, especially in the Iliad, of local knowledge of Ionia—or rather of the Asia Minor littoral as a whole. Autopsy of Troy, suspected by many ever since antiquity, cannot be proved, though something of the sort is suggested by the apparent knowledge that the bulk of Tenedos did not quite cut off from view the topmost peak of Samothrace (XIII. 12 ff.). Familiarity with small places like Thebe, Pedasus and Lyrnessus, or with the figure of Niobe on Mount Sipylus, may add further confirmation, and so more notably do many similes with an unmistakable local implication: the birds in the Asian meadow at the mouth of the Kaystros (II. 459 ff.), the storm in the Icarian sea (II. 144 ff.), the north-west winds from Thrace (IX. 5) or coasts lashed by south-west or west winds (II. 394 ff., IV. 422 ff., etc.). Some of these are inexact testimonies—for example waves could be driven onshore by a west wind in an indented part even of an east-facing coast—but together and in the mass they are persuasive for East Aegean experience by some at least of the poets involved. This applies in particular to many similes, which on the whole seem to have been carefully disposed (and I would say in many cases invented) by the monumental composer (pp. 202 f.). On the other hand there is comparatively little local information, except in the Achaean Catalogue and Nestor's reminiscences, about the mainland or Peloponnese. The Odyssey, the action of which lies in the west or in far-off and imaginary places, naturally contains less East Aegean reference. The account of Telemachus's journey displays some

Peloponnesian knowledge, such as could have descended largely from Mycenaean times and traditions, but more specialized descriptions—for example of the geographical position of Ithaca—often seem to have been misunderstood or distorted in transit.

§2. *Audiences and occasions*

What was Homer's own position in this Ionian background, and for whom did he sing his songs? This is an important question: for oral poems were directed at, or at least developed in front of, an audience, and important departures from traditional form or length were likely to be influenced either by the demand of a particular audience or at least by what some audience would tolerate. Monumental oral poems are quite exceptional. Avdo Međedović's longest version of the Wedding of Smailagić Meho was elicited by Parry's *specific and well-paid request* for the longest possible song—a kind of stimulus which obviously cannot have applied, in anything like this form, to Homer. What other situations and audiences can be imagined which could have given rise to poems of the length of the Iliad and Odyssey—or rather to the earlier and greater of the two, since once the Iliad existed its imitation is not hard to understand?

The two kinds of occasion repeatedly considered by Homeric scholars have been the nobleman's feast and the religious festival. That the first of these provided an important audience for ἀοιδοί at certain periods cannot seriously be doubted. The Odyssean descriptions of Phemius, the court poet of Ithaca, and of Demodocus, who, though he lived in town and outside the palace, was regularly summoned to sing for the Phaeacian βασιλῆες, show quite clearly that aristocratic entertainment was one function of the oral poet, at least at some periods.[1] The preoccupation of the great poems—the Odyssey less markedly than the Iliad, but still to a large degree—with the heroic upper classes, and the care devoted to certain heroic genealogies, suggest that many singers must have had aristocratic patrons in mind. Yet in the Dark Age, at least, the 'aristocratic' audience would in many parts of the Greek world be quite ordinary, quite un-aristocratic according to the normal associations of the word. The 'kings' would just be the chief men of the town or village, claiming descent, no doubt, from Achaean heroes, yet incapable of maintaining elaborate and exclusive establishments like those of the late Mycenaean *wanaktes* or even 7th-century relics like the court of the Penthelidae in Lesbos. In those circumstances a resident court singer would be out of the question, and visiting singers, even if they sang in the chieftain's house, would probably do so before many or most of the men of the village. Even in most Ionic or Aeolic towns of the 9th or 8th century one may doubt whether exclusively aristocratic audiences could be found for most singers; for although certain aristocratic titles and privileges were still maintained even in the 6th century, presumably much of the apparatus of palace life, and perhaps the distinction between hereditary nobles and a new aristocracy of wealth, were tending to disappear or diminish. Thus while it is right to emphasize aristocratic interest in the singers—and also the singers' probable interest in the aristocracy, whose gifts would be the largest—and while court poetry has been an important social phenomenon in other oral traditions, like the Teutonic and the Anglo-Saxon, we should also remember that aristocratic audiences were not likely to have been the only or even the predominant kind at all or most stages of the Greek epic tradition; and even aristocratic audiences would often be mixed, not very exclusive, and not particularly stable. The Ithacan palace-singer Phemius must have had his counterparts in real life, but he was probably not a typical singer, at least after the Mycenaean age; and many epic audiences were of a different kind from his.

This is a satisfactory conclusion, since it is hard to see how an exclusively court audience could have tolerated with any particular ease the singing of a monumental poem lasting for several evenings. Such an audience might have been less fluctuating than some others, and the wish to please a powerful host might have inhibited their most natural reactions; but court circles have rarely been notable for experiments, especially of a cultural kind, and genealogical attractions alone—

which are in fact totally absent from many parts of both poems—would not have given much extra incentive for welcoming the new and quite exceptional length. Heaven knows this is a flimsy enough type of argument, compounded of generalities and based on the haziest knowledge of the aristocratic circles involved; but unfortunately any evaluation of this particular problem must, for lack of concrete evidence, be of this vague and inferential kind. So long as conclusions are not treated as certain ones, not too much harm will be done: it is really a question of trying to isolate the possibilities and then arranging them in an order of plausibility and attraction.

The second special audience or occasion is that of the religious festival—not the small local festival, which was likely to have shared the exuberance and the almost chaotic informality of the modern ἑορτή, but rather the large inter-state gathering, of which the Delia at Delos and the Panionia at Mycale were the most important Ionian examples; about the Ephesia little is known. Something of what happened on such occasions is revealed for Delos by the probably 7th-century Delian portion of the 'Homeric' Hymn to Apollo. There, at 147 ff., the Ionians with trailing tunics are said to gather with their wives and children, their ships and rich possessions, and to enjoy themselves like gods with contests of boxing, dancing and ἀοιδή, singing, in honour of Apollo. In particular a Delian girls' choir sings a hymn to Apollo, Leto and Artemis, and then recalls men and women of old (160), somehow imitating the dialects of different regions. The blind singer of Chios who recounts these happenings was assumed by Thucydides and others to be Homer himself, and did much to cloud the issue of Homer's personality in antiquity.[1] In truth, however, a Homerid is the most he is likely to have been, and his prelude is so long that only quite a short epic song is likely to have followed: perhaps the singing contests were after this pattern. In any event the conditions described are not those of the 9th or 8th-century singer, and the curious song of the female choir, with its dialectal tricks, belongs to the time of Anacreon, Stesichorus or

Alcman rather than to the full creative oral period in which Homer flourished. The whole impression is of a large, gay and still slightly chaotic assembly. The Panionion was used for the more serious purpose of political deliberations too; but the festival itself, and its opportunities for long epics, might not have been very different from the Delia. Quite when contests of singers were started we cannot say; the Delian hymn may imply them before 600, and competitive singing may even be meant in the Thamyris reference at II. 595.[1] A tripod was won by Hesiod in a poetical contest at the funeral of Amphidamas at Chalcis (*Works and Days*, 654ff.); but the rhapsodic contests at the Panathenaea do not seem to have been regularized until the 6th century. Nevertheless the presence of large crowds of prosperous holiday-makers at the 8th-century Delia or Panionia must always have attracted singers, whatever the date of formal contests; and these singers would soon enough have been competing with each other, informally at least, for popular favour. The question is whether these conditions were still of a kind actually to elicit, or at least to provide a ready audience for, a poem on the scale of the Iliad. The evidence such as it is suggests to me that they were not, at least until the time when these festivals were organized on a more serious basis, partly for purposes of prestige and propaganda, in the 6th or at earliest the 7th century. Even then it is difficult to see the Iliad being recited whole, even if it could be squeezed into the same period, three days, as the performance of a tragic sequence at the Great Dionysia at Athens. For the drama possessed at the same time more variety and greater solemnity; the atmosphere of the Dionysia must have been markedly different from that of the Panathenaea; and it is doubtful whether the whole of the Iliad or Odyssey was recited at the Panathenaea even after the rhapsodic contests were regulated in the 6th century (p. 307). Thus while the great festivals cannot be disregarded as the possible milieu of Homer's great experiment, they do not seem to provide such ideal conditions for it as many critics have previously believed.

Neither the court nor the festival, then, seems to have

provided conditions which would particularly encourage the production of a large-scale poem. Indeed they do not seem to me to provide necessarily more favourable conditions than other popular audiences might do, in the different and more casual gatherings of day-to-day life. This is a theme I have already developed to some extent with reference to the Dark Age. Similar probabilities apply even to the later and more settled and prosperous period of the 9th and 8th centuries; and the singer would often and easily find an audience in town or village, after the day's work was done, whether in someone's house or in the market-place or in a tavern. This has been so in most places and at most periods in which oral heroic poetry has flourished. The heroic epic seems always to have quickly found, and then to have retained, a large popular audience which often, indeed, becomes the main support of the generality of singers. There may be an important aristocratic audience as well, as in the Odyssey and in the courts of the early Middle Ages—and it was presumably for a primarily aristocratic audience that heroic and aristocratic poetry was normally in the first instance composed. It rapidly extended its audience, though; for in a Heroic Age or its immediate successor there is usually not enough organized social resentment to prejudice the people against the actions and ideals of the heroic class; and in Greece, where the downfall of the aristocratic structure so rapidly followed the Trojan *geste* and the acme of heroic saga, the popular audience would rapidly assume an exceptional importance.

Schadewaldt has drawn attention to the not too obvious popular affiliations of the Odyssean court singer Demodocus, who lives in the town of the Phaeacians but is frequently summoned to sing in Alcinous's palace.[1] His very name means something like 'pleasing to, or accepted by, the *demos*', and at *8. 472* he is described as 'honoured by the *people*', λαοῖσι τετιμένον. No less significant is Eumaeus's classification at *17. 383* ff. of the singer among the δημιοεργοί, together with seers, doctors and carpenters—to whom heralds may be added from *19. 135*. Now δημιοεργοί here must mean something like 'workers for, or among, the *demos*'. Admittedly the exact connotation of *demos* is often difficult to determine, but it must be something like 'community', 'commune' or 'village'—in the Linear B tablets *da-mo* appears to mean 'village', either the land or the people. Yet δῆμος in the archaic age included rich men and aristocrats, and we should not take 'worker for the community' or something similar to imply an exclusively proletarian functionary. This is shown, too, by the case of the herald, also a worker for the community: he is a civil servant, his activities affect the people and he is in close touch with them, but he is controlled by the rulers and belongs to their *entourage*. Doctors and carpenters are more popular and less aristocratic in their associations; indeed in no case can the connotation of *association with* or *effect on* the people, or the community as a whole, be excluded from the word δημιοεργός. Thus the singers as a class—not just one singer, or a special kind of singer, but all of them—are considered in the Odyssean passage to have professional connexions with the community at large. They are *not* regarded as an exclusively royal or aristocratic appurtenance, and the concentration on Phemius and Demodocus as court poets is to some extent misleading—in fact Demodocus is described in *θ* as singing in the market-place, too, after the athletic contest is over and when the young Phaeacians display their skill at dancing to his song of Ares and Aphrodite. Now the picture of the *aoidos* given in the Odyssey may be in certain respects a composite one, with elements derived both from the recent Ionian practice of the 9th or 8th century and from older traditions of the singer and his craft. The apparently deliberate insistence on the singer's status and god-given qualities may well belong to the more self-conscious era of the main composer; but in any case the rise of trade in Ionia is likely to have progressively increased, and certainly not diminished, the popular associations of the epic singer.

The conclusion of this line of argument is that in the 9th and 8th centuries many *aoidoi* must have sung for popular audiences in houses, taverns or market-place, as well as on special occasions in noble mansions or palaces and at large festivals. We have seen that these special occasions are not particularly likely to have provided the conditions to elicit an exceptionally large-scale poem, and I think it quite possible that the humbler and more frequent occasions would have been no worse, and perhaps better, in this respect. *Weddings* in Yugoslavia, Hungary, Greece and many other traditionally peasant communities sometimes still last for as long as a week, and are most commonly arranged for the slack times of a farmer's year. Eating, drinking, telling stories, singing and listening to songs are the main occupations. In Muslim Yugoslavia the month of Ramadan, with its nights devoted to eating and drinking, is the chief occasion for a singer to deploy his repertoire to the full, and best provides a continuous audience. No such comparable festival existed in ancient Greece, but weddings and perhaps funerals—humble no less than aristocratic—and small horse-fairs and the like would in some cases have lasted long enough for the development and singing even of a song as vast as the Iliad. It could have been in such circumstances as these that Homer first strung together elements of his Trojan repertoire—much of it acquired from older singers—so as to form a coherent poem with one or two strong central themes.

The truth remains that none of these possible occasions—feast or festival, fair or wedding or funeral or informal gathering in market-place or tavern—seems to possess any special quality that could easily and naturally have actually *elicited* a large-scale epic. The concept of the oral poem as functional is a useful one—but it is not going to help us much with the monumental poem, simply because by the normal canons of heroic song this kind of poem is an aberration. Rather I believe we should accept that the chief factor in the making of the new literary form was not function or occasion, but—and this is horribly obvious once one comes to say it, though it has been avoided like the plague by most Homeric critics in the last sixty years—the special ability, aims, imagination and reputation of a particular singer; the singer in fact who compounded the first large-scale Iliad and who was known as Homer. An outstandingly accomplished singer may be seen to acquire a tremendous reputation in any oral society, first in his own district and then further afield; often he may acquire a prestige equalling that claimed by Demodocus in the Odyssey. I am driven towards the provisional conclusion that it was this prestige that enabled Homer to outstrip normal performances, normal audiences and normal occasions—that enabled him to *impose* his own will and his own vast conception on his environment, so as eventually to produce an Iliad. Admittedly if circumstances were such that no one would listen to a poem of this length, or more or less take in its whole span, the Iliad would hardly have survived in the tradition—unless it could be recorded in writing without delay, which for reasons discussed on pp. 98ff. I regard as an improbable and unnecessary hypothesis. But there is no reason to suspect that circumstances *were* such—weddings and fairs, to look no further, could have provided audiences consistent enough to encourage the great singer, if only his own powers and reputation were high enough to hold them. The crucial factor was the creative imagination, the singer of outstanding brilliance and an exceptionally large Trojan repertoire who suddenly saw that many of its songs could be interlocked to make a complete and universal Trojan song. This was not like the evolution of tragedy, for example, each stage of which may have seemed a logical development from the last; it was more like the evolution of the monumental Geometric amphora or crater. The evidence of archaeology does not suggest that pots became systematically larger and larger until eventually one was made that was seven feet tall, but rather that there was a leap from the largeish pot to the perfectly colossal one, a leap which must have been made for the first time by a particular potter who suddenly had a flash of ambition and the inspiration of sheer size, and at the same time realized that he possessed the necessary materials and technique. This kind of leap, incidentally, is far easier to understand in one man than in a group or a corporation—though others will inevitably follow the example of magnitude once it has been given.

§3. *The date of the poems*

Postponing to the end of this chapter the question whether the Iliad and Odyssey are likely to be substantially the work of the same singer, we may now turn to their approximate date: for whatever their differences, their stylistic similarities are enough to suggest that they are unlikely to be separated by more than two or three generations. I take it that in any case the Iliad came first. Possible criteria of date may be divided into four main classes: datable phenomena within the poems themselves, datable external effects of the poems, the evidence of chronologists in antiquity, and the implications of literature and literary personalities in the 7th century.

Class I, internal criteria, may be subdivided into (i) archaeological criteria, that is, objects, customs and so on (here we shall be using the results of the survey in chapter 9, §1); (ii) language and style (chapter 9, §2). Both kinds of criterion are liable to be concerned with isolated passages and can be deceptive when applied so as to give a *terminus ante quem* for the poems as a whole. To take (i) first: nothing in the poems (except the apparently Attic custom mentioned at VII. 334f., which looks like a considerably later Athenian addition: p. 180) is necessarily later than about 700; and two or three well-distributed phenomena— the Phoenicians (after 900?), the pair of throwing-spears (after 950?), and separate roofed temples (after 850?)—suggest around 900 as a *terminus post quem*. Archaeological criteria which suggest an 8th rather than a 9th-century date are few and isolated: only, in fact, the implications of hoplite tactics (after *c.* 750?) on the one hand, and Gorgoneia (the same *terminus post*, but far commonest in the first half of the 7th century) on the other. The lamp and brooch (p. 185) are too uncertain to be used either way; so are comparisons between Homeric shields and bowls and those from Crete and Phoenicia respectively.[1] The language-and-style criterion, (ii), is not very helpful. It has been seen that there are no absolutely datable linguistic phenomena beyond Myceneanisms and precarious mainland Aeolisms, which give an equivocal *terminus ante*, and contraction

and the disappearance of digamma which give a *terminus post*
of perhaps around 1000—apart, as always, from the exceedingly
rare organic Atticisms, which again reflect Athenian interference with the text considerably later than the main stage of
composition. In general, though, the newer elements in the
mixed language of Homer, such as the use of the demonstrative
as a true definite article and the free formation of verbal
abstracts, do nothing to prejudice either a 9th or an 8th-century
date. The general style, including formular economy and
metrical criteria like the frequency of bucolic diaeresis, places
the Iliad and Odyssey somewhat earlier than Hesiod and the
earliest Homeric Hymns. The Hymns to Demeter and Delian
Apollo probably belong not before *c.* 650; Hesiod's date is not
objectively determinable, but there is nothing (except the
fallacious assumption that the Amphidamas mentioned at
Works and Days, 654 *must* be the king involved in the Lelantine
war) to place him earlier than *c.* 680.

Class II, the external effects of the Homeric poems, may be
subdivided into three groups: (i) datable quotations from and
literary references to Homer; (ii) epic scenes on vases; and (iii)
the foundation of fresh heroic cults, possibly as a result of a new
heroic interest generated by the spread of the Homeric poems
on the mainland. (i) Epithets, formulas and half-lines common
in Homer occur in the surviving fragments of 7th-century
iambic, lyric or elegiac poets, notably in Archilochus, Alcman,
Callinus and Tyrtaeus. Archilochus at least can be securely
dated, since the eclipse he mentioned must be that of 6 April
648 B.C. All that this absolutely proves is that *heroic poetry* of the
Ionian type was known in Greece by that time—but that the
influence was Homer and the new kind of massive epic is highly
probable. Semonides of Amorgos referred a line in the Iliad to
'the man of Chios', but the date of this reference is not quite
beyond dispute (n. 2 to p. 272). Another and more important
'literary' reference is the couplet on the Ischia jug (p. 70),
certainly not later than 700, which refers to the famous cup of
Nestor: this capacious vessel is described at XI. 632 ff., and the
Ischia reference must either be to the Iliad or to a separate

Pylian poem perhaps used by the main composer of the Iliad. More than this we cannot say.

(ii) No *certainly* identifiable epic scene is known from the Geometric period which ended *c.* 700. There is one highly probable mythological picture of a specific kind (Heracles and the Stymphalian birds on an Attic late Geometric jug in Copenhagen, pl. 5c) and more than one indubitable scene with centaurs—but these do not necessarily derive from poetical accounts, let alone Homeric ones.[1] An Attic jug of the late 8th century in Athens has a double figure which may well represent the Siamese twins, the Aktorione–Molione (pl. 5b); though they are not at all conspicuous in the Iliad and their public fame probably derived from non-Homeric epic.[2] Recently, too, a new and attractive interpretation has been offered of a scene on a late Geometric Attic jug (of around 730 B.C.?) in the Louvre, here plate 5a. K. Friis Johansen maintains[3] that the main scene represents the end of the duel between Ajax and Hector in the seventh book of the Iliad: the figure holding out a long staff is Idaeus, one of the two heralds who intervene (VII. 274ff.); the figure to his left is Ajax, that to the right of his staff is Hector, who has lost his shield in the fight (270ff.) and has already taken off and is now holding his sword with scabbard and belt as an exchange-offering (299– 304). The main difficulty is the recumbent figure under the herald's staff, repeated once more on the vase. Johansen takes it as a reference to the gathering of the corpses from the battle- field which takes place under truce later in VII, and argues that this confusion of one scene with another is typical of the Geo- metric artist's method of presentation. I am unconvinced by this in the present case, and the recumbent figure presents a grave difficulty in the proposed interpretation. Yet Johansen's extremely interesting and ingenious suggestion, of which I have summarized only the main points here, will need serious reflection and discussion. Meanwhile I am certain of one thing, that he is right in his contention that on this vase we find not a generic scene but, a rare thing for the Geometric age, a highly individual one—a reference not to warfare as such but to some particular and unusual episode of war, and therefore, perhaps, to some commonly recognizable scene from familiar heroic narrative.

The earliest indisputable figure-scenes derived from epic, indeed, are later than 700 and the Geometric style of pottery. Significant among them are two mainland paintings of the blinding of Polyphemus by Odysseus, one Proto-Argive (pl. 6c) and one Proto-Attic, and also the Proto-Attic Ram Jug with Odysseus's companions escaping from the cave under Polyphemus's sheep. All these were painted between 675 and 650.[1] The story of the Cyclops is of course age-old—but this sudden access of representations, *if it is not simply a question of artistic fashion*, must be symptomatic of a fresh and popular version of the tale, not improbably that of the Odyssey. At precisely this period other epic scenes, too, become predominant; some of them can be identified with complete certainty because of the new custom of attaching identifying inscriptions to characters in the pictures. It is interesting and significant that the majority of these heroic scenes of between *c*. 680 and 640 are taken from the subject not of the Iliad and Odyssey but of other Cyclic poems like the *Cypria* and *Aithiopis*; this may suggest that these supplementary poems had already begun to circulate on the mainland, as well as the great Homeric epics which inspired them.

The third possible external factor is, more doubtfully, (iii) the foundation of new hero-cults. This factor was suggested by J. M. Cook on the basis of the discovery in 1950 of a heroic precinct at Mycenae, which from dedications found there was evidently devoted to the cult of Agamemnon as early as the late 8th century.[2] This coincides with the reuse of Mycenaean chamber-tombs for cult purposes at Menidi in Attica as well as at Mycenae itself, and with the probable initiation of a cult of Menelaus and Helen at Therapne near Sparta. Cook suggests with some plausibility that the stimulus of these fresh heroic cults was the recent spread of Homer's Iliad on the mainland of Greece, and the coincidence with (i) and especially (ii) is in any case striking.

Class III contains two pieces of evidence. (*a*) Herodotus was the only important author of antiquity to pronounce (at II, 53) on the date of Homer: Hesiod and Homer, he said, were 400 years and not more before his own time. That puts Homer soon after 850; but Wade-Gery has argued that Herodotus, who knew that three generations to a century was a more realistic estimate than the forty-year generation favoured by some of his chronographical sources, is giving the *maximum* value for *ten* generations—as is shown by 'and not more'.[1] The true interval should therefore be more like 330 years, which would place Homer (with Hesiod) squarely in the 8th century. The (Homerid?) genealogical information on which this estimate would be based is unlikely to be completely accurate, but may well not be more than a generation out.[2] (*b*) The other objective chronological criterion is the date of Arctinus of Miletus, the composer of the *Aithiopis*. This poem is later than the Iliad by the criterion of subject, which was evidently designed to start where that of the Iliad left off. But according to the Suda's report of Hesychius's report of the opinion of one Artemon of Clazomenae, an annalist of perhaps pre-Hellenistic date who also wrote on Homer, Arctinus was born 'in the 9th Olympiad, 410 years after the Trojan war'.[3] At least his two dating standards do not conflict; they give a birth-date around 744 and a presumed *floruit* before 700. This again would put the composition of the Iliad not later than the late 8th century, and perhaps earlier. Artemon's reliability is unknown, but he was presumably using Clazomenian and perhaps Milesian records.

Class IV contains a single point: by the time of Archilochus, in the middle of the 7th century, the poet had become an individual. Personal poetry in the form of elegiac, iambic and lyric verse had made the anonymity of the *aoidos* obsolete; by this time the public had begun to be interested in the personality of the poets themselves, and the feelings and experiences of poets as individuals invade the subject-matter of poetry. This has begun to happen even in Hesiod. Partly as a consequence the biography of poets becomes much fuller, and even the Cyclic authors were better known than the man who far outstripped them in fame and public interest, Homer. It seems inconceivable that either of the great poems could have been constructed as late as the generation of Archilochus without far more being known about their composer or composers than antiquity could discover about Homer.

These, then, are the pieces of evidence on which any estimate of the date of monumental composition must be based. They are completely inadequate for any precise conclusion. The effort to supplement them by other and even more ambivalent arguments—for example that references to Cyprus reflect the restoration of Greek trade with the island in the 8th century, or those to Sicily the colonization of the late 8th and the 7th century (p. 185); or Schadewaldt's deductions from the prophecy at xx. 306 ff. that the descendants of Aeneas will rule Troy[1]— increases rather than diminishes the uncertainty. The evidence does point clearly enough, however, to the general period of the 9th and 8th centuries. Moreover there are almost no factors to favour the 9th rather than the 8th, and some to favour the reverse: notably the appearance of Trojan-cycle representation and heroic cult at the end of the 8th or beginning of the 7th century, and the hoplite references which give a probable *terminus post* around 750 (pp. 186–8) and which, though few in number, there is no special reason for regarding as additions to the Iliad. Thus provisionally and with due caution I accept the 8th century, as many others have, as the probable date of composition of the Iliad—and probably too, close to its end, of the Odyssey. Yet there is no overwhelming reason why we should not envisage the later 9th century as the time of main composition of the Iliad, with gradual accretions by the singers of the 8th (pp. 325 f.); after all, artistic techniques and fashions could account for the burst of epic scenes in the early 7th century, while religious innovations often tend to lie outside the sphere of strict causation. Again, the formation of the large-scale Odyssey might easily have been as late as the first years of the 7th century. In the light of our ignorance of so much that went on in the 9th and 8th centuries, and even in the first half of the 7th, it must be confessed that our inability to place the poems more precisely does not at present matter very much.

§4. *The relationship of the Iliad and Odyssey*

Finally we come to the problem discussed ever since antiquity: whether the Iliad and Odyssey are due to the same main composer. It will be plain from assumptions made earlier that I myself believe, though with certain reservations, that the main processes of composition of the two great poems were carried out by two separate singers. Once more this kind of choice, against a background of almost complete biographical and social ignorance, is of only limited significance; but in this case the analysis of their differences, on the evidence of which the choice must be made, is important for the understanding of the poems themselves—the only complete realities in the whole situation.

Instantly to be dismissed is the objection to separate composition that *two* such geniuses can hardly have appeared in so short a time. Geniuses are in part produced by situations (compare the Renaissance in Italy, not to mention classical Greece itself), and only come singly in situations like our own. In any case it is misleading to think of genius all concentrated in one man, the monumental composer. Behind him there undoubtedly lay oral heroic material of very high quality; his special gifts were those of integration, and above all the imaginative concept of a large-scale unity. This idea did not have to recur independently; if the Odyssey was subsequent to the Iliad it seems likely that there was some degree of imitation, whether by the same composer or another.

The different subjects of the two poems—war and heroic pride in the one case, dynastic crisis, adventurous journeys and private vengeance in the other—of themselves impose differences of ethos, treatment and style (pp. 160 ff.). Yet it is important—and unusual—to recognize that these different subjects could both be included in the same poet's repertoire. It is a mistake to think of nearly all heroic poetry as martial poetry, and of the Iliadic type as necessarily incompatible with the Odyssean. Heroic poetry of all periods often concerns marvels, outlandish adventures, and the uses of disguise and stratagem. The Iliad is indeed unusual in its suppression of these themes; at the same time the frequent theme of bride-stealing and wife-recovery is common to both it and the Odyssey. Granted that in origin the two different subjects might have appealed to, and been developed by, different types of singer, yet once the heroic repertoire had become fairly extensive, and once social conditions allowed the intermixture of regional varieties—as must have been the case long before Homer—then many different singers would have been ready to accept both kinds of song into their own repertoire. Thus a single one of them *could* have elaborated each kind on a monumental scale, developing for each construction a slightly different tradition and extending the application of a slightly different technique. It must be admitted, nevertheless, that the differences of structure and viewpoint in the Iliad and Odyssey suggest a considerable divergence of gifts and intentions on the part of their main composers. The Iliad seems to have reached its length and form mainly by planned accretions to two or more basic themes—on which Page points out that the vengeance theme has two different applications in the first and second part of the poem, first against Agamemnon and then against Hector. The Odyssey, on the other hand, takes three distinct thematic complexes and three different geographical settings and compounds them, with varying success, into an integral whole. The latter is a more ambitious and more difficult process, and perhaps a more advanced one; it would certainly be made easier if many of the problems of monumental composition had already been solved or emphasized by the Iliad. Yet these considerations do not of themselves exclude the possibility of a single singer making first the Iliad and then, later in his life, with greater practice, higher ambition, and I would say diminished freshness, the Odyssey. I shall point out in chapter 17 that the Odyssey in places seems to strive for sheer length—and not in places which seem to be seriously affected by later elaboration. This appears to presuppose a deliberate effort to match the Iliad; an effort which could again have been made by a separate imitator, or again be the response of the same singer at a later stage of his career.

A radical difference of treatment of a few subjects common to the two poems suggests at the very least a variation of tradition in the stage preceding large-scale composition. Odysseus himself is a conspicuous example. In the Odyssey his weapon is the bow; he is a great marksman, one who even resorts to poisoned arrows, and at *8. 215*ff. he boasts of having been a great archer at Troy (although he left his best bow at home, *21. 38*ff.). This is utterly different from the situation depicted in the Iliad, where with the exception of Teucros, Paris and Pandaros—of whom only the first is respectable, and he but a minor hero and also a spearsman—no hero uses the bow, and certainly not Odysseus, who is depicted as a spear-fighter and who presumably shared Diomedes's scorn for the archer Paris at XI. 385 ff. This is a major difference between the two poems, a difference that amounts to a marked inconsistency. It strongly suggests that the tradition about Odysseus had developed separately in different poetical environments, for some time at least before the era of monumental composition. The character of Nestor presents a similar but less conspicuous case: he is aged and patriarchal in both poems—that is perhaps the central characteristic of the early tradition about him—but in the Iliad he is garrulous and always ready to reminisce about the Peloponnesian exploits of his younger days, while in the Odyssey this obvious trait is hardly touched on, and one of his typical Iliadic expressions, 'would I were as young as when...', can even be reused in completely different circumstances and put into the mouth of the disguised Odysseus (*14. 468, 503*).

Another significant difference lies in the handling of the gods, the emphasis placed upon the Olympic pantheon and the way in which deity is thought to operate. After the opening scenes of the Odyssey divine assemblies and debates virtually cease to occur; and divine control over the events of the story is exercised almost exclusively either by Poseidon pursuing a private and rather exaggerated grudge or more conspicuously by Athene acting as Odysseus's personal *daimon* and protector. Contrast this with the Iliad and its repeated and long-drawn-out divine assemblies, its pro-Achaean and pro-Trojan parties of gods, its obvious delight in the details of life on Mount Olympus, in the intimacies and quarrels of gods and in the mechanisms of Zeus's supremacy! Did the composer of the Odyssey find these things less worth-while for their own sake—though he was not averse from a sophisticated Ionian story about the infidelity of Aphrodite; or did he think they had been exhausted by the Iliad, or did he simply not know about them? None of these hypotheses is *a priori* very attractive, and once again one must probably posit regional divergences in the heroic tradition at a pre-Homeric stage. Once again, too, one is left with the consequent question of whether and in what circumstances this difference of approach would have been allowed to stand, without attempts to reduce it more obvious than any to be detected in our Homer, by the same composer for both poems— or even by different ones of which the later knew the whole work of the earlier. In the Odyssey, too, the gods show more concern —though it is still extremely intermittent—with justice. The gods of the Iliad, indeed, are almost wholly indifferent to this concept, and determine events like the fate of Troy from motives of their convenience. Admittedly Zeus is reluctant to see the destruction of such a regular sacrificer as Hector; but this is a very different picture, and superficially at least a more primitive one, than that of the Odyssey, in which the concept of arbitrary Fate almost disappears, in which the gods are frequently referred to as rewarding the just and punishing the unjust, and in which the destruction of the evil suitors is god-supported. This replacement of the heroic irresponsibility of the Iliad by the inklings of an ethical theodicy in the Odyssey is hard to reconcile with the operation of a single singer on the materials of both poems, even accepting that these materials may have contained such divergences. It may even be said that the same is true of a more concrete disparity over the identity of the divine messenger: as is well known, Iris invariably performs this function in the Iliad but goes unmentioned in the Odyssey (where admittedly there are fewer divine messages to be carried), while Hermes is the Odyssean messenger, whose function in the Iliad is solely as escort. Once again one asks oneself—and receives no unequivocal reply—what circumstances and what intentions can have produced this far from trivial divergence in two poems which achieved their large-scale form quite close together in time and place.

These are important variations, not to be explained solely on the grounds of a mere change of subject. Surprising differences can be found, too, in the language of the two poems. This is a topic that requires particularly careful treatment, and for the time being English readers are fortunate to have two recent discussions from rather different points of view. D. L. Page reached the conclusion that the Iliad and Odyssey were composed in places which, though not necessarily far apart, had long been isolated from each other at least so far as oral poetry was concerned; the composer of the Odyssey did not know the Iliad. 'The stream of the Greek Epic divided, at an early date in the dark ages, into two reaches: the main flood was more or less equally distributed between the two, but the courses which each followed, and the tributaries which ran into them, were different.'[1] Page based his judgement to a great degree on the consideration of many words and formulas that occur in one poem but not in the other; in the light of the economy seen in most parts of the epic formular system this in itself implies a breach in the unity of the tradition. Against the more extreme part of these conclusions T. B. L. Webster has argued that some of the evidence adduced is not wholly relevant, while the rest points to a less drastic divergence in the tradition than that inferred by Page.[2] He contends that many important formulas common to both poems include organic and relatively late characteristics like contraction and neglected digamma, and are therefore unlikely to go back far into the Dark Age; that the words and formulas cited by Page are only a minute proportion of the whole Homeric vocabulary and formular system, most of which is shared in common by both poems; and that many of the vocabulary differences between the poems are due, directly or indirectly, to their difference of subject-matter. The point about the presence of organic contractions in some common formulas is a substantial one, though we cannot yet determine very precisely when such linguistic habits began (pp. 196ff.); at least they seem to exclude separation 'at an early date in the dark ages'. It is also germane to emphasize, as Webster and many other critics have done, the vast amount of common vocabulary material shared by the poems; the overriding impression, which is a correct one, is that their linguistic expression and style is substantially the same, though with minor— but perhaps significant—divergences. The similarities of words and formulas, lines and half lines, greatly outweigh the exclusively Iliadic or Odyssean material, and suggest to me very strongly that, if the tradition had separated, whether wholly or partially, then it separated only quite shortly before the era of large-scale composition or perhaps even during that era.

At the same time Page's conclusions cannot be disregarded, and the case he presents, even if one decides not to accept it in its totality, is a valuable one. The words and formulas he instances are, as he claims (and as Webster does not mention), only a sample; but they surely include the most striking part of the whole linguistic evidence for divergence. A proportion of the sample—notably words or expressions which occur but once or twice in one poem and not at all in the other—is probably not significant one way or the other; but what is left, even though it may affect only two or three per cent of the Homeric vocabulary, demands the most serious consideration. In the pages that follow I give a further, smaller, and I hope slightly less vulnerable selection, mainly derived from Page's useful material but with a few additions—which many readers will be able to supplement—and omitting cases where the number of uses in either poem is too low to be significant or where difference in subject could adequately account for the divergence.

First, single words that are frequent in one poem and absent from or exceedingly rare in the other (complete absence admittedly being the safest criterion, but a disparity of e.g. 10 to 1 still having significance): $\dot{\epsilon}\rho\iota\beta\hat{\omega}\lambda\alpha\xi$, -os, 'fertile', 21 × Iliad, 2 × Odyssey; $\epsilon\hat{l}\theta\alpha\rho$, 'forthwith', 9 × Il., not in Od.; $\check{\epsilon}\theta\epsilon\nu$, one form of 'his' or 'her', 16 × Il., 1 × Od.;

χραισμεῖν, 'help', 19 × Il., not Od.; λοιγός, λοίγιος, 'destruction, -ive', 25 × Il., not Od.; ποινή, 'requital', 10 × Il., 1 × Od.;
οὔνομα or ὄνομα, 'name', 20 × Od., 2 × Il.; δέσποινα, 'mistress',
10 × Od., not Il.; θεουδής, 'pious', 6 × Od., not Il.; ἄεσα, etc.,
'sleep', 5 × Od., not Il.; εὐφροσύνη, 'gladness', 5 × Od., not Il.
None of these words is likely to be excluded by the subject-
matter of either poem; 'mistress', for example, might be
expected to occur more often in the circumstances of the
Odyssey than of the Iliad, but scarcely to the extent of 10 times
against not at all.[1] Words with martial connotations would of
course occur far more often in the Iliad, and in many cases
would not be expected to occur at all in the Odyssey. Even so
it is surprising that αἰχμή, 'spear-point' or 'spear', 36 × Il.,
does not occur even once in the Odyssey—where book 22, for
example, which is much concerned with spears, makes do with
δοῦρα, etc. The same surprise is elicited by φόβος, 'rout',
39 × Il., 1 × Od.; κλόνος, -έω, also meaning something like
'rout', 28 × Il., not Od.; ἕλκος, 'wound', 22 × Il., not Od.;
and in spite of Webster (op. cit. p. 277) I agree with Page that
the absence from the Odyssey of δήιος, 'hostile', which comes
no less than 46 times in the Iliad, is still remarkable even if the
Odyssey has five instances of related δηιόω, δηιότης. Perhaps
these words of fighting, many of which entered the common
speech of classical Greek, were in the oral period associated
exclusively with poems of primarily martial type, and regarded
as part of a technical vocabulary which was avoided in
primarily non-martial poems even when concepts covered by
these terms happened to arise. This is by no means an obviously
valid hypothesis, but something like it may provide the true
explanation. Many of the procedures and conventions of oral
poets are not obvious to us, and at least we should hesitate to
fall back on the theory that much of the martial vocabulary of
the Iliad was entirely unknown to the makers of the Odyssey—
though this theory cannot be automatically excluded.

Next may be considered the formulas or fixed groups of
words that occur commonly in one poem and not in the other.
In many ways complex formulas are more significant for sepa-

rate composition than single words were; for since a formula is a standardized unit designed to express a particular meaning in a set form for a particular metrical length, and since it is less susceptible to variation than most single words (although we have seen that even single words can be used in a formular manner), the failure to use a known formula for a common concept in one poem or the other may seem to suggest that this formula was missing from the epic equipment of the main composer of that poem and his predecessors. How rigidly this argument can be applied depends on how complete was the scope and economy of formulas throughout the Ionian tradition as a whole. Unfortunately we can only attempt to answer this question on the basis of the Iliad and Odyssey; and it might be contended that the restriction of a number of formulas to only one of these poems shows that formular economy was *not* complete for poems of different genres, in any case, and therefore that one is not entitled to argue for independent regional traditions in order to explain the difference. At the same time so large a majority of the formular vocabulary is held in common by both Iliad and Odyssey that genre differences are most unlikely to have operated except in well-defined fields like martial terms on the one hand or sea-faring terms like ὑγρὰ κέλευθα, 'wet paths' (4× Od., not Il.), on the other. Thus the more general the meaning of formulas used in one poem but absent from the other, the greater their significance for these problems is likely to be. Exclusive to the Odyssey, then, are the following formulas among others (again the selection is a small one, but includes most of the more conspicuous and frequently used non-technical examples): κακὰ (φρεσὶ) βυσσοδομεύων, etc., 'pondering evils (in his heart)' (7×); τετληότι θυμῷ, 'with steadfast spirit' (9×); ἤρχετο μύθων, 'began words' (5×); ἐμπάζετο (etc.) μύθων, 'took heed of words' (5×); μεταλλῆσαι καὶ ἐρέσθαι, 'to question and ask' (5×); κατεκλάσθη φίλον ἦτορ, 'dear heart was broken' (7×); ἄπτερος ἔπλετο μῦθος, 'wingless were his (her) words' (4×); ἐλπωρή τοι ἔπειτα, 'there is hope then for you' (4×); Κακοΐλιον οὐκ ὀνομαστήν, 'evil-Ilion not to be named' (3×). It may be noticed that χθόνα δ' ἤλασε παντὶ μετώπῳ, 'he struck the ground with his whole forehead' (twice in the Odyssey), is an addition to the many Iliadic phrases for the collapse of a casualty of war; possibly it is an invention of the main composer of the Odyssey or an immediate predecessor— for even formulas have to be invented at some time, though it usually takes the lapse of more than a generation (it may be thought) for their use to become established and very frequent— and so was not available to the Iliad, which certainly tried to vary the expression of this particular concept as much as possible. Complete formular economy would in this case have produced intolerable monotony. Turning to the Iliad, one finds that the list of exclusive formulas includes the following: φρεσὶ πευκαλίμῃσι, 'with subtle mind' (4 ×); δέμας πυρός..., 'like fire...' (4 ×); ἐρεβεννὴ νύξ, etc., 'dark night' (6 ×); μοῖρα κραταιή, 'mighty destiny' (9 ×); ὄσσε φαεινώ and ὄσσε κάλυψε, etc., 'bright eyes' and 'covered his eyes' (6 × and 14 ×); αἰσχροῖς ἐπέεσσι, 'with shameful words' (3 ×); πυκινὸν ἔπος, 'subtle word' (4 × —though the Odyssey uses πυκινόν in the same formular position with other nouns like δόμον); οὐκ (οὐδ') ἀλεγίζω, 'I take no account of' (3 ×). One or two of these would naturally occur somewhat more frequently, but not exclusively, in a martial poem.

A small number of whole-line formulas are significant, if they are frequent in one poem and very rare in the other; at least they argue for a drastic change in formular habit, albeit on the part of a single hypothetical composer. Thus ὣς εἰπὼν (-οῦσ') ὤτρυνε μένος καὶ θυμὸν ἑκάστου, 'thus speaking he (she) urged on the might and spirit of each' (10 × Il., 1 × Od.), which contains both contraction and ignored digamma; here, though, it may be argued that the formula, though appearing ten times in the Iliad, is entirely absent from its last eight books—and so could be entirely absent, as it is, from most of the Odyssey. Again, ἀλλ' ἄγε, ὡς ἂν ἐγὼν εἴπω, πειθώμεθα πάντες, 'but come, let us all obey what I say' (8 × Il., 2 × Od.), is absent from the last quarter of the Iliad; it is not inappropriate to warfare, but could have been used much more often by Odysseus to his companions in the Odyssey—which can counter with the line ἀλλ' ἄγε μοι τόδε εἰπὲ καὶ ἀτρεκέως κατάλεξον, 'but come, tell me this and truthfully declare it'. This occurs 13 times as against 4 uses in the Iliad, and those restricted to two in the late Doloneia and two in xxiv, which has obviously undergone considerable expansion in an Odyssean style and vocabulary (pp. 320 f.); so also ἦμος δ' ἠριγένεια φάνη ῥοδοδάκτυλος Ἠώς, 'when early-born rosy-fingered Dawn appeared', 20 × Od., 2 × Il. The exclusive Odyssean line δύσετό τ' ἠέλιος σκιόωντό τε πᾶσαι ἀγυιαί, 'set the sun and shadowed were all the streets' (7 ×), may have been absent from the Iliad because streets were usually not in question, except in Troy-scenes like those of vi. Another exclusive line, γιγνώσκω, φρονέω· τά γε δὴ νοέοντι κελεύεις, 'I recognize, I understand: your orders are given to one who knows', only occurs thrice, but is none the less formular and probably significant.

To the evidence represented by this selection may be added the Odyssey's increased use of short datives plural, retention of short vowel-values before a mute and liquid or nasal (with which may be compared its treatment of short vowels before λίσσεσθαι, etc., lengthened only in one of 6 occurrences as against 8 out of 9 in the Iliad), and by its fuller use of most classes of abstract nouns; also its greater propensity for probable linguistic archaisms, terms like τηυσίην, ἀλφηστῇσιν, βυκτάων, δασπλῆτις, ἀμφουδίς, ὀλοφώια and so on. These might be explained, however, simply on the grounds of later date of composition, even within the limits of a single lifetime. There are probably many significant syntactical differences, too (for example, why is ὡς meaning 'when', almost always followed by a verb of perceiving, at least twice as frequent—47 × against 15 ×—in the Iliad as in the Odyssey?); but these require further isolation and study.

In assessing all these vocabulary differences we must remain keenly aware of the truth that even a single author will often favour certain words and certain expressions at different stages of his development and decline, so that particular words, phrases and locutions, often of quite general and trivial meaning, will occur relatively frequently at one stage and very rarely, or even not at all, at another. This has been adequately demonstrated in the case of Aristophanes, Milton and others; and it may be recalled that the dialogues of Plato have been set in order of composition, to the satisfaction of generations of Platonic scholars, by the 'stylometric criterion'—in particular by Plato's changing habits in the use of connecting particles.[1] These are all literate composers; at first sight the variation in vocabulary might be expected to be even stronger in the case of an illiterate composer who cannot revise his manuscript or make conscious comparisons with his earlier style. Yet this is a misleading argument, for there is another important difference between literate and illiterate poets which has just the opposite effect: the literate poet's earlier work lies in the past, unless he makes a deliberate effort to reuse it, and its effect on his present composition is only indirect; but the illiterate singer never forgets and never (unless he regards it as quite unsatisfactory) drops from his repertoire a song that once has entered it. The language of the earlier songs that he has acquired and elaborated is always with him; it is indeed a traditional language, a very highly conventionalized one, which is common to all the oral poets of his region and to a lesser degree to all those of his whole culture. Supposing that the Iliad and Odyssey were due to the same main composer: the Iliad seems from all points of view to be the earlier, so that when he came to expand the Odyssean material into an Odyssey he would have in his mind—and surely would still be frequently singing, in whole or part—the Iliad. Could he then depart from the vocabulary of the Iliad by even so much as he is seen to have departed in the examples given above? Even supposing that martial and non-martial songs were allowed to retain some differences of vocabulary in the epic convention, would this have allowed the same singer to abandon certain familiar locutions like 'with subtle mind'—how convenient for the Odysseus of the Odyssey, yet never used of him!—or even to avoid inserting new favourites like 'began words' into his most recent versions of the Iliad? Here one must remember that the hypothesis of a poet always slightly altering the shape and expression of his songs might help to account for certain phenomena in the Iliad, notably the strong Odyssean colouring of parts of xxiv; but even so I find great difficulty in the thought that an Iliad and Odyssey could be composed successively—and even to some extent simultaneously, for the reasons I have just suggested—by a single singer, without an even higher degree of homogeneity than are in fact to be found in them.

Apart from this consideration it is difficult to assess the implications of the linguistic divergences between the two poems. Once doubtful examples are removed the essential evidence, much of which is contained in the selection of material given above, is not really very extensive. While I absolutely deny Page's contention that the differences of vocabulary entail complete regional isolation in the development of the two poems, not only for the main act of composition but for several generations beforehand, I agree that the vocabulary differences probably imply a difference of main composer, and am prepared to take seriously the possibility of different (though not completely separate) regional traditions. Here I am partly influenced by the non-linguistic differences between the poems, which were discussed earlier in this section. Indeed I do not believe that the linguistic evidence can be used in quite such a concrete and statistical way as many critics have evidently hoped, for the simple reason that too many relevant factors concerning the habits of singers and the degrees of regional difference remain unknown. Within the boundaries of a single poem, which can be expected to have developed in a single channel of the heroic tradition, greater certainty can be achieved.

One argument of Page's for isolated composition of the Odyssey may be seriously questioned: it is that the Odyssey makes no reference to events included within the compass of the Iliad, though it contains many other allusions to conspicuous incidents of the Trojan war, especially those subsequent to the content of the Iliad.[1] Many critics, and I among them, feel that this characteristic of the Odyssey points in precisely the opposite direction, and suggests rather that the main composer of that poem was deliberately avoiding reference to events that he knew had been fully treated in the Iliad. This avoidance is not in itself an obvious or necessary procedure; but at least it is a possible one which explains the situation as we have it. Page's conclusion hardly does this; for if the Odyssey refers freely to conspicuous Trojan incidents known to its particular regional tradition, we have to assume that the quarrel of Agamemnon and Achilles and the death and indeed the very existence of Hector were probably quite unknown to that tradition. This seems unlikely, and presupposes both an independence and a degree of local invention in the different poetical centres of Greece after about 950 B.C. which seem inherently improbable.

None of the problems considered in this chapter is susceptible of final decision, at least in the existing state of the evidence; the present one no more than the others. In arguing in favour of a separate main composer for each of the two great poems I do not wish to pin my faith to one particular class of evidence; and even within the general category of linguistic or expressional evidence my feeling is that the consideration of exclusively Iliadic or Odyssean vocabulary-elements should be supplemented by more general considerations of manner and style. What I have to say about this may be found in chapters 8, 16 and 17, and may be summarized in the contention that the style of the Odyssey is smoother, fuller and also flatter than that of the Iliad. This result could not be absolutely dissociated from the effects of advancing age in a single main composer (so Aristotle and 'Longinus'), but like other differences it is probably better explained on the assumption of separate composers, of whom the poet of the Odyssey was already familiar with the Iliad, though he probably had not assimilated the whole poem into his own repertoire. For further progress in this field we shall require a detailed and perceptive study of the Iliadic, non-Iliadic and contra-Iliadic phenomena in the Odyssey.

14

THE CRUCIAL PHASES
OF TRANSMISSION

HERE only those stages of Homeric transmission can be considered that seriously affected the state of the text. Consequently the history of the tradition from Aristarchus in the 2nd century B.C. onwards will be virtually ignored; for Aristarchus's editions and commentaries can be seen to have produced a comparatively stable and satisfactory vulgate text of Homer. This was transmitted in many different uncial manuscripts—for Homer was still the favourite author of later antiquity—to the Byzantine world, and was reproduced in minuscule copies after the rebirth of interest in pagan literature from the 9th century A.D. onwards. Superb annotated manuscripts of the 10th and 11th centuries, of which Venetus A of the Iliad, preserving critical extracts primarily from Aristarchus, is outstanding, were recopied and eventually formed the basis of the earliest printed editions. Modern collations of the whole rich manuscript tradition, including the numerous but fragmentary ancient papyrus copies, have altered our own texts comparatively little, and essentially the Aristarchean vulgate became the Byzantine and then the modern version.

Assuming that the main stage of large-scale composition was completed for both poems before 700 B.C., or perhaps very soon afterwards in the case of the Odyssey—an assumption which will be further examined in the next chapter—it may be concluded that the poems subsequently passed through two distinct periods of comparative inaccuracy and flux, each being ended by a determined attempt at stabilization and the restoration of an accurate text. The first main period of flux, it can be inferred, was the 7th century B.C. and the first part of the 6th, when early written texts of the poems were still unskilled and probably incomplete and when their oral preservation lay in the hands of reproductive singers and rhapsodes. Perhaps 'reproductive singers' is an unfair characterization, for oral composition, perhaps occasionally with some dubious help from writing, was still practised during the 7th century, which saw the production of the Hesiodic poems, the earlier and more important 'Homeric' hymns and some of the earlier and probably better poems of the Epic Cycle. None of these matches the technical standards or the freshness and descriptive power of most parts of Homer, and their fragmentation and unnecessary ornamentation of the traditional formular vocabulary is evidence for their diminishing connexions with the pure and *illiterate* creative tradition of heroic verse. Yet the predecessors of these singers, in the first part of the 7th century, must in many cases have been capable of composition and elaboration almost up to Homeric standards. For an important but obscure interval, then, the great poems were in the hands of singers whose alterations we can hardly hope to detect. Some such alterations there must have been, by the very nature of oral poetry; yet they need not have been profound ones, for reasons summarized on pp. 319f. Later and more decadent singers were more dangerous, while the rhapsodes, whether or not they occasionally used partial literary aids (for they did not need written texts, nor were complete texts easily feasible in the probable conditions of writing at that time), were too prone to the exhibitionism of the virtuoso performer to be reliable. They were professional reciters, true singers no longer but histrionic interpreters of the great poems of the past, who seem to have concentrated at first on the most spectacular passages to the neglect of the rest and to have elaborated those, in many places, by laboured and fantastic 'improvements' of their own. This is to be inferred partly from later descriptions of rhapsodes and their aims and methods, of which Plato's unwholesome portrait of Ion is the most important, and partly from the probability that by the 6th century B.C., when Homeric recitations were accepted as a regular part of the programme of the reorganized four-yearly Panathenaic festival at Athens, special legislation was needed to ensure that the Iliad and Odyssey were recited in due order, without arbitrary omissions and also, presumably, without unauthorized additions. This enactment, which will be further examined below, initiated an era of important Athenian influence on the dialect and orthography of the poems—an era extended by the dominance of Athens in the Greek book-trade of the 5th and 4th centuries.

The second and more successful attempt to restore stability formed part of that outbreak of scholarly and bibliographical activity which was centred on the new foundation of Alexandria, in the early Hellenistic period, and culminated in the great critic Aristarchus of Samothrace, head of the Alexandrian Library in the middle of the 2nd century B.C. This second attempt was prompted by two complementary causes: first the organization, for the first time, of a comparatively accurate system of copying and textual recension under the auspices of the Library; secondly the chaotic state into which most texts of Homer seem to have fallen by the time of Aristarchus's precursors Zenodotus of Ephesus and Aristophanes of Byzantium. Quotations by classical authors like Aristophanes, Isocrates, Plato, and Aristotle imply considerable textual divergences even by their time, and this is confirmed by the few surviving pre-Aristarchean papyrus fragments of Homer from the 3rd or early 2nd century B.C. (pl. 8a). These contain few omissions but comparatively frequent additional lines or groups of lines, some of them displaced or repeated from other Homeric contexts and others apparently spurious additions due to the taste of rhapsodes, poetasters, library-owners and men of culture. In other words the 6th-century Panathenaic text—if there ever was a complete one, rather than a mere summary of the content of each poem in its correct order—was no longer closely followed as a standard; all sorts of variants had arisen or re-established themselves which were irregularly incorporated in different written copies of either poem. The situation was complicated by the fact that transmission was still to some extent oral. The quotations in Plato and Aristotle, for example, show that the

exact reproduction of Homer's words was not a necessary ideal
—that an unchecked memory of a passage was good enough for
students or even for publication in a literary form.[1] The less
creative and more pedantic values of Alexandria were required
to ensure the preservation of the Homeric poems in something
like their true or at least their earlier form. Before this period
scholarship, such as it was, was romantic, naïve and uncontrolled. Apart from the Panathenaic activity, critical work on
the Homeric texts had been attempted in the late 5th century
if not before; associated with it are the names of Antimachus,
Democritus, Euripides the Younger and Theagenes. Yet much
of this work seems to have been concerned with attempts to
explain unfamilar terms or inconsistencies arising for the most
part from the methods and technique of oral poetry—a subject
that was little better understood in the 5th or even the 2nd
century B.C. than in the 18th century A.D. Even if such critics
had separately achieved useful results, it would still have been
difficult to affect the common view of what Homer sang; for this
was more often learned by heart than read in papyrus rolls, and
Xenophon reported that in his time rhapsodes who knew the
Homeric poetry by heart could be heard on most days in
Athens.[2] These oral versions were virtually impossible to control
in the absence of a consistent written text. The difficulties are
summarized by an anecdote reported by Plutarch in which the
master of one school visited by Alcibiades had no text of Homer,
while the master of another had a copy containing his own
corrections.[3] Presumably the first one knew the poems by heart,
more or less; but the kind of transmission he represents is
unlikely to have been adequately corrected by the every-man-
his-own-editor attitude of the other.

These, then, were the two most dangerous phases of flux and
the two operations designed to check it. Before the historical
difficulties of the 6th-century stabilization are considered,
something needs to be added about the subsequent stage of
Alexandrian activity. I touch only on three points. First,
Aristarchus's detailed variants and emendations, involving
single words or phrases, were often, like those of his predecessors,

THE CRUCIAL PHASES OF TRANSMISSION

inadequate, and had no permanent effect on the later tradition. The influential part of his critical activity concerned the *numerus versuum*, the number of verses: it was in his defence of lines or passages previously doubted or more notably in his total omission of obviously spurious repetitions or additions that his criticism was best; and here posterity, to judge from the post-Aristarchean manuscripts, seems to have accepted his verdict. He only omitted those passages which he held to be unmistakably false; those he thought merely suspicious he marked with an *obelos* or stroke but left in the text—fortunately so, since on these points his judgement was sometimes more doubtful. Secondly, scholars have debated for the last two centuries about the *reasons* for Aristarchus's omissions, obelizations and variants: were they conjectural or were they based on earlier manuscript evidence? This is a misleading and unreal disjunction.[1] No profound examination of the form of Aristarchus's judgements, even as summarized in the scholia, is needed to show that they were at least in many cases primarily conjectural—for example in his use of 'unseemliness' as a criterion of the un-Homeric. For his systematic application of not always accurate grammatical preconceptions it is highly unlikely that he had manuscript support in every case. Elsewhere he is just as clearly following the authority of certain written texts of Homer, of which the Library had many and to some of which special value seems to have been attached, while others (by no means always the worst by modern standards) were classed as 'the indifferent' or 'the more casual' texts. Surely Aristarchus's decisions were founded partly on the readings of particular copies, partly on other scholarly opinions, and partly on his own sense of what was best. Thirdly, the second pseudo-Plutarchean Life of Homer states that it was the circle of Aristarchus that first divided the Iliad and Odyssey into twenty-four books. Paul Mazon noted that both this statement and a much later report in Eustathius emphasize the use of the letters of the alphabet to distinguish the twenty-four books, and suggested that it must have been just this minor innovation that was made by the Alexandrian librarians.[2] It is possible that the number of earlier units had fallen short of twenty-four in one or other poem—though hardly in both, for in this case the new numeration system would be unlikely to have presented itself—and that this was adjusted in the Library. That the whole division was made for the first time in Alexandria, on the other hand, is most improbable—though as a matter of fact three pre-Aristarchean papyri mark no book-divisions.[1] For one thing we know that different major episodes, like the Catalogue of Ships or the Diomedeia, were distinguished and referred to by these titles even in the 5th century B.C., even though their implied limits do not always coincide with the occasionally arbitrary book-divisions as they survive in our texts. More important, however, is the following consideration: that if the present division had been made by Zenodotus or Aristarchus, methodical librarians as they were, they would certainly have seen to it that the resulting book-lengths were more or less consistent, which would greatly help both copying and storage. As it is there is a most striking variation between the longest and shortest books in each poem, for example between 909 verses in v and 424 in xix. This degree of variation also annihilates the theory that the book-division as we have it is very old since each book represents what could conveniently be sung at a single session.[2] In short it may be said that a division into major episodes and sections probably went back to the period when written texts of Homer became common, and beyond that to the rhapsodes and the singers themselves; but that in the course of time the dividing lines changed, until they were finally fixed in Alexandria. Much remains obscure in all this; but at least there is no reason for thinking that division or re-division ever of itself caused the suppression of Homeric material or the introduction of non-Homeric.

The assessment of the evidence for 6th-century Athenian activity on the text of Homer is from the point of view of composition a more crucial matter. This evidence falls into an earlier and a much later group. The earlier consists of two statements from the 4th century B.C., some two centuries after the events being discussed. The orator Lycurgus declared that 'our fathers...made a law that at each four-yearly Panathenaea Homer's epic poetry alone, of all the rest, should be recited by the rhapsodes' (*contra Leocratem*, 102); while the pseudo-Platonic dialogue *Hipparchus*, composed probably quite soon after Plato's death, contains the statement at 228 B that 'Hipparchus...first brought the epics of Homer into this land, and compelled the rhapsodes to go through them one taking over from the other, successively'—ἐξ ὑπολήψεως, ἐφεξῆς. This was expanded much later by Diogenes Laertius, I, 57, using an earlier authority of unknown date; he assigned to Solon the rule that the poems of Homer had to be recited without gaps. I agree with Mazon that this does not necessarily imply that the whole of the Iliad or Odyssey had to be recited at each festival.[1] Of the later group of references the earliest and most important is Cicero, *de oratore*, III, 137: 'Pisistratus...who is said to have first arranged as we now have them the books of Homer, which were confused before (*confusos antea*).' Cicero may have been thinking partly of the kind of tradition represented by the Townleian scholion on the opening of the tenth book of the Iliad: 'They say that this rhapsody was separately arranged (τετάχθαι) by Homer and was not part of the Iliad, but was arranged into the poem by Pisistratus'; but as stated by Cicero the situation was more drastic, and other testimonies in the late group, Pausanias and a relatively early anonymous epigram of the Palatine Anthology, emphasize that the poems of Homer had become totally scattered and were reshaped in monumental form by Pisistratus.[2] Josephus, on the other hand (*c. Apionem*, I, 12), simply states that the poems were first transmitted orally and only later written down. This probably reproduces a separate, and I would say correct, phase or element of the tradition.

Now it is unlikely that there is much truth in the main theory of this later group. The strong Homeric echoes in the literature and art of the 7th century probably tend to support the unanimous opinion of the classical age that a conspicuous and coherent Iliad and Odyssey were widely and continuously familiar before Pisistratus. Moreover it is quite possible, and I myself feel probable, that the later group of evidence is not founded on new or special information but is simply a perversion of part of the complex tradition represented, already with some distortion, by the earlier group. This tradition must have included the implication that the rhapsodes were getting out of hand, so that when the recitation of Homer was established on a regular and exclusive basis in the reorganized Panathenaea a rule was made that, whatever major part of the poems was chosen by the *athlothetes* for recitation, it had to be recited continuously by one rhapsode after another with no omissions. It is true that the Lycurgus passage says very much less than this; it simply implies that at some stage legislation was made to the effect that only Homer was to be recited at the Panathenaea, but presumably this was at the time of the Pisistratean reorganization of the festival. Lycurgus has simply selected what is important for his context, namely an indication of the pre-eminence of Homer. As for the *Hipparchus*'s assignment of the law to Hipparchus rather than his father, this is unimportant and may again depend on the special concerns of the author. On the whole the later group's concentration on Pisistratus is probably justified, not only because it was he who first reorganized the festival in its classical form but also because he was blamed by the Megarians for having inserted into the text of the Catalogue of Ships that couplet (II. 557f.) which asserts that Ajax stationed his Salaminian ships next to the Athenians. The couplet as it stands will not do; it is highly probable that it has replaced something else, and undeniable that Athens at the time of Pisistratus was anxious to justify her claim to Salamis.

The interpretation of this admittedly unsatisfactory collection of testimonies has given rise to bitter disputes among Homeric scholars. A large part of the trouble, at least in more recent years, has been caused by the ambiguity of the term 'Pisistratean recension' that was generally used in the last century to describe the hypothetical Athenian stabilization of the text. That there was some such stabilization, and that it was connected with the Great Panathenaea, is a possible theory that can be dismissed out of hand only by fools. That the monumental poems required to be completely reassembled in Athens, or that they never *were* assembled as such before the Attic phase, is highly unlikely, and if this is what 'Pisistratean recension' now connotes to some scholars then they are right to reject it. The first theory, it will be noticed, corresponds roughly with the Hipparchean group of evidence, the second with the Ciceronian.

That the Homeric poetry passed through a stage of influential Attic transmission is proved by the superficial Atticization, in dialect and orthography, of the texts that have come down to us. Yet that this stage must have occurred in the 6th century B.C. is far from proved; it could conceivably have been due to the predominance of Athens in the production of literary texts in the 5th and 4th centuries. Thus Rhys Carpenter's much-quoted dictum that 'if antiquity had neglected to record for us the Pisistratean recension of Homer, we should have had to invent it for ourselves as a hypothesis essential to explain the facts' contains an element of exaggeration.[1] Yet the Attic colouring of the text, like the tradition of Pisistratus's tampering with the Catalogue of Ships, *could very easily* be explained by an effort at stabilization made when the recitation of Homer was established as an essential part of the new Panathenaic festival. A tradition to this effect was known in the 4th century; and that some sort of stabilization was necessary at about this time is precisely what we should expect from our knowledge of rhapsodes, from the probable effects of literacy on an oral tradition, and from the qualities of certain anti-traditional passages that survive in our versions of Homer.

One factor which persuades me to accept the *Hipparchus* passage as containing a substantial kernel of truth is that there is no obvious motivation in other stories, either for example in Pisistratus's political manipulation of the Catalogue or in the idea of introducing a special manuscript or making a first written copy, for the emphasis on orderly and consequential rhapsodic recitation. The only intelligible reason for such emphasis is the belief that rhapsodes had previously tended to concentrate on some passages and neglect others—precisely the result that uncontrolled virtuoso performances would be likely to achieve. Yet a puzzle remains in the *Hipparchus* statement:

how did Hipparchus (or more probably Pisistratus himself) *first introduce*, πρῶτος ἐκόμισεν, the poems of Homer into Attica? If this implies that Homer was completely unknown before (as might well be implied in the parallel tradition that Kynaithos first ἐρραψῴδησε Homer to the Syracusans just before 500), then it is surely wrong; the Iliad and Odyssey must have been familiar, in some large-scale form, in late 7th and early 6th-century Athens. Rather we may see in these words, which obviously contain a certain amount of distortion, an early version of the story developed in later traditions, that before the Panathenaic activity Homer existed only or mainly in oral versions, which would naturally be assumed in a literate era to be incomplete and ill-arranged; Hipparchus then (or whoever it was) prescribed the writing of a complete text—perhaps, alternatively, with the aid of a special manuscript brought from abroad. The word ἐκόμισεν, 'introduced', could be either general or specific in meaning and does not necessarily imply the special copy.[1] In fact this part of the tradition is probably misleading, and may have arisen from the attempt to reconcile and make sense of several separate pieces of information: that the poems were for long transmitted orally, that this had led to expansions, omissions and confusions, that the rhapsodes were partly or wholly to blame, and that a fixed text or at least an accepted order of episodes was established soon after the reorganization of the Panathenaea.

There seems, in short, to have existed by the late 4th century B.C. a complex and already rather confused tradition about the first phase of flux and consequent stabilization. It probably included the following themes in varying degrees of emphasis: the idea of oral transmission, the making of a first written text, the procuring of specially authentic versions, propagation by the Homeridae, the insertion of the Doloneia, the unique position of Homer at the Panathenaea, the activities of the rhapsodes at this festival, and the rule or law that nothing should be omitted. Whether a full Panathenaic text was made remains uncertain, though there is no evidence that it was; and if so it was surely not the first written version of Homer, although it might well have been the first to aim at completeness and to use variant sources. Some standard arrangement of episodes there must have been—and this would be important for the recognition or rejection of many different lines and passages. How accurate was this Attic arrangement, many of the effects of which were presumably permanent, is again uncertain. In any case the Panathenaic version would differ to some extent from any of those sung by the main composers themselves, and it certainly did not succeed in expelling all rhapsodic elaborations. The tradition that the *Doloneia* was added at this stage may well be true; it was a separate and post-Homeric composition, perhaps of similar date to the central poems of the Cycle, but too short to survive for long on its own. Moreover it seems to have been designed to fit into the action of the Iliad, or at least it was able to do so; doubtless some rhapsodes were already including it in their Iliadic recitations, since it was a piece full of excitement and flamboyance which accorded well with their methods of declamation. Other and shorter pieces of doubtful authenticity may well have been accepted into the canon at this stage—indeed it may have been now that the present ending of the Odyssey replaced a simpler lost predecessor (pp. 248 ff.). Yet I am reluctant to believe that many major manipulations of the plot of either poem were carried out at this time, for example the coalescence in the Odyssey of different versions of the recognition of Odysseus (pp. 244 ff.); though Amphimedon's knowledge in 24 of different, non-Odyssean versions of Penelope's web and the trial of the bow may perhaps be explained as well on this hypothesis as on any other. Such large manipulations would have been a much more complicated operation than the insertion of a self-contained piece like the Doloneia or even the substitution of a new ending. It seems more probable that the sometimes clumsy amalgamations that can be detected in the structure of the poems as we have them were carried out in the process of their formation on a monumental scale; and that the already formed large-scale poems had eclipsed minor alternative versions by the time of Pisistratus. At all events a clear distinction should be drawn between rhapsodic embellishments, or even imitative *tours de force* like the Doloneia, and alternative versions of major developments in the plot. Some of the former may have found official acceptance at Athens; but that the latter should have been amalgamated at this stage in the tradition, without leaving marked traces of late language in transitional passages and at the same time without achieving the consistency to be expected from a deliberate endeavour aided by the use of writing, seems much less probable. That the poems *might* have disintegrated in the generations of post-Homeric but pre-rhapsodic transmission cannot be denied. That they did not in fact do so to any serious extent is indicated, for me, by this total absence of marked 6th-century qualities. I see no reasons for believing that Pisistratean Homerists were capable of exactly imitating Homer, and several for believing that they were not.

Finally a closer look must be taken at that important but fallible link in transmission, the rhapsode, and at his relationship to the ἀοιδός or true oral singer. Direct evidence for the rhapsode in the archaic period is distinctly thin, and it must be clearly recognized that the interpretation of his effects on the text of Homer advanced in this book is to some extent conjectural. The ῥαψῳδός is the 'stitcher of songs', one who ῥάπτει ᾠδάς, and the Homeridae according to Pindar (*Nem.* 2, 1f.) were 'singers of stitched words'; though the name was often also associated, falsely it seems, with the ῥάβδος or staff which the rhapsode carried. The 'stitching' metaphor refers probably not to the joining of different poems but to the interlocking of phrase with phrase, verse with verse and theme with theme; it is sometimes applied, especially in the verb ῥαψῳδεῖν, to the activity of presumed free composers like Homer and Hesiod who could also be loosely described as rhapsodes, for example by Plato in a context that laid emphasis on their travelling from place to place.[1] It is plain from Homer, who uses neither ῥαψῳδός—which contains a contraction first seen in *Hymn to Apollo*, 20, ᾠδῆς—nor ῥάπτειν, ῥαπτός in any association with poetry, that the traditional term for a singer was simply ἀοιδός; and the Odyssey gives a familiar and evidently recognizable picture of the oral singer and his methods in the persons of Phemius and Demodocus. Not long afterwards, however, Hesiod seems to have used the expression ῥάψαντες ἀοιδήν, 'stitching song', of himself and Homer (fr. 265 Rzach); the noun-form must soon have been invented, and soon applied to the new kind of reciter who was making himself felt just at this time—a man who was not an *aoidos*, among other reasons because he did not sing, and who needed a new and special kind of name to describe his quite new kind of activity. There is little positive evidence to go on: Herodotus wrote of rhapsodes as reciters of Homer in early 6th-century Sicyon, and there are vase-paintings of rhapsodes reciting, staff in hand, from the early years of the 5th century onwards (pl. 7b).[1] Yet we are in a position to recognize and define, more clearly for example than Pindar, a most important distinction: the appurtenance of the *aoidos* is the φόρμιγξ or κίθαρις, a predecessor of the lyre, while the appurtenance of the rhapsode is the staff. The *aoidos* sings or chants to music, the rhapsode declaims. Now musical accompaniment is an almost essential and invariable part of oral poetry. A very few Slavic regions are known where it has fallen out of use, but the vast majority of oral traditions, and all rich and prolific ones, have depended on a musical accompaniment. This is because the accompaniment is functional, not merely decorative: not only does it help to stabilize the rhythm of the verse but, more important, it provides emphasis, covers hesitations, fills gaps, and in general allows the singer time to marshal his next phrase or verse. The transition from lyre to staff, then, is closely associated with the transition from the true oral singer to the reciter, the performer, the reproducer by rote.

It may only have been in the 4th century that the reputation of rhapsodes as unusually stupid, as it appears for example in Plato, became fully established. Yet presumably this reputation took some time to crystallize, and was founded on rhapsodic behaviour at least in the 5th century if not earlier. What this behaviour was can be deduced from Plato's description of the ambitious, superficial and sensationalistic Ion of Ephesus. It is possible that some 6th-century rhapsodes may have been more respectable; yet here we have the tradition of the *Hipparchus* to confirm that the dramatic and rhetorical qualities of the classical rhapsode were no sudden innovation. If we project ourselves back into the 7th century the darkness is deeper still. Written poetry is establishing itself, the oral epic is in corresponding decline; yet poems like those of Hesiod and the earlier Hymns and Cyclic epics are still being made—many of which, without doubt, are wholly or primarily oral. There are still some creative *aoidoi*, then, and there may have been many more reproductive ones of the Novi Pazar type; these are singers who still composed or reproduced with the aid of the lyre, and they played an essential though inconspicuous part in the transmission of the Homeric poems—see especially pp. 319f. Yet the undeniable decline in the quality of these new poems, whether in spontaneity as in the Hymns or in fluidity as in Hesiod, together with the demonstrable pollution of the careful traditional vocabulary, strongly suggests that by the close of the 7th century, at least, true oral composition was virtually dead. It would be wrong to try and fix this turning-point too accurately, or to imply that oral composition and rhapsodic reproduction did not for a time probably overlap; but there was a stage of which it can be said that before it the Homeric poems were still preserved primarily in the minds of singers, after it they survived primarily in the repertoires of a new class of reciters who lived largely, no doubt, on the merits of the already famous Iliad and Odyssey. I should be inclined to place this stage, provisionally, at some time between 625 and 575.

Schadewaldt has suggested that the musical accompaniment was abandoned when the Homeric poems had to be performed for very large audiences who could no longer hear it.[1] This may be so, but I would add that in any case the accompaniment was, from the reciter's point of view, not only a needless luxury but also an actual impediment, since it occupied not only a portion of his attention but also both his hands. It is perhaps more revealing to ask what was the origin and purpose of the rhapsodic staff. It cannot have been a symbol of inspiration or poetical authority, like the branch or wand with which Hesiod was touched by the Muses, for it was much too large. It was in fact a traveller's staff in origin, and is often shown with a crook as in pl. 7b; it was used by the vagrant reciter (as perhaps by some of his creative predecessors) in his journeys from town to town and village to village. It became especially associated with the rhapsode, I suggest, because from the beginning it was used during his performance to give emphasis to his words. In this aspect it was a descendant of the σκῆπτρον or sceptre, a somewhat more elaborate kind of staff, which was passed from speaker to speaker in heroic assemblies and which is exemplified by the sceptre of Agamemnon hurled down by Achilles at I. 245f. Properly a symbol of royal permission to speak, and consequently of royal protection, the σκῆπτρον was normally also used as a means of emphasis and gesture. That can be inferred with absolute certainty from Antenor's description of Odysseus as an orator at III. 218f.: he used to fix his eyes on the ground, and

> σκῆπτρον δ' οὔτ' ὀπίσω οὔτε προπρηνὲς ἐνώμα,
> ἀλλ' ἀστεμφὲς ἔχεσκεν, ἀΐδρεϊ φωτὶ ἐοικώς,

the sceptre neither backwards nor forwards he wielded, but held it unmoved, like an ignorant man.

The hero who is not an ignoramus, therefore, makes full use of the sceptre to emphasize his argument. Thus the use to which the rhapsode put his staff while reciting can even be said to be in the heroic tradition—but in this case it was a rhetorical and not a poetical tradition. This accords well enough with those rhetorical tendencies which we have suspected in even the earliest rhapsodes, tendencies which can still be seen in the detectable post-oral or anti-traditional elaborations embedded in the text of Homer (pp. 204–8), and which caused that concentration on the most spectacular passages which is probably implicit in part of the evidence for the Panathenaic stabilization.

15

STAGES OF DEVELOPMENT

ONE of the difficulties of Homeric studies is that the critic tends to get caught up in the web of his own hypotheses. He starts out by determining to keep them in their place, but from time to time they take on the deceptive appearance not of hypothesis but of fact. The picture presented so far of the development of oral poetry and the origin of the Homeric songs is bound to be false or distorted in some places and over-simplified or excessively *a priori* in others. In this chapter, as well as extending the range of conjecture about the ways in which the poems may have developed, I wish to re-examine certain basic assumptions more closely and finally to emphasize once again the complexities of oral poetry and the utter impossibility of assigning its threads and themes to particular, determinable people or influences.

One of the primary assumptions is that of the monumental composition of each poem in the 8th century. By 'monumental composition' I have meant the making, on the basis of pre-existing traditional materials, of an aggregated and expanded poem of great size and with a strong central theme; and as the agent of such composition it has seemed necessary to imagine a single singer for most of each poem. Neither a corporation of singers nor a later rhapsodic effort could have achieved the same result—the first because it would be both ineffective and improbable, unmotivated in 8th-century Greece and un-paralleled elsewhere, and the second because from all we know of rhapsodes or many 7th-century *aoidoi* they would have been incapable of the task, *at least without leaving manifest signs of their taste and technique.* Nor can the poems have gradually coalesced, in some other way, without individual design—not even the Iliad, in which the degree of composition by sheer aggregation is much higher than in the Odyssey; and not even the half-way stage towards an Iliad, for I have emphasized that any poem of over three or four thousand verses would require a quite deliberate and unique effort. It would not arise either naturally or by accident from the conditions and aims of oral singers, any more than did the two or three poems of shorter but comparable monumental length which have been elicited from South Slavic singers by itinerant professors or the challenge of printed song-book versions.

A further possibility is that there was progressive expansion by gifted singers over several generations, perhaps from *c.* 750 to *c.* 650, so that a central wrath-theme, for instance, was expanded at intervals by an Embassy, a Shield, a Diomedeia and so on. Even this theory, however, presupposes an initial poem of peculiar unity, authority and scale. There are indeed a few major and more or less self-contained episodes like the Embassy, the Telemachy, the Sea-adventures, which could in theory have been accreted in this way—rather as the Doloneia was, but earlier. In general, however, the evidence of cross-references and transitional passages, and our knowledge of post-Homeric standards, do little to support this more complicated assumption against the simpler one that these episodes were added by the main composers themselves.

One variant of the assemblage-by-rhapsode possibility is the theory supported by those who believe in the most extreme type of 'Pisistratean recension': that a body of Trojan poetry, already associated with the name of a famous singer called Homeros and perhaps composing the greater part of an out-standing repertoire of separate but sometimes loosely inter-related songs, was subsequently worked into a large-scale Iliad in 6th-century Athens by those concerned with the Panathenaic recitations; and that the same sort of thing was then done for the Odyssey—or alternatively that a large-scale Iliad existed at an earlier period, but that the Odyssey was formed after its pattern by Athenian editorial activity. Such theories can be absolutely dismissed, in my opinion, for the following reason, already adumbrated on p. 312: that in this case we should expect the

Attic qualities of the poems to be much more conspicuous than they are—to exceed the merely superficial dialectal and orthographical influence and the two or three short interpolations of a patriotic character that are to be found in our texts. No amount of respect for the traditions of the Ionian epic—and if the monumental poems did not yet exist there is no reason why that respect should have been excessive—could have prevented the importation of deeply-rooted Attic qualities; and not only of Attic qualities, but also of *post-oral* qualities of taste, belief and vocabulary such as we see in detectable expansions of the poems. The process would not be simply the juxtaposition of earlier materials, which could in theory have been done without anachronistic importations; rather the making of the large-scale poems involved a great deal of elaboration and reshaping of older materials and the supply of many new structural and transitional elements. These necessary new sections can occasionally be identified, and their fully traditional quality is an additional guarantee that the great poems achieved large-scale structure before the end of the unadulterated oral period.

The hypothesis of monumental composition, then, remains unshaken. A secondary hypothesis, that anti-traditional language reveals post-traditional elaboration, can now be re-examined against the discussion of singers and rhapsodes in the last chapter; and the first statement of it on p. 208 will be seen to need but slight adjustment. If oral composition continued during the 7th century, as it did with varying degrees of influence from literacy, then some of the apparently later expansions of the Homeric poems would be due to the post-Homeric *aoidoi* as well as to the rhapsodes. The least original and most debased among these singers would presumably be capable of many of those anti-traditional locutions that we previously associated primarily with the rhapsodes. Indeed in expansions which show a considerable element of new composition, rather than the re-hashing of traditional language over a mere line or two, it would be logical to see the work of declining singers rather than of rhapsodes in the strict sense; for the latter were in essence reciters, for whom anything approaching extensive fresh composition, even in the limited oral sense and of however low quality, was difficult or impossible. Expansions like the Doloneia, then, though they may loosely be classed as 'rhapsodic', should strictly be associated with singers, not reciters, though with singers who shared most of the defects of the reciters or rhapsodes proper. Indeed one should not draw too firm a line between the rhapsode and the late 7th-century and perhaps semi-literate *aoidos*. The latter would in some cases be prone simply to memorize and then recite, whether with or without musical accompaniment; while certain rhapsodes might have been able to achieve, laboriously and unspontaneously, not in the oral manner, a limited amount of semi-traditional hexameter composition.

The weakest and most impure of the post-Homeric singers would have resorted in places to wildly un-Homeric expressions, and it is therefore sometimes possible to recognize their influence. But what of those earlier or purer singers of the 7th century, those who were post-Homeric but still traditional, and who were responsible for transmitting the Iliad and Odyssey, for a time at least, without obvious and therefore detectable distortion? Sir Maurice Bowra has contended that if the poems had depended for their transmission on such singers then they would contain palpable signs of 7th-century interference, in the shape of intruded ideas and language: they do not contain such signs, therefore the poems cannot have been transmitted like that and must have been committed to writing at the time of monumental composition.[1] I have already argued (pp. 99f.) that Bowra and others probably exaggerate the degree in which a poem in the Greek oral tradition must have changed in the re-singing; but even apart from differences between Greece and Yugoslavia, once the Iliad and Odyssey existed they must quickly have gained a *special* authority which introduced an important and entirely new element into the problem of freedom and accuracy in transmission. The monumental poem immediately becomes a special case. Once a post-Homeric singer started to sing something from these quite exceptional poems it is reasonable to expect that his audience might insist on the greatest possible accuracy in its reproduction. The accuracy would be far from total, even so, and it is plain that on any other hypothesis than the extremely improbable one of a *complete* text from the time of Homer we must accept the presence of some 7th-century singers' omissions and elaborations; but there is no reason to think that these would be very extensive, very inferior or necessarily detectable by us.

Relatively early but probably post-Homeric aoidic expansion may occasionally be detected *in the Iliad* by Odyssean phraseology—language which is comparatively common in the Odyssey but otherwise not found in the Iliad—when it is unaccompanied by post-traditional or anti-traditional characteristics. A very complex example, and one which requires to be considered for its own sake too, is xxiv. Parts of this book contain conspicuous agglomerations of Odyssean words and formulas. So do the Doloneia and the funeral and games of xxiii; but in the first and part of the last of these episodes the Odyssean language is mixed up with much anti-traditional expression and is presumably due to the 'rhapsodic' type of elaboration. Now some of the Odyssean language of xxiv has the same sort of post-oral associations, but much of it has not and probably reflects an earlier stage of embellishment; for it is certain that xxiv was among the most favourite parts of Homer in antiquity, and that it was constantly selected for separate singing or reciting all through its history. It has sometimes been supposed, however, that its partial Odyssean colouring means either that the whole of our xxiv is a later addition to the Iliad or that it has replaced an earlier ending. The first alternative is extremely improbable: the Iliad can never have ended with the funeral or the funeral-games of Patroclus, since that left unresolved the question, crucial for a Greek audience, of what happened to Hector's body. This question must have been settled, and its settlement necessitated Achilles's surrender of the body for burial—for that he should have been allowed to achieve his threat of throwing it to the dogs is contrary to the tenor of the entire poem. That xxiv replaced an earlier ending is less unlikely, but there is no special reason why it should have done; and unless the language of our version is found to be consistently post-Iliadic it is reasonable to assume that substantial portions of something like Homer's ending survive, but have been subjected to later elaboration and alteration of different kinds. The language is *not* in my view consistently post-Iliadic, though many Analytical critics have blindly followed W. Leaf, for example, in assuming that Odyssean usages occur throughout.[1] In fact they seem to occur significantly in the following sections: in the opening, and in the assembly of the gods down to the despatch of Iris to Thetis at 77; occasionally in the conversation of Hecuba and Priam and the latter's preparations, 194 to about 280; in the encounter between Priam and the disguised Hermes, especially around 358 to 409; in the first part of Priam's address to Achilles, 486–92, and in the moralistic portion of Achilles's reply (which may well be an expansion of 518–23), at 524–51; in the preparations for food and sleep around 621–55; finally in the lament of Helen, 762 ff., and in one or two verses of the passage describing the funeral of Hector at 788 to the end. This leaves the most important part of the divine assembly, Thetis's visit to Achilles, and much of Achilles's meeting with Priam—not to speak of portions of other episodes like Priam's journey—free from markedly Odyssean language. Yet these form the most essential parts of the action of xxiv; they are vigorous and not at all un-Iliadic in style; and there is no reason for considering them as post-Homeric. Of the remainder, much may have been supplemented or to some extent rephrased at the time of the Odyssey or soon after, by singers who knew the vocabularies of both poems; but passages like the first meeting of Hermes and Priam at 349 ff. combine the Odyssean with the confused and the anti-traditional, and are presumably due to a later stage of elaboration; there was much in this book for Aristarchus to mark as conspicuously un-Homeric, and with good reason. Some of the Odyssean phraseology, it should be remembered, is caused by subjects like the preparation of beds or mule-carts which are to be found in the Odyssey but not elsewhere (for good reason) in the Iliad, and other assumed cases are not necessarily Odyssean at all.[2]

Are other non-decadent aoidic expansions only to be identified by lower quality, structural anomaly or an exceptional use of apparently untraditional (but not anti-traditional) language? The critic is almost, but not quite, confined to the use of these three extremely fallible criteria; but he can probably assume that markedly *Hesiodic* features reflect the interests of singers of the first half or middle of the 7th century. The list of Trojan rivers at XII. 20–2, followed at 23 by the mention of demi-gods, is definitely Hesiodic (cf. *Theog.* 340–5, *Erga*, 160), and it is possible that the whole passage from 6 to 37 belongs to the same stage of elaboration. Other lists with Hesiodic affinities are the Boeotian heroines of *11.* 225–97 and the Nereids of XVIII. 39–49, and an example of a different Hesiodic quality is to be seen in the personification of Deimos, Phobos and Eris at IV. 440 ff. Other apparent additions that do not have this Hesiodic colouring but are suggested by one or more of the less satisfactory criteria mentioned above, mainly by lack of suitability or oddity of expression, might be exemplified by VIII. 185–97, Hector's address to his (four) horses with its odd reference to Nestor's shield and Diomedes's breastplate, otherwise unknown; XXII. 487–99, athetized or marked as spurious by Aristarchus, the part of Andromache's lament which contains a bizarre, exaggerated and not very effective picture of the probable treatment of Astyanax as an orphan; and XXIII. 344–8, the ending of Nestor's advice on chariot-racing, with its illogical claim of invincibility for him who overtakes at the turning-point and its mention of the horse Arion, famous in the *Thebais*— though Nestor's tactical advice of any kind is liable to be curious and might possibly be derived from some earlier source. Additions of this kind and indeed of all other kinds—except for obvious and well-documented cases of interference like the ending of the poem and parts of the Nekyia—are much harder to find or suspect in the Odyssey; indeed this was a difficult poem from the point of view of casual expansion, since it was so much more tightly-knit, systematic and uniform than the grander, cruder and more uneven Iliad. Additions of the more harmless aoidic type are likely to have been relatively few;

though this does not exclude the probability of frequent re-wording or rearrangement within the verse.

In considering different types of addition and elaboration we should not overlook those liable to have been made during the 5th and 4th centuries B.C., particularly in Athens as centre of the literary world. Many of these must have been eradicated in Alexandria, and the modern critic cannot often hope to distinguish surviving examples from the few recognizable Attic interpolations that more probably originated at the 6th-century Panathenaea. Thus the Salamis-couplet (II. 557–8) presumably belongs to the latter class, but references to Theseus are more doubtful. Another class of addition, those made in the Alexandrian period itself, is equally hard to isolate. Fortunately the activity of Zenodotus and Aristarchus, the former more drastic than the latter, was chiefly directed to removing additions rather than to increasing them, but Aristarchus himself tended to accept lines whose main purpose seems to have been to supply a verb to a preceding original verse which legitimately omitted one; and certain other unnecessary 'improvements' are probable. Sometimes an earlier corruption seems to have given rise to a subsequent explanatory expansion: for example at II. 318 the vulgate keeps ἀρίζηλον, 'conspicuous', although Aristarchus himself, who obelized but did not omit 319, presumably read ἀίζηλον, 'invisible', correctly. 318 on this explanation means that the god who revealed the snake as a portent also made it invisible when its work was done; once the word for *invisible* was misinterpreted as *conspicuous* an explanatory line had to be added, 'for the son of Kronos made it into a stone'! That the vulgate reading had earlier textual authority is suggested by Aristarchus's half-hearted reaction to the consequent gloss, which may be early Alexandrine but might be earlier still. Certain other pedantic glosses, however, were evidently frowned on by all the Alexandrian critics: for example XII. 450, the addition that Zeus must have made lighter a huge boulder lifted by Hector, and *11. 602–4*, the explanation that the Heracles seen by Odysseus in the underworld must have been a wraith or copy. The scholiast declares this to be an insertion by Onomacritus, a tame scholar sponsored by the Pisistratids; and it seems indeed as though many or most of these 'scholarly' additions are not Alexandrian, as one might at first expect, but earlier.

That additions were made to the Homeric poems in most periods between their creation and the Aristarchean stabilization of the text is now clear; but it is equally important to observe how many opportunities for expansion were *not* taken. I instance the Viewing from the Walls at III. 161 ff., in which Helen identifies for Priam some prominent Achaean heroes. Agamemnon, Odysseus, Ajax and Idomeneus are the only ones identified; how easy it would have been to add descriptions of Menelaus, Diomedes and others, and how tempting to expand the jejune dismissal of Ajax in a single line at 229! The Shield of Achilles in XVIII, too, was ripe for elaboration, though it contains few signs of it; yet it must often have been chosen for separate singing or recitation, and its extraordinarily abrupt ending in our texts may be connected with this. The laments for Hector at the end of XXII and XXIV were also a good occasion for elaboration, and would presumably have appealed to the rhapsodic taste; some expansion there almost certainly is, but it does not seem very extensive. In the Odyssey, where the opportunities for aggregation were fewer, the missed opportunities are naturally less conspicuous; but the Phaeacian games, for example, could have been expanded much as the games for Patroclus were in the Iliad, and some of the songs ascribed to Phemius and Demodocus could have been extended beyond the existing title or summary.

The conclusion to be drawn from this argument is that the Iliad and Odyssey were *not* subjected to wholesale elaboration, in spite of the recognizable addition of certain quite substantial segments like the Doloneia and parts of the Nekyia. That they were not is presumably due to the reverence in which the *ipsissima verba* of Homer were held at many stages of transmission, the effectiveness of the controls set up when laxity of transmission began to make itself conspicuous, and a certain minimal understanding and good taste that must have prevented even the worst of the rhapsodes from the most serious excesses —or at least prevented their audiences from applauding them. In general it remains true that favourite episodes or sections, like I, VI, IX, XXIII in the Iliad or the Telemachy, Nekyia and ending in the Odyssey, are most exposed to elaboration and most prone, too, to special prologues, curtailed endings and abrupt transitions. It is also important to remember that the identification of additions is a hazardous business that should be carried out as conservatively as possible; for the oral style is itself cumulative by nature, the singer constantly has afterthoughts which might look like additions—they *are* additions, in a sense, but ones made by the Homeric singer himself. Sometimes these additions become a convention, for example in the type 'Penelope came downstairs—not alone, but two maidservants followed with her', in which the addition fills a complete extra verse.[1] To classify this kind of cumulation as a later elaboration would be a very serious mistake.

Now that the different stages in the development and history of the poems have been approximately defined, a further question may be aimed at one of our hypotheses. If the poems passed through a phase of fully oral transmission by post-Homeric *aoidoi*, before the semi-literate rhapsodic stage, is it possible that this phase has been wrongly placed on the provisional time-scale—and with it the period of monumental composition itself? In other words, if the later datable phenomena in our poems are to be set shortly before *c.* 700, is it possible that these were due not to the main composers but to subsequent singers, and that the monumental composition of the poems is to be placed earlier, perhaps around 800? This possibility certainly cannot be excluded, and it is true that the meagre objective evidence for the date of Homer points almost as well to the later 9th century as to the 8th—for example Herodotus's remark that Homer and Hesiod were not more than four hundred years before his time, if this is interpreted literally and without refinements (p. 286). On the other hand there is no special reason for treating the rare hoplite passages as post-Homeric additions, though some at least of the mentions of

Gorgon-heads, which likewise cannot be much earlier than the end of the 8th century, could very well be added (p. 186). Moreover the outbreak of references to the Trojan story in the art, literature and cult of the first part of the 7th century (pp. 283–5) is most plausibly, though not certainly, explained by the influence of the great poems, which were presumably fairly new at that time. The sum of evidence, such as it is, still favours the 8th century for monumental composition rather than any earlier period; though the possibility that our view of large-scale construction is over-simplified (p. 317) should not be forgotten.

The identification of probable additions to the Iliad and Odyssey is a precarious task, not only because of the cumulative tendencies of oral singers but also because of probable differences in quality between different parts of their repertoire according to differences of source and degrees of assimilation. Yet many additions there obviously were, and it is helpful to have isolated the more conspicuous types before attempting to consider the methods and stages by which the main composers might have built up their large-scale poems. Here again the essential preliminary is to recognize and classify different types of material which these composers had available in their existing store of song. These types would have included the following. First of all other stories outside the range of events covered by the poems themselves—earlier stories like the Seven against Thebes, the Meleagria and parts of the Heracleia in the Iliad, Cretan tales and extra-Iliadic Trojan stories in the Odyssey. The Meleagros tale is used as a paradigm, or example of the consequences of a certain sort of behaviour, and other paradigms are to be found in Niobe (xxiv) and the centaurs (21); above all the Odyssey uses the tale of Clytemnestra, Agamemnon and Orestes as a warning and example for Odysseus and Telemachus. The Iliad has a greater range of references to completely separate, non-Trojan stories and to events of earlier generations, while the Odyssey concentrates on filling gaps between the close of the Iliad and Odysseus's return home to Ithaca. Much of the material of both kinds must have been poetical, and some of it appears in the Homeric poems in the abbreviated style which seems to suggest simple condensation from a poetical prototype—for example in tales of Tydeus, Heracles, and Meleagros in the Iliad and in the first description of Theoclymenus and his family at *15. 222*ff. in the Odyssey. The Nestor reminiscences presuppose a special source, a Pylian song or group of songs. There has been some compression, and no doubt a good deal of re-wording, in their transposition to the Iliad, though they do not show the extreme symptoms of the abbreviated style. The subject-matter reflects the Dorian invasion and some earlier events, but the geography is not always clear; I doubt if the source-poetry was itself very old in the form used by Homer. It is not surprising that Pylian material should be available in places like Athens, Colophon and Smyrna, all of which had Neleid connexions.[1]

A second category of pre-existing material consisted of poetical catalogues, of which the Achaean catalogue in II, though much re-worked, is the most important product. Many lesser ones, though, have Hesiodic affiliations and may well be due to post-Homeric expansion; though there is no reason to predicate this of the list of Phaeacian sailors, for example, at *8. 111–20*. Thirdly, typical scenes like setting sail, sacrificing, preparing a meal, receiving strangers and so on; these are commoner in the Odyssey than in the Iliad, which may be said, however, to have a special class of typical martial scenes. These scenes are formular in character and unlikely to have been novelties at the time of earliest monumental composition—though the possibility cannot be neglected that certain phrases and passages were both invented and so frequently used by a single singer that they became fully formular within his own songs. Fourthly we may count certain similes among the earlier material used by the great poets. Short similes are not unusual in earlier Near Eastern literature, and it seems likely that some of the very common lion and animal comparisons existed, perhaps in no very elaborate form, before Homer. At the same time similes of the length and frequency of those in the Iliad would have been quite out of scale in normal oral songs of say between 400 and 2000 lines; and both the placing and the internal qualities of most of the longer Homeric examples, of which there is no hint in apparent reproductions of earlier poetical material in the Iliad and Odyssey, are so artful that one is tempted to assign the chief credit to the main composers, particularly to the main composer of the Iliad in which these images are so much more conspicuous. No doubt a few of them were added later.

A fifth and important type of earlier material must have consisted of poetry about the gods, their life on Olympus or elsewhere and their dealings with mortals. Such scenes were again not uncommon in Near Eastern poetry; and in the present case, unlike that of similes, there are many divine references in the earlier stories summarized in the great poems: the imprisonment of Zeus and his release by Briareos at the instance of Thetis, his maltreatment of Hephaestus, Hera's opposition to Heracles and so on.[1] It is impossible to be sure of a poetical original for all these stories, but the influence of the gods, and particularly of Athene, is an important element of many of the non-Trojan stories in the abbreviated style, for example in references to Tydeus, Bellerophon and Meleagros in the Iliad. These show, what is more, that the theme of divine protection of some human favourite by an individual deity was well developed in poetry before the Odyssey: for Tydeus was constantly helped by Athene, the young Nestor singled her out in his prayers, and Hera at *12. 72* loved and protected Jason. Elaborate divine councils may have been foreshadowed in some earlier Greek poetry, but it seems probable that it was the poet of the Iliad who raised them to the level of a major narrative and dramatic element. Sixthly, certain unusual material, like the bizarre tactical advice usually attributed to Nestor (perhaps because he was so venerable), or the cosmogonical information that appears in the Deceit of Zeus in XIV and XV but practically nowhere else in either poem (if it is not a later elaboration of Hesiodic origin), may have been found by the main composer in his sources; he is unlikely to have invented it himself.

Most of these identifiable earlier elements are only incidental to the main subject-matter of either poem, namely fighting in the Iliad, adventure and return in the Odyssey. There must have been a great quantity of existing poetry on these subjects too; it must in fact have been far more important than the extraneous or incidental material, but is harder, indeed impossible, to isolate. Unlike some of the external stories it was not merely summarized, but re-thought and expanded; it passed into the poet's repertoire and was there mixed both with other material and with his own invention. It must have been given a new leisureliness, a new degree of detail and a new scale; for the scale and deliberation of most of the monumental narrative far exceeds what one could reasonably expect from most shorter poems of a maximum of two or three thousand lines.

How extensive was the monumental poet's new creation likely to have been? Here one must be careful of terms: the oral poet does not create *de novo*, he extends themes and discovers new thematic variants, he conflates and expands material absorbed from others and gives it a new and perhaps much wider application. He makes up new lines and sequences of lines, but always on the basis of an acquired formular apparatus; these lines are his own, but they also belong to the tradition, and he only needs to make them when there is nothing in his repertory to fulfil, with or without adaptation, his required function. I have already tried to emphasize that this kind of procedure is not merely mechanical and unoriginal (pp. 80–3); it can demand the highest imagination and creative gifts, it can entail the transformation of an arid and bare list of events into a detailed, coherent, completely poetical and dramatic unity. One can see a limited degree of novelty even in the expansions of an Avdo Međedović, although the chief basis of these is the extreme and in my view often tiresome elaboration of detail.[1] The Homeric poets, though they probably started from a much higher level of contemporary heroic song, reached artistic heights that were altogether beyond the imagination of any recent Yugoslav singer whatever, and in doing so they themselves contributed far more than a prodigious repertory and an unusual technique. Fresh composition is most likely to occur regularly in joining-passages designed to lead from one theme to another, where the two have been juxtaposed by the monumental poet. These structural passages must occur frequently throughout the Iliad and Odyssey, and it is a sign both of their skill and of our ignorance that it is almost always hard to be sure which are joining-passages and which are not. The introduction to the wounding of the Achaean chieftains in XI, Achilles allowing Patroclus to fight at the beginning of XVI, the divine assembly in *1* and despatch of Hermes to Calypso's isle in *5*, much of the conversation in Eumaeus's hut from *14* onwards—all these must include fresh composition by the main composers, but it is impossible to distinguish the point at which fresh transitional material ends and elaborated thematic material begins. This demonstrates that earlier material bearing on their central themes was completely absorbed by the main singers, and emerged more or less indistinguishable from their own free composition. Sometimes this kind of skill may be tentatively applied as a criterion; for example the repeated duel in VII contains a curious ending, but the introductory passage with its conversation between Athene and Apollo is so harmonious that one is prevented from classing the whole episode as post-Homeric.[1] Alternatively where transitional passages are discordant or confused, as in the connexions between Circe and the underworld in *10* and *11*, it is prudent to consider the possibility of post-Homeric interference.[2]

The analysis of the poems should include the isolation and classification of obvious additions; also the recognition and definition of a few clearly marked stylistic categories, as exemplified in chapter 8, and likewise of different kinds of subject-matter or content. The analyst should then attempt to discover whether certain types of subject are connected with certain manners of presentation or with the few datable linguistic or archaeological phenomena: for example the Nestor reminiscences are not obviously abbreviated in the manner of the Meleagros paradigm; they do not contain a marked degree of primarily Odyssean language on the one hand or Hesiodic on the other; they do contain certain archaic or archaistic information. The main result of conflating many different analyses of this kind will probably be anomaly, incomprehension and confusion; but it may also be possible provisionally to assign certain less obvious passages to more clear-cut categories, and to associate certain categories with different stages of development—pre-Homeric, Homeric or monumental, post-Homeric but traditional, decadent and anti-traditional. These analytical processes can only be carried a short way, and will shed but little light, and that possibly deceptive, on the greater part of the poems. This part will remain unanalysed—or rather it will be assigned to the large and vague category 'Homeric, making use of earlier materials, with slight later variations in places'.

Great circumspection is needed both in this kind of analysis and in forming theories about how and in what order each poem was developed. Certain provisional generalizations can, indeed, be made. It is undeniable that the Iliad shows signs of aggregation, and that the various episodes which delay first the Achaean defeat and then the vengeance of Achilles—the catalogues, duels, deceit of Zeus, shield, fight with the river and so on—could have been gradually added as the main composer, in session after session of singing, month by month and probably year by year, compounded a great part of his repertoire into a consequential whole. Presumably the theme of the wrath of Achilles was prominent from the first; though even this could have assumed the role of nucleus quite gradually. Certain other elements were probably magnified as the large-scale structure became clearer: the embassy to Achilles, for example, and the figure of Hector. One is tempted to wonder whether Hector or any other Trojan hero except Paris had been conspicuous in heroic poetry before Homer; and in book vi one may perhaps see part of the main composer's effort to create a sympathetic character and a worthy opponent for Achilles. Nestor, too, who is assumed to need explaining when he is first mentioned in i, is probably new in Trojan poetry. The Odyssey, on the other hand, is built on a more complex principle; the agglomeration of small episodes and narrative units is far less prominent. The story of Odysseus's return, vengeance and recognition seems to have existed in at least two versions which were elaborated and conflated, not quite impeccably, in the monumental poem. The sea-adventures were perhaps selected from a fairly extensive cluster of existing poetry, some of which might need comparatively little adaptation. The Phaeacian episode seems to have been the main singer's most original contribution to this part of the poem, though once again it must have been elaborated on the basis of familiar thematic material. Calypso, too, may have been developed on the lines of Circe; and the whole Telemachy, with its complex relationship between Telemachus, Penelope and the suitors, not to speak of Athene, must have demanded much original work—though some of the episodes and reminiscences in the Peloponnese may well have been closely modelled on existing songs. In the second half of the poem, after Odysseus's return to Ithaca, the main composer must have had many passages to compile with little direct help from his predecessors, and here the effects are visible of a new compositional motive, the effort to match the scale and force of the Iliad (p. 357). After monumental composition came further elaboration, some of it no doubt post-Homeric, notably of the underworld episode and of the poem's ending, which was re-composed at greater length. The end of the Iliad, too, was progressively elaborated so as to throw greater emphasis on the hazards of Priam's journey and the pathos of his encounter with Achilles.

These are broad guesses about the construction of the two great poems, some of them based on the kinds of classification outlined above and others inferred less systematically from obvious aspects of the poems. In general such conjectures should be carefully restrained—though neither care nor restraint has been conspicuous in most branches of Homeric study in the past. The growing knowledge of oral poetry, in particular of the Yugoslav singers who can be studied in the Parry–Lord publication as it progresses, shows that the process by which a single song, even a short one, establishes itself in a singer's repertoire and takes on its form of a particular moment is so complex that, without the opportunity to examine his technique over a wide range of themes and without direct information from the singer himself, it is quite impossible to reconstruct. Even such direct information is often extraordinarily unhelpful, since it is characteristic of these and other illiterate poets that they are unselfconscious and naïve about their methods and quite vague about the history and descent of particular songs and particular versions. The situation is further complicated by the facts that some singers vary their vocabulary and style from time to time, for one reason or another, and that most repertoires include a few unusual songs acquired, perhaps, in special localities or from a representative of some other regional tradition. If we try to apply analysis by subjects and styles to the Novi Pazar songs, for example, and then to assign different songs or sections of songs to different singers, different influences, and different generations, we shall rapidly be reduced to manifest and demonstrable confusion. Precisely the same danger unfortunately exists with the attempt to analyse and explain the composition and structure of the Homeric poems, at least beyond a certain rather elementary point. An oral tradition is an almost infinitely complex entity; the way in which a particular theme or group of themes has developed as between different regions, different generations, different singers and different occasions is not easily determinable, to say the least, even with the amount of information collected by a Parry. Not all this information is yet available; but when it is we shall see, I suspect, that even the whole of it is inadequate for that degree of understanding, even of a single short song, that many Homeric scholars think they can achieve for the massive and remote Iliad or Odyssey. To some extent, it is true, the Homeric tradition is likely to have been more consistent, better organized and therefore more predictable than the Yugoslav or any other modern oral tradition of which we know; but how much less information we have! Nearly the whole of it has to be tortuously levered out of the poems themselves. Comparatively speaking a great deal has been inferred, some of it reasonable and helpful and much of it, I hope, to be found within these covers; though I am aware of having occasionally transgressed in other chapters beyond the austere limits defined in this one. Yet I have already stated my conviction on pp. 228f., and it is repeated here: that classical Analytical theories which claim to distribute particular elements in the Iliad and Odyssey between two, three or more separate, successive and distinguishable poets utterly founder—except in a few cases where a short passage is repeated with progressive or degenerative variants, and even there a single singer is often possible—on precisely this complexity and *impenetrability* of oral traditions, in which each singer, according to his own tastes and qualities, takes over material from others and then conflates it with other material and then conflates that conflation with other conflations.

In the light of these difficulties, and in constant awareness of the plurality and complexity of oral poetry, it is not without value to do, at least for some of the time, what every oral singer intends his audience to do: to take his poem as it stands, as a unity, whatever its history and however diverse or even fortuitous the means by which it achieves its effects. The obvious and identifiable post-Homeric additions should never be ignored; but for the rest, in the closing chapters which follow, I propose to regard the Homeric poems primarily as poetry, albeit as oral poetry, and not as mere concentrations of diverse and disparate elements.

PART VI

❋

THE SONGS AND THEIR QUALITIES

16

THE ILIAD

FOR the modern taste, and for continuous reading, the Iliad may seem too long. It would have greater dramatic impact if the battle-poetry were cut by about a third, and if some of the reversals of fortune which delay the required Trojan success were omitted or drastically curtailed. Yet one cannot say that such a contraction would seem desirable by the completely different canons of oral poetry—in particular by those of monumental oral poetry, which remain to a large degree obscure. Until there is some reliable means of knowing the kinds of audience to whom a large-scale oral poem was sung, precisely how it was sung, and the status of the singer, it is impossible to contend that the Iliad is too long or contains too much battle-poetry. Poems on such a scale were quite untypical in the Greek context; but the mere fact that the Iliad was allowed to attain its present length, not to speak of its subsequent oral transmission, strongly suggests that it was *not* too long by the artistic standards of its audience. In any case Homer's Iliad was shorter than the 5th-century Iliad, which our text not too distantly resembles. There is little reasonable doubt that our poem contains at least two or three sizeable expansions and elaborations. Many other passages, most of them quite short, probably accrued after the main act of monumental composition had been completed—or, to be more precise, after the main singer (Homer) had developed a complete large-scale song on the fighting at Troy and the wrath of Achilles and its consequences. Yet this poem, though it may have been shorter than the elaborated version that became standardized by the 5th century, must still have been on a vast and quite unusual scale and must still have contained broad tracts of battle-poetry. And it was this poem that was thought successful enough, and brilliant enough in its scope and construction, to be the pattern for another *tour de force* in a slightly different genre, the Odyssey, which set out to emulate—under occasional strain, as I shall argue in the next chapter—precisely the scope and scale and fullness of the great new poem on Troy. Nor did the Greeks from the 6th century onwards, by which time the Iliad had probably been expanded, find fault with its length and structure or the apparent similarity of many of its descriptions of warfare. Their criteria, it is true, were no longer those of the original oral audiences; but they confirm what has become clear from many points of view, that any judgement of redundance and excessive length tends to arise from a modern literary taste—a taste which may still have some value, and reveal characteristics of the poem that the Greeks themselves ignored, but which must be clearly recognized as extraneous and academic.

A poem of the length of the Iliad, even if we imagine it stripped of post-Homeric excrescences and elaborations, must have taken several days in the singing. That in itself involves different standards of cohesion and dramatic effect from those usually applied to a written work of literature or even a poem designed for continuous single recitation. In the monumental poem, unless the main themes are allowed to drop altogether out of sight—which they never are, even in our expanded Iliad—it does not matter that they are diffused and separated by masses of other and secondary material. The wrath of Achilles did not need to be often mentioned between the second and the fifteenth books (of course it reasserts itself strongly in the Embassy in IX); his absence from the fighting must have been conspicuous all through, and must have reminded an audience that knew from other poetry, or from Homer himself, that Achilles was the greatest warrior on either side that the wrath-theme was there in the background, waiting for its inevitable development and conclusion. This being so it mattered less, from the standpoint of structure, how often the battle raged to and from the Achaean ships. Eventually one of those ships had to be fired, Achilles had to be drawn back into the fight. The audience on the first or second day of singing was not, in any case, going to hear of those things. They lay in the future; meanwhile the question was whether the intermediate episodes, the advances and retreats, the digressions and all the incidents of camp and city and battle, were brilliant and compelling in themselves; or whether their scale and complexity, together with the remoteness of their known outcome, were likely to prove tedious and confusing to a possibly shifting audience.

Almost certainly they were not found tedious. If they had been, as I have already suggested, the audience would have made their reactions felt and the singer would have altered his song. The Iliad as it has survived would not exist. There is no good reason for thinking all these parts of the Iliad too long, once the basic facts and circumstances of oral poetry are borne in mind. Indeed to convey a true poetical impression of such a war, fought out brilliantly through ten whole years between the greatest heroes of the Achaean world and an enemy not unworthy of them, is a task that positively demands a treatment massive in scale, detail and depth. To convey this kind of impression, as much as to tell of Achilles's quarrel, seems to have been Homer's aim. His poem was an Iliad, a summation of all the years of fighting in front of Ilios. His choice of the wrath of Achilles as its main theme was an intelligent one, since apart from being intensely dramatic in itself it served as an effective skeleton for the whole organism. It promoted radical changes of fortune within a limited period; it immediately involved the gods; it emphasized the pre-eminence of Achilles and the underlying dangers of the whole expedition, yet gave a foretaste of the ultimate fall of Troy. It subjected the heroes on each side to exceptional emotional stresses and showed their reactions to abnormal events, which allowed the poem to explore and reveal the whole heroic idealism of pride, honour, loyalty and courage. Finally the wrath-theme enabled the veering progress of battle, under the interested guidance of the gods, to maintain some special relevance to the development of the central plot.

Indeed it is only at three or four points that unrelieved descriptions of the fighting are protracted for long enough to run the risk of becoming excessive. The first occasion is the fifth book, which for most of 900 lines describes the triumphant foray of Diomedes. Here, however, there is little doubt that post-Homeric expansion has taken place: some of it in the rhapsodic stage, some probably by other singers in the fully oral period. Certain passages, not least in the descriptions of Diomedes's encounters with gods, contain an unusually high proportion of untraditional language; they misuse certain established formulas and show many signs of an extravagant taste. In one sequence, for instance, the following curious phrases occur: 'and they bore straight on the might of their hands' (v. 506, οἱ δὲ μένος χειρῶν ἰθὺς φέρον), 'neither the strengths of the Trojans did they fear nor the routs' (521, οὔτε βίας Τρώων ὑπεδείδισαν οὔτε ἰωκάς), and 'O my friends, be men and take for yourselves a defensive heart' (529, ὦ φίλοι, ἀνέρες ἔστε καὶ ἄλκιμον ἦτορ ἔλεσθε—a gratuitous and somewhat unsatisfactory variant of the standard exhortation 'Be men, my friends, and remember brave defence' (ἀνέρες ἔστε, φίλοι, μνήσασθε δὲ θούριδος ἀλκῆς), and one in which the use of ἔλεσθε with the ἄλκιμον ἦτορ formula seems rather harsh. Such expressions, the first two distinctly Hesiodic in style, are a strong indication of the rhapsodic or quasi-rhapsodic kind of expansion, carried out in the period when true oral composition was in decline and was imitated perhaps with the equivocal help of writing.[1]

Rhapsodic expansion, as well as the earlier, more harmless and ofter undetectable aoidic type, would be particularly liable to occur in those Iliadic episodes that were most often sung or recited. This explains what otherwise seems puzzling, that there are many short anomalous passages even in books essential to the main structure of the Iliad, and which consequently have special claim to be considered as part of what was sung by the monumental poet. Important among these are the books that composed the 'original Iliad' or *Ur-Ilias* that was once a standard and misleading concept of Analytical scholarship: I, XI, XVI, XXII, which describe respectively the beginning of the wrath, the first and crucial Achaean defeat, the sally and death of Patroclus, and the vengeance of Achilles on Hector. Even these sections of the poem have suffered sporadic elaboration;

yet their richness in essential narrative content, together with their outstanding literary quality, prevented large-scale interpolations or very widespread later interference. An episode like the Diomedeia of book v was different. It is in no way essential to the main plot, indeed like most of the first half of the poem it delays its development. It was worked into the poem to give breadth and scale and to increase the effect of omnipresent war. It must often have been chosen for special performance, since it contains many felicities, concentrates on the exploits of a single hero and thus possesses an obvious unity of its own, and makes a powerful impression of heroic invincibility and Achaean triumph. In addition its nucleus of divine encounters, expanded as it may have been, must have given the whole episode a special appeal.

The Diomedeia has often, indeed, been taken as a supreme example of Homer's art as a poet of battle, and many critics have failed to recognize the degree of later elaboration to which it was probably subjected. In fact the concentrated descriptions of fighting in the twelfth book (after the probably added opening) or the sixteenth—the former describing the fight to break through the Achaean wall and ditch, the latter the *aristeia* and death of Patroclus—are more magnificent and more typical of Homer at his best. The fighting of v is better paralleled by that of the seventh and eighth books, or the seventeenth. The last, which describes the long-drawn-out tussle for Patroclus's body, resembles the Diomedeia in its unevenness, and perhaps for a similar cause: it is a more or less self-contained episode which was probably often chosen for special recitation and thus for post-Homeric exaggeration.

It is possible to feel that books v or xvii are too long, but most of the descriptions of warfare do not run a serious risk of this effect. That is largely because of the force and variety of Homeric detail and digression. The accounts of battle are far more than mere lists of victors and victims. They are varied by many differences of approach and treatment, used with feeling and dramatic understanding. Even the unadorned list of victims has its use at times: not as a mere resource for filling out a few more lines, but rather to drive home the savagery and invincibility of a great hero in a moment of inspired rout, and the confused and almost anonymous mass of those he slaughters.[1] Homer can use even the most arid methods with success. Usually, though, the devices that bring reality and life to the scenes of warfare are the reverse of arid, are luxuriant and sometimes fantastic. The two main ones, which are used with almost unlimited richness and variety, are the lapidary sketch of the minor victim—for it was a difficulty that most of the victims *had* to be insignificant figures, almost unknown to the rest of the poem—and the elaborate slow-motion account of the fatal wound. Hundreds of otherwise obscure Trojan and Achaean warriors are brilliantly illuminated at the moment of their death. A vignette of three or four lines describes how one of these lesser fighters came to Troy, or gives the name of his homeland and father or wife, or describes some special quality or skill that he possessed in his lifetime, or combines all these elements: he came to woo a daughter of Priam, or to win glory with the Achaean army, his father had lost two sons already and was now to lose a third, his wife was newly married and had hardly known him, soon she would be shrieking in her halls, he was faster at running than his friends, or better at throwing the spear—but now this did not avail him, for he was face to face with the god-like Hector, or Patroclus, or Diomedes. And then the manner of death: anatomical, often fantastic, stereotyped in the dark cloud that comes over the eyes or the clatter of armour about the falling corpse, but curiously moving and pathetic, and, even more surprising, bringing a feeling of variety and freshness rather than the satiation and sterility one might expect.

There can be few parts of the body that were not pierced or shattered in the myriad different deaths of the Iliad. I once read a remark by a continental scholar of the old school that went something like this: 'Homer's knowledge of the human anatomy was so profound that a Surgeon-General of the Imperial German Army did not hesitate to salute him by the name of colleague.' This endearing comment is in fact as inaccurate as it is absurd. The description of wounds must have been an established theme of oral heroic poetry, and successive singers brought their own particular observation or imagination to extend the range of possible alternative formulations. It was not just one singer, Homer, who thought up all these different deaths; though it could be that he first used them in such profusion and variety and as a deliberate stylistic element. He and his predecessors may have seen some of the disagreeable things that spears can do to flesh and bone, and these things must have been a commonplace of experience in any of the more martial periods of Greek history before his time. There is a strong element of accurate description in these accounts of wounds; but there is often, too, a strong element of fantasy and exaggeration. We know for a fact that eyeballs do not drop out on to the ground when heads are shattered, that marrow does not spurt out of the spinal column when it is severed, that spear-shafts do not vibrate under the action of the heart when their points pierce into it. Sometimes the course of the spear-head is minutely described as it penetrates first neck, then jaw, and so on; and sometimes too this course is impossible to reconcile with the arrangements of human anatomy, a fact which has needlessly worried many an Analytical critic. Sometimes these excesses of inaccurate fantasy are probably due to the tasteless and inept ambitions of rhapsodic elaborators, but in their less extreme forms they reflect simply the vagaries of the poetical imagination working on the basis of distant or indirect observations. The result, nearly always, is brilliant. It is both horrifying and, whatever the actual and surgical imprecisions, vividly realistic in its effect; and it stresses over and over again the brutal finality of war, the feebleness of human aims and ambitions and delusions, the harshness and dynamism of the hero in action, and the pathos, cruelty and completeness of human mortality. Here is an example of one such encounter, not of the shortest kind. It describes a minor Trojan in the act of dragging away the corpse of Patroclus:

ἤτοι τὸν Λήθοιο Πελασγοῦ φαίδιμος υἱός,
Ἱππόθοος, ποδὸς ἕλκε κατὰ κρατερὴν ὑσμίνην,
δησάμενος τελαμῶνι παρὰ σφυρὸν ἀμφὶ τένοντας,
Ἕκτορι καὶ Τρώεσσι χαριζόμενος · τάχα δ᾽ αὐτῷ

ἦλθε κακόν, τό οἱ οὔ τις ἐρύκακεν ἱεμένων περ.

τὸν δ' υἱὸς Τελαμῶνος ἐπαΐξας δι' ὁμίλου
πλῆξ' αὐτοσχεδίην κυνέης διὰ χαλκοπαρῄου·
ἤρικε δ' ἱπποδάσεια κόρυς περὶ δουρὸς ἀκωκῇ,
πληγεῖσ' ἔγχεΐ τε μεγάλῳ καὶ χειρὶ παχείῃ,
ἐγκέφαλος δὲ παρ' αὐλὸν ἀνέδραμεν ἐξ ὠτειλῆς
αἱματόεις· τοῦ δ' αὖθι λύθη μένος, ἐκ δ' ἄρα χειρῶν
Πατρόκλοιο πόδα μεγαλήτορος ἧκε χαμᾶζε
κεῖσθαι· ὁ δ' ἄγχ' αὐτοῖο πέσε πρηνὴς ἐπὶ νεκρῷ,
τῆλ' ἀπὸ Λαρίσης ἐριβώλακος, οὐδὲ τοκεῦσι
θρέπτρα φίλοις ἀπέδωκε, μινυνθάδιος δέ οἱ αἰὼν
ἔπλεθ' ὑπ' Αἴαντος μεγαθύμου δουρὶ δαμέντι.

Him did Hippothous, the glorious son of Lethus the Pelasgian, drag by the foot amid the powerful throng of battle, having bound the heel-sinews with his shield-strap, doing favour to Hector and the Trojans; but soon upon him came evil, which no one diverted from him, wish it though they may. Him did the son of Telamon, darting through the mass of men, strike from close to through bronze-cheeked helmet; and the horsehair-crested helmet grated round the spear-point, struck by great shaft and thick hand, and the brains ran out beside the spear's socket, out of the wound, all bloody; and there his might was unloosed, and from his hands he let fall to the ground the foot of great-hearted Patroclus, to lie there. And he close to him fell flat upon the corpse, far away from strong-furrowed Larisa, nor to dear parents did he pay back the cost of his rearing, but short was his lifetime, subdued as he was with the spear by great-spirited Ajax (XVII. 288–303).

These are the basic ways in which the singer varies and enlivens that necessarily recurrent theme, the death of a minor figure. Different resources prevent the battle scenes from being a mere succession of such encounters, however brilliant some of them may be in themselves. Often the greatest heroes do combat with each other, meeting either by chance or because one sets out to track the other through the mêlée of battle. Then a more elaborate duel takes place—more elaborate, at least, in its preliminaries and consequences, for the fighting itself never lasts for long and the alternation of spear-cast and sword-stroke is never fully developed (pp. 373–5). The elaboration consists in an initial conversation, a challenge or threat or boast on one side met by a determined reply and an affirmation, perhaps, of race or prowess; and then perhaps in a dying speech, a detailed stripping of the arms, and the capture or rescue of the body. Sometimes the duel does not result in a death, but the weaker participant is saved by a divine protector, as Aeneas is saved by Aphrodite, Apollo or Poseidon; sometimes he is merely wounded and manages to retreat to the safety of his companions. The gods provide other forms of diversion: often the description of battle is suddenly interrupted, and the scene shifts to Olympus or Ida where the gods plan to help their favourites or where Zeus weighs fates in his scales. These divine scenes successfully avert the threat of monotony, because they provide a total change of atmosphere and behaviour—domesticity and humour and all sorts of not very heroic qualities are allowed to enter the lives of the gods. Yet such scenes are not objectionably irrelevant or structurally heavy-handed; and they usually lead to a reversal in the progress of battle, or to some new factor like the personal intervention of Hera or Apollo, disguised or invisible, to chide a favourite or make his limbs lighter and fill him with might, or deflect a spear by catching it or blowing it aside, or rescue a damaged warrior by covering him in a cloud or flicking him over the heads of his companions to a place of safety, or removing him, in the case of Paris, to his wife and bedchamber.

These different kinds of individual intervention or encounter are occasionally interspersed by scenes of mass fighting: armies preparing or moving against each other, slowly and inexorably, packed tight like stones in a wall, or armies in panic and pursuit like deer before a ravening lion. These generic scenes are used sparingly, because in themselves they tend to be uninteresting; they are synoptic glances at the whole battlefield, the whole Trojan plain, designed to emphasize and define a movement which has so far been suggested in terms of individuals. Even so they are invested with some specific life, because these mass movements are nearly always illuminated by an image or a group of images. The use of imagery, of course, is one of the basic resources of the poet of the Iliad: regularly the developed simile intervenes to vivify the actions of armies or individuals,

345

THE SONGS OF HOMER

or of deities as they tread like doves or dart downwards like sea-birds or plummets. The expanded simile, in which the details of the image are developed far beyond the point of comparison, and for their own sake, is one of the chief glories of the Iliad. The simile is a deliberate and highly wrought stylistic device, as careful in its language—which is often untraditional in appearance, because the subject-matter is often untraditional too—as in its variety and its placing in the narrative. Some similes have a complex or a changing point of reference, like XIII. 795 ff.:

οἱ δ᾽ ἴσαν ἀργαλέων ἀνέμων ἀτάλαντοι ἀέλλῃ,
ἥ ῥά θ᾽ ὑπὸ βροντῆς πατρὸς Διὸς εἶσι πέδονδε,
θεσπεσίῳ δ᾽ ὁμάδῳ ἁλὶ μίσγεται, ἐν δέ τε πολλὰ
κύματα παφλάζοντα πολυφλοίσβοιο θαλάσσης,
κυρτὰ φαληριόωντα, πρὸ μέν τ᾽ ἄλλ᾽, αὐτὰρ ἐπ᾽ ἄλλα·
ὡς Τρῶες πρὸ μὲν ἄλλοι ἀρηρότες, αὐτὰρ ἐπ᾽ ἄλλοι....

They advanced like the blast of grievous winds, which descends to earth under father Zeus's thunder, and with marvellous din mingles with the salt sea, and in it are many foaming waves of the boisterous ocean, arching and crested, some in front, others behind; so the Trojans were ranged, some in front, others behind....

Others are more abstract in point of comparison: the Danaans defend their wall at XII. 417 ff., and the Lycians cannot dislodge them,

ἀλλ᾽ ὥς τ᾽ ἀμφ᾽ οὔροισι δύ᾽ ἀνέρε δηριάασθον,
μέτρ᾽ ἐν χερσὶν ἔχοντες, ἐπιξύνῳ ἐν ἀρούρῃ,
ὥ τ᾽ ὀλίγῳ ἐνὶ χώρῳ ἐρίζητον περὶ ἴσης,
ὡς ἄρα τοὺς διέεργον ἐπάλξιες...,

but as two men quarrel about boundaries, holding measures in their hands, in a common field, and they in a narrow space strive about a fair division; so then did the battlements keep them apart... (421–4).

In both examples there is a certain looseness which is not so much due to carelessness as to the exploration of extreme possibilities in a medium which is completely mastered. The similes have a double purpose: to crystallize, in a sphere close to the listener's own understanding, a sight or a sound or a state of mind; and to give relief from the harshness and potential monotony of warfare by suddenly actualizing a quite different and often peaceful, even domestic, scene—the shipwright who fells a tall pine-tree to make a ship's timber, or the shepherd who from his watch-point sees a dark cloud growing over the sea.

Grouped in profusion such images can create a new effect of massive and complex movement or appearance, as when the Achaean forces move out in II or as in the fighting at the end of XVII. Sometimes, too, a simile fills a simple structural need by serving as transition from one scene or one manner of narrative to another: to lead back to individual fighting after a generic description at IV. 452 ff., for instance. Not all these comparisons are peaceful ones, obviously; but even the many variants of the ravening-lion motif, which is the commonest of all Homeric images and must have been long established in the epic tradition, depend upon violence *in a peacetime context*. In these cases the intention is less to relieve a surfeit of horrors than to emphasize and colour the rage, determination or invincibility of a great hero. In the lion-similes and some of the nature-similes there is an occasional danger of monotony. Not all examples are successful, though most are, and a few are aggressively inappropriate, ponderously vague, or muddled in their detail. v. 864 ff., for example, is not easily intelligible, though it still has a powerful emotive effect:

> οἵη δ' ἐκ νεφέων ἐρεβεννὴ φαίνεται ἀήρ
> καύματος ἐξ ἀνέμοιο δυσαέος ὀρνυμένοιο,
> τοῖος Τυδεΐδῃ Διομήδεϊ χάλκεος Ἄρης
> φαίνεθ' ὁμοῦ νεφέεσσιν ἰὼν εἰς οὐρανὸν εὐρύν.

Such as is the dark mist that appears from clouds, out of heat
when an evil-blowing wind arises, such did brazen Ares appear
to Diomedes as he went together with clouds into the broad sky.

No doubt lesser singers than the monumental poet, and then in their turn the rhapsodes, played their part in introducing such confused or conflated images.

The singer of the Iliad had many other ways of varying his story, apart from essential devices like the switch to Olympus, the simile, or the brief biography of a lesser victim, and apart too from stylistic variants like apostrophe and rhetorical question.

The warfare itself can be varied by descriptions of movement by chariot, or of irregular kinds of fighting like the hurling of vast stones or the shooting of arrows—about the respectability of which the tradition was equivocal (p. 290). A greater relief was achieved by the reminiscence of heroic events before the Trojan war. Nestor indulged in such reminiscences at inordinate length, and it was hard, too, to stop Diomedes from bringing up in council the deeds of his father Tydeus in the Seven against Thebes. The doings of Heracles were often recalled, for example in Dione's list of outrages perpetrated by mortals against gods at v. 383 ff. These Heracles stories seem to be based on earlier—though not very early—poetical accounts, just as the Pylian reminiscences of Nestor summarize some kind of independent Pylian saga. Nestor also gives the oddest kinds of tactical advice, which were probably the prized invention of a particular singer and were associated with Nestor because of his role as a counsellor in touch with earlier generations of men (p. 322). Longer versions of earlier stories are exemplified by Glaucus's tale of his ancestor Bellerophon in vi and Phoenix's recital of the paradigm of Meleagros and his wrath in ix; but even these passages show signs of condensation from fuller poems, and exemplify what has been termed the abbreviated style (pp. 164ff.). Events from the earlier years of the Trojan expedition are occasionally mentioned—Achilles's expeditions against Thebe and Lyrnessus, the omen when the fleet was delayed at Aulis—but no doubt many Trojan episodes were reserved for incorporation in the action of the Iliad itself, and historical digressions in this poem, unlike the Odyssey, are concentrated on the experiences of earlier generations. Sometimes, again, the whole tenor of the narrative is broken or transformed by some unique and fantastic occurrence: not so much by standard portents, birds or thunderclaps, which are less frequent though more convincing in the Iliad than in the Odyssey, but by special signs of divine emotion or heroic transfiguration, like showers of bloody rain or sudden darknesses that enclose a part of the battlefield, or a tremendous bellow from Ares or Achilles that frightens men out of their wits or their lives, or Agamemnon

waving a red flag, or the prophecy of Achilles's horse Xanthus.[1]
These odd occurrences derive their power from their unique-
ness; they are not traditional, but there is no need to claim them
as later elaborations for this reason alone, and often they make
a powerful climax that could have been planned by the monumental poet himself. His, too, must be the subtle observation
that diversifies the egregious heroic personalities of many of the
chief figures—for instance in the hysterical pride and intermittent defeatism of Agamemnon, the tetchiness of Priam,
Hector's unfairness to Polydamas and the resentment towards
him shown by Aeneas or Sarpedon; not to speak of the complexities and introspections of Achilles which give such solidity
to the main theme of the poem.

To consider these and other variations of style, subject and
feeling as mere mechanisms for keeping monotony at bay in a
poem of exceptional length is clearly wrong. They prevented
monotony, but they did much more too. Yet the monumental
singer was aware of the dangers of so long a poem; so much is
clear from the care he took in arranging the larger structural
elements of his song. The Iliad is constructed so as to provide
variation and colour in the background action while the central
plot moves intermittently towards its climax and the great battle
makes its massive impression, swaying to and fro across the
plain. After the opening book and the setting of the plot the
first half of the poem consists largely of a series of special
episodes, which conceal the truth that Zeus's promise to Thetis,
to drive back the Achaeans to the ships, is not being fulfilled. It
is in this part of the poem that the poet's work of expansion,
magnifying and diversifying a few independent themes so as to
represent a whole war, is most apparent—to those who look. It
is not *obtrusive* in the way in which the effort to draw out a
scene, apparently for the sheer sake of length, is occasionally
obtrusive in the Odyssey. Yet all sorts of episodes are thrown in,
some of them clearly based on stories of events earlier in the war.
The dream of Agamemnon and his curious testing of morale is
followed in II by the long catalogues, themselves justified by
the march-out of the two contingents. The expected clash is

349

prevented by the arranged duel between Paris and Menelaus in III and by the viewing from the walls, in which Helen identifies for Priam some of the leading Achaean warriors—a procedure, as is well known, that properly belongs earlier than the tenth year of war. Danger of a premature armistice is prevented by Pandarus's treacherous wounding of Menelaus, and this leads in IV to Agamemnon's inspection of his contingents. Battle is at last joined, and the triumph of Diomedes occupies V; in the next book variation is achieved first by the encounter with Glaucus, then by Hector's withdrawal to Troy and his meetings with Andromache, Helen and Paris—all of which enlarges sympathy for the Trojan side. VII presents another duel, a truce for burial, and the construction of the Achaean wall and ditch which are often ignored later in the poem; these events show signs of strain, and VIII, too, consists mainly of rather meaningless advances and retreats. It leads, however, to the embassy to Achilles in IX, an episode of a new character and one which, while it is inessential to the main plot, deepens the hearer's interest in Achilles and his motives and contains some of the subtlest poetry in the Iliad. Next comes the night expedition of Odysseus and Diomedes in X—a post-Homeric insertion according to most modern scholars and some ancient ones, and such it must certainly be (p. 311). It was probably made for separate recitation; it is untraditional and inconsistent with the Iliad at many points in respect of weapons, clothes and behaviour, and its language is strained or anti-traditional in the rhapsodic manner. It can be removed from the Iliad without a tremor of disturbance and could be inserted just as easily. It is quite exciting, though, and so long as I am not required to associate it with the monumental composer I am happy to accept it as part of that Iliad to which we have grown accustomed. Its irrelevance to the progress of the main plot is no greater than that of much which preceded; and such is the interest of the various components of this first part of the poem that the audience remains happily unconscious of any strong deception.

Book XI for the first time effectively advances the promise of Zeus to Thetis by putting many of the Achaean chieftains out of action, and XII sees the Trojan penetration of the camp. XIII delays the expected crisis, for Poseidon rallies the Achaeans; and in the next book, with the help of Hera who lulls Zeus to sleep in a major digression and a splendid episode in its own right, he inspires a revival in which Hector is wounded. Zeus awakes and restores the Trojan fortunes in XV, and at the beginning of the next book Patroclus is allowed by Achilles to wear his armour and fight in his place. The wrath-plot is firmly in hand again: Patroclus is killed, his armour stripped, and the struggle for his body forms the content of a long set-piece in XVII. Achilles mourns and awaits new armour; the making of the shield by Hephaestus is described in charming detail. In XIX Achilles is formally reconciled with Agamemnon; the next book contains the prelude to a battle between the gods, and some inconsequential and not very effective human fighting. Hector must be killed in revenge for Patroclus, but first comes Achilles's fight with the river in XXI. In the following book Hector is lured to death, his body is misused, and he is mourned in Troy. That is an obvious climax of the wrath and its consequences; but Patroclus has yet to be duly burned, and the games at his funeral are elaborately described in XXIII. The last book of all describes the divine displeasure at the mutilation of Hector, and Achilles's relenting, and his return of the body unharmed to Priam, who travels through the night to retrieve it and prepare for the funeral with which the Iliad ends.

Thus the main events of the Iliad, as well as its detailed treatment, are solid and various enough to accommodate the masses of battle narrative and to cover all necessary gaps between different phases of the central theme. The result, as is obvious, is a poem of acceptable unity and great dramatic force. A close examination—which the poem was not designed to withstand—soon shows that it has been swollen to its present length by the incorporation of all sorts of material which does not particularly suit the main thematic structure. Much of this material must have existed in embryo, at least, in the repertoire of many Ionian singers; and it demanded to be incorporated in a poem that aimed at presenting the Trojan war in all its magnitude.

Some elements, like the second formal duel in VII—which by its hopeless ending suggests itself as a doublet of the duel in III—or the frenzied sequence of events in VIII, or the futile argument in XIX about whether or not Achilles will take food, are not really successful. In general, however, the process of inflation, most drastic in the first half of the poem, is inconspicuous and technically well accomplished. A certain proportion of the poem, it must constantly be remembered, was elaborated after the main composer's aims had been fulfilled. Elaborations of this kind may be recognized with less or greater certainty in parts of the Diomedeia (v), the whole of the Doloneia (x), the unconsummated Hesiodic introduction to the clash of the gods in xx, and certain events in the funeral games (XXIII). Failures like those mentioned for VII, VIII and XIX may have had, in part, a similar cause. In any event it seems highly probable, virtually certain in fact, that the 8th-century Iliad was less inflated and dramatically stronger than the 5th-century version which, with only minor corruption, has come down to us. Whether or not it was less polished is impossible to say. On the one hand successive handlings of the poem by singers who learned it from Homer may have removed certain imperfections—though they may also have added others; on the other the period of mainly rhapsodic transmission during the latter part of the seventh century and the first part of the sixth undoubtedly introduced certain acute anomalies of taste and language.

Leaving aside technical matters of composition, what kind of dramatic impact did the Iliad make on its more assiduous and sensitive listeners? It was obviously more than a great anthology of battle-poetry or a great compendium of heroic conduct, though it was these things too, and Plato, for one, sometimes treats it as little else. It is also much more than the working out of the wrath-theme—in the sense that the Odyssey is mainly the working out of the theme of a hero's return and vengeance. Rather it is the exploration of a wrath-theme supplemented and made more profound, and set against a monumental background of the whole Trojan war concentrated into the action of a few days. Admittedly the wrath of Achilles, properly so taken,

352

is only part of the whole dire and dramatic aspect of the poem. Yet it possesses a complexity and a profundity that is quite absent from the rather prosaic anger of Meleagros, which was recited to Achilles as a cautionary tale in book IX and which some critics believe to have been the thematic basis of the Iliad.[1] That seems unlikely: it was probably just another and much simpler example of a well-known theme that underlay many epic songs. The important thing to recognize is the degree to which the monumental composer extended and deepened this kind of theme. The withdrawal of Achilles entails not just the loss of prizes but the loss of his closest friend. This in its turn increases the rage and infatuation of Achilles, diverting it now to Hector. Achilles returns to the fight and saves the Achaeans, but this is almost incidental; he lives for the moment when he can slay Hector in return for Patroclus, and when he has done so he maltreats Hector's body and commits yet another atrocity by cremating twelve Trojan prisoners on the pyre of his friend. By these actions he half-expurgates his grief, and is ready to accept, though at first with bad grace, the divine instruction to abandon his infatuation and return the body of his enemy. It is the addition of these other consequences that sublimates the prosaic motif of heroic sulking into the complex, touching and tragic plan of the Iliad.

It would be falsifying the balance of the poem to claim that it is the mental and emotional history of Achilles that chiefly matters; but the transformation of his pride and anger, first in the Embassy into doubt of the whole heroic code, then into indecision and the compromise that leads to Patroclus's death, then into self-reproach and grief, then into obsessional madness, and finally into some sort of reluctant acceptance of the basic laws of society and at least a similitude of generosity—all this is the moral core of the whole poem, and that which raises it beyond the level of reiterated cruelty and death to a more universal plane of pride, purgation and divine law. There is little doubt in my mind that this deepening of the themes of war is the work of Homer, the main composer of the poem. So much of the Iliad presents the heroic way of life with implied approval:

that was the tradition which had descended from the heroic age itself, and in a sense the first questioning of the ultimate perfection of heroic standards was, as well as its consummation, the beginning of the epic's decline. It is in the Embassy, in Achilles's rejection of the offers of the Achaeans, that the new and profounder attitude to the old ideology reveals itself most clearly. Probably this episode was subjected to minor alterations and conflations; certainly it must have been one of the most popular parts of the whole poem for rhapsodic performance; yet the portrayal of Achilles there must surely belong to Homer and to the original form of the great poem. The last book, too, contains strikingly Odyssean features and again has been subjected to post-Homeric re-handling, primarily by later *aoidoi* (pp. 320f.); yet again the reactions of Achilles must belong to Homer's conception of how the whole poem should develop. That conception finds no real parallel either in the Odyssey or in identifiably earlier elements of the Iliad itself, and is the supreme justification for the development in Greece of the monumental epic form.

17

THE ODYSSEY

THE Odyssey is a poem of greater structural sophistication than the Iliad. This is seen particularly in the division of the action between Ithaca, the Peloponnese, Calypso's island, Scherie and, by reminiscence, the scenes of Odysseus's preceding adventures. The coalescence of these parts was in no way beyond the powers of a great oral poet working with the example of the Iliad in his mind and with the help of a highly developed system of formulas and minor themes. Moreover the composer of the monumental Odyssey seems to have had the advantage of using certain quite extensive poems on important elements of his subject-matter: certainly on the courting of Penelope and her treatment of the suitors, on the recognition of Odysseus and the concerting of a plan for killing the intruders. It may be that some of this material had been worked up previously by the monumental singer himself, into a song of say four or five thousand lines; we cannot tell. Yet there were also other pre-existing versions, as can be seen from signs of inconsistency and conflation in the matter of when and how Odysseus made himself known to his wife. The adventures of Odysseus, too, were certainly founded on earlier poems of wanderings in far-off lands; and the journey of Telemachus to the Peloponnese, though it bears every sign of having been put together by the main composer, probably makes use of much existing material on the Νόστοι, or Returns of the Achaean heroes from Troy, and perhaps on life in the great Mycenaean palaces. It seems probable, then, that the poet of the Odyssey worked with larger prepared units than the poet of the Iliad, and that made the interweaving of major themes correspondingly easier.

The main plan of the poem is not difficult: the decision of the

gods to release Odysseus, the crisis in Ithaca between Telemachus and the suitors, Telemachus's journey, Odysseus's stay
among the Phaeacians and the retrospective recital of his adventures, his arrival in Ithaca and at Eumaeus's hut, Telemachus's
return and meeting with his father, Odysseus in disguise at the
palace, the plan for vengeance and its successful accomplishment, his recognition by Penelope. This narrative falls into
well-defined and substantial episodes: for example the journey
of Telemachus (first Pylos, then Sparta, with reminiscences of
Achaean fortunes), the adventures of Odysseus, the scenes with
Eumaeus, Odysseus in disguise among the suitors. The main
difficulty lay in passing from one field of action to another and in
adjusting and relating the temporal sequence. Here the Iliad,
which is much more strictly annalistic, provided little help. In
fact the solution of these problems was often made very simple:

> ὣς οἱ μὲν τοιαῦτα πρὸς ἀλλήλους ἀγόρευον,
> καδδραθέτην δ᾽ οὐ πολλὸν ἐπὶ χρόνον, ἀλλὰ μίνυνθα·
> αἶψα γὰρ Ἠὼς ἦλθεν ἐύθρονος. οἱ δ᾽ ἐπὶ χέρσου
> Τηλεμάχου ἕταροι λύον ἱστία. . . .

Thus they [*sc.* Odysseus and Eumaeus in Eumaeus's hut] spoke
such words to each other; and they slept for no long time, but
a little while, for fair-throned Dawn quickly came. But they, by
the shore, Telemachus's companions, loosed the sails. . . (*15.
493–6*).

Sometimes there is a slight chronological deception, but nothing
that is detectable in recitation or indeed in ordinary reading;
the regular epic convention is observed that events, wherever
they take place, follow each other successively and leave no
gaps. The inconsistencies and harsh transitions in the Odyssey
do not in general arise out of this complex structure, but rather
from the conflation of variant accounts on the one hand and
from rhapsodic expansions on the other—whether by the later
insertion of summaries designed to introduce an episode chosen
for special recitation, or by the expansion of the main underworld scene and the supplementation of the ending.

The narrative of the Odyssey stands out in retrospect as tense,
varied and compelling. Taken as a whole this story of return

and vengeance is satisfying and successful: no one in his senses can deny that the poem is a marvellous accomplishment. Nevertheless it contains weaknesses, especially when judged by some of the standards that we apply to the Iliad; and it is essential to recognize and understand those weaknesses, even at the risk—which anyone runs who treats either poem with less than open-mouthed and uncritical adulation—of being accused of boorish impercipience. I shall consider these first and at much greater length than the positive qualities of felicity and genius, which in this poem are unusually self-evident where they exist and which tend to wilt under the blast of exposition.

The main fault of the Odyssey is that at many points the narrative content is drawn out to excessive length. At these points one feels that the monumental singer is consciously and almost painfully elaborating his material so as to make a great poem which will match the scale of the Iliad. He is doing the kind of thing that Avdo Međedović did when encouraged by Parry to expand a theme to monumental length; though with the difference that the singer of the Odyssey did not simply drag in every kind of thematic accretion and accessory of detail from the oral singer's repertoire, but rather expanded his scenes either by free composition of an excessively leisurely kind or by sheer repetition. This does not happen, or rather it does not become noticeable as a fault, in scenes where the action is rapid and enthralling and the plot-content relatively high. On the contrary there are many points, for example in some of the adventures (like the Lotus-eaters, the Laestrygonians, the Sirens) or in Telemachus's evading of the ambush set by the suitors, at which the narrative is all too brief and elliptical. At these points expansion and elaboration would have been well justified; though admittedly the main singer was right not to make the recital of Odysseus's adventures too long in total. There it might have been better to omit one or two of the lesser episodes and to have expanded certain of the others; though it seems profane to suggest a course by which the world might never have known of the Lotus-Eaters, and one cannot wish it on absolute grounds. It is not at points like these, then, that expansion becomes vicious: rather it is in conversations between some of the main characters—between the suitors and Telemachus, or the disguised Odysseus and Eumaeus or later Penelope herself—that a certain lack of tension, an excessive leisureliness, becomes obtrusive. These conversations are perhaps largely the work of the main composer himself; he sought to gain length not so much in the expansion of pre-existing narrative elements as by an increase in scale in the preparatory and transitional passages that he had to supply in order to make a unified poem. Some reservation is necessary, since the same excessive leisureliness shows itself in books 3 and 4—in Telemachus's visit to the palaces of Nestor and Menelaus and in the long conversations and reminiscences that take place there. Here the poet was probably expanding well-known epic themes of the Returns of the heroes from Troy and the fate which met them at home. His method and technique differ, then, from those of book 14 or 19. Yet the effect of slowness and monotony and the excessive use of repetition remain the same. It is no use arguing that a deliberate slowing of the pace was necessary at these points. I doubt whether such compositional subtleties occurred to the oral poet, even to the monumental poets themselves; and though their experience and good taste might instinctively achieve variations of tempo where necessary, it is doubtful if extreme leisureliness *was* necessary either so early in the poem as *3* and *4* or between *13* and *19*, in which there is comparatively little action anyway and many plans and minor movements have to be described. In short, then, if such long-drawn-out sections of the poem exist, they exist because of a fault of method on the part of the main composer; or perhaps a fault of intention, to produce a poem to match the Iliad in length and scale.

That *longueurs* do exist can be confirmed, though admittedly with some risk of error, by reading the poem through, fairly rapidly and preferably in Greek, and at least with an open mind. It will be observed that in *3* and *4* genre passages of the preparation of food, sacrifices, and arrival and departure are very frequent, as is perhaps inevitable, and that such repeated passages are commoner throughout the Odyssey as a whole than in the Iliad. Similes are almost wholly absent from these books, partly because much digressionary material was being offered in the form of reminiscences by Nestor, Menelaus and Helen, and partly because similes are almost entirely restricted to narrative and do not come easily in speeches. Indeed one might almost say that these reminiscences, and the information they supply about what happened between the end of the Iliad and the beginning of the Odyssey over ten years later, are the main point of the third and fourth book. Certainly Telemachus discovers little about his father, and apart from the subsidiary theme of his education and development the so-called Telemachy contributes little to the main plot of the poem. This is no reason for suspecting its authenticity or supposing that it must have existed as an independent poem before the formation of the Odyssey. It seems to me to be a potentially entertaining episode which has the advantage of giving a certain interest to the character of the boy Telemachus, and showing how up to this moment he has been too young and too weak to prevent the suitors from establishing themselves in his mother's house. It also summarizes events from the end of the Trojan war, which had to be referred to somehow—even though the audience of the Odyssey may be presumed to have known many of them from short poems like those that seem to have been used as source by the monumental composer; and it gives them additional point by the contrast between Agamemnon's wife and Odysseus's and by the exemplar of the heroic son Orestes which is constantly stressed by Athene–Mentes and others. The leisureliness of narrative in these books, the rambling and repetitious reminiscences and the wordy conversations, the emphasis on food and drink, sunrise and sunset, going to bed and getting up, and on the small details of life in a peacetime palace, the flatness of the particular formular style and the absence of similes (to all of which Menelaus's story of his encounter with Proteus, *4. 351* ff., is an exception)—all this reminds one strongly of the methods of books 14 to 19, the preparations for action in Ithaca, and persuades one that the

Telemachy, though it uses earlier material, is essentially the work of the main composer of the Odyssey.

It is tenable that this main composer elaborated the conversations between Odysseus and Eumaeus, or Odysseus and Penelope, in order to deepen the characterization and explain the motives of the main figures of the poem. If so he was not particularly successful. One cannot feel that Odysseus's false tales, or his claim to have seen the real Odysseus in Thesprotia and his assertions that this Odysseus is or soon will be in Ithaca, met as they are by obstinate and despondent disbelief on the part of the swineherd or Penelope, really do much to illustrate character in depth; nor indeed is this a common epic intention. They substantiate Odysseus's craftiness, but that is already well-established—his false tale to the disguised Athene in *13*, at which she is so delighted that she smiles and fondles and praises him, has already made this point in the same kind of way but infinitely better. They also substantiate Penelope's habit of despair, her repeated disappointment caused by visitors who tried to please her by claiming to have news of her husband—but in fact this theme is over-emphasized, and eventually leads to the highly improbable picture of Penelope maintaining complete disbelief even in the face of a perspicuous dream plainly interpreted and other information that clearly portends her husband's return. The flagging tempo after Odysseus has reached Eumaeus's hut is emphasized by one of the poorest digressions in the whole poem (*14. 457* ff.), the story which the hero tells Eumaeus in order to secure the loan of a cloak or other warm clothes for the night. No such elaborate trick was necessary, since Eumaeus had already shown himself the soul of hospitality; and the story that Odysseus concocts, of how he had once won the use of a cloak in an ambush on a cold night, is weak and rather pointless. This complicated wrangle about cloaks is unfortunately a not completely inappropriate conclusion to the fourteenth book, which is surely the least satisfactory, poetically and dramatically, of any in either poem. The preoccupation with trivialities reminds one of the tiresome arguments about whether Achilles will or will not take any food in book XIX of the Iliad—a theme repeated, with little more success but at least more briefly, at 7. 215ff.

This occasional weakness in the narrative is sometimes aggravated by the language. In general it is true that the language of the Odyssey is smoother and flatter than that of the earlier poem. It is more polished, less stark and angular, yet more diffuse and much less lively. It is not particularly that its formular vocabulary is slightly different from that of the Iliad, for though there are significant differences there are far more similarities; and the harshness of some of its untraditional neologisms is balanced by the occasional linguistic crudity of the Iliad. Nor is a tired or second-hand formular style (as it was termed in chapter 8), in which in certain passages the high proportion of repeated lines and half-lines and the overworking of certain common formulas begin to obtrude themselves, particularly to blame. Indeed the formular phrases of the Odyssey give the impression of being less mechanically used, more variegated by minor adjustments and alterations, than those of the Iliad. The language is in a way less stereotyped, and I conjecture that the proportion of more or less free composition to strictly formular composition is higher in the Odyssey than in the Iliad; in certain respects the main poet of the later poem is technically superior to the singer of the monumental Iliad. The main trouble with this smoother and less angular language is precisely parallel to that of the narrative structure, that it is plethoric, redundant and over-digested. It is typical that the formular stock of the Odyssey contains far more tautologous phrases than the Iliad, phrases like $\tau\epsilon\lambda\epsilon\upsilon\tau\acute{\eta}\sigma\eta\varsigma$ $\tau\epsilon$ $\kappa\alpha\grave{\iota}$ $\check{\epsilon}\rho\xi\eta\varsigma$ ('have accomplished and done'), $o\^{\iota}\delta\acute{\epsilon}$ $\tau\epsilon$ $\kappa\alpha\grave{\iota}$ $\delta\epsilon\delta\acute{\alpha}\eta\kappa\epsilon$ ('knows and has learned'), $\check{\epsilon}\pi o\varsigma$ $\kappa\alpha\grave{\iota}$ $\mu\^{\upsilon}\theta o\nu$ ('word and tale'), $\pi\iota\phi\alpha\acute{\upsilon}\sigma\kappa\epsilon\tau\alpha\iota$ $\mathring{\eta}\delta$' $\mathring{\alpha}\gamma o\rho\epsilon\acute{\upsilon}\epsilon\iota$ ('utters and declares'); see also p. 167. Admittedly the repeated use of functional half-lines tends to encourage the unnecessary expansion of an idea to fill the other half of the verse, and the language of Homer in general is often rather full and imprecise—so that one finds sentences like $\acute{o}$ $\delta\grave{\epsilon}$ $\phi\rho\epsilon\sigma\grave{\iota}\nu$ $\^{\eta}\sigma\iota$ $\nu o\acute{\eta}\sigma\alpha\varsigma$ / $\theta\acute{\alpha}\mu\beta\eta\sigma\epsilon\nu$ $\kappa\alpha\tau\grave{\alpha}$ $\theta\upsilon\mu\acute{o}\nu$ ('and he perceiving it with his mind marvelled in his spirit', 1. 322-3). Yet the Odyssey goes further in this way than the Iliad—taken as a whole, that is; obviously there are parts of the earlier poem that are 'Odyssean' in style and vocabulary, like much of XXIV, and parts of the Odyssey, like book 22, which possess the greater sharpness and force of most of the Iliad.

The impression of redundancy in language is heightened not only by the Odyssey's greater use of repeated genre passages, of food and sacrifice and ships, but also by its tendency to reuse a preceding passage in a shortened form—so that one has an impression not of archaic simplicity, directness and economy but of anti-climax and repletion. The repetition of the prophecy of Odysseus's last journey at different points throughout the poem is dramatically effective, and the repetition of Penelope's ruse with the web is acceptable for the same reason; but Odysseus's false tales are too similar to each other, and the recital to Antinous at *17. 427–41* of part of a longer story told to Eumaeus in *14* makes a frigid effect. One has no right to complain of the magnificent scenes of shipwreck in the Odyssey, but the brilliant description of the destruction of Odysseus's ship at *12. 403–25* is sadly and unnecessarily attenuated by being dragged into one of the false tales at *14. 301* ff. A large part of the nineteenth book consists of repetitions. Finally the epic convention by which a messenger's speech is repeated more or less verbatim, when the messenger receives it and when he delivers it, is seriously overworked at certain points in the Odyssey, where it is applied to prophecies, instructions, and the actual performance of those instructions: thus Circe tells Odysseus how to pass the Sirens, then Odysseus tells his crew, and finally the actual journey is narrated in much the same language, by now all too familiar. The same feeling of extensive repetition is produced by Circe's instructions to Odysseus at the end of *10* about his visit to Hades, and the description of the actual visit that follows early in *11*; though it is possible that constructional difficulties played some part in this instance.

The main events of the Odyssey are more varied in themselves and allow a more varied and therefore potentially more lively treatment than those of the Iliad, which is so heavily

concerned with the progress of battle and the martial reactions
of its chief participants. In fact, however, the vitality and
tension that fill even some of the slightest episodes of the Iliad
are often absent from the Odyssey. And yet, of course, the later
poem still contains many brilliant evocations and descriptive
tours de force: the landing in Scherie and the encounter with
Nausicaa in 6, the semi-lyrical picture of the islet facing the
island of the Cyclopes at 9. *116*ff., Polyphemus's tender speech
to his ram and his furious prayer against Odysseus later in the
same book, the famous episode of the dog Argos in *17*, the
description of the early morning bustle of the palace servants at
20. *147–65*, the strange but powerful episode of the suitors' mad
laughter and Theoclymenus's vision and departure—the one
and only time when his appearance has any dramatic force—at
the end of that book, the rout of the suitors and the bloodthirsty vengeance on the treacherous servants in *22*—these and
more reach the heights of inspiration and virtuosity. Apart
from such set-pieces the singer of this poem, and presumably
some of his immediate predecessors, were capable of extraordinary touches of irony, subtlety, tenderness and fantasy—
indeed in these gentler qualities they exceeded the normal range
of heroic poetry and at least equalled the powers of the singer of
the Iliad. The description of the Phaeacians, though it contains
some odd anomalies, shows all these qualities, and particularly
the gift for fantasy and lyrical other-worldliness which is one of
the special splendours of the main composer of this poem. This is
seen as the Phaeacian ship carries Odysseus homeward:

Then they leaned back and threw up the salt sea with the oar, and for
Odysseus delightful sleep fell upon his eyelids, unbroken and very
sweet, most like to death. And the ship—as in a plain stallions four-
yoked all leap forward together at the lashes of the whip, and rising
high swiftly achieve their course, so did the ship's stern rise, and
behind, dark and huge, the wave of the boisterous sea rushed along.
Safely the ship ran all the time, nor would a falcon have kept pace
with it, the fastest of birds: so swiftly running along did it cut the
waves of the sea, bearing a man who possessed counsel like the gods,
who before did suffer very many griefs in his heart, wars of men
and cleaving the grievous waves, yet then slept motionless, in

THE SONGS OF HOMER

forgetfulness of all that he had undergone. When the star rose that is brightest, which most of all comes announcing the light of early-born Dawn, then it was that to the island approached the sea-travelling ship. There is a certain harbour of Phorkys, the old man of the sea, in the community of Ithaca...' (*13. 78–97*).

To the shore of this harbour Odysseus is carried, still sleeping, by his magical escorts, who are destined to be turned to stone by Poseidon on their return to Scherie: Athene disguises the landscape by shrouding everything in mist, and when Odysseus wakes he does not recognize it but everything remains fantastic, menacing and strange.

Despite such marvellous scenes the Odyssey as a whole fails to achieve the profound monumental effect of the Iliad. This is partly because the main theme is less universal and less tragic; but to a large extent it is caused by the actual character of Odysseus. The man of many trials and many devices, the canny, suspicious, boastful and ruseful victim of fortune and his own qualities, is obviously less magnificent than the god-like Achilles, the swift and insanely proud warrior; he is also less real, strangely enough, and less credible. Achilles is often petty and unimaginative, in many ways like a destructive and acquisitive child, but there is something sympathetic in him: he represents some of the commonest aspirations and failings of human nature, though on a superhuman scale. Odysseus is a more specialized being, a curious mixture of heroic and intellectual qualities that can never have been frequent in any society. Moreover he is not drawn in much depth: partly the difficulty lies in reconciling the Iliadic Odysseus, who is clever and persuasive but still a great warrior in the classic mould, with the ingenious braggart, poisoned arrows and all, that he has become in some parts of the Odyssey. For even within the Odyssey itself his character is inconsistent in—for the unitarian audience—a rather unfathomable way. The faithful husband who rejects a life of divinity with Circe and Calypso is estimable enough; he makes a nice symbol of the conservative and social demands of man and the power of his affections, even at the cost of survival; yet he does not accord with the dangerously conceited victor over the Cyclops. In fact this Odysseus of the sea-adventures makes too strong an impression for the good of the whole poem, in the rest of which the hero's character is more consistently sound and gentle—though always suspicious. Admittedly the hero of the false tales is not usually an appealing figure, and one suspects that the real Odysseus quite admired his creations; but otherwise the generous master of servants, the patient victim of insults, the determined and ultimately affectionate husband, is admirable enough. The trouble is that he does not turn out to be very interesting. Largely this is because of the role the main poet has seen fit to assign to Athene, and to the altered conception, different from that of the Iliad, of the way in which the gods rule the life of mortals. During the sea-adventures, at least, Athene is absent from Odysseus's side—because she could not risk offending Poseidon, as she explains later, but also perhaps because some of the earlier sea-tales did not have this kind of divine participant;[1] and, though the audience still knows that the hero will survive, his ordeals seem more terrifying as a consequence. Once he is accompanied at almost every step by the goddess, either heavily disguised or in her plainest anthropomorphic form of a tall, beautiful and accomplished woman, the tension of Odysseus's actions and dangers is surely reduced. This may not seriously affect his moral stature, but it diminishes his interest as a hero developing with his circumstances. The growth of Telemachus's character under the goddess's guidance is heavily emphasized; but his father is too mature and too cunning for this kind of unfolding, and the only quirks and anomalies of his character, as we have seen, are probably the rather worrying product of the conflation of different themes and different kinds of epic material. The Achilles of the Iliad stands in contrast: he is fascinating because he occasionally rebels against the traditions of the hero. In ix he sublimates his personal affront into a temporary inquietude with the whole concept of heroic warfare and heroic guest-friend obligations, and shows a touch of schizophrenia (or at least hysteria) in the process; while at the poem's end his frenetic mutilation of Hector is followed by a mercurial and heroic acceptance of Zeus's rebuke, and his treatment of Priam reveals a touchy and evanescent humanity that was neither impossible nor entirely expected of him.

A similar difference affects the drawing of other figures in the two poems. Although they are placed in fewer situations that might be expected to reveal the finer points of character, Agamemnon, Nestor, Hector and Paris stand out more solidly from the Iliad than do Eumaeus, Telemachus or Antinous from the Odyssey. Even Ajax, whose main role is martial, is better defined than most of the second-rank personalities of the later poem, of which there are many. Helen in the Iliad enters the action at only a few points, yet she still seems more a creature of flesh and blood than Penelope, who is described and talked about throughout the Odyssey. Perhaps it is partly because flesh and blood are Helen's speciality, and there is little moral complexity about her; while there is all too much complexity in Penelope, in fact a great deal of doubt about what precisely she is up to—some of which doubt, it is fair to say, probably arises from structural anomalies and the conflation of two variant accounts. Nevertheless Penelope never becomes much more than a paradigm of wifely constancy or of feminine illogicality, uncertainty and despair: an adult figure, but lacking the spark of life that touches the lesser female characters, Nausicaa and Circe and Calypso. It is a commonplace that Homer's most felicitous descriptions are often brief, allusive, and almost accidental: 'No cause for reproach that Trojans and well-greaved Achaeans for such a woman so long a time should suffer griefs; marvellously like the immortal goddesses is she to look upon' (III. 156–8)—that is how Helen's signal beauty was described in the Iliad. The same unemphatic allusiveness distinguishes Nausicaa, and even more the two demi-goddesses, and makes them more remarkable in retrospect than Penelope herself. It is admittedly harder for the poet to vivify a middle-aged wife than a divine mistress; but one senses the same flatness in many of the lesser characters of the Odyssey, too, in comparison with their counterparts in the Iliad. Admittedly the martial poem almost completely neglects the humble people below heroic rank; steersmen, stewards and the common ruck of soldiers are occasionally referred to in the mass, and so are a favourite captive-woman or two; the upstart Thersites is beaten up by Odysseus; but the Odyssey has the advantage in social universality, and in places—as in the description of the anonymous corn-grinding woman who, weaker than the others, was kept working even at dawn and prayed aloud for the destruction of the suitors (*20. 105* ff.)—it achieves great pathos. Yet scores of Iliadic fighters both on the Achaean and on the Trojan side come alive, if only for a line or two; the poet imagines them as people, with a home and a living background, and this turns their death or their moment of triumph into something more than a mere statistic of warfare. This simply does not happen in the Odyssey: Odysseus's crew in the adventures, even the demoralized Eurylochus, hardly exist except as a necessary group, labouring or complaining, weeping or expiring as events demand.

The same reproach can be made to a lesser degree about the suitors. In terms of sheer bulk of description they play a large part in the poem. Yet my own feeling is that most of them are uninteresting—Antinous and Eurymachus mere bully-boys and cheats, Amphinomus a bit better because unusual, with signs of decency, Ctesippus a mere replica of Antinous, and most of the rest anonymous until the moment when, as the victims of Odysseus, they gain a name and a patronymic and a brief semblance of actual existence. None of these men makes a dangerous suitor for Penelope, someone really likely to turn her head. In a way the treatment of the suitors as an indistinct, sinister and almost anonymous *bloc* might be dramatic; but this effect is spoiled by the poet's plain efforts to give individuality to some of them. An even more serious criticism concerns Eumaeus. The story in *15* of his kidnapping as a child is a brilliant digression, but otherwise comparatively little about him is subtle, memorable or deeply interesting: he is shown at length as the faithful swineherd, conscientiously guarding his master's property, wishing for his return, cursing the suitors, and acting as a loyal friend and retainer of Telemachus and (in spite of her neglect) of Penelope. Country life and servitude have sapped the heroic qualities that his noble birth promised; Odysseus does not take him into his confidence before he has to, and then his role in the plan against the suitors is relatively minor. Eurycleia, the faithful elderly nurse, again has an important part in the narrative, especially in her recognition of Odysseus by his scar, but only comes powerfully alive in her rather gruesome approval of the horrors perpetrated later.

The Odyssey shares with the Iliad the great virtue of a well-defined central theme which is worked out at length but inexorably. By its nature, though, the Odyssean theme is less profound and less pathetic. The restoration of Odysseus to his home and fortune and family, the reward of Penelope's constancy and the removal of the manifold dangers to Telemachus, are not rendered trivial simply because they are not tragic, but nevertheless these things lack the depth and severity of the wrath of Achilles and its dire consequences. At times the complicated narrative of Odysseus's return, his intricate plan, his disguise, his methodical and cool-headed progress to the goal that Athene has guaranteed him, entail stretches of narration in which major events are lacking. That is particularly so of books 13 to 19 or 20; and the same leisureliness of action is apparent in many parts of the journey of Telemachus. In these places the possibility of tedium, a slight wilting of attention in the audience, might be excluded by spirited composition and by flashes of digression. A similar danger existed with much of the battle-poetry in the Iliad, but the earlier poet was more successful in meeting it. One of his devices for doing so is the extended simile. Now while it is true that an image can be used almost anywhere for its own sake, it is rightly accepted that frequent similes are more necessary in the battle-poetry of the Iliad than in much of the Odyssey; yet there are many places in the latter poem where the greater use of imagery would have been a welcome improvement. The Odyssey contains far fewer similes than the Iliad, and they are not a very conspicuous element in the Odyssean style. They are almost entirely absent from the Telemachy and the preparatory period in Ithaca; they become more frequent, indeed, in places where the action itself quickens up and where they are consequently less necessary. One disadvantage, already remarked, was that convention evidently excluded their use in speeches. Book 22, which describes the slaughter of the suitors, has many good similes to add to the Iliadic effect of the poetry of battle. Doubtless this is intentional: the model of the Iliad showed that similes were commonest in poetry of action and warfare. Yet there they were commonest in such contexts because the contexts themselves were so numerous that there was danger of monotony. In the Odyssey, though, martial contexts are rare and the danger of monotony exists elsewhere; could the main composer with advantage have used more similes in the quieter passages and fewer in the violent ones? Some of those he does use, at least, are fresh and lively and come up to the highest standard of the Iliad.

In other digressionary devices, too, the Odyssey lags behind the Iliad. The abolition of scenes among the gods, once the poem is under way, removes one glorious and effective kind of diversion. The singer may have felt that to introduce a fourth major scene of action into an already complicated plot would be too much, but the chief reason for the change is the new and less dramatic conception of a daimon-like personal protector. The lack of life and detail in the minor characters, in comparison with the Iliad, has already been noticed; Nestor's reminiscences have no real parallel in the Odyssey, and Theoclymenus is a less successful diversionary figure; portents come thick and fast in the second part of the poem, but many of them are obscure in significance and casual in description. One new device, which belongs to a poem about noble courts and not to one about expeditionary war, is the description of singers in action and the report at less or greater length of some of their songs: the illicit love of Ares and Aphrodite, sung by Demodocus for a Phaeacian dance and lasting a hundred lines, is a brilliant and unusual episode. Most of the Odyssean references to happenings outside the action of the poem are to the Trojan war and the returns of the heroes; the first four books are full of these—for example Helen's tale of Odysseus's entry into Troy in disguise, at *4. 240*ff., in which the emphasis on his disguise may be a deliberate echo of what is to happen later in the action; and Menelaus's subsequent account of the Trojan Horse. There is less relief and less contrast in these references to recent events, though no less intrinsic interest, than in the Iliadic type of historical digression on the vanished world of earlier generations. The boar-hunt on Parnassus is one example of an Odyssean digression which succeeds in evoking a fresh atmosphere, and so do certain parts of Odysseus's fabrications. The exchange of gifts and the description of rich and unusual objects, as at *15. 99*ff., excited the Homeric audience more than a modern reader, and had something of the effect of an extended simile. One common Iliadic diversion arose from a request to be told a hero's parentage—such a request stimulated, for example, the whole Bellerophon story in VI. This device is used only rarely in the Odyssey, though Theoclymenus's genealogy is given at length, and in a confused and abbreviated style, at *15. 225–56*; a more successful example, again in a convoluted style suggesting a more extensive poetical model, is seen in the description of Iphitus, the previous owner of Odysseus's great bow, who was treacherously murdered by Heracles (*21. 13–41*).

Sometimes a lack of realism, permissible in the more impressionistic narrative of the Iliad, damages the tension of the Odyssey, which relies more heavily on the careful, logical and progressive narration of events. Occasionally this is due to the difficulties of binding together the complex elements of the poem and is a hardly avoidable consequence of large-scale oral poetry. Often this reason does not apply, as when Odysseus's manifest distress at hearing songs about the return from Troy is only very belatedly and hesitantly recognized by Alcinous (who is, however, a bit of a fool); or in the failure of either Telemachus or Leodes to demand another attempt at stringing the bow once Antinous had had the new idea of softening it with grease. Yet this is a small complaint, less important than those that preceded it. They, I believe, have real substance. Different people will have different opinions here, but I think the conclusion will stand that the Odyssey is stylistically flatter and less continuously moving than the Iliad; also that there are long sections where the interest is allowed to flag, partly because of an abandonment of some of the technical resources of the earlier poem but also because the main composer was trying to draw out the pure narrative thread to an excessive length, with little more than brute magnitude in view. The plain fact is, though, that if there had been no Iliad many of these criticisms would not, and perhaps could not, have been made. By any but quite exceptional standards the Odyssey is a superb narrative epic. The technical analysis of its relative strengths and weaknesses neither disguises this truth nor rivals it in importance.

18

MAN, FATE AND ACTION: SOME SPECIAL QUALITIES OF THE HOMERIC POEMS

GREEK epic, like Greek tragedy, dealt with stories whose general outcome was already familiar. This meant that the kind of interest it sought was often different from that of a work of fiction, for example, in which the result of the action is entirely unknown. Uncertainty may still exist over how a poet will dispose and elaborate the essential themes; but the dramatic impression of the Iliad, at least, did not depend to any serious extent on the treatment of the unexpected. It depended rather on the qualities of the central plot and the scale and ruthlessness of the fighting. The Odyssey relies more on the systematic unfolding of a relatively complicated action. Its happy ending was presumably known to most of the audience, for it is plain that the poem had shorter predecessors concerning the vengeance and recognition of the returning warrior; but the means by which Odysseus escaped from many dangers to reach Ithaca, and the accomplishment of his plan by disguise, reconnaissance and ruse—these were the object of real suspense of a quite straightforward kind. Even so there are some points at which the Odyssey follows the Iliad in avoiding what we should consider, at a more sophisticated stage of literature, as the most effective way of exploring and developing dramatic potentialities.

The Iliad achieves over-all suspense by its ingenious delay of the unfolding of Zeus's purpose and so of the main plot. This allows many digressions which were valued for their own sake, but which also increase the curiosity of the audience about when and precisely how the wrath of Achilles is to be fulfilled and appeased. Yet in the detailed progress of the action there is often an apparent lack of interest in the creation of suspense for its own sake, particularly in the battle narrative which is the core of the poem. Is this lack of interest simply a failure of technique, a complete ignorance of the devices for exploiting tension in momentary action? The triumph of a great hero often consists in his slaughter of a succession of lesser victims. The exact manner of their death is narrated with clinical brilliance, but there is little to make us fear deeply for the safety of the hero himself. A spear may strike his shield or corslet and be broken or turned aside, or else he swerves and is only scratched; but that is all. The same is so with more elaborate duels between heroes more closely matched: usually one of them is plainly in a winning vein, the other is destined to die or at best be rescued by a god. Despite the length and elaboration of many of these encounters there is little real urgency about who shall win and how. The elaboration is devoted to the preliminaries of the fight and to its aftermath: challenges, genealogies or threats beforehand, the nature of the wound, parting insults or the stripping of the corpse afterwards; but the fight itself is described at scarcely greater length than were the minor encounters. The combat of Patroclus and Sarpedon, for example, is one of the great duels of the poem and surely belongs to the main composer. What happens after the introductory setting—in this case not taunts but the temptation of Zeus to save his son—is this (xvi. 462 ff.): Patroclus casts first but misses Sarpedon and kills his squire instead; Sarpedon casts and misses Patroclus but hits one of his horses; Sarpedon throws his second spear but misses again; Patroclus throws *his* second spear and hits Sarpedon in the lungs. Sarpedon dies after calling on Glaucus to rescue his body, round which a general fight develops. The description of the fight lasts for forty lines, and so the singer was prepared to spend time on its details; but he fails to give the progress of the combat either tension or special grandeur, and seems deliberately to reject nearly every device of emphasis or elaboration. The killing of another victim by mistake admittedly makes some variety—it is quite a common minor thematic variant, and three or four others may occur, like the hurling of a stone, the breaking of a sword, the interference of a god. Most encounters, though, consist in the routine discharge of weapons until one happens to hit; sometimes only a single spear-cast on each side ends the whole cursory affair.

The Homeric singer never describes, for example, the way in which one of the combatants strains himself for a supreme effort in the final spear-cast, leaning far back for greatest force and gripping his weapon with bulging muscles and white knuckles. This simply was not part of the epic convention, though it has become a cliché in other literatures. The Homeric equivalent might be the prayer to a god and the consequent lightening of a warrior's limbs; but even this rarely happens in the middle of a fight, to increase its vividness and the feeling of approaching climax. It was not that the Ionic singers were uninterested either in the detailed observation of physical effects or in the minute anatomy of action; the description of wounds shows that. So, in another and probably less traditional narrative genre, does the tense realism of the chariot-race in XXIII. Yet this in a sense undramatic treatment probably arose from something deeper than the accident that tradition hit upon certain themes and dramatic devices and not on others, though that assuredly had much to do with it. First, the preliminaries and consequences of a heroic death *were* important—indeed in the heroic morality they were in many ways more important than the actual fight. Then with Hector and Achilles and Patroclus and Ajax there was no sense that being beaten was in itself disgraceful, or that the duel was a crucial test of *virility*. The epic sense of fate prevented this. A man would die when fate or the gods willed it; his part was to do his best, to fight honourably (which meant being as unpleasant as possible to one's enemy without offending the basic conventions), to show no fear—though even if one should panic, as Hector did when finally he met Achilles, that could still be justified as a god-sent infatuation. Thus what really matters in a duel is the way one confronts the enemy and pays back taunt with taunt; the way one leaps upon him and triumphantly strips his armour or faces the agony of the fatal

374

wound and uses the last moments of life to fling back one more word of noble defiance. It was partly for this reason that Homer and his forerunners did not enlarge too much on the antics of the fight itself; another reason, perhaps, was that with so many combats throughout the poem much variation in detail might have produced an effect of fussiness and confusion; an effect which would not strengthen but weaken the monumental aspect of continuous and relentless battle. In other respects, too, the obsession with τιμή, honour, together with the awareness of fate and sporadic rejection of will-power, often alters the expected colouring of a scene and makes it flat and *un*heroic in the modern sense of the word. Thus when Agamemnon finally renounces his quarrel at XIX. 78 ff. he blames the whole thing on Ἄτη, divine infatuation. There is nothing magnanimous, let alone morally interesting, about his admission of wrong, merely an arid and complacent legalism and the citation of a long exemplary tale about the power of Infatuation even over the gods.

Many minor examples of the same tendencies can be discovered in the Odyssey; but the later poem shows a change of method and intention in this respect as in certain others. When the suitors try to string Odysseus's bow in *21*, for example, their physical efforts are passed over without emphasis, as in the case of Eurymachus who 'moved the bow in his hands, warming it here and there in the light of the fire; but even so he could not stretch it, but groaned greatly in his glorious heart; in distress he spoke out and addressed himself: "Alas, in truth for me is grief..."' and so on (*21*. *245* ff.). It is his reaction to failure, not the process of failure itself, that is accorded the more careful description. In this, as I shall shortly try to show, a common Homeric tendency is exemplified. Yet here the main reason for not elaborating the suitors' efforts may be that the poet did not want to detract from the force and detail of the magnificent scene that he was planning, in which Odysseus himself, after tense argument between Penelope, Telemachus and the suitors, at last gets his old weapon into his hands. The stringing itself is quickly described, so easy is it—as easy for Odysseus as stringing a lyre (*21. 404*ff.); but then he tested the string and it rang shrill as a swallow's cry, and the suitors felt grief and their skins changed colour; Zeus thundered and Odysseus rejoiced at the sign, and took a swift arrow which lay by him on the table— no one can argue that the tension is not built up in this passage with the greatest deliberateness and brilliance.

Yet this climax is not wholly typical of Odyssean methods, and it has already been observed on pp. 171 f. that the moment of Odysseus's self-revelation to the suitors at the beginning of *22*, which is the natural corollary of the climax of the bow, is described quite briefly and in rather unemphatic language. There are many other places where the Iliadic canons persist. An unfamiliar assessment of the different moments of action is something the modern reader must understand and accept. It is often complicated by the oral singer's unscientific view of the nature of time and sequence. Leisureliness and elaboration of description were not felt to detract from the urgency and excitement of the event described (e.g. XVI. 124–277), nor did the insertion of a simile or long diversion in a vivid and exciting action seem to disturb the sequence of events or reduce their power. The best example of this comes in the Odyssey, where Eurycleia recognizes Odysseus by his scar at *19. 392*, yet the audience has to wait through a digression of some seventy-five verses about how Odysseus received the scar before it learns the consequences of recognition. This kind of interruption is up to a point, no doubt, deliberate, a deliberate device for provoking suspense; but it is only acceptable in relation to what might be termed an analytical rather than a mechanical view of time. It was the essential moment that mattered. 'The spear pierced his tunic, and he swerved and avoided black doom' (e.g. III. 359f.): he must have started swerving before the tunic was pierced, but that does not really matter. Similarly Teucros complains at XV. 467ff. that a god has cast the bow from his hand and broken the string—the reverse of the logical sequence. The neglect of sequence is reflected in the indifference to logical subordination in the paratactic style; it may also be true that the reversal reproduces Teucros's thought-process ('the bow has fallen out of my hand; the string must have broken'); but the essential point is that the verbal reconstruction of temporal sequence is unimportant.

This notion of time and causality is another concomitant of the heroic sense of fate, which was seen to condition the hero's attitude to battle and the traditional account of it. In Homer fate is usually embodied in Zeus, though sometimes Zeus himself is subject to it; but from the point of view of mortals the gods are in complete control. Yet not all or most human actions, even heroic ones and even in the Iliad, are envisaged as due to the direct action of gods, nor could all divine interventions be explained as symbolic statements of natural causes and events.[1] This was the origin of the tendency, perhaps, but by the time of the Iliad, and doubtless for long before that, the gods had established independent existence for themselves outside the events of nature and the psychology of men. When Patroclus's armour is knocked off him by Apollo, as the hero stands dazed and helpless in the midst of battle at XVI. 791 ff., this is no natural event symbolically described but the doing of an enemy, though a divine enemy who at the moment is invisible. In the Odyssey, with its slighter interest in the convocation of gods disputing about their mortal favourites and its conception of the individual divine protector standing when possible at the hero's side (as Athene stands by Odysseus, whether in her own shape or that of Mentor or some other mortal), the power of fate takes on a new form which eventually culminates in the classical concept of the personal daimon. Present even in and before the Iliad, where Tydeus for example is remembered to have had Athene's special protection, this almost intimate relationship between divine and human—Athene fondles Odysseus for his lies in *13* and Odysseus is positively rude to her for what he considers as her neglect—brings with it a confidence and even complacency on the part of the favoured mortal which produces a different and flatter effect than the moments of special and unexpected divine visitation in the Iliad, when Ares or Aphrodite is felt to enter the limbs or when Apollo or Poseidon brings sudden aid or counsel.

The close support and constant intervention of the gods, whether in its Iliadic or its Odyssean form, seems once again to weaken the dramatic force of much of the action—if modern standards are applied. Achilles, for instance, is known to be invincible for the time-span covered by the Iliad; can we ever feel that he is seriously endangered by an enemy, except perhaps once in the brilliant fight with the river? So clearly established is this that the poet becomes almost careless in invoking divine inspiration for Achilles—without it he would have been killed a dozen times over. This weighting of the scales reduces the interest of victim's resistance and victor's triumph alike. In xxII the panic and flight of Hector is progressively enthralling, but once he decides to stand and fight he is doomed and the tension drops: he fights not so much Achilles as Athene, who deludes him by creating a phantom ally and who when Achilles misses returns his spear (226ff., 276f.). Thus when these two champions finally come to grips—a climax of the poem and the whole war—the contest is quite unequal: after one miss on each side Hector has only his sword, while Achilles fights with his spear once more. The description of what follows, at 306ff., escapes through its majestic style and brilliant use of simile the apparent perfunctoriness of many Homeric duels; but ultimately its vividness is reduced by the god-given advantage of Achilles and the ease and speed with which in the end he lays Hector low. Similarly when Odysseus doubts at *20. 38*ff. whether he will be able, alone, to kill all the suitors, Athene abruptly reminds him that he has an immortal helper: 'I am a god, who continuously guard you in all your labours. I declare to you openly: even if fifty squadrons of men surrounded us, eager to slay us in war, even *their* cattle and fat sheep would you be able to drive away' (*47–51*). This declaration and others like it reduce the listener's concern for Odysseus, temporarily at least; for the final preparations, the test of the bow, the revelation of Odysseus and the spear-fight in the banqueting-hall are nevertheless intensely exciting, and the poet allows Athene and her guarantee of success to recede into the background. It is true, also, that even the gods are fallible, and that Athene in spite of all her boasts might conceivably have been restrained at a crucial moment by Zeus or Poseidon.

The constant divine interventions and the known protection of certain heroes do undeniably reduce the tension of many episodes in the Iliad and a certain number in the Odyssey. Yet it must be stated quite bluntly that suspense, tension, or excitement is not the primary or necessarily an important purpose of the heroic poet, even—where it may legitimately be expected— in the narration of rapid or violent action. It is equally mistaken to think that the creation of suspense lies entirely outside the canons of Greek literature; Euripides's melodramas disprove that hypothesis, and so do many parts of the Odyssey itself in which *what is to happen next* is of first importance. All the same the dramatic power of most of the action of the Iliad is of a different kind. The epic audience knew that Hector would die at the hands of Achilles; the moment of his downfall must have a kind of forceful sublimity, and achieves it through the noble similitudes of the eagle and the star;[1] but it need not be suspenseful or twisted nearly to breaking-point, since now that the position of the two champions is clear what matters most is not how many spear-casts Hector will be able to make or sustain, or how near he comes to wounding Achilles, but rather how he will react to approaching death, what he will say as he dies, and how Achilles will tolerate the strain of triumph. Pathos in death and the power of fate are the impressions that this encounter and other lesser ones are intended to convey. The sense of inexorability and human impotence which pervades the Iliad, and which must have been specially emphasized by the monumental singer, would not survive the attempt to extract the last ounce of excitement from every situation, or the implication that its outcome was always genuinely uncertain. When Patroclus is knocked silly by Apollo and bared to the thrusts of Euphorbus and Hector the poet is not just arbitrarily rejecting the chance of a good clean fight and a gentleman's death, he is emphasizing the power and the pathos of fate, the way in which Achilles's anger involved those he least expected to involve, and the inevitability of retribution once Patroclus had exceeded his orders and his nature.

If the sense of inexorability is an essential element of the Homeric poems, and especially of the Iliad, yet it is not allowed to exceed its natural limits. Events may be predetermined, but not human reactions to them—or at least those reactions are often unpredictable. What distinguishes the Ionian epic from most other narrative oral poetry (though not always from the Icelandic) is its preoccupation with motives and reactions; it is not only the objective event that counts, the duel of two chieftains or the insulting of the disguised Odysseus, it is the subjective effect of the event on its participants. It is this combination of divine determination and vivid human response, of arbitrariness and involvement, that allows these poems to be at the same time heroic and humane. One indication of this is the way in which an inanimate function is so often carefully related to an animate response:

> ὡς δ' ὅτε χείμαρροι ποταμοὶ κατ' ὄρεσφι ῥέοντες
> ἐς μισγάγκειαν συμβάλλετον ὄβριμον ὕδωρ
> κρουνῶν ἐκ μεγάλων κοίλης ἔντοσθε χαράδρης,
> τῶν δέ τε τηλόσε δοῦπον ἐν οὔρεσιν ἔκλυε ποιμήν·
> ὡς τῶν μισγομένων γένετο ἰαχή τε πόνος τε.

As when winter torrents flowing down the mountain-sides mingle their weight of water into a valley-bottom, coming from great springs, within a hollow gorge, *and their roar from afar in the mountains the shepherd hears*—so was their shout and toil as they joined in combat' (IV. 452 ff.).

The point of comparison is complex, both the clash of forces from different directions and the din that results, and is exactly enough maintained; its exactitude, indeed, is surprising for Homer, and what prevents it from becoming pedantic, or the whole simile from appearing frigid, remote, and 'literary', is the brilliant verse italicized above: the distant shepherd not only emphasizes the strength and solitude of these mountain torrents, he also connects the phenomena of nature with the feelings and experiences of men.[1] The same insistence on man as focus and measure of the objective world may be seen in other similes: for example in the comparison of the Trojan watch-fires at the end of VIII to the stars in a clear sky, 'and all the stars are seen, *and the shepherd rejoices in his heart*' (559). The shepherd occurs once again, since alone in the hills or country-side he is an obvious and powerful symbol for this humanistic intuition. Many other similes, of course, have no such prominent human focus; on the whole, inanimate phenomena require human illustration, human emotions do not—so that the rage and vigour and ruthlessness of a great warrior in action are compared over and over again to a consuming fire or the obsessive fury of a ravening lion. Sometimes, again, there are no such subtle overtones, and a simile is chosen simply because, without being completely exact, it has some obvious visual resemblance to the real situation—as when Odysseus as he scrabbles at the rocks of Scherie is compared with the octopus whose tentacles are torn from the walls of his cavern (*5. 432*ff.).

These are similes, and the style and character of the similes are often distinct from those of the narrative. Yet the same kind of emphasis on human reactions to events is seen (as I have already suggested) in the main narrative of the poems. One of the crucial turning-points of the Iliad is the firing of the Achaean ships, the point at which Achilles has decided to intervene. Yet when it happens this dramatic and significant event is thrown away in a line or two, and it is the urgent response of Achilles himself that marks the occasion:

> τοὶ δ' ἔμβαλον ἀκάματον πῦρ
> νηὶ θοῇ· τῆς δ' αἶψα κατ' ἀσβέστη κέχυτο φλόξ.
> ὣς τὴν μὲν πρύμνην πῦρ ἄμφεπεν· αὐτὰρ Ἀχιλλεὺς
> μηρὼ πληξάμενος Πατροκλῆα προσέειπεν·
> 'ὄρσεο, διογενὲς Πατρόκλεες...'.

And they cast unwearying fire on the swift ship; and over it immediately unquenched flame was poured. Thus did fire beset it at the stern; but Achilles smote his thighs and addressed Patroclus—'Arise, divine-born Patroclus...' (XVI. 122ff.).

Naturally this kind of treatment is not invariable, and another great crisis of the action, when Hector and the Trojans break down the gates of the Achaean camp at the end of XII, is described in elaborate and dramatic detail. Here Hector is inspired by Zeus (437) and is portrayed as superhumanly strong and majestic:

ὁ δ' ἄρ' ἔσθορε φαίδιμος Ἕκτωρ
νυκτὶ θοῇ ἀτάλαντος ὑπώπια· λάμπε δὲ χαλκῷ
σμερδαλέῳ, τὸν ἔεστο περὶ χροΐ, δοιὰ δὲ χερσὶ
δοῦρ' ἔχεν· οὔ κέν τίς μιν ἐρύκακεν ἀντιβολήσας
νόσφι θεῶν, ὅτ' ἐσᾶλτο πύλας· πυρὶ δ' ὄσσε δεδήει.

In he leapt, glorious Hector, like swift night in his countenance; he shone with fearful bronze, which clothed him round his skin, and two spears he held in his hands; no one who met him could have kept him back, save the gods, when he leapt in through the gates; and his eyes burned with fire (XII. 462–6).

Even in this case, then, the climax of the fight to break through the Achaean defences is sublimated into the triumph and transcendence of Hector; the drama of the objective action is not here neglected, but it is still emphatically allied with the personal reaction and participation of a great heroic figure.

It is easy to concentrate on moments of pathos and insight and to forget the limitations of the heroic outlook. How far the percipience of the tragedy of mortality or the questionable merits of continual warfare belonged to the monumental poets, and how far it had already entered the oral tradition before their time, is hard to say. What is certain is that in the Homeric poems the restrictions of the heroic mentality are often transcended or broken: the outbursts of Thersites and Achilles, the weakness of Agamemnon, Odysseus's experience of the humiliations of a beggar's life, all these show that the tradition is no longer a purely heroic one. The Dark Age and Ionian sophistication played their part in this; but the Trojan war itself, round which the traditional picture of the Achaean heroic age seems to have crystallized, came in a period of decline when many of the complacencies of nobility were being severely shaken. Be that as it may, the fascination and subtlety of these poems lies to a considerable extent in the contrast between the simplicity and crudeness of traditional and conventional attitudes and the brief flashes of criticism and deeper understanding; or conversely in the harsh realities beneath the polished surface. Behind the pleasant conversations of Pylos, Lacedaemon and Scherie in the Odyssey or the courtesies of Glaucus and Diomedes in the Iliad lies a different and more barbaric world. Hector is not always the devoted husband of the sixth book, the kind brother-in-law to Helen and the just critic of tiresome Paris; he is not always so careful of other men's corpses as he obsessively wishes Achilles to be of his own. At XVII. 125 ff. he starts dragging away the body of Patroclus 'so as to cut head from shoulders with sharp bronze, and to drag the corpse and give it to the dogs of Troy'; and at XVIII. 176f. it transpires that what he wants to do is to stick Patroclus's head on a stake. When he dares to face Achilles his mother implores him from the walls, holding up her breast as the sign of her claim on him— an unsophisticated gesture, reminding us that relationships between parents and children were cruder and more practical than our own. Telemachus is sometimes almost brutal to Penelope (who in turn could be unpleasant to Eumaeus);[1] Phoinix had to leave home because of a sordid domestic imbroglio in which his mother persuaded him to sleep with his father's concubine (IX. 448ff.). The episode in the seventeenth book of the Odyssey in which the dog Argos recognizes his master and then dies has justly been admired for its sensitivity and pathos, but this pathos must be seen against its true background, in which the dog is utterly neglected because his master is absent and he is past the age for hunting. Priam, in fact, fears that his own dogs will devour his corpse.[2] Again, Odysseus does not think it odd to win the sympathy of a stranger by making out that he had left home after deliberately murdering a prince who was trying to deprive him of his share of booty; though the sense of pride and property was so strong that murder might seem almost normal in these circumstances.[3] What do not seem normal are the atrocities at the end of the Odyssey. The poet of 22 and the first part of 23 was perhaps trying to outdo the martial qualities of the Iliad, and in some places, indeed, he brilliantly equalled them. All the same it is revealing that the agreeable Telemachus improves on his father's orders to cut the

guilty maidservants' throats, and himself devises the line of
twitching bodies on a rope (*22. 443, 462*ff.); he too is there when
Melanthios has his nose, ears and privates cut off to be thrown
to the dogs (*474–7*). Finally Eurycleia, admittedly a gruesome
hag, tells Penelope 'Your heart would have leapt to see
Odysseus spattered with blood and gore like a lion':

$$\mathrm{\mathring{\iota}}δοῦσά\; κε\; θυμὸν\; \mathring{\iota}άνθης$$
$$αἵματι\; καὶ\; λύθρῳ\; πεπαλαγμένον\; ὥς\; τε\; λέοντα\; (23.\; 47\; \mathrm{f.}).$$

The crudities give power and passion to the poems and remind
us that their characters cannot be sentimentalized. Many such
passages are, in a sense, emotional archaisms, and in certain
cases the contrast—in the character of Hector, for instance, and
his attitude to the treatment of the dead—may be accidental
and arise from the juxtaposition of elements derived from
different stages of the tradition. Yet if there are such accidents
they have been gratefully accepted by the main composers, in
full consciousness, perhaps, that human nature contains such
contradictions. How much of the intuition and pathos of the
Iliad and Odyssey was present in the shorter songs of earlier
singers will probably never be known; less, certainly, than in
the great poems themselves. Yet ultimately these owe their
qualities to a rare and almost unique coalescence of virtuosity
and, precisely, tradition: to the directness and inevitability of
a language evolved over many generations of singers, to the
formalized and severe repetition of descriptions and themes, but
also to a deeper vision in which infatuation and mortality, the
stresses of heroic personality and the tensions and rewards of
existence in peace and war, are subjected to an oblique but
penetrating scrutiny.

About the effects of this felicitous combination a hundred
other things might be said, some well and some not so well.
Best of all, though, these effects shine out from the poems
themselves, and in particular from the greater of the two:

*Thus did Lykaon the glorious son of Priam beseech Achilles with
words, but heard a relentless voice: 'Fool, of ransom speak not,
address me not; for before Patroclus encountered the day of doom,*

then was it dearer to me in my heart to spare Trojans, and many did I take alive and sell overseas. But now there is none who shall escape death, of all whom God before Ilios casts between my hands—of all Trojans, but above all the children of Priam. But, my friend, do you die too; why do you grieve in this way? Patroclus also died, who was far better than you. Do you not see my own beauty and stature? My father was a nobleman, a goddess bore me as my mother; but yet for me too there is death and the irresistible portion: there shall be either dawn or afternoon or midday when someone shall take my soul, too, in warfare, striking me either with spear or with arrow from the bowstring.' Thus did he speak, and Lykaon's knees and dear heart were loosened; he let go of Achilles's spear and sat back spreading out both hands. Achilles drew his sharp sword and smote him on the collar-bone beside the neck, and the whole of the two-edged sword sank in. And he on his back on the ground lay outstretched, and black blood flowed forth and moistened the earth. Him did Achilles grasp by the foot and fling into the river to be borne away, and boasting declaimed winged words over him: 'There now lie among the fishes, who from your wound will lick the blood without sorrow; nor shall your mother place you on the bier and lament you, but eddying Scamander shall bear you within the broad gulf of the salt sea; leaping in the wave many a fish shall dart up under the shivering black surface to eat the shining fat of Lykaon....' XXI. 97–127

NOTES

LIST OF ABBREVIATIONS

AJA	*American Journal of Archaeology.*
BSA	*Annual of the British School at Athens.*
CQ	*Classical Quarterly.*
CR	*Classical Review.*
Desborough, *PGP*	V. R. d'A. Desborough, *Protogeometric Pottery* (Oxford, 1952).
Dow, *GBA*	Sterling Dow, 'Greeks in the Bronze Age', *XIe Congrès International des Sciences Historiques* (Stockholm, 1960).
Finley, *WO*	M. I. Finley, *The World of Odysseus* (London, 1956).
HSCP	*Harvard Studies in Classical Philology.*
JHS	*Journal of Hellenic Studies.*
Lord, *Singer*	A. B. Lord, *The Singer of Tales* (Cambridge, Mass., 1960).
Lorimer, *HM*	H. L. Lorimer, *Homer and the Monuments* (Oxford, 1950).
Mazon, *Introduction*	P. Mazon (ed.), *Introduction à l'Iliade* (Paris, 1948).
Page, *HHI*	D. L. Page, *History and the Homeric Iliad* (Berkeley, 1959).
Page, *HO*	D. L. Page, *The Homeric Odyssey* (Oxford, 1955).
Parry, *Épithète*	M. Parry, *L'Épithète traditionnelle chez Homère* (Paris, 1928).
Parry–Lord, *SCHS*	M. Parry and A. B. Lord, *Serbocroatian Heroic Songs*, vol. 1 (Cambridge, Mass., 1954).
Schadewaldt, *Homers Welt*	W. Schadewaldt, *Von Homers Welt und Werk* (3rd ed., Stuttgart, 1959).
Starr, *Origin*	Chester G. Starr, *The Origin of Greek Civilization* (New York, 1961).
Ventris–Chadwick, *Documents*	M. Ventris and J. Chadwick, *Documents in Mycenaean Greek* (Cambridge, 1956).
Webster, *MH*	T. B. L. Webster, *From Mycenae to Homer* (London, 1958).
Whitman, *HHT*	C. H. Whitman, *Homer and the Heroic Tradition* (Cambridge, Mass., 1958).

page 3   1 The date of Hesiod is a perennial problem, but I incline to place him not earlier than the early 7th century. See p. 286; and, for the dates of the Iliad and Odyssey themselves, ch. 13, §3.

page 4   1 Chester G. Starr, *The Origin of Greek Civilization* (New York, 1961), pp. 21 ff.; Sterling Dow, 'The Greeks in the Bronze Age', *XIe Congrès international des sciences historiques* (Stockholm, 1960), pp. 4 ff. Both these are valuable for this and other problems of the period, and contain useful bibliographical references. See also now G. L. Huxley, *Crete and the Luwians* (Oxford, 1961).

         2 Dow, *GBA*, p. 3 and nn. 4 and 5; Starr, *Origin*, p. 25.

         3 Predecessors of 'Minyan' pots are known from the Early Helladic period, but the vast improvement in technique and increase in numbers found is still significant.

         4 Dimini in Thessaly and Lerna in the Argolid were fortified in the Early Helladic period, but they were exceptional.

page 6   1 This is disputed by L. R. Palmer, *Trans. of the Philol. Soc.* (1958), pp. 86–100; *Mycenaeans and Minoans* (London, 1961), ch. 7. Palmer also thinks that the palace at Knossos was burned not round 1400 but round 1150 B.C. (*op. cit.* ch. 6), but does not so far seem to have presented a convincing or an adequately documented case. Some adjustments of the Egyptian synchronisms for the beginning of the Middle Minoan/Middle Helladic period are also in the air. The chronology of the 2nd millennium B.C. may not yet be finally fixed for the Aegean area: but it seems to me unlikely that the main outline of events as I have presented it in this chapter will be very seriously altered.

         2 The case for this is clearly put by Dow, *GBA*, pp. 9 f.

page 7   1 Thucydides, 1, 9, 2; Pindar, *Ol.* 1, 67–89; T. B. L. Webster, *From Mycenae to Homer* (London, 1958), p. 121 (Myrtilus).

page 8   1 Cf. Dow, *GBA*, pp. 16–19, who favours destruction and abandonment by Mycenae because of the intransigence of the native Cretan population.

         2 In favour of some kind of Minoan thalassocracy: Dow, *GBA*, pp. 8–13; against, Starr, *Origin*, p. 38. Piracy ('a great sea raid'): N. G. L. Hammond, *A History of Greece to 322 B.C.* (Oxford, 1959), p. 35. Sicily: Herodotus VII, 170.

page 9   1   Cf. Webster, *MH*, pp. 28 f. and in general ch. 2, which if anything exaggerates the international character of Mycenaean art.

page 10   1   A. J. B. Wace, *Mycenae* (Princeton, 1949), pp. 132–4, placed these events in the later part of LH III A, around 1350–1330 B.C. G. E. Mylonas, *Ancient Mycenae* (London, 1957), pp. 32 ff., argues for LH III B and the 13th century. Mylonas may be right (see also Mrs Vermeule's review, *AJA*, 62 (1958), 115–18); but it would be surprising if the luxurious Lion Gate was built so soon before the attack on Troy—if, as many think, this attack was a symptom of economic pressure.

page 11   1   Wace, *op. cit.* p. 33; Mylonas, *op. cit.* p. 39.

page 12   1   Thebes: A. D. Keramopoulos, *Arkhaiologikon Dheltion*, 3 (1917), esp. pp. 253 ff.; but this is not now very satisfactory, and Thebes in the Mycenaean age badly needs fresh consideration. Orchomenus: H. Bulle, *Orchomenos*, 1 (1907), 69 ff. Pylos: progress reports by C. W. Blegen (or Blegen and M. Lang) have appeared each year in *AJA* from vol. 57 (1953) onwards.

page 14   1   Helen's suitors promised to avenge any infringement of her marriage: Hesiod, fr. 96 Rzach, lines 40–9 (from the *Catalogue*). Homeric hints: II. 286, IV. 267, cf. XIII. 669, XXIII. 297. Thucydides: I, 9, 1.
            2   Finley, *WO*, ch. IV.

page 15   1   O. R. Gurney, *The Hittites* (Pelican, 1961), pp. 28–32.
            2   Gurney, *op. cit.* pp. 46–58; D. L. Page, *HHI*, ch. 1; G. L. Huxley, *Achaeans and Hittites* (Oxford, 1960).

page 16   1   C. W. Blegen and others, *Troy* (4 vols., Princeton, 1950–58). On the size and character of Troy VI and VII a, Page, *HHI*, pp. 53–74.

page 17   1   1184/3 B.C. was the date arrived at by Eratosthenes: Clement of Alexandria, *Stromateis*, I, 21, 139.

page 18   1   See J. Mellaart, *AJA*, 62 (1958), 9 ff.; J. M. Cook, *Archaeological Reports for 1959–60* (supplement to *BSA* and *JHS*), p. 29.

page 19   1   For example Echepolus king of Sicyon is called 'descendant of Anchises' at XXIII. 296, and Anchises is only known as the Trojan father of Aeneas; but there may be a confusion with a *Trojan* Echepolus, descendant of Thalysias, killed at IV. 458. There is a king Erich-

NOTES

thonius in the Trojan royal line as well as in that of Mycenaean Athens, and the name of his father Dardanus was Arcadian according to e.g. Pausanias (VIII, 24, 3).

2 Homeric names on the tablets: Ventris and Chadwick, *Documents*, pp. 103 ff.; D. H. F. Gray, *JHS*, 78 (1958), 43 ff.—Even if Troy really was 'barbarian', only a few major non-Greek names might be preserved, such as Priamos, Hekabe, Paris. Alexandros has often been explained as an assimilation of Hittite Alaksaundos, but *a-ra-ka-sa-da-ra*, Alexandra, has now turned up on a Linear B tablet excavated at Mycenae in 1958.

page 22   1 Menelaus: *4. 90*f.; Odysseus: *14. 245*ff.; Thersites: II. 211 ff.; Nestor: VII. 132 ff., XI. 670 ff., 690 ff. (Heracles).

page 23   1 See especially Ventris and Chadwick, *Documents*; and J. Chadwick, *The Decipherment of Linear B* (Cambridge, 1958).

page 28   1 On possible bilingualism in the late 2nd millennium see also E. Pulgram, *Glotta*, 38 (1960), 180.

page 29   1 This inference is repeatedly made by Webster in *MH*; first on p. 11.

page 32   1 L. R. Palmer, *Achaeans and Indoeuropeans* (Oxford, 1955), pp. 12 f.; criticized by K. Murakawa, *Historia*, 6 (1957), 385 ff., who still writes as though the term must be of Mycenaean origin. Of this there is no indication.—δημιοεργός does not appear in the index of Palmer's latest work, *Mycenaeans and Minoans* (London, 1961).

page 35   1 These views are represented respectively by Webster, *MH*, *passim*, and M. I. Finley, *The World of Odysseus* (London, 1956), pp. 159–62; 'Homer and Mycenae: Property and Tenure', *Historia*, 6 (1957), 133 ff.—a valuable antidote to the epidemic of brash interpretations of the tablets and their contents. A well-balanced survey is to be found in the 5th chapter of Page, *HHI*; another survey by Palmer in *Mycenaeans and Minoans*.

page 37   1 *Historia*, 6 (1957), 133–59, especially 140–4.

page 42   1 Page, *HHI*, n. 1 on pp. 21–3; and comments in my review, *CR*, n.s. 11 (1961), 9 f.

page 43   1 Herodotus, IX, 26.

page 44   1 Fall of Mycenae: before 1125 B.C. according to A. Furumark, *The Chronology of Mycenaean Pottery* (Stockholm, 1941), p. 115 and n. 2; around 1100 according to A. J. B. Wace, 'The Last Days of Mycenae', *The Aegean and the Near East* (New York, 1956), pp. 126ff., also G. E. Mylonas, *Ancient Mycenae* (London, 1957), p. 17.

page 45 1 O. Broneer, *AJA*, 52 (1948), 111–14; Hellanicus, fr. 125 (F. Jacoby, *FGrH*, 4F125).

2 On cremation see p. 130. On the developments of late Mycenaean, Submycenaean and Protogeometric pottery Starr, *Origin*, pp. 89–94, is sensible. On the early Kerameikos material see W. Kraiker and K. Kübler, *Kerameikos*, I (Berlin, 1939); and on Protogeometric pottery and its origins see V. R. d'A. Desborough's important monograph *Protogeometric Pottery* (Oxford, 1952).

page 46 1 Strabo, XIII, 1, 4; also Thucydides, I, 2, 6; I, 12, 4; Herodotus, I, 149. On Athens's part see C. Roebuck, *Ionian Trade and Colonization* (New York, 1959), pp. 25ff.

2 *BSA*, 53–4 (1958–9), 10.

page 47 1 Herodotus, I, 146 (inter-marriage). On the date cf. N. G. L. Hammond, *A History of Greece to 322 B.C.* (Oxford, 1959), pp. 84f. The archaeological picture of early Miletus is still far from clear: see now C. Weickert in *Neue Deutsche Ausgrabungen im Mittelmeergebiet und im vorderen Orient* (Berlin, 1959), pp. 181ff.

2 This agrees with J. M. Cook's conclusion in *Archaeological Reports for 1959–60* (supplement to *JHS* and *BSA*), p. 40: the discovery of Protogeometric pottery from scattered sites 'suggests that the Ionic settlement of the coast was probably well advanced in the tenth century B.C....'.

3 *BSA*, 53–4 (1958–9), 11 n. 11.

4 H. T. Wade-Gery, *The Poet of the Iliad* (Cambridge, 1952), pp. 8f.

page 48 1 *BSA*, 53–4 (1958–9), 10ff.

2 R. M. Cook, 'Ionia and Greece in the Eighth and Seventh Centuries B.C.', *JHS*, 66 (1946), 67ff.; G. M. A. Hanfmann, 'Ionia, leader or follower?', *Harvard Studies in Classical Philology*, 61 (1953), 1ff. See also C. Roebuck, *Ionian Trade and Colonization* (New York, 1959), especially ch. 1.

3 Particularly C. H. Whitman, *Homer and the Heroic Tradition* (Cambridge, Mass., 1958), especially chs. 3–5. Webster's *MH* shows the same leanings.

page 49   1   At Cos and Rhodes there was a break in the 11th century, after which Protogeometric pottery occurs, to be dated well before the end of this style in Athens: Desborough, *PGP*, pp. 232 f.

page 57   1   See H. M. and N. K. Chadwick, *The Growth of Literature* (3 vols., Cambridge, 1932–40); H. M. Chadwick, *The Heroic Age* (Cambridge, 1912); C. M. Bowra, *Heroic Poetry* (London, 1952); and for the Near Eastern parallels *Ancient Near-Eastern Texts*, ed. J. B. Pritchard (Princeton, 1955), pp. 44–52, 72–99 (Gilgamesh), 142–9 (Keret), 60–72 (creation-hymn).

page 58   1   See works cited in previous note. The pioneering book was H. M. Chadwick's *The Heroic Age* (1912).

page 59   1   Of Parry's works see particularly *L' Épithète traditionnelle chez Homère* (Paris, 1928); 'Studies in the Epic Technique of Oral Verse-making', *HSCP*, 41 (1930), 73 ff. and 43 (1932), 1 ff.; also *Serbocroatian Heroic Songs* (Cambridge, Mass., 1954–), in which Parry's Yugoslav material, supplemented by songs collected by Lord himself, is being carefully published by A. B. Lord. See also next note.

page 66   1   M. Parry, *Les Formules et la métrique d'Homère* (Paris, 1926).

page 68   1   *Yale Classical Studies*, 8 (1942), 103 ff.

           2   Though the fourth and sixth chapters of Page's *HHI* carry the matter considerably further. Much remains to be done in this as in other important fields of Homeric study.

           3   For Hesiod see A. Hoekstra, *Mnemosyne*, n.s. 10 (1957), 193 ff., and my essay cited in n. to p. 340.

page 70   1   Between 735 and 725 according to the thorough-going study of Jean M. Davison, 'Attic Geometric Workshops' (*Yale Classical Studies*, 16, 1961), pp. 73 ff. and 129. She does not deal with the inscription, only with the pot (Athens N.M. (192) 2074); theoretically the incised inscription could have been added at any time after the pot was made and before it became damaged or stylistically obsolete—the last being datable, with the end of the true Geometric style in Attica, around 700. Probably, though, the jug was fairly new when offered as a prize. For the inscription see P. Friedländer, *Epigrammata* (Berkeley–Los Angeles, 1948), no. 53, pp. 54 f. Friedländer allows himself to consider the early 7th century as a possible date *for the pot*: this is quite wrong.

NOTES

2 Ithaca cup: *BSA*, 43 (1948), 80f.; Ischia jug: G. Buchner and C. F. Russo, *Accademia dei Lincei: Rendiconti*, 10 (1955), 215ff.; D. L. Page, *CR*, n.s. 6 (1956), 95ff.

3 Hymettus cups: C. W. Blegen, *AJA*, 38 (1934), 10ff. Mantiklos bronze: Friedländer, *Epigrammata*, no. 35, p. 38; Perachora inscriptions: Friedländer, nos. 10, 34, pp. 17f., 37; H. Payne, *Perachora*, 1 (Oxford, 1940), pp. 261–3.

4 *BSA*, 49 (1954), 184–6.

5 Phrygian alphabetic writing, which can hardly have antedated the Greek alphabet, has been found on vases at Gordion which must be placed not later than 700 (R. S. Young, *Illustrated London News*, 17 May 1958, p. 828). This confirms the evidence of the Greek material.

6 P. Dikaios, *A Guide to the Cyprus Museum* (Nicosia, 1953), pp. 183f.; exact provenance in Cyprus unknown. Dikaios dates to the first half of the 9th century B.C.

page 71
1 See R. M. Cook and A. G. Woodhead, *AJA*, 63 (1959), 175ff.; and an important recent treatment by Miss L. H. Jeffery in her *The Local Scripts of Archaic Greece* (Oxford, 1961), pp. 1–20. She considers Rhodes and other places as well as Al Mina (site of an 8th-century Greek colony at the mouth of the Orontes), and summarily dismisses Cyprus; she favours *c.* 750 as the date of introduction of the alphabet into Greece.

2 Ahiram: cf. e.g. Lorimer, *HM*, pp. 126f.

page 81
1 Page, *HHI*, p. 160; cf. pp. 117f. of the present book.

2 C. M. Bowra, 'Homeric Epithets for Troy', *JHS*, 80 (1960), pp. 16–23.

3 Thus W. Whallon, *Yale Classical Studies*, 17 (1961), 97–142, rightly refers to the 'indispensable variety', as well as to the 'remarkable economy', of the Homeric formular system. His article emphasizes the individual character of many formular epithets, and with Page's treatment in the fourth and sixth chapters of *History and the Homeric Iliad* it forms a useful complement to Parry's rather exaggerated emphasis on their generic and arbitrary qualities.

page 83
1 Parry, *Épithète*, pp. 197ff.

page 85
1 Parry–Lord, *SCHS*, p. 111.

page 86
1 *Ibid.* p. 98.

393

page 88   1 A. B. Lord, *The Singer of Tales* (Cambridge, Mass., 1960), ch. 3.

page 90   1 J. C. Pope, *The Rhythm of Beowulf* (New Haven, 1942), pp. 88–95.

page 91   1 'Homer and Modern Oral Poetry: some Confusions', *CQ*, n.s. 10 (1960), 371 ff.

page 92   1 Lord, *Singer*, p. 22.
             2 *Ibid.* pp. 78 f.

page 93   1 *Ibid.* pp. 272 ff.

page 94   1 Parry–Lord, *SCHS*, nos. 8 and 9, pp. 366–70 and 116–18.

page 95   1 A hypothetical exception being the case where a developed creative singer from another country wins disciples and imitators who then initiate an oral tradition without a true originative stage.

page 98   1 *Homer and his Forerunners* (Edinburgh, 1955), pp. 10–14.

page 99   1 A. B. Lord, 'Homer's Originality: Oral Dictated Texts', *Transactions and Proceedings of the American Philological Association*, 84 (1953), 124 ff.; also *Singer*, pp. 9 (which is too dogmatic in tone) and 124–38.
             2 J. A. Notopoulos, *AJA*, 73 (1952), 225 ff.
             3 Cf. e.g. Webster, *MH*, pp. 77 f.
             4 Sterling Dow, *Classical Weekly*, 49 (1956), 117; C. M. Bowra, *Heroic Poetry* (London, 1952), p. 368.

page 105   1 Simple lyres and pipes were of course familiar in the Aegean world of the 2nd millennium B.C.; cf. the Cycladic marble figurines from Keros and Thera (C. Zervos, *L'Art des Cyclades* (Paris, 1957), figs. 302, 317, 333) and the lyre-player on the Haghia Triada sarcophagus (e.g. Webster, *MH*, fig. 6). The bird on the Pylos fresco (*ibid.* fig. 9) is flying away from in front of the singer, which mars the suggestion that 'some such scene misunderstood gave rise to the myth of Orpheus' (Webster, *MH*, p. 47).

page 106   1 Webster, *MH*, pp. 16 f.

page 107   1 Gilgamesh: *Ancient Near-Eastern Texts* (Princeton, 1950), ed. J. B. Pritchard, pp. 47–52 and esp. 72–99; Webster, *MH*, pp. 79 ff. Keret: *Ancient Near-Eastern Texts*, pp. 142 ff. For an extremely liberal view of the significance of these and other parallels between Greek and Near Eastern literature one may refer to C. H. Gordon, 'Homer and Bible', offprinted from *Hebrew Union College Annual*, 26 (1955), 43 ff.

2 L. A. Stella, *Il poema d'Ulisse* (Florence, 1955), pp. 146 f. and 175, with other references.

page 109 1 See pp. 93 f. and n. to p. 94; and add *SCHS*, no. 7, which Ugljanin knew only in prose, *ibid.* p. 359.

page 110 1 See M. P. Nilsson, *The Mycenaean Origin of Greek Mythology* (Berkeley, 1932).

page 111 1 See in general Lorimer, *HM*, which however is already becoming out of date in relation to e.g. greaves, corslets and hoplite armour; and my article 'Objective Dating Criteria in Homer', *Museum Helveticum*, 17 (1960), esp. 190–2.

2 See H. Gallet de Santerre and J. Tréheux, *Bulletin de Correspondance Hellénique*, 71–2 (1947–8), 156–62 and 243–5.

3 There is now some evidence, not known to Miss Lorimer in her survey in *HM* (pp. 250–4), that bronze greaves were sometimes used by Achaeans after the abandonment of the body-shield: see C. M. Bowra, *Mnemosyne*, 14 (1961), 100–2, for a convenient summary. Otherwise metallic greaves have not been found in Greece until the hoplite period. It seems probable, therefore, that ἐυκνήμιδες does represent a reminiscence of the Mycenaean period and its armour—though a very vague one.

4 It is right to criticize the old parallels drawn between Nestor's cup and the shaft-grave cup, as S. Marinatos has, *Festschrift B. Schweitzer* (Stuttgart, 1954), pp. 11 ff.; but it is surely wrong to imply that the description of Nestor's cup is not based on a Mycenaean type, as Starr does (*Origin*, p. 47 and n. 6, with other references).

5 For a preliminary description see *Archaeological Reports for 1960–61* (suppl. to *JHS* and *BSA*), pp. 9 f.

page 112 1 D. H. F. Gray, *CQ*, n.s. 5 (1955), 7 ff.

page 114 1 *Contra* Webster, *MH*, p. 107, Page, *HHI*, p. 188, and others. For a fuller statement of this point see my 'Dark Age and Oral Poet', *Proc. Camb. Philol. Ass.*, n.s. 7 (1961), 36 f.

2 Lorimer, *HM*, p. 273.

page 115 1 ἐυκνήμιδες 'Αχαιοί, for example, does not come in the same category. Even if the reference is sometimes to

Mycenaean armour, the detailed form of the expression—which is obviously an old one—need not go back to the Bronze Age itself, or even to within a century of it.

2 See my 'Objective Dating Criteria in Homer', *Museum Helveticum*, 17 (1960), 189 ff., especially 199 f.

page 117 1 C. J. Ruijgh, *L'Élément Achéen dans la langue épique* (Assen, 1957), which is criticized in the article cited in the preceding note. Ruijgh's study nevertheless contains much valuable material.

2 Page, *HHI*, ch. 4, especially pp. 123 f.; reservations expressed in my *Mus. Helv.* article above, pp. 200 f., also *CR*, n.s. 11 (1961), 12; and by A. Parry and A. Samuel, *Classical Journal*, 56 (1960), 85.

page 118 1 See e.g. C. M. Bowra, 'Homeric Epithets for Troy', *JHS*, 80 (1960), 16 ff.

2 D. H. F. Gray, *JHS*, 78 (1958), 47.

page 119 1 The difficulties are perhaps diminishing: see for example L. R. Palmer, *Minoans and Mycenaeans* (London, 1961), pp. 147 f.

page 124 1 Cf. e.g. Bowra, *Homer and his Forerunners*, pp. 21 f.

page 126 1 Gilbert Murray, *The Rise of the Greek Epic* (Oxford, 1924), pp. 71 f.; Webster, *MH*, p. 159.—Much of what I have written in this chapter is based on my article 'Dark Age and Oral Poet', *Proceedings of the Cambridge Philological Society*, n.s. 7 (1961), 34 ff.

page 127 1 There is no really satisfactory discussion of the problems of the Dorian migration and Dark Age as a whole. Dorians: H. Bengtson, *Griechische Geschichte* (Munich, 1950), pp. 46 ff.; N. G. L. Hammond, *A History of Greece* (Oxford, 1959), pp. 74 ff.; Starr, *Origin*, pp. 62 f., 69 ff., with other references. Dark Age: Desborough, *PGP*, especially pp. 296 ff.; Emily Townsend Vermeule, *Archaeology*, 13 (1960), 69 ff.; Starr, pp. 77 ff.

2 Dow, *GBA*, p. 33 n. 65, thinks that the exhaustion caused by the Trojan war may be exaggerated.

page 128 1 See the preliminary notice in *Bulletin de Correspondance Hellénique*, 82 (1958), 707; and cf. p. 112 above.

page 129 1 Emily Townsend Vermeule, *AJA*, 64 (1960), 1 ff. On Submycenaean pottery finds see the site-index of Desborough's *PGP*, pp. 316 ff.

2 See *Ergon* for 1960 (issued 1961), p. 58.

3 W. Kraiker and K. Kübler, *Kerameikos*, I (Berlin, 1939), 1–165.

page 130 1 Herodotus, v, 65; Pausanias, VII, 2, 3.

2 Athens: *Kerameikos*, I, 10f.; Perati: *Praktika* (1955), pp. 100–8.

3 *Contra* Emily Vermeule, *Archaeology*, 12 (1960), 71. Hers is an unusually acute discussion, but I feel that at this one point she exaggerates the necessary effects of material poverty.

4 Iron: Lorimer, *HM*, pp. 111–17; Desborough, *PGP*, pp. 308–12; Starr, *Origin*, pp. 87 f. Proof of local iron-working is provided by the iron knives found with lumps of local ore at Malthi/Dorion: M. N. Valmin, *The Swedish Messenia Expedition* (Lund/Oxford, 1938), p. 103, cf. Lorimer, *HM*, p. 112. These were found with pottery of LH III c type, which is rightly held to be considerably later at provincial Malthi than in the main centres.

page 131 1 The wall across the isthmus of Corinth built in the second half of the 13th century B.C. is evidence for some kind of united effort (*AJA*, 62 (1958), 322f.); but is more likely to have been built to check infiltrations than a large army.

2 C. W. Blegen, *Zygouries* (Cambridge, Mass., 1928); *Korakou* (Concord, N.H., 1921); *Prosymna* (Cambridge, 1937). Aegina: G. Welter, *Aigina* (Berlin, 1938), pp. 25–7. Crete: see especially 'Karphi: a City of Refuge of the Early Iron Age of Crete', *BSA*, 38 (1937–8), 57ff.; and Starr, *Origin*, pp. 81 ff.

3 Herodotus, I, 146.

page 134 1 *HHI*, pp. 267, 242. On pp. 132, 139, 142, 153, 173 a rather rigid choice is presented between creation in the Mycenaean period or creation in 9th or 8th-century Ionia.

2 *Homer and the Heroic Tradition* (Cambridge, Mass., 1958), p. 58.

page 135 1 Parry–Lord, *SCHS*, I, p. 60.

2 Webster, *MH*, p. 186.

3 J. A. Notopoulos, *Hesperia*, 29 (1960), 190.

page 136 1 Bowra has some interesting observations on this topic in 'The Meaning of a Heroic Age' (Earl Grey Memorial Lecture, Newcastle upon Tyne, for 1957), pp. 15ff. See also the works cited in n. to p. 57.

NOTES

page 137 1 *The Heroic Age*, pp. 88f.

2 Court poetry is envisaged in the peacetime conditions of the Odyssey, though Phemius and Demodocus reflect developed Ionian conditions rather than those of the Bronze Age. Here the invention of the early Dark Ages is unlikely. It may be significant that the Achaean princes, according to the Iliad, took no singers with them to Troy. See also pp. 274 ff.

page 141 1 See A. Andrewes, 'Phratries in Homer', *Hermes*, 89 (1961), 129–40; '. . . the homeric army belongs perhaps somewhat earlier [*sc.* than the 10th and 9th centuries], to an age when the Greeks were still unsettled' (p. 138 *fin.*).

page 142 1 See also Finley, *WO*, pp. 97–9.

page 143 1 P. Chantraine, *Grammaire Homérique*, 1 (Paris, 1958), pp. 44–7; Ventris and Chadwick, *Documents*, pp. 78f.; Webster, *MH*, pp. 163f.

page 144 1 Webster, *MH*, p. 164.

page 145 1 W. Porzig, *Indogermanische Forschungen*, 61 (1954), 147ff.; M. Lejeune, *Traité de phonétique grecque* (Paris, 1955), pp. 7–18; E. Risch, *Museum Helveticum*, 12 (1955), 61 ff. The last of these is of exceptional importance.

2 One may also note that the East Thessalian and 'pure Aeolic' way of saying 'into' was ἐν followed by the accusative, as distinct from the Ionic and also Lesbian usage common in Homer, εἰς or ἐς with the accusative. Yet traces of ἐν with the accusative only survive in two words used in the poems, ἐνῶπα (in the solitary phrase κατ' ἐνῶπα at xv. 320) and ἐνδέξια which occurs four times. So Chantraine (II, 100); but I am not convinced that, although Ionic derived εἰς or ἐς from an earlier form ἐνς, *ἐνσδέξια might not for the sake of euphony have turned into ἐνδέξια rather than *ἐσδέξια, even in Ionic. It would be safer, then, to neglect this point in the discussion of probable Aeolisms; especially since ἐν (ἰν) was certainly Mycenaean.

page 146 1 *po-si*: E. Risch, *Museum Helveticum*, 12 (1955), 66.

page 147 1 Cf. Risch, *op. cit.* p. 69.

2 Chantraine, *Grammaire Homérique*, I, 430f.

page 149 1 C. D. Buck, *The Greek Dialects* (Chicago–Cambridge, 1955), p. 116; also pp. 147 ff. for references to his detailed and useful discussions of Aeolic characteristics.

NOTES

page 151   1 *Sitzungsberichte der preussischen Akademie der Wissenschaften* (1906), pp. 61 ff.

page 152   1 P. Cauer, *Grundfragen der Homerkritik* (Leipzig, 1921–3), especially pp. 224–95.

page 169   1 For a good brief account of the paratactic style see Chantraine, *Grammaire Homérique*, II, 351 ff.

           2 See A. Parry, 'The Language of Achilles', *Transactions and Proceedings of the American Philological Association*, 87 (1956), 1–7.

page 171   1 Though the Homeric singers had a different approach from our own to the problems of dramatic emphasis: see chapter 18.

page 177   1 This is the important methodological weakness of M. Leumann's otherwise useful book *Homerische Wörter* (Basel, 1950).

page 180   1 On the datable objects in Homer see my 'Objective Dating Criteria in Homer', *Museum Helveticum*, 17 (1960), 191–6; also e.g. D. H. F. Gray in *Fifty Years of Classical Scholarship*, ed. M. Platnauer (Oxford, 1954), pp. 28 f. All such surveys are heavily indebted to Miss Lorimer's great *Homer and the Monuments*.

           2 F. Jacoby, '*Patrios Nomos*', *JHS*, 64 (1944), 37 ff.

page 182   1 Iron weapons and tools: IV. 123, 485, XVIII. 34, XXIII. 30; in the Odyssey in the phrase 'iron of itself draws a man on', *16. 294 = 19. 13*, and then in several references to the iron axes of the trial of the bow in *21*.

page 183   1 C. W. Blegen, *Hesperia*, 21 (1952), pp. 286 f.

page 185   1 P. Jacobsthal, *Greek Pins* (Oxford, 1956), p. 141.

page 186   1 Though M. I. Finley points out to me that the role of the βασιλεύς accords better with the earlier colonization of Aeolis and Ionia.

           2 G. Karo, *Führer durch Tiryns* (Athens, 1934), pp. 47 f. and fig. 17; R. Hampe, *Frühe griechische Sagenbilder* (Athens, 1936), p. 63 and pl. 42.

page 187   1 H. L. Lorimer, 'The Hoplite Phalanx', *BSA*, 42 (1947), 76 ff.; Argos armour: P. Courbin, *Bulletin de Correspondance Hellénique*, 81 (1957), 322 ff., esp. 340 ff.

           2 *Contra* Webster, *MH*, pp. 217 f.

page 192   1 Webster, *MH*, p. 167. See also Miss D. H. F. Gray, 'Homeric Epithets for Things', *CQ*, 41 (1947), 109 ff.

page 193 1 'Les atticismes...sont superficiels et presque unique-
ment orthographiques': P. Chantraine, *Grammaire
Homérique*, I, p. 513; see his discussion, *op. cit.* pp. 12,
15 f., also the basic work, J. Wackernagel, *Sprachliche
Untersuchungen zu Homer* (Göttingen, 1916), pp. 1–159.

page 197 1 E. Risch, *Museum Helveticum*, 12 (1955), 65, 68.

page 201 1 *Museum Helveticum*, 17 (1960), 202–5.

page 202 1 *Revue de Philologie*, 29 (1955), 73.
2 Such arguments are set out by Page, *HHI*, pp. 133 f.
with nn. 44–8 on pp. 166–8, and references there to
Jacoby, Burr, Wade-Gery.

page 209 1 For a clear summary see nn. 13–15 on pp. 161 ff. of
D. L. Page's *The Homeric Odyssey* (Oxford, 1955).

page 218 1 Page, *HHI*, p. 297; conclusions: pp. 310–13.

page 219 1 Thucydides, I, 11.

page 223 1 W. Leaf, *The Iliad* (2 vols., 2nd ed., London, 1900–2),
ad loc. Leaf's commentary, in spite of its excessive
analysis, is still one of the best and most acute treatments of the Iliad.

page 224 1 See nn. 2 to pp. 117 and 202.
2 H. T. Wade-Gery, *The Poet of the Iliad* (Cambridge,
1952), p. 54.

page 225 1 Page, *HHI*, ch. 4.

page 228 1 R. Merkelbach, *Untersuchungen zur Odyssee* (Munich,
1951); P. Von der Mühll, Pauly–Wissowa–Kroll, Suppl.
VII, 696 ff.; E. Bethe, *Homer* (Leipzig, 1914–22);
E. Schwartz, *Die Odyssee* (Munich, 1924); U. v.
Wilamowitz, *Die Heimkehr des Odysseus* (Berlin, 1927);
Homerische Untersuchungen (Berlin, 1884); A. Kirchhoff,
Die homerische Odyssee (Berlin, 1859, 2nd ed. 1879).

page 231 1 E.g. by Page, *HO*, p. 61.

page 232 1 *Ibid.* pp. 70 f.
2 *Ibid*, pp. 66–8.

page 233 1 T. Zieliński, *Philologus*, Suppl. 8 (1901), pp. 407 ff.
2 Page, *HO*, pp. 70 f.

page 234 1 K. Meuli, *Odyssee und Argonautika* (Basel, 1921).

page 239 1 R. Merkelbach, *Untersuchungen zur Odyssee* (Munich,
1951), pp. 142–53 (on the Telegony; an elaboration of
Schwartz, *Die Odyssee* (Munich, 1924), pp. 148 ff.).
The wider operations of Merkelbach's B-composer (in

whom, needless to say, I do not believe) are described in many other parts of his book.

2 Thus κατέκειτ' is appropriate at *11. 45* but not at *10. 532*: see Page, *HO*, pp. 29 f., and in general his excellent discussion of the difficulties of this part of the poem in his second and fourth chapters.

page 242 1 E.g. Page, *HO*, p. 87.

page 249 1 Lord, *Singer*, p. 184, misses this point.

page 250 1 Lord, *Singer*, p. 178.

           2 Finley, *WO*, p. 95 n.

page 259 1 Whitman, *HHT*, pp. 129, 132, 143.

page 260 1 W. Schadewaldt, *Iliasstudien* (Leipzig, 1938), especially pp. 150 ff. Schadewaldt was chiefly concerned with forward references and preparations for future action: see also his index, *s.v.* 'Vorbereitung'. Webster, *MH*, pp. 265-7.

page 261 1 Whitman, *HHT*, pp. 259 f.

page 263 1 J. L. Myres, references in Webster, *MH*, p. 200 n. 1; Webster, *MH*, esp. pp. 200-7; Whitman, *HHT*, chs. 3, 5, 11.

page 272 1 U. v. Wilamowitz, *Vitae Homeri et Hesiodi* (Kleine Texte, Bonn, 1916); *Homer*, vol. v (Oxford Classical Texts), ed. T. W. Allen, pp. 192 ff. (contains the essential parts of the *Lives*, including the *Certamen*).

           2 According to ps.-Plutarch, *Homeri Vita*, II, 2, Pindar described Homer as Χῖόν τε καὶ Σμυρναῖον (= Pindar fr. 264 Schroeder). The Semonides reference is fr. 29 Diehl; though there is still a faint possibility that the author was not *Semonides* but *Simonides* of Ceos, in the early 5th century B.C.

page 274 1 Demodocus: *8. 43* f., *13. 27* f.; W. Schadewaldt, *Von Homers Welt und Werk* (Stuttgart, 1959), p. 69.

page 276 1 Thucydides, III, 104, 4-6.

page 277 1 *Hymn to Apollo*, 149 f.; date, T. W. Allen and W. R. Halliday, *The Homeric Hymns* (Oxford, 1936), pp. 183-5. Thamyris: Schadewaldt, *Homers Welt*, p. 64.

page 278 1 Schadewaldt, *Homers Welt*, pp. 67 f.

page 282 1 E.g. M. P. Nilsson, *Homer and Mycenae* (London, 1933), pp. 125, 135 f.; Schadewaldt, *Homers Welt*, pp. 357 ff., containing some rather mystical judgements; Webster, *MH*, p. 213.

page 284   1 F. Brommer, *Herakles* (Münster/Köln, 1953), p. 25. The shipwreck scene on the well-known Munich jug (no. 8696, see e.g. Webster, *MH*, pl. 28) does *not* correspond with *12. 420* ff.; and the restoration of the Athens sherd (Johansen, *op. cit.* n. 3 below, fig. 13; *Antike Kunst*, pl. 17) is quite speculative, *contra* Johansen pp. 38 ff.

2 R. Hampe, *Frühe griechische Sagenbilder* (Athens, 1936), pp. 45–50. Pl. 5 b might refer to Nestor, cf. XI. 750.

3 In 'Ajas und Hektor', *Historisk-filosofiske Meddelelser*, 39 (1961), 55 ff. The vase is Louvre no. CA 2509.

page 285   1 Proto-Argive: P. Courbin, *BCH*, 79 (1955), 1 ff. Proto-Attic: blinding of Polyphemus, *AJA*, 59 (1955), 224 and pl. 67 (from Eleusis), Starr, *Origin*, pl. 15 a; escape under sheep, J. M. Cook, *BSA*, 35 (1934–5), 189 and pl. 53—the 'Ram jug' in Aegina museum; Courbin, *op. cit.* fig. 17. The blinding of Polyphemus also appears on the Aristonothos crater from Caere (Rome, Museo dei Conservatori), which may be a little later than 650 B.C. and is probably of South Italian manufacture.

2 *BSA*, 48 (1953), 30–3.

page 286   1 H. T. Wade-Gery, *The Poet of the Iliad*, pp. 25–9.

2 H. Strasburger, 'Herodots Zeitrechnung', *Historia*, 5 (1956), 129 ff.

3 Suda (Suidas) *s.v.* ’Αρκτῖνος: cf. P. Mazon, *Introduction à l'Iliade* (Paris, 1948), pp. 264–6.

page 287   1 Schadewaldt, *Homers Welt*, p. 95.

page 292   1 Page, *HO*, pp. 149–59, with notes. The quotation is from p. 156.

2 Webster, *MH*, pp. 276–83.

page 294   1 I agree with Page against Webster that one might expect to find ποινή more than once in the Odyssey. ἄποινα is more difficult; and the virtual absence of φλόξ from the Odyssey is adequately accounted for by J. B. Hainsworth, *JHS*, 78 (1958), 49 ff.

page 298   1 Aristophanes: e.g. C. J. Ruijgh, *L'Élément achéen dans la langue grecque* (Assen, 1957), pp. 19–21. Milton: D. C. C. Young, *Greece and Rome*, n.s. 6 (1959), 96 ff., especially his remarks on pp. 107 f. and reference to G. Udny Yule, *The Statistical Study of Literary Vocabulary* (Cambridge, 1944). Much of Mr Young's article is

amusing, but as one-sided as anything he is attacking.
Plato: R. Simeterre, *Rev. des Études grecques*, 58 (1945),
151 ff.

page 299 1 Page, *HO*, pp. 158f. D. B. Monro, *Homer's Odyssey*
(XIII–XXIV) (Oxford, 1901), whom Page quotes, drew
the opposite conclusion to Page's.

page 304 1 See J. Labarbe, *L'Homère de Platon* (Liège, 1949).
2 Xenophon, *Symposium*, III, 6.
3 Plutarch, *Vita Alcibiadis*, 7.

page 305 1 The most notable recent defenders of something close
to these two extreme positions are respectively
M. H. A. L. H. van der Valk, in his *Textual Criticism of
the Odyssey* (Leiden, 1949), and G. M. Bolling, e.g. in
his *Ilias Atheniensium* (Baltimore, 1950).
2 Ps.-Plutarch, *Vita Homeri*, II, 4; Eustathius, 5, 29;
Mazon, *Introduction*, pp. 139 ff.—The use of a decimal-
alphabetical notation for numbers (by which e.g.
$\iota\alpha' = 11$) is seen in papyri of the late 4th and early
3rd century B.C., and is probably much earlier. Where
24 items had to be numbered, it was not difficult to
change to $\lambda = 11$ and so on down to $\omega = 24$.

page 306 1 See now W. Lameere, *Aperçus de paléographie homérique*
(Les Publications de *Scriptorium*, IV, Brussels etc., 1960),
pp. 37 ff. In addition to the three pre-Aristarchean
(3rd c. B.C.) papyri, which include the fine P. Louvain 1
published here by Lameere, there are also several
extant *post*-Aristarchus papyri with no divisions between
books—which proves that scribes could be unreliable
witnesses on this matter.
2 A theory held by Mazon, *Introduction*, p. 138, and most
recently by G. P. Goold, *Trans. and Proc. of the American
Philol. Ass.* 91 (1960), 288f. Goold thinks that the 24
letters of the Ionic alphabet were attached to the
Homeric books before the Alexandrian period, in fact
by 'Homer' himself. This does not convince me; but
the main thesis of his paper, that there was no μετα-
χαρακτηρισμός, or transposition of the written text of
Homer from the Attic to the Ionic alphabet, probably
in the 5th century B.C., deserves serious consideration.

page 307 1 Mazon, *Introduction*, pp. 234 ff.
2 Pausanias, VII, 26, 13; the epigram, *Anthologia Palatina*,
XI, 442, is 'certainly Hellenistic or soon after', D. L.
Page (by letter), who adds that its appearance in an

epigram for popular consumption 'shows that the σποράδην-motif was a matter of common knowledge'.

page 309   1 Rhys Carpenter, *Folk Tale, Fiction and Saga in the Homeric Epics* (Berkeley–Los Angeles, 1946), p. 12.

page 310   1 *Contra* Mazon, *Introduction*, p. 270.

page 312   1 Plato, *Republic*, 600 C–D.

page 313   1 Herodotus, v, 67: the tyrant Cleisthenes forbade rhapsodes to compete in Sicyon because of the Homeric glorification of Argos, with which Sicyon was then (first half of 6th cent.) at war. Vase-paintings: the earliest is on the Attic red-figure vase by the Kleophrades Painter, here pl. 7 b: B.M. no. E270, shortly after 500 B.C. (Beazley, *Attic Red-figure Vase-painters* (Oxford, 1942), p. 122).

page 314   1 Schadewaldt, *Homers Welt*, pp. 60f.

page 319   1 *Homer and his Forerunners*, pp. 9f.

page 321   1 *The Iliad*, II (London, 1902), p. 536.
     2 It is notable, however, that Odyssean characteristics appear even in the closing lines of XXIV and the whole poem: ἐρικυδέα δαῖτα (4 × Od., not otherwise Il.) at 802 and more significantly ἦμος δ' ἠριγένεια φάνη ῥοδοδάκτυλος 'Ηώς (20 × Od., only once else in Il., and then in the first book, which like XXIV carries many marks of its later popularity) at 788.

page 325   1 *1. 331, 18. 207*, cf. XXIV. 573 ff.

page 327   1 Herodotus, v, 65; Mimnermus, fr. 12 (Diehl).

page 328   1 I. 396 ff. (Briareos); I. 590 ff. (Hephaestus); XIV. 249 ff., XIX. 95 ff. (Heracles).

page 329   1 As in the arming-scene quoted by Lord, *Singer*, pp. 87 ff.

page 330   1 Ending of duel in VII: see pp. 216f. Introduction to duel: especially VII. 17–42.
     2 Transitions in *10* and *11*: see pp. 239f.

page 340   1 Even in the *Theogony* expressions of this kind may be suspected of rhapsodic distortion: see my essay 'The Structure and Aim of the Theogony', *Entretiens Hardt*, VII (Geneva, 1962), especially p. 75–83 ff.

page 342   1 E.g. XVI. 694 ff., of Patroclus, or XXI. 209 f., of Achilles among the Paeonians.

page 349   1 XVI. 459 ff. (bloody rain); XVII. 368 f., 645 ff. (darkness); v. 859 ff. (Ares's shout), XVIII. 228 ff. (Achilles's); VIII. 220 f. (red flag); XIX. 404 ff. (Xanthus).

page 353   1 Notably J. T. Kakridis, *Homeric Researches* (Lund, 1949), especially pp. 1–64.

page 365   1 *12. 72*, however, shows that Hera supported Jason in an earlier version of the Argo story.

page 377   1 See now A. Lesky's 'Göttliche u. menschliche Motivation im homerischen Epos', *Sitzungsberichte der Heidelberger Akademie der Wissenschaften* (phil.-hist. Kl.), 1961, pp. 4–52, which deals politely but firmly with some extravagant and widely-held views on the sources of human motivation in Homer.

page 379   1 Eagle: XXII. 308–11. Star: XXII. 317–21.

page 380   1 I have stated this somewhat differently from H. Fränkel, *Die homerischen Gleichnisse* (Göttingen, 1921), p. 26.

page 383   1 Hecuba's appeal: XXII. 80; Telemachus: e.g. *1. 345* ff.; Penelope: *15. 374* f.
         2 Argos: *17. 291* ff.; Priam's fear: XXII. 66 f.
         3 *13. 259* ff.

❋

PLATES

PLATE I

a. Mycenae, from Mount Zara, looking down towards the edge of the Argive plain: 'a small fortress containing a palace, surrounded by houses that have left only few traces, secreted in a rocky corner of the fertile Argive plain' (pp. 10 f.). The palace is to the right, grave circle A and the Lion gate to the left (what looks like a river beyond is a tarmac car-park). The surrounding fortification wall (left) and the figures give some idea of the smallness and steepness of the site.

Photograph by courtesy of J. Walter Graham and 'Archaeology'

b. Pylos, the east corner of the palace, with the so-called 'Queen's Megaron' conspicuous in the centre; looking northward over moderately fertile country down to the sea. See p. 10.

Photograph by courtesy of C. W. Blegen and 'Archaeology'

PLATE 2

a. Late Helladic gold ring from Tiryns, made perhaps between 1450 and 1350 B.C.: Athens, Nat. Mus.,
no. 6208. The ring, which depicts fantastic theriomorphic daimons bringing offerings to a seated goddess, illustrates the profound difference between actual
Achaean cult-practices and those described in Homer
(p. 35). The ring is part of the 'Tiryns hoard' (*Athen.
Mitteil.* 55, 1930, pp. 119 ff.), evidently a tomb-
robber's hoard of mixed date which was buried and
lost in the early Iron Age. The circumstances are
rather odd, but there is no good reason for suspecting
the authenticity of this ring (unlike some others).

Photograph by courtesy of National Museum, Athens

b. Linear B tablet from Knossos: SO 894 = *Docs.*,
no. 278; Oxford, Ashmolean Mus., no. 1910.211. The
tablet lists different types and numbers of chariot-
wheel (p. 33): note the five wheel-ideograms. Line 2
reads: *ka-ki-jo* WHEEL ZE [= ζεῦγος, 'pair'] 1 *ka-ko-
de-ta* WHEEL ZE...: 'of bronze, one pair of wheels;
bronze bound, ... pairs of wheels'. (⊕ is not to be
confused with the ideogram but is the syllabic sign
for *ka.*)

Photograph by courtesy of Ashmolean Museum, Oxford

c. Late Helladic ivory plaque from Delos: Delos
mus., no. B 7069. Shown slightly less than real size,
it represents an Achaean (or Minoan?) warrior with
figure-of-eight shield, boars'-tusk helmet and thrusting-spear. The workmanship is perhaps Cypriot or
Levantine, and the date might be as late as *c.* 1250 B.C.,
but is probably somewhat earlier (pp. 111, 181).

Photograph by courtesy of École française d'Athènes

a

b

c

PLATE 3

a. Late Helladic III B goblet from Calymnos, *c.* 1250 B.C.: Brit. Mus., no. A 1008. This vase, which is probably of Peloponnesian manufacture, is an average example of a common 'Mycenaean' or Achaean type. The shape itself is elegant, though here the stem is heavy and the handles are a little crude. The schematized naturalistic motif is somewhat perfunctory both in execution and in positioning. See pp. 13, 130.

Photograph by courtesy of British Museum

b. Late Helladic III B tankard from Ialysos in Rhodes, *c.* 1250 B.C.: Brit. Mus., no. A 848. Here is exemplified the coarser, less Minoanized, more baronial aspect of the Achaean Heroic Age; the shape is practical but stolid, the decoration crude and automatic (p. 130).

Photograph by courtesy of British Museum

c. Submycenaean cup from Argos, *c.* 1100–1050 B.C.: Argos museum (École française d'Athènes, photo no. 27522). It is of moderate fabric and pleasing though perfunctory decoration, and is aesthetically superior to 3 *b* at least (pp. 45, 128–30). Much of the decorated Submycenaean pottery was rougher and less successful, e.g. pl. 4 *b*; though some from the Kerameikos cemetery at Athens was more elaborate.

*Photograph by courtesy of P. Courbin
and École française d'Athènes*

d. Protogeometric cup from the Agora at Athens, *c.* 1000–950 B.C.: Agora museum, no. P 3953. An average, not a particularly fine, representative of a style whose aesthetic merits are sometimes exaggerated; but the fabric is consistently good and the decoration careful—note the compass-drawn circles. See pp. 45 f., 130–2.

*Photograph by courtesy of Agora Museum, Athens,
and American School of Classical Studies*

PLATE 4

a. Fragmentary bronze helmet, with cheek-piece, from a Submycenaean grave at Tiryns: Nauplia museum, (Tiryns) 1342. This is an unusual but extremely fine helmet, presumably fitted originally round a felt or leather cap. It is impossible to say from its shape and decoration whether or not it is a Late Helladic III survival; it might, too, have been imported from outside Greece. In any event its presence in a burial in Submycenaean Tiryns, together with a bronze spearhead and shield-boss and an iron dagger, as well as the jar (4*b*) which dates the grave, suggests that conditions there in the generation or two following the collapse of the Achaean world were better than catastrophic (pp. 45, 128, 130).

Photograph by courtesy of N. M. Verdelis and
Deutsches Archäologisches Institut, Athens

b. Submycenaean stirrup-jar, *c.* 1125–1050 B.C., which approximately dates the burial at Tiryns in which the helmet, 4*a*, was found: Nauplia museum, (Tiryns) 1380. See above, and compare pl. 3*c* for another example of pottery from the Argolid in this decadent but not utterly destitute period.

Photograph by courtesy of N. M. Verdelis and
Deutsches Archäologisches Institut, Athens

a

b

PLATE 5

a. Part of the figure-scene on a late-Geometric Attic jug, *c.* 725 B.C.: Louvre museum, no. CA2509, from the Lambros collection. The photograph is a composite one, with very slight distortion at the centre. The third figure from the left must be a herald, since what he holds is a staff and not a sword. He is separating two combatants, one with a shield and the other without. K. Friis Johansen (see p. 284) suggests that the left-hand combatant is Ajax, the right-hand one Hector, with reference to their duel in book VII of the Iliad or some other similar account. They are being separated by Idaios (VII. 274 ff.); Hector has lost his shield (270–2) and is preparing to offer his sword and belt in an exchange of gifts (303–5); Ajax is still fully armed. The horizontal corpse presents a problem; the small figure on the extreme left is identified by Johansen as Eris. In spite of difficulties the proposed identification is attractive, and at least the scene is a very specific one which seems to illustrate some presumably familiar heroic incident; it is unlikely to represent an experience of the vase's owner.

Photograph by courtesy of P. Devambez and Musées du Louvre

b. Detail of the shoulder-decoration of a late-Geometric Attic jug, *c.* 710–700 B.C.: Ny Carlsberg museum, Copenhagen, no. 3153. It is hard to avoid concluding that the unusual scene of a man apparently strangling one of a series of birds refers to the story (not necessarily in poetical form) of Heracles and the Stymphalian birds (p. 284).

Photograph by courtesy of Ny Carlsberg museum, Copenhagen

c. Late-Geometric Attic jug, *c.* 730 B.C., from the Agora at Athens: Agora museum, no. P4885. The curious double figure, for which there are other parallels in the art of this period, probably represents the Aktorione–Molione, Eurytos and Kteatos, who were legendary Siamese twins (cf. XXIII. 638–40). They are mentioned as past opponents of Nestor at XI. 750–2, and that incident, whether derived from the Iliad or from some shorter poem, could be referred to here. See p. 284.

Photograph by courtesy of Agora Museum, Athens, and American School of Classical Studies

a

b

c

PLATE 6

a. Late-Geometric Attic jug, *c.* 735–725 B.C., from the Dipylon cemetery at Athens: Nat. Mus. no. (192) 2074. Incised on the shoulder is probably the earliest Greek alphabetic inscription so far known: the complete hexameter line Ϝος νυν ορχεστον παντον αταλοτατα παιζε, 'who now of all the dancers sports most gracefully', is followed by two or three more words, now partly obliterated, perhaps forming half a verse and probably meaning something like 'shall win this as a prize' (pp. 69 f.). The inscription reads from right to left; as far as ατα (of <u>αταλώτατα</u>) can be seen in the photograph.

Photograph by courtesy of National Museum, Athens

b. Bronze helmet and cuirass from Argos, in the Argos museum (École française d'Athènes, photo no. 26359). This armour comes from a late-Geometric grave, near the Roman Odeon, excavated in 1953 by M. Paul Courbin; the pottery found in the grave is to be dated round 720 B.C., possibly a decade later but probably not more. This kind of complete panoply, with the probable but not essential addition of metal greaves, was needed for the tactics used by hoplite fighters in closely packed ranks. Such tactics, previously considered as later than 700 B.C., are perhaps already implied occasionally in the Iliad: see pp. 186–8.

Photograph by courtesy of P. Courbin and École française d'Athènes

c. Fragment of a Proto-Argive crater from Argos, in the Argos museum (École française d'Athènes, photo no. 26322). The fragment, *c.* 660 B.C., shows the blinding of Polyphemus, a scene evidently popular in the art of this period (p. 285). The details of the story in the Odyssey are not reproduced at all exactly (P. Courbin, *BCH* 79, 1955, pp. 35–49). Perhaps the painter had a different version in mind; but the representation of epic scenes tended to be very free, at least until late in the 7th century B.C.

Photograph by courtesy of P. Courbin and École française d'Athènes

a

b

c

PLATE 7

a.   Part of the figure-scene on a late-Geometric Attic jug, *c.* 730–725 B.C.: Athens, Nat. Mus., no. 17497. The seated *kitharis*-player may be an *aoidos*, a singer. He is flanked by two figures (not in the photograph) wielding rattles (probably) which can just be seen. This kind of scene appears on several vases of the period, and is probably funerary. The *kitharis*-player *may* be singing a dirge for the dead; he is the closest we can get, at present, to a contemporary illustration of a Homeric singer.

Photograph by courtesy of National Museum, Athens

b.   A rhapsode reciting, from an Attic red-figure amphora found at Vulci, *c.* 490 B.C.: Brit. Mus. no. E270. Notice the rhapsode's staff, its size and its handle and its use for emphasis (pp. 313–15).

Photograph by courtesy of British Museum

PLATE 8

a. Pre-Aristarchean papyrus fragment of the Iliad, *c.* 250 B.C.: P. Brit. Mus. 639*a* (= P. Grenfell II, 2). The photograph shows the right-hand surviving column only, the left-hand one being fragmentary. The first half of verses VIII. 249–53 is given, together with 252*a* and *b*—two additional verses, evidently added during the course of transmission, which were subsequently extruded from the tradition presumably by Aristarchus and his circle (pp. 303–6). These plus-verses are lines 5 and 6 of the photograph:

ΖΕΥC ΔE ΠΑΤΗΡ ΩΤΡΥΝΕ Φ[

ΕΙΞΑΝ ΔΘ ΤΡΩΘC ΤΥΤΘΟΝ ΔΑ[

Photograph by courtesy of British Museum

b. A Yugoslav *guslar*, or oral heroic singer, with his *gusle* or single-stringed violin. He is Halid Bihorac from Bijelo Polje, the town of Avdo Međedović. See pp. 83 ff. *Photograph by courtesy of A. B. Lord*

c. The degeneration of oral traditions: this posed tourist photograph shows one modern form of the decline of oral poetry (p. 98). Antiquarianism, folklorism and pretty girls are new elements; but the self-consciousness and emphasis on external trappings— completely absent from the genuine and unassuming exponent in 8*b*—are probably common to the degeneracy of all oral traditions. The spread of literacy is the main hidden factor.

*Photograph by courtesy of Yugoslav
National Tourist Agency*

a

b

c

INDEX OF PASSAGES

GENERAL INDEX

Odyssey (*cont.*)
316 f., 322, 324, 326, 337 f., 348, 352, 354, 355, 359, 361–71, 372, 375, 383; monumental, 51, 159, 184, 200, 202 f., 214, 237 f., 242, 252, 265, 285, 287, 298 f., 301, 308 f., 311, 316–18, 355; ending of, 97 f., 168, 189, 208, 212, 248–51, 260, 266 f., 311, 322, 332; transmission of, *see* Homer; development of, 234–6, 239 f., 245 f., 247, 252, 311, 316–34, 355; tension in, 372–80; *see also* Homer, Iliad, Nekyia, similes
Oenomaus, 7
Oineus, 119, 165
Olympus, 76, 122, 152, 161, 189, 250, 290 f., 328, 345, 347
O'Neill, Eugene, Jr., 67
Onomacritus, 324
oral poetry, 55–101, 152, 172, 180, 190, 210, 212, 233, 253–8, 262, 266, 288 f., 325, 328, 332 f., 337, 357 f. and *passim*; elaborate conditions unnecessary for, 49, 133 ff., 135, 136, 278–81; defined, 55 f.; and Heroic Age, 56–9, 274; formulas in, 59 ff., 64; and Homer, 59–68; and writing, 68–72, 98–101; themes in, 72–80, 288 f.; originality in, 80–3; in Yugoslavia, 83–95; in Russia, 57, 83, 136 f.; in Crete, 99, 133; Teutonic and Anglo-Saxon, 57, 137, 275; kinds of, 95–8, 137 f.; originative, 95 f., creative, 96, 133 f., 208; reproductive 91–5, 96 f., 133 f., 138, 208, 302; degenerate, 97 f., 194, 204 f., 213, 302; decline of, 134, 302; transmission of, 99–101, 133 f., 212 f., 228, 319 f.; learning of, 135; inconsistencies in, 212 f., 243, 256–9; conflation in, 192, 194, 213, 220, 334; artificial language of, 194, 253; modernization of, 92, 199; impenetrability of tradition, 332–4; monumental, 274, 319 f., 337; musical accompaniment of, 89 f., 313; see also *guslar*, rhapsodes, singers
Orchomenus, Mycenaean palace at, 10, 389 (n.); reputation for wealth, 11 f., 155

Orestes, 326, 359
Orpheus, 235, 271, 394 (n.)

Page, D. L., 42, 81, 117 f., 126, 133, 134, 154, 204, 215, 218, 225 f., 230, 233, 236, 242, 289, 292–4, 299 f., 389 (n.), 390 (n.), 392 (n.), 393 (n.), 395 (n.), 400 (n.), 401 (n.), 403 f. (n.)
palaces, Cretan, 7 ff., 11, 12; Hittite and Near Eastern, 15, 105 f.; at Troy, 16; Achaean, 9 ff., 12, 20, 22, 23 ff., 36, 38 f., 105 f., 123, 153, 155, 193, 275, 355; administrative and economic system of, 15, 21, 23–39, 43, 123, 125, 132, 141; collapse of, 44, 127, 129, 132
Palaikastro, 12
Palmer, L. R., 388 (n.), 390 (n.), 396 (n.)
Pamphylia, dialect of, 15
Panathenaea, regulations for reciting Homer at, 277, 302 f., 308, 310 f., 315; stabilization of text at, 100, 193, 303, 308–11, 317, 323
Panionion, 47 f., 277; Panionia at, 276, 277
Pandarus, 217, 290, 350
papyri, of Homer, 301, 403 (n.); pre-Aristarchean, 303, 306; post-Aristarchean, 305
parataxis, 169
Paris, 290, 331, 345, 366; duel of, 74, 191, 217, 265, 350; *see also* Alexandros
Parry, A., 396 (n.), 399 (n.)
Parry, Milman, 59 f., 63, 66, 68, 83, 84, 87, 88, 94, 98, 99, 135, 137, 259, 274, 332, 357, 392 (n.)
Payne, H., 393 (n.)
Peiraeus, 240, 242
Patroclus, 77–80, 174, 213 f., 330, 374; and Achilles's armour, 190, 220 f., 351; and Sarpedon, 191, 373; death of, 74, 266, 340 f., 343 f., 351, 353, 377, 379 f., 383, 384 f., 404 (n.); funeral of, 73, 320, 324
Peleus, 77, 154, 174; name of, 119; spear of, 78, 173, 190 f.
Peloponnese, 7, 29, 41, 51, 125, 153, 161, 273 f., 355; invaded by Dorians, 43 f., 127–9; Achaean survivors in, 128–31; refugees from, 44, 46, 130; hoplite tactics in, 187
Pelops, 7

Yugoslavia (*cont.*)
    prose tradition, 93 f., 109; prize
    poets in, 98; *see also* Avdo Međe-
    dović, Novi Pazar, Ugljanin
Yule, G. Udny, 402 (n.)

Zenodotus, 303, 306, 323
Zeus, 76, 78, 79, 86, 106, 165, 170, 205,
    221 f., 236, 250, 261–3, 291, 323,

328, 345, 370, 373, 377, 379, 381;
epithets of, 61, 63; on tablets, 34;
promise of, to Thetis (plan of), 73,
170, 226, 266, 349, 350, 372; Beguilement of, in xiv–xv, 69, 74,
172, 189, 227, 266, 328, 351;
dreams sent by, 73, 216, 221
Zieliński, T., 400 (n.)
Zygouries, 131